Citizenship in Modern Britain

Second edition

Cavendish
Publishing
Limited

London • Sydney • Portland, Oregon

This book is supported by a Companion Website, created to keep *Citizenship in Modern Britain* up to date and to provide enhanced resources for both students and teachers.

Key features include:

- ◆ termly updates
- ◆ self-assessment tests
- ◆ links to useful websites
- ◆ links to 'ebooks' for introductory and further reading
- ◆ revision guidance
- ◆ guidelines on answering questions

www.cavendishpublishing.com/citizenship

Citizenship in Modern Britain

Second edition

Trevor Desmoyers-Davis

Cavendish
Publishing
Limited

London • Sydney • Portland, Oregon

Second edition first published in Great Britain 2003 by
Cavendish Publishing Limited, The Glass House,
Wharton Street, London WC1X 9PX, United Kingdom
Telephone: + 44 (0)20 7278 8000   Facsimile: + 44 (0)20 7278 8080
Email: info@cavendishpublishing.com
Website: www.cavendishpublishing.com

Published in the United States by Cavendish Publishing
c/o International Specialized Book Services,
5824 NE Hassalo Street, Portland,
Oregon 97213-3644, USA

Published in Australia by Cavendish Publishing (Australia) Pty Ltd
45 Beach Street, Coogee, NSW 2034, Australia
Telephone: + 61 (2)9664 0909   Facsimile: + 61 (2)9664 5420
Email: info@cavendishpublishing.com.au
Website: www.cavendishpublishing.com.au

© Trevor Desmoyers-Davis 2003
First edition   2001
Second edition   2003

British Library Cataloguing in Publication Data
Desmoyers-Davis, Trevor
Citizenship in modern Britain – 2nd ed
1 Citizenship – Great Britain
I Title
342.4'1'083

Library of Congress Cataloguing in Publication Data
Data available

ISBN 1-85941-808-2

1 3 5 7 9 10 8 6 4 2

Printed and bound in Great Britain

To Yoann, Kelvin and Martine,
my mother,
and the memory of my father.

'Let the teaching of Citizenship open up fields of enquiry rather than deliver settled doctrines.'

ACKNOWLEDGMENTS

I am extremely grateful to all the people who have helped in some way with this book. Trying to figure out who to thank and how to thank them has been a challenge, and, although it may not be obvious to all, there is a logic to the organisation of the following acknowledgments.

I must initially express my gratitude to Liz Sherratt, for it was Liz who started the ball rolling and had enough faith to invite me on board. I hope all is progressing well.

I must also thank all the people at Cavendish for their support. Throughout this project, I have always received positive and enthusiastic responses to even the most obvious of questions. However, the 'sooper' and wonderful Ruth Massey must receive special thanks for all her encouragement, support and hard work. I have decided that it takes a special kind of person to apply such attention to detail and as a result, Ruth has now been elevated to the three 'o' category of being simply soooper.

Between these two extremes, I must thank everybody who happily responded to what must have seemed like a series of random and pointless questions, along with those students at my own school who read (or said they had read) the text. I am very appreciative of all your comments. However, it is those students who commented on the early drafts of the book that deserve special thanks; the enthusiasm of Dominic was motivation in itself to complete the book.

The greatest burden, however, fell to the reviewer of the first draft. To comment succinctly and perceptively on a first draft is a skill that I had not appreciated until I read the comments provided by Professor John Greenwood, who reviewed the initial manuscript. John's detailed, incisive and thoroughly professional review, pointing out omissions and anomalies, helped considerably in the shaping of the final text.

It was obvious to me that the book would benefit considerably from the inclusion of illustrations and my thanks are extended to Yoann, who provided a cartoon. Thanks also to Tanja, Brian and Nadia. The cartoonist in chief cannot pass without a particular mention. Special thanks are extended to Bob Cummings, aka BobZ, who rose to the combined challenges of translating my notes and transforming a vague idea into the cartoons within this book.

Lastly, I need to thank those members of my immediate family who provided the time and space to allow me to disappear to the solitude of the workroom for long periods of time in order for the text to be completed. I am a little concerned, however, by their enthusiasm for me to complete another text!!

Stop press: at the time of going to print, Tony Blair had announced the Cabinet reshuffle, including the abolition of the role of Lord Chancellor and proposals for the creation of a Supreme Court. These changes have been met with considerable shock and are currently regarded as controversial; because of this and constraints of time, they have been omitted from this edition. Readers can keep themselves updated on the companion website that accompanies this book: visit www.cavendishpublishing.com/citizenship.

Every effort has been made to trace all the copyright holders, but if any have been inadvertently overlooked the publisher will be pleased to make the necessary arrangements at the first opportunity.

Trevor Desmoyers-Davis
15 June 2003

CONTENTS

Contents

PART 2
THE CITIZEN AND THE POLITICAL PROCESS

Contents

Contents

PART 3
THE CITIZEN, SOCIETY AND THE COMMUNITY

KEY TO SYMBOLS

Within the text are a number of boxes containing symbols. The symbol indicates the nature of the suggested 'activity' within the box. Some boxes clearly fall into one type of activity, whilst others can incorporate more than one single purpose. Many boxes will provide an opportunity for students to add to their *key skills* portfolio.

Aims

These boxes begin every chapter and are a summary of the issues that will follow.

Review

These boxes appear at the end of each chapter and highlight terms and concepts that have been introduced. Use this box as a review of the content of the chapter and test your ability to apply the words in these boxes in a meaningful way.

Community involvement

These boxes require the student to do something – to be active in the community. They present activities that have a focus on the application of knowledge or specific concepts, with the intention of testing understanding.

Discussion

These boxes also appear at the end of each chapter and present issues, one-sided interpretations or biased views. The student is invited to use their knowledge and understanding of concepts and evidence to justify the view or present an alternative view.

Research

These boxes invite the student to extend their studies beyond the classroom. Some research tasks are easier to complete than others. However, they provide an opportunity to be liberated from the constraints of books and specifications – to pilot the *CitizenShip Enterprise* and boldly go where no student has gone before.

CHAPTER 1

Why Citizenship?

The aims of this chapter are to:

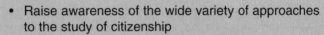
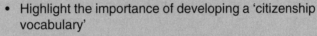
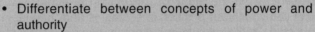
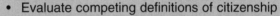

- Raise awareness of the wide variety of approaches to the study of citizenship
- Highlight the importance of developing a 'citizenship vocabulary'
- Differentiate between concepts of power and authority
- Evaluate competing definitions of citizenship
- Appreciate debates surrounding the introduction of citizenship education
- Appreciate the problems involved in measuring citizenship
- Appreciate controversies surrounding national identity cards

The following two extracts were recently submitted in a competition set on the theme of 'The Young Citizen and the Twenty-First Century'.

ALICE

I have no rights; there are no human rights, that's why I don't have any rights. I cannot change anything. I cannot change society, I cannot change the government. I can't even influence politicians. In the eyes of a politician, I'm too old to be kissed and too young to be important. Anyway, all they do is argue between themselves, so why bother? I only get told what they feel I should know. I'm subjected to their laws and rules, I don't want to follow them. As for the rest of society. Whenever anybody talks about doing something in everybody's interest what they really mean is doing something in their own self-interest. Responsibilities? Don't make me laugh. If you want some guidance to the 21st century, follow my advice: be yourself, do nothing, say nothing and you will survive; this is 21st century citizenship.

ARLO

My advice to other young people for the twenty first century would be to say that a good home life is important. Pass on good values to your children, have family discussions about topics on the news, recycle the rubbish and ration the computer games. At work I would like the boss to adopt a charity and listen to staff if they felt that the company policy was wrong. In my community, I would suggest that everybody should adopt an elderly neighbour and buy their goods at the local shop. Go out and organise a tea party, this will make you a good citizen.

The two extracts are very different. The extract written by 'Alice' is very negative and suggests that she does not have any power or influence. 'Arlo', on the other hand, seems to be seeing life through a pair of rose-tinted spectacles. What Alice and Arlo have in common is that neither actually represents what the study of Citizenship is about. Citizenship is not about telling you what your position in society is and then leaving you to it. Neither is the study of Citizenship about presenting you with a shopping list of virtues and 'good behaviour' to be ticked off once accomplished. So, what is the study of Citizenship and what will it involve? Citizenship involves questioning:

- your role as a citizen and your influence as a citizen;
- how much power you have as a citizen;
- who has authority over you;
- what is going on in society and how it will affect you and other citizens;
- your understanding of why things happen in the way that they do and why they are presented in the way that they are;
- the role of other citizens; and
- questioning the role and function of institutions in society.

This is not going to lead to the situation where there are more questions than answers, because the study of Citizenship will provide a range of different answers. In fact you'll find that the problem is the reverse: there will be more answers than questions! However, the study of Citizenship will give you an understanding of issues, institutions and people from which you can formulate your answer to any question and, most importantly, justify your reasons in a logical and systematic manner using a range of evidence, examples and theories. From this position, the world is at your feet: you will be able to apply your knowledge and become active, or more active, in setting out to achieve change, or preservation, or any other personal goal.

The study of Citizenship does not revolve around the student who can shout the loudest. It is not a chance to express any irresponsible or ill thought out view. If you wish to do that, go to Speakers' Corner in London and get on your soapbox! The study of Citizenship involves a consideration of debates, ideas, concepts and evidence and it is from this that mutual understanding of the differences between students (citizens) can be understood.

It is important in the study of Citizenship to discuss and attempt to clarify many issues and ideas that are already in the public domain. The result of this process is to transform your often generalised and vague understanding with a set of meanings and definitions of terms, ideas and concepts that are precise and unambiguous; an exercise that would also benefit many other citizens in society. There may not be agreement about these ideas and concepts, but the process will help to establish a base from which a shared understanding of issues essential to the study of Citizenship can develop.

'Power' and 'authority'

To illustrate this point, consider the issue of the difference between 'power' and 'authority'. Both terms are used in the public domain: they are used in everyday conversation, often without any realisation that there is a difference between the two. However, in the study of Citizenship, they have quite distinct meanings and need to be used correctly.

When one individual has 'power' over others, the individual with power can dictate other people's behaviour. They can, through physical or economic power, force others to act in a certain way regardless of their feelings. The same is also true for organisations. Some organisations have more power than others and will use this power to achieve certain goals.

Power is transformed into authority when an individual believes that another person, or organisation, has the right to dictate how they should behave. They believe that the person or organisation has a legitimate right to expect obedience or a certain type of behaviour and, as a consequence, people behave accordingly.

The terms have been transformed from generalised, interchangeable words into two distinct concepts that can now be used to tackle the following exercise.

Develop a list of people and organisations that you think have power over you.

Develop a list of people and organisations that you think have authority over you.

If you were a leader of an organisation or a political leader, or even 'just a teacher', would it be better to have power or authority? Justify your answer.

As a result of this activity, it should be apparent that there is little agreement about the terms, concepts and ideas associated with the study of Citizenship. This disagreement is perfectly acceptable and can be a distinct advantage, especially when a student is able to understand *why* there are different views, meanings and explanations attached to the same event.

It is unlikely that every reader and student will agree entirely with all these definitions. However, it is important to try to establish definitions, because this allows for an informed exploration to develop from which you can then use your knowledge and skills to apply, interpret and evaluate issues, debates and discussions surrounding Citizenship in a framework that avoids confusion and ambiguity.

Giving meaning to Citizenship

Once the importance of definitions has been established, it is now essential to raise questions and issues as to what is actually understood by the term 'Citizenship'.

A useful starting point might be to simply look the word up in a dictionary. Dictionary definitions tend to take either the narrow form, which emphasises an individual's legal right to belong to a country, or a broader version emphasising the social obligations of an individual to accept various rights and responsibilities that are all part of being a citizen of a country.

The advantage of dictionary definitions is that they do provide a base that can offer some explanation as to what Citizenship involves, and also provide a platform from which further discussion can develop. However, in general, dictionary definitions are far too clinical and will not allow you to develop a full appreciation of what Citizenship encompasses.

It could be argued that even when the narrow view, emphasising the legal right to belong to a country, is combined with the broader view with its emphasis on social obligations to accept rights and responsibilities, this still does not fully represent the breadth of what Citizenship is all about.

For some, to fully appreciate what Citizenship is about, there must be a move from the passive 'belonging to a country with rights and responsibilities' to a greater emphasis on active citizenship: being a citizen in society, not being a spectator of society. Active citizenship should have as its focus shared participation, from the neighbourhood to the nation, with the aims of connecting people from different backgrounds, tackling segregation and exclusion, and overcoming hostility and ignorance. It should encompass issues of exclusion, social class, education, housing and racism. Such a concept of Citizenship, it is argued, would consequently contribute to the development of a shared identity between diverse communities and would achieve integration with diversity.

This view of Citizenship demands that Citizenship issues cannot be ignored and should be actively taught in schools. It also suggests that, for new members of the community, there should be an introductory programme on what it means to be British.

Education for Citizenship

After the 1997 General Election victory by the Labour Party, the incoming Education Secretary, David Blunkett, was quick to set up the 'Advisory Group on Education for Citizenship and the Teaching of Democracy in Schools', under the chairmanship of his old university professor, Bernard Crick. The brief that Crick was given was 'To provide advice on effective education for citizenship in schools – to include the nature and practices of participation in democracy; the duties, responsibilities and rights of individuals as citizens; and the value to individuals and society of community activity'.

One conclusion reached as a result of Bernard Crick's research was that Citizenship education 'can no longer be left as unco-ordinated local initiatives that vary greatly in number, content and method', and September 2002 witnessed a revolution in the secondary school curriculum when Citizenship education became compulsory. But what is Citizenship education? This question was effectively answered before the Crick Report was published, when the view as to what the focus of Citizenship education should take was clearly identified in a press release (June 1999) from the then Schools Minister, Charles Clarke. Clarke said: 'Citizenship is about responsibility and the ability to discuss and resolve differences constructively.' He further stated:

> It is important that young people learn about the value of democracy and the way in which they can play a part as responsible adults in society. Citizenship education can give young people the skills to cope with the demands that modern society places on them and are able to make informed choices and decisions in their adult life.

Clarke's press release pre-empted Crick's report, which stated that Citizenship education should focus on social and moral responsibility, community involvement and political literacy. For Crick, Citizenship education would tackle a wide range of issues. Some questions of political literacy – like issues surrounding the advantages and disadvantages of the political system known as representative democracy, and issues surrounding the balance between a citizen's rights and responsibilities – would be addressed. Other essential issues for Crick would be raising issues surrounding equality of opportunities and citizens' appreciation of community and cultural diversity. Crick also wanted to develop the skills that would allow participation within society. These included emphasising two different sets of skills: learning skills, including the ability to discuss, communicate and co-operate; and practical skills, to be developed through active participation in voluntary and/or community projects.

If you wanted to understand why these elements became the main focus of Citizenship education, it would be necessary to read Crick's complete text. However, a more realistic approach, which might be able to shed some light on the reasons why 'Citizenship Education 2002' has the interpretation that it does, would be to look at the context from which Citizenship education was born.

David Blunkett (whilst he was Education Secretary 1997–2001) was the motivational force behind the introduction of Citizenship education. Blunkett, an enthusiast for voluntary work, was also extremely concerned about the very poor levels of political knowledge in Britain. When the annual British Social Attitudes survey published (in November 1999) the finding that 'the percentage of teenagers who had no interest whatever in politics had increased from 27% in 1994 to 34% in 1999', Blunkett released a press statement revealing that the Government was 'determined to reverse the trend'. He also expressed the view that:

> We [the Government] want young people to be informed, critical and responsible. That is why the Government will be introducing citizenship as a subject into secondary schools with effect from September 2002. This ... will help young people become fully involved in the life of their schools, neighbourhoods and communities.

It could be said that the level of political participation among young people does leave a little to be desired. A MORI poll published in May 2001 found that 73% of 18–24 year olds were unable to name their MP or their constituency and only 38% of 18–24 year olds voted in the 2001 General Election.

The other strand to Citizenship education – issues concerning social responsibility and the constructive resolution of differences – can be best understood if divided into two sections. First, issues concerning 'social responsibility' are at the heart of the ideas within 'New Labour' policy, and a further section of Charles Clarke's press release stated this policy clearly:

> We want to encourage young people to be responsible citizens, recognising that they have duties as well as rights, showing respect for rules and laws whilst developing the knowledge and skills to change laws in a peaceful and responsible manner.

The second section, that revolving around the constructive resolution of differences, may well derive from issues revolving around social diversity and racism, especially in the light of the Stephen Lawrence enquiry (discussed later).

The extension of Citizenship education

One conclusion that can be drawn from the above discussion is that David Blunkett, whilst he was Education Secretary, was the central influence in the establishment of Citizenship education, so it should come as little surprise that when he changed his Cabinet post in 2001 from Education Secretary to Home Secretary, issues concerning Citizenship transferred with him.

Although the change in Blunkett's appointment is significant, it would seem that it is only after two worldwide events are combined with his appointment that the extension of Citizenship education from schools to all those wishing to become citizens can be understood.

The first of the two events that help to explain why Citizenship education has been extended is the increase in and the greater complexity of migration throughout the world. In the year 2000, according to Blunkett ('What does Citizenship mean today?'), there were 168 million people living outside the country in which they were born, of whom 21 million were refugees or displaced persons.

The second world event that needs to be introduced into the debate is the attack on the World Trade Center, New York, on 11 September 2001. For Blunkett, this attack was not just a terrorist attack, but 'a fundamental rejection of the values of democracy'.

Managing asylum

For Blunkett, the combination of migrants, displaced persons and asylum seekers entering Britain needed to be 'properly managed'. If it was not properly managed, these migrants, displaced persons and asylum seekers could be 'perceived as a threat to community stability and good race relations'.

With the existence of an anti-democratic international terrorist group combined with the potential for destabilisation through migration, Blunkett felt that there was a need for democratic governments to make sure that there was enough trust in the system to ensure that it would not be rejected in favour of extremist solutions. As a result of these events, minds began to focus on issues of social order, community cohesion and cultural diversity. One way of introducing or maintaining order and cohesion within a diverse population, it is believed, is through the introduction of Citizenship classes for migrants to Britain.

The debate focusing on whether migrants and asylum seekers to Britain should take Citizenship classes and a Citizenship test before they can become citizens culminated in the publication of 'Secure Borders, Safe Haven' by the Home Office in February 2002. This White Paper proposed the introduction of compulsory Citizenship tests and a Citizenship ceremony. In the ceremony, which should be seen as a 'significant life event', the oath of loyalty would be made to the local mayor or provost and could take the following form:

> I do solemnly and sincerely affirm (or swear by almighty God) that, from this time forward, I will give my loyalty and allegiance to her majesty Queen Elizabeth the Second, her heirs and successors, and to the United Kingdom. I will respect the rights and freedoms of the United Kingdom. I will uphold its

democratic values. I will observe its laws faithfully and fulfil my duties and obligations as a British citizen.

This oath mirrors those taken in countries like Canada, the USA and Australia.

The loyalty oath, which is relatively straightforward and not particularly controversial, contrasts sharply with the complexities of introducing a Citizenship test. However, for new members to the British community, any study programme relating to what it means to be British creates further complications and needs to be discussed.

Measuring Citizenship

To try to test an individual's 'Britishness' assumes that there is something that is identifiably 'British'. If there are things that are identifiably 'British', how well are they established? Are they static and unchanging or permanently evolving? Would 'Britishness' be measured in terms of roast beef and Yorkshire pudding or chicken tikka masala? Devising any test that will reflect the realities of the British character and examine core British values is fraught with problems. Would applicants score extra 'Britishness' points if, for example, in the queue for their test papers they started to twitch nervously at the sight of an individual hovering at the front of the queue about to push in? For more 'Britishness' points, what should the correct answer be to the question of what to serve as an appropriate accompaniment to spaghetti bolognaise: a light sprinkling of parmesan cheese and a glass of Chianti, or a large portion of chips, two slices of white sliced bread and a pint of beer? Would the wearing of long grey socks combined with summer shorts and sandals score bonus 'Britishness' points for male candidates?

Attempting to measure 'Britishness' in terms of food illustrates how difficult the task could be. If an alien arrived from outer space and took a short walk through almost any town centre, the alien would conclude that British eating habits revolve around burger bars, kebab shop, pizza restaurants, Chinese take-aways, curry houses, pasta restaurants, espresso café bars – along with the ubiquitous 'greasy spoon' serving all-day breakfasts. Apart from the versatile sandwich, the evidence that the alien would collect about British eating habits would provide data that in effect questions the very notion of 'Britishness'.

With the continued growth of the internet and the marketing strategies of multinational companies, the world has become, for many of the leisure industries, a single market, and products are designed to cater for, and targeted towards, a worldwide audience. When the latest DVD, PC game and/or cinema release is aimed at an international market, attempting to measure 'Britishness' becomes even more difficult. What in effect might be being measured is not 'Britishness' at all, but how much an individual is exposed to the media.

The 'Britishness' quiz

 Your task is to develop a test of 'Britishness' in order to score 'Britishness' points.

1 What qualities are essential in order to be able to pass as 'British' and what qualities are decidedly 'un-British'?

Make a list of qualities that would provide an answer to the question above. One way to achieve this task is to use a combination of categories that could include:

- Food
- Culture
- Hobbies and sports
- Clothing
- Personal characteristics
- Music
- Skills
- Media obsessions

2 Using a scoring system in which the British qualities score 10 points and the 'un-British' score 1 point, take a small sample of people and ask them to rate, on a scale of 1 to 10, how closely the qualities listed in your test apply to themselves.

3 Calculate the score for each person in your sample.

4 Is the person with the highest score the most typically 'British' of your sample and the person with the lowest score the least 'British'?

5 How useful are Citizenship tests? Justify all your reasons.

The fundamental problem associated with tests of 'Britishness' is the difficulty in identifying the national characteristics and the common values that are regarded as making up 'Britishness'. If 'Britishness' is not easily definable and is ever-changing, how can it be realistically tested without becoming a crude test of old stereotypes? If Britain is a multicultural society, which by definition places an emphasis on cultural diversity, how can there be a test of 'Britishness' that is essentially testing cultural conformity? Are some elements of 'Britishness' going to be more highly valued than others?

Although David Blunkett, in his essay 'What does Citizenship mean today?' (September 2002) argues that there is shared ground between diverse communities, he also argues that there are limits to cultural differences. He highlights 'forced marriages' as being 'incompatible with our basic values'. Interestingly, Blunkett does not state which section of the community he is referring to and one is left to make the assumption that he is describing the practice associated with elements of the Asian community rather than the royal family.

In 2003, the first report from the Home Office team devising the 'Britishness' tests for all who want to become British citizens was published. The report recommended that there should be a focus on practical issues about housing, benefits and using the National Health Service. How to find a job, how to get help and issues surrounding the minimum wage would also be emphasised. British national institutions like the monarchy and Parliament would also be covered, as would the need to know about the 'etiquettes of everyday life'. Here the report stated that issues like 'how to be a good neighbour' and assumptions of equality between the sexes would provide the backbone to this element of the Citizenship test. The report also emphasised that applicants would have to learn about how Britain is a 'changing multicultural society'.

The report has already been criticised, even by David Blunkett, as it excludes knowledge of British history and compulsory language lessons as part of any Citizenship test. The report argued that learning about historical events will not give any real understanding about what it is to be British. According to the report, understanding what it is to be British can only be achieved through time and experience, and this is quite different to learning British history. The report was optimistic, however, that as a consequence of 'the pride and security' of becoming British, new citizens would be so proud of their new status that the study of British history would become an interest that would be pursued.

The report suggested that the test would be available in the language of the applicant and rejected the view that applicants must have reached a certain level of skill in the English language before being able to pass the test. The report did, however, suggest that each individual applicant should improve their competence in English by one level according to a standard set by the Department for Education and Skills.

One problem with any test of 'Britishness' is to be found in the very title of the test: 'Britishness'. Such a test assumes that 'Britishness' is accepted as a national identity, yet the 2002 General Household Survey found that, on average, only 31% of citizens describe themselves as 'British'. The description of 'British' in fact shrank to only 23% of citizens over the age of 65. The vast majority of citizens used the terms Welsh, Scottish, Irish or English to describe themselves. This issue raises a related question as to whether there is a series of past events that would constitute such a thing as 'British history'. Would citizens who see themselves as Scottish, Welsh, Irish or English as opposed to 'British' have the same interpretation of past events? If Blunkett feels that there should be more British history in future 'Britishness' tests, would these tests be different in various parts of the country so as to take into account regional differences?

Another issue that needs exploring revolves around the question of why Citizenship tests have only recently been seen to be necessary. Since migration and asylum have been continuing for centuries, why is there felt to be a need for Citizenship tests to be introduced?

One answer to the question rests with the publication of the Ouseley Report into the 2001 civil disorder in Bradford. This report spoke of a community fragmenting along social, ethnic and religious lines, with race relations worsening, attitudes hardening and the city being characterised by segregated housing and schools. Ouseley believed that the introduction of Citizenship lessons should not stop at primary and secondary schools but should be introduced to all new migrants in order to develop in them a sense of belonging, promote cultural diversity and widen understanding between communities.

Although the proposed tests have met with positive approval from many within politics, they have been criticised due to their one-sided nature. Whilst it is seen to be important for the migrant to attend an induction course into the British way of life, would it not also be important to educate others about why people are seeking asylum, where they have come from, and what they have experienced in order to arrive in Britain? Another criticism of such classes revolves around Blunkett's declaration that some migrants will need to 'question their deeply held beliefs and prejudices'. One could ask the same question to the lager-carrying shaven-headed gentlemen with red and white painted faces whose lack of tolerant and liberal attitudes is frequently exhibited.

From Citizenship education to Citizenship identification

There can be little doubt that, as a result of the attack on the World Trade Center in September 2001, there has been an increase in political activity under the general banner of 'counter-terrorism'. One possible result of such political activity is the recent interest in the possible introduction of identity cards for all citizens.

David Blunkett established his views on identity cards at the launch of his book *Politics and Progress* on 26 September 2001, when he stated that he was attracted to a national identity card scheme although it would not be the type of scheme that gave the police the power to stop people and demand to see their identity card. He suggested that an identity card scheme would be, in effect, a move towards a citizens' 'entitlement card' which would give the individual access to various government services and could be combined with driving licence, passport and even credit cards. However, at a later date, Blunkett started to talk of the national identity card scheme in terms of a 'high quality common population register' that would assign every citizen 'a unique personal number that could be used across the public sector'.

Following Blunkett's initial thoughts, an opinion poll published at the same time (September 2001) suggested that 86% of citizens supported some form of identity card. Such cards have been introduced in Britain on two previous occasions: in 1915 and 1939. Significantly, both of these occasions came at a time when Britain was engaged in a world war; recent claims justifying the introduction of identity cards because Britain is now involved in a worldwide 'war against terrorism' seem a little hollow by comparison. Other arguments used to support the idea of identity cards rest on a series of very generalised assertions suggesting that identity cards will reduce illegal immigration, reduce benefit fraud, reduce crime, reduce terrorist attacks and make life easier for the police. These arguments are further supported by the notion that, as a society, the British already carry a vast array of cards, all with the purpose of establishing identity. One more would not make any difference and one official identity card might make some of the other cards redundant and thus save citizens from an ever-expanding wallet of pointless plastic. Supporters of identity cards also point towards the continent, where 11 European Union countries have some form of identity card. However, there is no similarity in the nature of the cards among those 11 countries. They range from Belgian identity card, introduced in 1919, to the new Italian cards, to be operational by 2005; from Portuguese identity cards, that include photographs and fingerprints and must be carried at all times and can be inspected by police, customs, private security guards as well as government officials, to the voluntary identity card scheme operating in the Netherlands.

 Just how many countries have identity cards and in what ways do they vary?

Although Tony Blair stated that he did not see any great civil liberties objections to carrying national identity cards, many other criticisms have been levelled at the idea. Historically, they were abolished by Winston Churchill in 1953 following an incident on 7 December 1950 in Finchley, North London, when PC Harold Muckle demanded to see the identity card of car driver Clarence Willcock. It is significant that PC Muckle never made the suggestion that Willcock was driving dangerously. Willcock took exception to the demand and refused to accept a form that Muckle produced requiring Willcock to show his identity card at a police station within 48 hours. Willcock had no defence against the 1939 law requiring citizens to carry their identity card and was convicted. However, in his judgment, Lord Goddard, the Lord Chief Justice, declared that 'to demand production of the card from all and sundry ... is wholly unreasonable', and continued by stating that 'random demands to see identity cards tend to make people resentful of the acts of the police and incline them to obstruct the police instead of to assist them'. This view was echoed by the Association of Chief Police Officers 50 years later; the Association believes that requests to see a citizen's identity card could damage community relations.

At first, arguments seemed to deal blow after blow to the likelihood of acceptance of the idea that ID cards would be introduced. A Cabinet Office report published in July 2002 suggested that they would only save 1% of benefit fraud whilst allowing for the potential increase in the crime of 'identity fraud' in which one citizen's 'identity' is stolen through the purloining of other citizens' identifying numbers. This can be set against the cost of establishing a national identity scheme, which has been estimated at £3 billion.

The notion that identity cards will automatically reduce crime or terrorism can also be questioned. If present day passports can be forged and credit cards manufactured, why can't those skills be transferred to the production of fake identity cards? Even more extreme, an identity card is going to do little to stop the suicide bomber or hijacker. Indeed, if a criminal or a terrorist does acquire ownership of an identity card, the card will, in effect, give them credibility and allow them to move freely within society.

However, for many, the greatest problems associated with identity cards are that they have the potential to penalise law-abiding citizens. If a citizen lost or forgot their identity card, they could be committing a criminal offence. Equally, identity cards destroy one of the oldest principles of law which establishes that any citizen who is neither committing an offence nor behaving suspiciously can go about their business without official harassment. Finally, if, as Blunkett suggested, it would not be compulsory for a citizen to carry their identity card, the whole scheme would be rendered entirely useless.

Although some citizens believe that the introduction of a non-compulsory ID card is an expensive and questionable exercise that infringes a citizen's privacy and liberty, creates new crimes and is an ineffective weapon against fraud, such details have never stopped a determined Home Secretary. Towards the end of May 2003, David Blunkett made clear in a series of interviews that he intends to introduce legislation to establish ID (or 'entitlement') cards after the next General Election. The cards would be self-financing, which means that citizens would have to pay an estimated £25 for the privilege of owning their card.

It would appear that the proposed card will hold a citizen's name, sex, address and date of birth, accompanied by a photograph. Additionally, it will detail a citizen's employment status, National Insurance number, and information that can currently be found on their passport and driving licence. The proposed card could also contain a PIN (personal identification number) or password so that it can be used to buy goods and services, or simply to get money from a cash point. The card might hold 'biometric' information such as an eye scan or electronic fingerprint to guard against fraud.

Debates about cards that are designed to establish a citizen's identity are likely to be ongoing and may arrive from unexpected sources. To illustrate this point, at present British holiday-makers can obtain an 'E111' form which allows them to access medical treatment anywhere in the European Union. Similar forms are available in all the other countries of the European Union. Anna Diamantopoulou, the EU Commissioner for Employment, stated that with '15 different E111s, it is red tape from the age of the dinosaurs', which accounts for the proposed introduction of the EU health card by 2005.

For some, debates surrounding identity cards and citizenship are viewed as being a single issue. For others, however, it is felt that it can be useful to make a distinction between citizenship concerns revolving around political issues and those of identity which revolve around an individual's innate characteristics. This distinction, if it actually exists, can be used to illustrate that the study of citizenship is fraught with debates and controversies. However, all these debates and controversies are an essential part of the lifelong study of this subject. But always remember: it is not what is believed that is important, but how that belief is justified. This is to be the starting point for the study of Citizenship.

 In order to illustrate the diversity and confusion surrounding debates and concepts that are essential to the study of Citizenship, try this simple questionnaire on a small sample of people.

Questionnaire

- What do you think the word 'citizen' means?
- Do you think that a citizen has any rights?
  - If yes, can you list any of these rights?
- Do you think that a citizen has any responsibilities?
  - If yes, what are your responsibilities?
- Do you think that there is only one definition of the word 'citizen'?
- What do you think the word 'society' means?
- What do you think the word 'state' means?
- Do you think that you are influenced by society?
  - If yes, can you suggest how?
- Do you think that you are influenced by the state?
  - If yes, can you suggest how?
- Why do you think that politicians from different political parties always seem to disagree?
- Is the Queen a citizen?

As a matter of interest, if you used any member of your Citizenship group as part of your sample, keep your results in a safe place and repeat the questionnaire at the end of the course. In theory, the responses should be quite different!

There are many places where you can complete the following activity. A voyage around the politics and sociology sections of your school, college or local library would be one means of research. Another productive source would be some form of encyclopaedia. An alternative approach is to use an internet search engine. Don't forget to make a note of all your sources for your definitions.

- How many different definitions of the term 'citizen' can you discover?
- How many different definitions of the term 'the state' can you discover?
- How many different definitions of the term 'society' can you discover?
- How many different definitions of the term 'community' can you discover?
- Can you discover what the phrase 'human rights' refers to?

From your individual results, it is interesting to establish the range of definitions and the way in which the definitions vary.

Compare the range of definitions for the terms:

- citizen
- the state
- society
- community

that you have researched either with other members of your group or within your own collection.

Consider the following issues:

- How do those from a political source differ to those from a sociological or legal source?
- How similar or how different are the definitions?
- How useful are they as a set of terms?

Identity cards – for your benefit or theirs?

Part 1

The Citizen and the State

INTRODUCTION

The citizen and the state, or should it be the state and the citizen? A citizen's rights and responsibilities, or should it be responsibilities and rights? The citizen's right to know, or the state's right to keep a secret? Confused? Getting into a state over it? Is that what this part is about? Questions, questions and more questions. What the student of citizenship needs is answers, answers and more answers, and Part 1 sets out to help provide some of these answers.

Some of the key areas that will be addressed concern exactly what is understood by 'the state' and whether it is more influential than society in determining behaviour and attitudes. Exactly what is meant and understood by the term 'citizen' and how and why the meaning of the term has changed is also addressed. Why do different groups of citizens have different ideas about 'right and wrong' and why is it that politicians always seem to disagree?

Once the student of citizenship has an understanding of these areas, they are able to develop and apply discussions and debates to issues that affect students' lives today. These issues concern freedom of information and the interaction between citizens and the police, along with issues surrounding the law and the welfare of citizens in society.

CHAPTER 2

The State, Society and Citizens

The aims of this chapter are to:

- Establish an understanding of what a state is and how it is distinguished from government
- Develop the notion of being a citizen
- Understand the significance of the influence of society on the attitudes and behaviour of its citizens

In Chapter 1, the terms 'state' and 'society' were introduced. There is probably general agreement that both have an influence on individuals. It is true to say that individuals are born into a society and they learn the laws of that society. But where do those laws come from? It is the state that has made the laws. So, what came first, society or the state? This is equivalent to trying to find an answer to the chicken/egg conundrum, and it is impossible to give an answer. However, the question as to whether it is society or the state that has the greatest influence on the general values held by the majority of people has to be the starting point in the study of Citizenship.

What is 'the state'?

The 'state' is often described in terms of a definite territory in which a legitimate government has the ability to control its own activities without interference from other organisations. An oft-quoted definition comes from the German sociologist Max Weber (1864–1920) who saw the state as 'an institution which claims the monopoly of legitimate violence for a particular territory'. The 'state' is also seen as something that is continuous. It has a set of rules, or constitution, in which the powers of its officials, like the Prime Minister, are defined and in effect, therefore, limited. However, although Prime Ministers will come and go, the 'state' will continue. The state will make laws that are binding on all of the people. It will also act on behalf of the people living in that territory and, as a counter-balance to this, the 'state' would expect that, at certain times, people will either voluntarily or through coercion undertake activities which will be for the benefit of the 'state'. The coercive elements would include all of the organisations, like the police or the army, which could use force in order to make people undertake activities that will benefit the state.

The 'state' is not the government. In simple terms, the government, consisting of a combined total of around 100 people, is headed by the Prime Minister and is made up of Cabinet Ministers, Secretaries of State and junior ministers, all drawn from Parliament. The monarch, who normally plays no part in government, heads the 'state'. The state does, however, include institutions like the civil service, the judiciary, the armed forces and the police. Whether the mass media are included as part of the state is open to discussion.

This balance between the state and the people living in that state results in the state undertaking activities on behalf of its people. This could include, for example, education and welfare. People are often heard talking about the state education system or the welfare state. The other side of this relationship is that the state expects its people, for example, to pay taxes and to obey its laws. In case a person chooses not to do this, the state can impose a range of penalties on the individual that could include fining them or imprisoning them.

The notion of being a citizen

To develop this a little further, the use of the word 'people' in the paragraph above is now unsatisfactory. If a relationship between the state and those individuals who have legally defined sets of rights and obligations exists, then both sides of this relationship need to distinguish themselves from those who do not have the same sets of rights and obligations.

In order to make this distinction, the notion of being a *citizen* developed. If an individual does have a legally defined set of rights that are balanced by a series of responsibilities and obligations, then that individual is said to be a citizen of that state.

There is considerable agreement and disagreement as to what a citizen's 'legally defined set of rights' should include. The right that probably generates the greatest agreement is the right for citizens to participate in the elections of the state, usually by means of voting. Another example of a right that generates agreement is a right to equal treatment before the law. However, although there is general agreement about the principle, there is less agreement as to whether all groups of citizens, in practice, receive equal treatment from the law or have equal access to the law.

Even if the right to vote confers being a citizen of a state, this will not automatically create a common identity between citizens, as inevitably there will be a combination of political, economic and social divisions. This lack of common identity creates diversity that is sometimes used as a justification to put limits on, or to withdraw, some of that 'legally defined set of rights'. But what is the cause of this diversity within a nation-state? The fundamental reason why there is not a common identity among citizens within a nation-state is because of the influence of society. This is a very broad statement and needs some further discussion to make it meaningful.

The influence of society

There have been many millions of words previously written on the subject of society and its influence(s) on human behaviour. However, some would not regard the idea that society influences human behaviour as being correct. These people take a different approach to human behaviour and believe that humans are pre-programmed in such a way that makes behaviour inevitable: the 'whatever will be will be' approach. The alternative view suggests that humans are moulded and shaped by social processes and patterns of organisations. The crucial question, which cannot be definitively answered, is whether human behaviour is shaped by 'nature' and therefore pre-determined, or is shaped by society and, therefore, socially constructed.

For many, it is because so much of our behaviour is socially constructed that there is not a common identity between citizens. The role and influence of society is immeasurable and it is this influence that manages to create diversity from a single human 'product'. To understand how society achieves this, it is necessary to discuss some of the key elements of human society.

From the moment of birth, babies are engaged in a learning process. This learning process continues, for example, when the child first starts school, when they become a teenager and start their first part time job, when they start university or full time employment, right up to when they become a pensioner and attend their first OAP social event. This learning process is not about 'facts'. It is about learning how to become part of that group and how to 'fit in'. To be a member of any group, the individual has to learn, and ultimately accept, the norms and values of that group's culture. The ongoing process of learning the norms and values of different groups is a process of socialisation. Since no two humans will ever have an identical set of learning experiences, due to the influences of their family, their education, their gender, their ethnicity, their social class and their region, it is unsurprising but at the same time paradoxical that there exist simultaneously both a common identity between citizens and substantial differences between those same citizens.

The cause of the paradox lies in the process of socialisation; in this process, norms, values and culture are established. A 'norm' is behaviour that is defined as being acceptable. Norms influence, for example, what is the 'correct thing to do or say' or the 'proper set of clothes to wear'. Not only do norms determine what behaviour is acceptable, they also determine what behaviour is *un*acceptable. Norms legitimate some behaviour and prohibit other behaviour.

However, what is defined as being 'acceptable, right and proper' is neither going to be universally accepted by all members of society nor appropriate to all members of society. The age of the person involved, the location where the activity takes place, the role of the individual and status of the individual will all influence definitions of acceptable behaviour. Norms are relative – relative to specific situations – and consequently will produce differing definitions of acceptability in relation to the same actions, depending on where an activity occurs, when it occurred, who was doing it, how it was undertaken and for what purpose.

Values are somewhat different to norms, in that they are less specific. Values are associated with what a society generally regards or defines as being worthwhile, and provide guidelines for behaviour. Values first provide shared standards of behaviour. They also provide the consensus that underpins the shared moral principles that are believed to be important. Because values are shared, they are important for reinforcing social cohesion and generating a sense of belonging to the group and/or society.

Like pepper and salt, the two terms 'norms' and 'values' are associated and make more sense when they are used in conjunction with each other. They are an essential element to the understanding of what constitutes the 'learned, shared behaviour' that defines culture and which is learned through socialisation. The overall result of this process is the fascinating paradox of society; the grouping together of large numbers of people who (usually) peacefully co-exist whilst simultaneously having both quite distinctive cultural differences and cultural similarities.

What do you understand by the following terms and concepts?

- State
- Government
- A citizen

- Socialisation
- Culture
- Norms and values

There are many ways that a citizen's behaviour can be influenced by the state and by society. Complete the chart, illustrating the different ways in which both the state and society can influence the behaviour and attitudes of a citizen.

The state	Society

Although the right for citizens to participate in state elections by means of voting is generally accepted in society today, this right is relatively modern. To illustrate how modern this idea is, it is worth a quick diversion into the modern history of politics section of your local library. Alternatively, many encyclopaedias, books or CD ROMs will also provide reference to the Electoral Reform Acts below.

Listed below are a series of dates in which changes have occurred in the voting rights of UK citizens:

- 1832
- 1884
- 1918
- 1928

- 1948
- 1969
- 2000

For each of these dates, show who was and who was not allowed to vote in UK elections. Try to estimate the percentage of the population who were excluded from voting for each date.

Should some citizens have their voting rights removed?

CHAPTER 3

The Changing Concept of Citizenship

The aims of this chapter are to:
- Introduce the concept of ideology
- Introduce individualistic and collectivist approaches towards citizenship
- Introduce inclusive/exclusive approaches towards citizenship
- Introduce Marshall's three stage model of citizenship

What is ideology?

The starting point for any discussion that tackles ideology is to restate that as part of everyday existence, all citizens are subject to numerous norms and values that govern and structure their behaviour. Although individual citizens may have quite different norms and values, there are enough similarities between these norms and values to enable citizens to live together. There is sufficient similar behaviour that is learned and shared to unite citizens within a common culture.

Citizens in society will, through their norms and values, have a point of view about many different issues. Ask a number of citizens to look out of the same window; will they all see the same thing? One could see a landscape worth sketching, another could see the opportunity to build a housing estate and make 'loadsamoney'. Another could see land that is suitable for planting GM crops whilst another could see a perfect environment for an adventure playground. In short, citizens will interpret the same view differently.

The reason for this is that as a result of cultural differences, citizens have quite different ideologies. An ideology can be described as all of those assumptions and ideas that a citizen holds which are then used to classify, order or generally make sense of their world. Ideology provides the framework in which judgments are made. For the artist, builder, scientist or agriculturalist, the view from the window was identical, but each judged what they saw differently. Each citizen's ideology allowed them to see something different. The same is also true whenever one citizen interacts with another citizen. Some are seen to be wise whilst others are judged to be foolish. This judgment is a result of a citizen's ideology based on those ideas that the citizen holds to be correct, true and right. This is their ideology and it provides

'Back again to pester Britain', *The Perishers,* Daily Mirror Publications, 1968

the assumptions, ideas and actions that allow one citizen to judge another as 'right' or 'wrong', 'good' or 'bad', or 'clever' or 'stupid'. Although many people do not talk about themselves in these terms, all citizens have an ideology, even if it is related to the best football team or the best soap. If a citizen holds a religious view or a political view on an issue, they are in fact adopting an ideological position. In theory a citizen's views should be consistent, but in reality, many citizens' views on other citizens and events are full of inconsistencies.

Politicians are, believe it or not, human, and they also take a view on a wide range of issues. When these views are similar to those of other politicians, the individuals can group together with the consequence that political parties develop. Each political party usually represents a broad range of views and opinions. In other words, each political party has a distinctive ideology, and it is these differences in ideology that lead to quite distinctive views on what is considered to be 'the right policy' or 'the right solution' and what 'citizenship' is.

Citizenship: individualistic versus collectivist

One major ideological division towards citizenship is the contrast between those whose views of citizenship tend to focus upon individuals compared to those who tend to focus upon society. To put it another way, there is a contrast between those who tend towards individualistic approaches and those whose outlook is more collectivist.

Within an individualistic approach, the role of the state is reduced. There is greater emphasis on a citizen's individual rights, with a corresponding stress on what citizens are entitled to do. This allows citizens the freedom to act independently and provides the conditions in which citizens can pursue their own self-interests. This contrasts to the collectivist or communitarian view, in which the role of the state is much more active. There is a much greater emphasis upon duties and the role of the state. Communitarianism stresses the importance of community in which citizens' shared goals are more important than individual self-interests.

This, however, is only one dimension to a concept that has potentially many differing connotations. If 'citizenship' is a term that is applied to those people who are formally recognised by the state, the concept of citizenship is essentially legalistic and, as a consequence, citizens are those who have legal status and legal rights within a nation-state, like the right to vote, balanced against a range of responsibilities such as paying taxes or completing jury service.

To illustrate these contrasting approaches, it is illuminating to explore briefly how they apply to the UK. Historically, there have been a series of laws passed in Britain which, when combined, provide legal rights that would pass any test of citizenship. The most obvious example is the extension of the right to vote in ever increasing numbers until universal suffrage has been achieved. With these legal rights, citizenship is conferred.

Inclusive and exclusive approaches to citizenship

An alternative approach, however, is to view the concept of citizenship as being related historically to those who were 'included' within the system. This discussion centres on the view that, for some, merely having the right to vote was not significant enough for them to be able to consider themselves part of the state and 'included' within that state. The existence of substantial differences in life chances and rewards created citizens who were, in effect, excluded in practice from effective participation in the state.

To solve this situation, attempts were made to generate conditions that would allow these citizens to participate in the state and thus become included. Two waves of welfare reforms, the first initiated by the Liberals between 1905 and 1914, the second occurring after 1945, were designed to allow those groups who were previously excluded to be included. Some groups, even after these welfare reforms, were still effectively denied full citizenship. A striking example of groups who found themselves in this situation were members of racial minorities who were denied employment opportunities or housing through prejudice and discrimination.

The Conservative years: 1979–97

Approaches to citizenship were radically changed during the Conservative years of 1979–97 when the Thatcher Government remoulded the whole inclusive/exclusive approach to citizenship. Between 1979 and 1997, policies were developed that placed greater stress on the responsibility side of citizenship. New policies were developed which were designed to reduce dependence on the role of the state and allowed citizens to assert their rights though the 'market'. A citizen would be asserting their rights through the market when they took their 'right to buy' opportunity and bought their council home or purchased shares in a privatised industry. (A more detailed discussion of these policies will follow later.) Although these policies arrived in a number of different forms, the most significant fact was the change in economic policy that now placed a much greater emphasis on a free market economy. This resulted in the creation of those citizens who were able to participate within this free market economy and benefit from it. These citizens were 'included'; they could visibly display the trappings of success. Not all citizens, however, were able to benefit from this policy and those who could not were basically excluded and came to represent the (economic) underclass.

Another way in which the approach to citizenship changed during the Conservative years is reflected in the promotion, in 1988, of 'active citizenship' by the then Home Secretary, Douglas Hurd. To understand why 'active citizenship' was introduced at this time it is necessary to understand it within the context of 1988. There was, at this time, a rising rate of crime and a rising rate of public spending. Both of these were unwelcome news for the government of the day. However, if the reasons for these problems could be deflected from the government and placed on the citizens of the state, then the citizens would have a duty to provide actions that would ultimately solve these problems. Thus, taking part in schemes like neighbourhood watch, care in the community, charitable and voluntary work constituted being an active citizen. If an individual could participate in such schemes they would, in effect, be included as a citizen. If circumstances did not allow an individual to, for example, care for a long-term sick relative, they would be excluded from the view of what constitutes being a citizen.

Change in government, change in citizenship?

Although there was a change in government in 1997, from the Conservative Party to the Labour Party, there is very little real evidence of a fundamental change in the approach towards citizenship. A citizen's responsibilities are still emphasised and, considering the lack of action on developing a written constitution, it could be suggested that citizenship issues are good for rhetoric, but poor for winning votes.

However, it has to be remembered that as a result of the Maastricht Treaty of 1992, UK citizens are also citizens of the European Union and can vote in European parliamentary elections. If the euro should become the currency of the UK, with a common currency and voting rights, surely questions should be raised as to whether citizenship can extend beyond the boundaries of a single state.

Global citizenship

It is true to say that the boundaries of a state do not present a barrier to various worldwide threats. AIDS will cross state borders as silently and as frequently as the flying birds. State borders do not provide a barrier for ecological problems, drug traffickers and global terrorists will not respect state boundaries; they are international issues. Equally, but more positively, the United Nations Organisation has promoted human rights across the world. If both problems and solutions can international, why shouldn't citizenship be international? If an individual's status as a citizen was not related to a nation state but was defined in the contexts of 'global citizenship' and 'global human rights', then the issue of exclusion could be tackled in a number of ways. Within this approach, international human rights could be used to incorporate different and diverse groups within the ideals of equality and universality that lie at the heart of being a citizen. It could be possible to achieve this through 'reactive' legislation that could, for example, help to develop the type of positive discrimination programmes that are designed to counteract disadvantages, both past and present. Proactive legislation could also be incorporated into the legislative framework with the aim of developing strategies for greater inclusion of some citizens within the state. One example could be officially recognising the languages and religious festivals of minority groups. Global citizenship, for some, would solve the inclusive/exclusive issues surrounding citizenship at a stroke.

Although the debate so far has developed around contemporary concerns and issues relating to approaches to citizenship, there is a very long history of discussions and debate on the concept. There is little to be gained for the contemporary student of citizenship in a historical sweep that outlines the approaches to the study of the citizen commencing with the Ancient Greeks. However, an understanding of the more recent developments in the discussions relating to citizenship today is relevant and useful.

Women and effective citizenship

In *Citizenship: Feminist Perspectives*, Ruth Lister has developed the inclusive/exclusive approach to the restrictions that some groups face in achieving full and effective citizenship. She argues that, for any group to achieve effective citizenship, it must have the 'rights necessary to be able to participate as a social and political agent'. Historically, women have been excluded from formal citizenship. It was men who were active in the public arena. However, men were only able to be active in the public arena because women were active in the private, domestic arena. To adapt the old adage, 'behind every good man stands a good or even better woman'. A historical justification for this division was the gendering of the human emotions with impartiality, rationality and independence being regarded as male qualities, whilst caring and domesticity were regarded as female qualities.

The legacy of this initial exclusion and the gendering of human emotions must be acknowledged in the recognition that the public and private spheres of life operate in a different way for women as compared to men. Questions can be raised about the relative value placed on the unpaid caring work undertaken by some and the paid work undertaken by others. If citizenship is associated with the work ethic that dominates social, political and economic values, then those groups excluded or marginalised from that work ethic will not achieve full and effective citizenship. If caring is essentially seen as being outside this work ethic, then those groups who are involved with caring are essentially excluded. Society today has a disproportionate number of female carers, which results in differential access to citizenship. This situation will remain until strategies are developed that will create equality between the work ethic and the care ethic.

Other social groups

This inclusive/exclusive approach can be further developed when applied to other social groups which it is felt have yet to achieve full and effective citizenship. These groups could include sexual minority groups and the disabled, although it is equally possible to incorporate those groups which, through racial or ethnic discrimination, harassment and violence, have also been marginalised and alienated from the goal of achieving full and effective citizenship.

The meaning of citizenship according to TH Marshall

Particularly significant in this context is the work of TH Marshall, who, in the mid-1960s, proposed that the meaning of 'citizenship' had developed through three stages. These stages are the rights associated with civil citizenship, the rights associated with political citizenship, and the rights associated with social citizenship.

The first stage in this approach to the development of citizenship is based on the rights associated with civil citizenship. This refers to the individual's rights in law and relates to individual freedoms like the freedom of speech, freedom of conscience, freedom of belief, and rights like the right to own property and the right to equal justice. The second stage is associated with political citizenship. This refers to the individual's right to participate in the political processes by, for example, voting in elections or standing for public office. The third and final stage is associated with social citizenship, which is essentially concerned with the individual's right to welfare provision. In this stage, Marshall asserts that citizenship is related to the ideals that involve establishing certain minimum standards of welfare and security. Social citizenship would be achieved when the incorporation of, for example, rights to a minimum wage, the right to education, the right to sickness benefit and health care were established. This third approach to citizenship quite clearly relates to the provision of those services that are usually referred to as the 'welfare state'.

Problems associated with the work of Marshall

The work of Marshall, however, has been criticised for a number of reasons. Initially, and maybe most significantly, is the criticism that the work is not explanatory; it is merely an evolutionary description of the changes in UK society with the assumption that the three stages of citizenship outlined are sequential. It does not explain why there was an expansion in citizenship or why those changes occurred in that sequence, or indeed why they occurred at all. It also fails to recognise that the experience of citizenship is not the same for all citizens. Citizens are not a homogeneous group and, as a consequence, they will experience citizenship differently, depending on gender, ethnicity, disability, social class and even locality.

Another problem of the approach adopted by Marshall was that central to his view of citizenship was the notion of the nation-state. It is not appropriate to criticise Marshall for not predicting the enormous changes that have resulted from developments in the electronics industry and the information and communication technologies. It is developments in these technologies that some argue have created economies that are no longer based on the concept of a nation-state but are essentially global. Within this view, there exists a globalisation of culture. To illustrate this point, it is not very many years ago that, if a UK citizen was asked whether they needed a 'Big Mac', they would have thought it might be about to rain, and that they may be a little overweight. They would not have considered their state of hunger.

BobZ

However, due to the activities of supranational institutions that spread supranational icons, the globalisation of culture occurs. These supranational institutions with their supranational icons are reducing the centrality of the nation-state in any debate relating to citizenship. If there is a globalisation of culture, then why not a globalisation of human rights from which a globalisation of the concept of citizenship could develop?

Active citizenship or passive citizenship?

Although the above discussion develops the idea that the process of globalisation could produce some unification of the concept of citizenship, at present, attitudes towards the concept of citizenship vary considerably between different cultures. The reason why there are radically different attitudes towards the concept of citizenship can be explained by reviewing the contrasting assumptions from which the concept developed. At the core of this division are the contrasting views as to whether citizenship rights were won through a combination of civil conflict and social struggle *or* whether citizenship rights were 'generously' handed down by the state to the population. This can be categorised as a division between a historical legacy based on 'active citizenship' or 'passive citizenship'. Active citizenship, which believes that rights were won through struggle and conflict, is going to generate a fundamentally different attitude towards citizenship from the passive citizenship view of rights being granted by some benevolent authority. Something that is fought for and won through struggle is going to be more precious than something that has been 'given' and could be taken away at some later date.

It could be argued that this passive view of citizenship rights is reflected in the underlying principle of the *Citizen's Charter* introduced by John Major's Government in 1991. The Charter was essentially designed to inform citizens about expected standards from public services and how to complain if those standards of service were not met. This is a one-way process, as it is the government (the benevolent authority) who is dictating to the consumer (the passive citizen) the expected standard of service. As an illustration of this one-way process, if at any time the expected standards of service outlined in the Charter were proving difficult to meet, the Charter, since it had been 'granted' by the government, could be amended, changed or removed. This contrasts with the active citizenship view, in which appropriate standards are demanded and, if those standards are not met, vociferous demonstrations follow. This could be the explanation to the frequently asked question as to 'why UK citizens are more likely to moan about the standard of their services whilst the French are more likely to go out and demonstrate about them'.

What do you understand by the following terms and concepts?

- Ideology
- Marginalisation
- Active citizenship

- Globalisation
- Citizen's charters
- Passive citizenship

What does it take to become a citizen of another country? In Australia, the Australian High Court has ruled that the ability to hold an Australian passport constitutes the major test of citizenship. In other nations, to become a citizen involves, for example, swearing an oath of allegiance.

Research how the test of citizenship differs in a number of different countries. To complete this research, possible sources could include using the internet or contacting the National Embassies of different countries.

Complete the chart, illustrating the main characteristics of the following approaches to citizenship.

Individualism	Communitarianism	Inclusive	Exclusive

The anti-war protest in London on 15 February 2003 was supported by an estimated 1.5 million citizens. Does the size of this protest indicate that UK citizens' attitudes are changing and that they are now just as likely to demonstrate as citizens in other European countries?

Ann Bates had been on her way to a meeting at the Department of Transport in the winter of 2002, to advise them on difficulties facing disabled people who travel by train. Unfortunately she was late for the meeting. This lateness was caused when she arrived by train at the northbound platform of the City Thameslink station to find that there was no lift available. There was a lift on the southbound platform but to reach it, she would have to travel from the northbound platform to Luton, 30 miles away, change trains, and return to the southbound platform.

When such problems are faced by some disabled citizens, it does not generate a feeling of being included within society.

What are the facilities like for disabled citizens in

- your school or college?
- your local community?

Research the facilities, suggesting where improvements could be made.

CHAPTER 4

The Role of the State in Citizens' Lives

The aims of this chapter are to:

- Introduce the Conservative 'New Right' and the 'anti-state' Liberal view of the role of the state
- Illustrate some examples of the role of the state within a Conservative 'New Right' context
- Illustrate some of the effects of the introduction of this view
- Introduce the changes in the role of the state after the 1997 General Election

To compound the difficulty surrounding the competing views of citizenship, there are, as previously discussed, different ideas and views as to what exactly is the appropriate role of the state. To appreciate this debate, it is necessary to look at how, over the last quarter of a century, there have been changes in the view of what exactly the role of the state should consist of in the life of a UK citizen.

The Conservative 'New Right' and the 'anti-state' Liberal view of the role of the state

To commence this discussion, it is necessary to focus on the differing opinions and debates that were becoming more and more intense by the 1980s and continued, in varying degrees of intensity, throughout the next decade of Conservative Governments. The reservations that were then being voiced by some elements of the Conservative 'New Right' and some elements of the 'anti-state' Liberal Party focused on the growing concern that the state was suffering from:

- a bureaucracy that was too powerful;
- a dependency culture;
- economic inefficiency in the public services;
- public spending that was too high.

The first area of concern relates to a large and powerful bureaucracy. At its very simplest, a bureaucracy refers to those civil servants who administer or run an organisation on behalf of other people. However, in order to understand the importance surrounding bureaucracies, it is necessary to introduce some ideas developed by the German sociologist Max Weber.

Weber (1864–1920)

Weber wrote extensively on the development of a bureaucracy. For Weber, the development of a bureaucracy was essential for the development of industrial society and was representative of a new form of power.

In Weber's view, in traditional societies, the leader is obeyed because he or she has, through long held customs and practices, some degree of traditional authority. Alternatively, the leader may be a great motivator and have such charisma, leadership and personal qualities that they have what Weber called charismatic authority.

However, in an industrial society, a tax collector would find it difficult to collect any taxes by relying only on traditional or charismatic authority. The tax collector needs to have laws that will allow him or her to legally 'rob citizens of their hard earned money'. Nobody likes paying taxes, but most would grudgingly agree that it is necessary.

For the tax collector, the existence of such laws gives him or her a legal and rational authority to collect taxes. An organisational structure with this rational legal authority is a bureaucracy. In Weber's words, a bureaucracy is 'a hierarchical organisation designed to rationally co-ordinate the work of many individuals in the pursuit of large scale administrative tasks and organisational goals'.

For Weber, a bureaucracy was advantageous and necessary, as it depersonalises potentially unpleasant situations. With a bureaucracy's emphasis on the importance of impersonal rules, the tax collector is not seen as a thief robbing an individual through personal dislike; they are only following the rules.

Increases in the role of the state after 1945

As the role of the state increased from 1945 onwards, more and more people were required to organise and run the system. The number of bureaucrats increased, which created another layer of bureaucracy; bureaucrats were needed to organise and run the affairs of other bureaucrats. With the increased number of bureaucrats, strategies and patterns of work were developed that were essentially designed to protect the interests of the bureaucrats and not the interests of the citizen. There was, in effect, a shift in the balance of power. The power of the bureaucracy increased whilst the power of the citizen decreased. The bureaucracy was, in the view of the Conservative 'New Right' and the 'anti-state' Liberals, becoming too powerful and, since a bureaucracy is neither elected nor accountable, there was nothing a citizen could do about it. A citizen could not use his or her vote to remove a bureaucracy that has not been elected.

Dependency culture

The second area of concern relates to the claim that the social welfare system creates a 'dependency culture'. A dependency culture is said to exist when a citizen who is faced with difficulties expects to find the solution to those difficulties provided by the state. The logical outcome of this situation ultimately is that, for those citizens who face multiple difficulties, either their existence will become increasingly controlled by the state or, in extreme cases, their whole existence will become controlled by the state. Since it is the state that provides solutions to problems, there is little incentive for a citizen to use their own initiative to seek a solution or to look for solutions within their family, friends or community. If the state provides money for a citizen when he or she is unemployed, what is the incentive for a citizen to get on, for example, a bike and go and look for work? Margaret Thatcher expressed the view that 'Welfare benefits, distributed with little or no consideration of their effects on behaviour, encourage illegitimacy, facilitated [helped] the breakdown of families and replaced incentives favouring work and self reliance with perverse encouragement for idleness and cheating' (*The Downing Street Years,* 1993).

Public spending

Inefficiency and increases in public spending were also seen as areas of concern. The view was taken that, as spending in the welfare services and the nationalised industries had increased, this had resulted in higher levels of taxation and borrowing. Inefficiency existed because the nationalised industries were not only subsidised but were also not subjected to free market forces. This combined lack of free market forces and, significantly, the lack of competition, it was argued, generated and perpetuated inefficient work and management practices, higher prices and poorer quality of service for the citizen.

These concerns about the role of the state are mirrored in a speech given by the then Secretary of State for Social Security, Rt Hon Peter Lilley at the 1992 Conservative Party Conference. He outlined six principles to guide future policy. These were:

- to focus benefits on the most needy;
- to restore incentives to work;
- to encourage personal responsibility;

- to simplify the system;
- to adapt it to the needs of beneficiaries not bureaucrats; and
- to crack down on fraud.

It booomoo oloar that tho rolo of tho otato and tho dovolopmonto and ohangoo in it are going to have an impact on the concept of citizenship. Whenever the government's attitude to citizenship changes, there will be a corresponding change in emphasis on what is regarded as important. These changes will ultimately influence how the citizen is able to participate within his or her community.

Monetarism

In effect, between 1979 and 1997, the Conservative Governments aimed to address the issues of dependency, high public spending, economic inefficiency and powerful bureaucracy by developing and implementing policies that were designed to reduce the role of the state. These policies ranged across the whole gambit of political activity, starting with the introduction of a view of economics that was known as 'monetarism'. The deployment of this view of economics was an attempt to control both inflation and high levels of spending by placing a limit on the amount of money in circulation. On this view, inflation is caused by an excessive amount of money in the economy. If the money supply can be reduced, inflation will decrease. With strict cash limits on the budgets of central government departments and local government councils, high levels of spending would be controlled. This would produce changes in the money supply that would influence and change the ability of some citizens to participate within their community.

As an economic system, monetarism demanded an economy that had a free market at its base. Inefficient work practices, inefficient management practices and lack of competition or subsidy were all seen as the enemy of the free economy and needed to be eliminated. Faith was placed in the forces of supply and demand in order to achieve efficiency. No more nationalised industries, state intervention or regional development grants. No more control over a citizen's spending through high taxation. Market forces were to be responsible for the establishment of a modern and efficient economy, and any organisation that was thought to be responsible for preventing the free market forces from working effectively needed to be controlled or removed. This became the justification for the unprecedented attacks against the rights and activities of the trade union movement. Clearly, the change in the role of the state had a significant impact on the concept of and the rights associated with citizenship.

Privatisation

A 'monopoly' exists when there is only one supplier of a service. Prior to the Conservative years (1979–97), many services were a state controlled monopoly. A free market economy, with its emphasis on the forces of supply and demand, cannot co-exist with monopolies. These state run monopolies were also seen within the context of increases in the role of the state, increases in the size of an inefficient public sector, increases in public spending and increases in the size and power of the bureaucracy. One policy which tackled at a stroke all of these problems for the free market was that of privatisation. Privatisation can take a number of forms. These range from the less obvious contracting of service provision to and the leasing of assets from the private sector, to the more publicised sale, through stock market flotations, of state owned and controlled assets. According to the advertising of the time, this form of 'popular capitalism', through the flotation of assets, which included the utilities of gas, water and electricity, the rail, coal and steel industries, British Telecom and British Airways, would allow citizens to become increasingly empowered through the purchase of shares in these industries. In reality, institutions purchased most shares. The ability of some citizens to purchase what they previously owned was either unaffordable or ideologically unacceptable.

Internal market

The second policy, which tackled those state run monopolies that were impossible to privatise, was to introduce an internal market. If a natural free market did not exist, then a quasi-free market could be artificially introduced by creating an internal market. One example occurred when an internal market was introduced into the National Health Service. Local surgeries or community health clinics became purchasers of the services provided by hospitals and surgeons. To explain how this internal market was to function, it is necessary to use the example of a local GP. When the GP needed to refer a patient who has a specific problem to a clinic, the doctor would have to 'purchase' this service from their allocated funds. If there were a number of different clinics or providers that could deal with the patient's problem, these clinics or providers would be in competition with each other. According to the forces of supply and demand that dictate the workings of a free market, the doctor, with limited funds, would search out the cheapest provider and send the patient there. All the different providers would want the profit from the maximum use of their facilities. This would generate competition between the providers, which, according to the theory of the free market, would make the providers improve their efficiency and ultimately force down the cost of the service.

BobZ

From this account, it is clear that there had been considerable change in emphasis relating to the role of the state in Britain from 1979. Such fundamental changes cannot occur without having considerable impact on the concept of citizenship. Within any set of relationships, it is the balance between the component parts that structure the reality of the relationship. For example, how high somebody will be elevated on a seesaw is dependent on the weight of the person sitting on the other end. The relationship on the seesaw is based on the necessity of having two people. The role of the state and the concept of citizenship are equally shaped by each other. If there is a change in one of the sets of views or assumptions, this will result in corresponding changes in the other side of the relationship. A vacuum cannot exist. Consequently, as changes were made to decrease the role of the state, there needed to be changes to increase the importance of alternatives to compensate for the decline in the state's role. The result of these changes in the emphasis and scope of the role of the state were compensated for by an increase in the emphasis and the importance of individual freedoms and the social unit of the family. As Mrs Thatcher famously stated, 'There is no such thing as society. There are only individuals, and their families'.

Changes in the importance placed on individual freedoms and the family unit

These changes in the emphasis and importance placed on the enhancement of individual freedoms and the family unit can also be explained within the context of the Conservative 'New Right' anti-welfare ideology of the 1980s. Within this view, the welfare system had come to be seen as a 'nanny state'. The implication of this term is that the 'nanny state' is over-protective and reduces a citizen's individual responsibility. The key to this view is the emphasis on the individual citizen. Individual citizens needed to be 'freed from state interference in their lives'. To illustrate this point, taxation came to be talked about as 'state theft' which should be reduced in order to allow individual citizens to spend more of their money in whatever way they chose. Organisations that stood in the way of allowing the individual citizen to take responsibility for their own lives needed to be removed or changed. This view was rather selectively applied, with some organisations, like the trade union movement, being subjected to many policies designed to make them either (depending on viewpoint) less effective or more democratic, whilst those organisations that controlled the professional work practices of those like doctors and lawyers remained untouched.

Another element in the desire to free the life of the individual citizen from state interference can be found with the encouragement and subsequent increase of private home ownership at the expense of local authority housing. Under changes introduced in the 1980 Housing Act, local authority housing had to be sold at discounted prices to those tenants who wished to purchase their home. A previously 'shackled' citizen became a private home owning citizen who now had the opportunity to benefit from being a part of this new 'property owning democracy'. Once the citizen was freed from local authority housing, other elements of the citizen's life could also be liberated from state interference, and policies were put into place to encourage private enterprise to promote private pensions, health and education. Implicit within all these areas of social life – housing, education, health and pensions – was the underlying importance of the family.

To elevate the importance of the family unit in the relationship between the citizen and the state was considered appropriate for the Conservative 'New Right', provided that the family unit that was being elevated was the 'right type of family'! Clearly, it would be the elevation of the family unit that would best encourage the continuation and development of private enterprise that would be regarded as the 'right type of family'. One type of family unit that certainly did not fit into this framework was the lone parent family, and it may be no coincidence that the lone parent family at this time came to be characterised as 'the root of all social problems within society'. This view can be graphically illustrated by referring to the then Conservative Local Government Minister, Dr Rhodes Boyson, who, at the 1986 Conservative Party Conference, condemned single parents as creating 'probably the most evil product of our time'.

Boyson condemns 'evil' single parents

People who choose to live as single parents were condemned yesterday by Dr Rhodes Boyson, the Local Government Minister, for creating 'probably the most evil product of our time'.

He launched his bitter attack at a fringe meeting organised by the Church Society at the Conservative Party Conference.

He blamed the one-parent family for many of the problems facing Britain, and said that such families would be increased by 'the rise of artificial insemination and casual sex relations'.

Dr Boyson said that one in seven children lived in one-parent families, with one in three in the inner cities. He blamed 'the wildness of the uncontrolled male young' on a lack of fathers.

'Boys can generally only be civilised by firm and caring fathers. The banishment of the father means that boys take their values from their aggressive and often brutal peer groups and are prepared for a life of violent crime, of football hooliganism, mugging and inner city revolt.'

The family was under attack from extreme feminists, the youth cults and homosexual lobbies, he said.

Adapted from 'Boyson condemns "evil" single parents',
David Hencke, *The Guardian*, 10 October 1988

Increasing divisions between citizens

The effects of these changes that have been outlined for citizens were very uneven. The free market economy did create considerable wealth. However, much of this wealth was not invested but was paid in the form of bonuses, dividends or large salaries for a minority of 'fat cat' executives. Undoubtedly, for some citizens, this was a time of unprecedented wealth creation. For others, however, it was a time characterised by increasing unemployment, increasing poverty and an increasing sense of disaffection with society. With an increasing number of disaffected citizens, society was becoming divided between those citizens who were empowered and included within society, and those that were becoming impoverished and facing social exclusion. Expressed another way, the unregulated individualism in the private sector produced the 'yuppies' and 'fat cats', in sharp contrast to the 'scroungers' on welfare benefits or those employed in the low paid public services.

This combination of rising unemployment, rising levels of visible poverty and rising disaffection culminated in a breakdown of law and order with a series of riots.

Daily Mail
TUESDAY, SEPTEMBER 16, 1995   20p

Autumn
fashion
special
See Centre Pages

Black petrol bombers attack police

RIOTING MOB ON RAMPAGE

The state responded to such disorders by changing the powers available to the police services. These changes had two effects: increasing the rights of the police whilst simultaneously reducing the rights of citizens.

The erosion of some of the rights of citizens during the 1980s influenced the balance of power between the rights of citizens and the police. In relationship to a citizen's right to protest and express dissent, the Public Order Act 1986 gave the police the right to ban processions and impose conditions on demonstrations. The Criminal Justice and Public Order Act, introduced in November 1994, created not only the new offences of 'collective trespass or nuisance on land', but also compromised a citizen's 'right to silence', a cornerstone of the English criminal justice system. The refusal to answer police questions could be drawn to the attention of a jury by a trial judge.

Rights attacked

Another area in which a citizen's rights were attacked and violated during the 1980s occurred with the introduction of a range of measures which effectively curtailed or removed citizens' previously assumed legitimate 'rights' associated with membership of a trade union, and indeed on the trade union movement as a whole. Restrictions were placed on the right to strike and picket, whilst the internal organisation of trade unions had to conform to new and unsympathetic regulations. Trade union funds were liable to be sequestrated and the culmination of these oppressive attacks on citizens' rights, for some, occurred when the right to trade union membership at the Government Communications Headquarters in Cheltenham was banned.

The effect of these Acts was to place restrictions on the rights of citizens and, although the changes were applicable to all citizens in society, some argue that the restrictions introduced by the changes were mainly directed against specific groups like the pro-environment activists, squatters and hunt saboteurs, who were becoming increasingly active and well organised.

Charter 88

Although it is impossible to suggest one single cause, by the end of 1988, there was in existence the pressure group, Charter 88. The aim of this pressure group was to promote the cause of constitutional reform and, by October 2002, Charter 88 had over 82,567 signatories. To check the current number of signatories, visit www.charter88.org.uk/politics/why88.html.

The original Charter

We have had less freedom than we believed. That which we have enjoyed has been too dependent on the benevolence of our rulers. Our freedoms have remained their possession, rationed out to us as subjects rather than being our own inalienable possession as citizens. To make real the freedoms we once took for granted means for the first time to take them for ourselves.

The time has come to demand political, civil and human rights in the United Kingdom. We call, therefore, for a new constitutional settlement which will:

- Enshrine, by means of a Bill of Rights, such civil liberties as the right to peaceful assembly, to freedom of association, to freedom from discrimination, to freedom from detention without trial, to trial by jury, to privacy and to freedom of expression.
- Subject Executive powers and prerogatives, by whomsoever exercised, to the rule of law.
- Establish freedom of information and open government.
- Create a fair electoral system of proportional representation.
- Reform the Upper House to establish a democratic, non-hereditary Second Chamber.
- Place the Executive under the power of a democratically renewed Parliament and all agencies of the state under the rule of law.
- Ensure the independence of a reformed judiciary.
- Provide legal remedies for all abuses of power by the state and by officials of central and local government.
- Guarantee an equitable distribution of power between the nations of the United Kingdom and between local, regional and central government.

> • Draw up a written constitution anchored in the ideal of universal citizenship that incorporates these reforms.
>
> The inscription of laws does not guarantee their realisation. Only people themselves can ensure freedom, democracy and equality before the law. Nonetheless, such ends are far better demanded, and more effectively obtained and guarded, once they belong to everyone by inalienable right.

The role of the state and citizenship and the 1997 Labour Government

Logically, the return to government in May 1997 of the Labour Party should have been marked by a change in political ideology, which would produce a corresponding change in the relationship between the role of the state and the citizen. Just like a large luxury liner that will take many miles to complete a 'three point turn', the relationship between the state and the citizen cannot be redefined overnight. The relationship between the two is shaped and given direction by the norms and values into which citizens have been socialised; after 18 years of Conservative government, the relationship between the state and the citizen, compared to the pre-1979 era, had fundamentally changed.

The Labour Party was faced with a dilemma. It had inherited a society that had experienced an increase in the number of citizens who had been marginalised. The trend towards greater inequality and social exclusion was a situation it wished to reverse, and thus produce a society that was more tolerant, with increased opportunities for citizens to participate effectively within society.

However, with such a prolonged focus on individualism during the Conservative years, there had effectively been a general reduction in the support for the collectivist view of citizenship. This resulted in the impossibility of introducing radically different policies characterised by large increases in public spending and wealth redistribution. Although there was general support and a focus on individualism during the Conservative years, there was little support for the unregulated individualism that had become associated with 'greed and sleaze'. It is a combination of these points that provide the essential elements of the Labour approach to citizenship – more inclusion, more tolerance and greater opportunity. Ultimately divisions between the 'included' and the 'excluded' disappear, as all citizens have a stake in society.

From shareholder to stakeholder

This shift in direction, from shareholder to stakeholder, was to produce a series of changes in emphasis and in ideology for the Labour Government after 1997. These changes, however, started from a declaration that the inherited market economic system would be supported, although future policies would be developed to ensure that those who had previously been deprived of work, prospects and power would be able to have a stake in society. On one level, two non-contentious aims could be achieved by the adoption of this 'third way'; economic efficiency and social justice. More significantly, however, two quite contrasting positions could also be achieved. Stakeholding could provide an individualistic focus on the acquisition of skills needed for wealth creation, and it could also provide a collectivist focus on the rights and responsibilities that are an essential part of being a member of a community. The dilemma between a collectivist legacy and an individualist framework was solved.

What do you understand by the following terms and concepts?

- Bureaucracy
- 'New Right'
- Privatisation
- Internal market
- The 'third way'

- A dependency culture
- Stakeholding
- Monetarism
- Marginalisation

It is impossible to justify any of the changes in the laws relating to trade unions that were introduced by successive Acts of Parliament between 1979–97, as the combined effect of these Acts was to deliberately reduce the power and influence of effective trade unionism.

Select a range of different policies that have been introduced since the mid-1960s, for example, the privatisation of public sector industries, or the introduction of comprehensive education.

For each policy, state:

- which political party introduced the policy;
- whether that policy would support a collectivist or an individualist view of Citizenship.

Party policy and the role of the state	Political party	Evidence to support differing views of citizenship		Justification for your decision
		Individualist	Collectivist	
Privatis- ation of public sector industries 1980s	*Thatcher Tory Party*			

Many different forms of research can be undertaken to get an idea of the changes that were occurring in the role of the state and citizens in the UK.

One method is to use the internet searching sites related to constitutional reform. A good example is www.charter88.org.uk/politics/why88html, the site of Charter 88.

Other sources of information include researching a specific event that encapsulates the changes. The miners' strike is a well documented example that will illustrate many elements of this chapter.

Equally, many novels and films are set in within this time and again provide a very useful alternative source of information. Examples include the BBC video collection of *Our Friends in the North* (1979–95) and the films *Brassed Off* and *Billy Elliot*.

CHAPTER 5

Rights and Responsibilities or Responsibilities and Rights?

The aims of this chapter are to:

- Introduce the issues surrounding the 'rights and responsibilities' of citizens
- Consider the balance or imbalance of power between the state and the citizen
- Consider the implications of an unwritten constitution
- Consider the Human Rights Act 1998
- Consider the implications of the Anti-Terrorism, Crime and Security Act 2001 on a citizen's civil liberties

Rights ...

Many countries have one single document that outlines and guarantees a citizen's rights and liberties. This statement of a citizen's rights and liberties is often referred to as a Bill of Rights, which forms the basis of, or part of, a written constitution.

The UK does not have either a written constitution or one single document outlining a citizen's rights and liberties. The rights and liberties of citizens in the UK are contained within a combination of Acts of Parliament that have been passed over the last eight centuries, common law traditions and unspoken conventions. Even the UK's 1688 Bill of Rights and the Human Rights Act 1998 are just Acts of Parliament and do not have any special constitutional status.

Although some claim that the strength of any unwritten 'constitution' is in its ability to evolve, adapt and change, the issue of a lack of one single document outlining the rights and liberties of citizens often results in the criticism that when the rights of citizens are 'vague and unstated [they] are not rights at all – but can be snatched back by government in a heartbeat. Witness the Major administration's alteration to the 1688 Bill of Rights, made solely to enable the disgraced Neil Hamilton to proceed with a libel action' (Freedland, J, *Bringing Home the Revolution,* p 204). Indeed, any government with an overall majority could change a citizen's rights simply by passing a Bill through Parliament.

... and responsibilities

The balance between the legally defined set of rights and the series of responsibilities and obligations is at the heart of this debate. An example can be found in the following extract from Tony Blair's speech at the Labour Party Conference, 28 September 1999:

> And I saw that what we said on drugs and new powers was attacked by civil liberties groups. I believe in civil liberties too. The liberty of parents to drop their kids off at school without worrying they're dropping them straight into the arms of drug dealers. The liberty of pensioners to live without fear of getting their door kicked in by someone thieving to pay for their habit ...
>
> ... Civil liberty to me means just that; the liberty to live in a civil society founded upon rights and responsibilities.

Tony Blair further outlined his vision for Britain in an article he prepared for publication on 10 November 2002. Although the language is not in the emotional style of a party political speech, the message is the same:

> Respect is a simple notion. We know instinctively what it means. Respect for others – their opinions, values, ways of life. Respect for neighbours; respect for the community that means caring about others. Respect for property which means not tolerating mindless vandalism, theft and graffiti. And self-respect, which means giving as well as taking.
>
> Respect is at the heart of a belief in society. It is what makes us a community, not merely a group of isolated individuals. It makes for a real contract between citizens and state, a contract that says with rights and opportunities come responsibilities and obligations.

Many would argue that there has been a long and historic development of citizens' rights in the UK which has resulted in a series of rights and liberties enjoyed by UK citizens. These rights and liberties include:

- Freedom of movement
- Freedom of speech
- Freedom of association
- Freedom of conscience
- Freedom of the person

- The right to be treated equally
- The right to privacy
- The right to a fair trial
- The right to own property
- The right to vote and to stand for public office

For others, there is the belief that many of the rights and liberties enjoyed by UK citizens are little more that an illusion that has come to be believed to be real through centuries of repetition, and even these rights and liberties, some would argue, have been systematically attacked recently. The following chart outlines the good news and the bad news on the state of rights and liberties in the UK.

Rights and liberties in the UK
The GOOD news and the BAD news

Freedom of movement

This freedom relates to the lack of restrictions on a citizen's right to move around the country ... even though there is no legal right protecting an individual's right of movement and the police can use a child curfew order to remove children aged 10–15 from the streets between 9 pm and 6 am.

Freedom of speech

This freedom relates to a citizen's right to express, publish and broadcast views and opinions on anything ... that the government has not placed a restriction on or that does not contravene the tough laws of libel.

Freedom of association

This freedom relates to a citizen's right to form groups and hold meetings ... However, there is no absolute right to freedom of association and, under the Terrorism Act 2000, simply being a member of a proscribed (banned) organisation carries a maximum penalty of 10 years' imprisonment.

Freedom of conscience

This freedom relates to the freedom to worship, with religious meetings being protected by law. Blasphemy is a crime ... but only against Christianity.

Freedom of the person

This freedom relates to the relationship between the citizen and the police and includes freedom from arbitrary arrest and/or arbitrary police searches and the right to silence ... unless the police are looking for any 'mark' that could be used to identify a citizen. The police can also photograph citizens without their consent, and these photos can be filed and permanently retained (established by the Police and Criminal Evidence Act, amended by the Anti-Terrorism, Crime and Security Act 2001).

The right to be treated equally

This right refers to the expectation that citizens will be treated equally in terms of political rights, employment and before the law. Discrimination on the grounds of race and sex is illegal ... although this does not extend to discrimination on the grounds of age, or to asylum seekers.

The right to privacy

This refers to the 'respect for a citizen's private life' and protects citizens from, for example, trespass and nuisance. It also includes protection from telephone tapping and interception of electronic and postal communications ... However, there is no right to privacy, as developments in and use of surveillance equipment has shown. Also, the Regulation of Investigatory Powers Act 2000 allows for the interception of private letters and emails whilst the Anti-Terrorism, Crime and Security Act 2001 permits the police and security services access to a citizen's personal information held by public authorities.

The right to a fair trial

This right refers to a citizen's right to a free trial following established procedures where the law is applied impartially without fear or favour. This openness also allows for citizens to be judged by their peers in the form of a jury ... However, the operational independence of the police and judiciary has been reduced by the Crime (Sentences) Act 1997. There is an ongoing debate relating to the right to trial by jury and, under section 23(1) of the Anti-Terrorism, Crime and Security Act 2001, a suspected international terrorist can be detained indefinitely if they cannot be deported or extradited.

The right to own property

This refers to a citizen's right to both own property and use it for any legal purpose ... unless it is terrorist property, subject to a compulsory purchase order, or is to be nationalised.

The right to vote and to stand for public office

The right to vote applies to all registered eligible UK citizens over the age of 18, and any UK citizen over the age of 21, subject to some conditions established in 1975, may seek election to public office ... However, the right to vote is lost if an eligible UK citizen is not registered and a UK citizen is not able to stand for election to the House of Commons if they cannot raise £500.

No UK citizen can stand for election to the House of Lords.

The Human Rights Act 1998

To redress some of the imbalance of power between citizens and the state, the Labour Government finally incorporated the European Convention for the Protection of Human Rights and Fundamental Freedoms (usually referred to as the European Convention on Human Rights), first signed in Rome in 1950, into UK law. Thus, on 2 October 2000, the Human Rights Act 1998, the biggest change in laws relating to rights and freedoms since the 1688 Bill of Rights, introduced not only a range of civil rights enforceable in all UK courts, but also provisions which demand that all courts 'so far as possible' take the Act and the interpretation given to the Convention by the European Court of Human Rights into account in their judgments. The significant Articles from the European Convention for the Protection of Human Rights and Fundamental Freedoms in the Human Rights Act include:

Art 2 The right to life of all citizens will be protected.	*Art 7* Retrospective criminalisation, except for war crimes, is banned.
Art 3 No citizen will be subjected to torture or to inhuman or degrading treatment or punishment.	*Art 8* All citizens have the right to respect for private and family life, their home and their correspondence. Restrictions on this right must be proportionate to the needs of a democratic society.
Art 4 No citizen will be subjected to slavery or forced labour.	*Art 9* All citizens have the right to freedom of thought, conscience and religion. Restrictions on this right must be proportionate to the needs of a democratic society.
Art 5 No citizen will be deprived of their liberty except in accordance with the law.	*Art 10* All citizens have the right to the freedom of expression. Restrictions on this right must be proportionate to the needs of a democratic society.
Art 6 All citizens are entitled to a fair trial within a reasonable time.	*Art 11* All citizens have the right to the freedom of peaceful assembly and the freedom of association with others.

Art 12	Art 14
Citizens of marriageable age have the right to marry.	All rights outlined in the Convention shall be applicable to all citizens regardless of sex, race colour, language, religion, political or other opinion.

The Human Rights Act has impacted on all citizens' lives, even if they do not fully realise it. Judges now have the power to amend and change laws without any input from Parliament by reinterpreting laws so that they are compatible with the Human Rights Act and, although a judge cannot remove a law if it offends the principles of the Act, a judge can declare that a law is incompatible with the Act. When this occurs, the government has to either introduce new legislation or face the possibility of being taken to the European Court of Human Rights. In reality any declaration of incompatibility will result in a change in the law as the likelihood of the government either wanting to face, or winning, a case at the European Court of Human Rights in Strasbourg is less than certain. In the first year of the Act, nearly 200 cases raised human rights issues and the courts used their power to rewrite a law in 10 cases.

The Human Rights Act, it would seem, has permeated UK culture. Indeed it would seem that some UK citizens are becoming increasingly aware of their rights and the Act is being used increasingly frequently. One area where the Act is being used frequently is where citizens, often 'celeb citizens', are using it to gain privacy injunctions to stop the exposure of elements of their behaviour. The *Sunday People* was, as they described it, initially 'gagged' in November 2001 from naming a married footballer who was having two affairs with other women. Almost a year later, Angus Deayton, the ex-presenter of BBC's *Have I Got News For You*, got an injunction to stop the *Mail on Sunday* from printing revelations that would, according to the newspaper, have 'shocked even his closest friends'.

After the first year of the Human Rights Act the senior Law Lord, Lord Bingham, described the introduction of the Human Rights Act 1998 as an unquestionably major advance. He felt that the Act had produced a sense of popular confidence in the system of justice.

Although the Human Rights Act was introduced by the Labour Party in their first term of office, the rights introduced for citizens were soon under attack as the Human Rights Act was followed, after the attack on the USA on 11 September 2001, by the Anti-Terrorism, Crime and Security Act (ATCSA) 2001. As will be discussed soon, the ATCSA 2001 challenges both citizens' civil liberties and elements of the Human Rights Act and indeed necessitated the opting out of Article 5 of the European Convention on Human Rights.

However, before the ATCSA 2001 can be introduced into the discussion, it is necessary to consider the balance between rights and responsibilities.

Rights with responsibilities; responsibilities with rights

A consistently recurring theme throughout the development of new Labour is the emphasis on rights and responsibilities. There are many illustrations of this emphasis. In an early Blair speech in 1996, he stated that 'rights and responsibilities are at the heart of everything new Labour stands for' and continued by stating that 'for every right we enjoy, we owe responsibilities'. In a later article, published in November 2002, he reconfirms the view that: 'Respect is at the heart of a belief in society. It is what makes us a community, not merely a group of isolated individuals. It makes for a real contract between citizens and state, a contract that says with rights and opportunities come responsibilities and obligations.'

To illustrate the balance between a citizen's 'rights' and 'responsibilities' it is possible to use the issue of parenthood. On the one hand, citizens have a 'right' to become a parent; a 'right' that is not contestable or considered unacceptable, and indeed, it is a 'right' that is pursued by many citizens. However, for some, the number of children who are abandoned by one of their parents is evidence that those 'responsibilities' that accompany the 'right' to parenthood have not been accepted.

The example of parenthood illustrates that the issue of a citizen's rights and responsibilities, when applied to a non-controversial area, will generate some discussion but will not generate a great chasm of opinion within society. The same, however, is not true when it is applied to issues that have much greater potential to harm large numbers of citizens. Indeed, there is a range of issues that need to be addressed which commence on the one hand with the question of 'whether it is indeed possible to have any rights without accompanying responsibilities' and culminate on the other with questions that take the form of 'what are the responsibilities that accompany a citizen's rights?'. Should the views of, as Blunkett put it, 'airy fairy liberals' who are concerned about minor erosions to citizens' right to privacy, stand in the way of a reforming government that seeks to root out groups who are prepared to bomb, kill and maim for some extremist political or religious cause? For responsible politicians, the right to privacy must be balanced against the right to live safely and freely.

Citizens have the right to privacy. However, the right to privacy is not an absolute right and can be eroded: the European Convention on Human Rights permits the state to invade a citizen's privacy providing this is done legally and is necessary to prevent crime. This compromise to a citizen's privacy might not be seen as an intrusion on a citizen's rights because both the citizen and the state would citizens to live freely and in safety.

The Anti-Terrorism, Crime and Security Act 2001

The problems, however, start to arise when the state increasingly intrudes into a citizen's privacy. If, in the view of the state, there exists 'the spectre of global terrorist networks, perpetrating outrages beyond our wildest fears', combined with 'an explosion in communications ... offering to a deadly minority greater ability to work across national borders and outfox national security and policing forces' (David Blunkett, 'Civic rights', in 'Big Brother', *The Guardian*, September 2002), this may be used to justify new laws on the grounds that they are necessary to prevent crime. As has been seen, this may further compromise a citizen's right to privacy. The fact that the Terrorism Act 2000 and the ATCSA 2001 have been introduced shows how easily a citizen's rights and civil liberties can be removed in the name of responsible government.

The Terrorism Act 2000 and the ATCSA 2001 are clearly intended to address the issue of terrorism. But what is a terrorist act? The answer, according to the Terrorism Act 2000, is:

> ... any act or threat of action which involves serious violence against the person or serious damage to property, endangers a person's life, creates a serious risk to the health or safety of the public, or is designed to seriously interfere with or disrupt an electronic system.

The act must also be designed to influence the government or to intimidate the public or a section of the public and to further advance a political, religious or ideological cause.

'I'm not a terrorist, get me out of here!'

If the broad definition of terrorism adopted in the Terrorism Act 2000 had been applied throughout history, to what extent would the following historical figures be regarded as terrorists?

- *The suffragettes*
  - ○ Emily Davison
  - ○ Christabel Pankhurst
  - ○ Annie Kenny
- *The 'match girl' striker*
  - ○ Annie Besant
- *The Digger*
  - ○ Gerald Winstanley
- *The Chartists*
  - ○ Feargus O'Connor
  - ○ John Frost
- *The IRA member*
  - ○ Michael Collins
- *The Syndicalist trade unionist*
  - ○ Tom Mann
- All citizens who demonstrated against the 'poll tax', London 1990

This is a very broad definition of terrorism and has the potential to encompass many activities which, although they may be unlawful, cannot be construed as terrorism. Activities that could be included within such a broad definition might be some forms of industrial action, some forms of civil disobedience and animal rights activism.

When such a broad definition is employed, the powers required will be substantial and the ATCSA 2001 has been criticised for its wide scope that changes the balance of power between police and citizens. Many would go further and argue that the ATCSA 2001 has, in reality, very little to do with 'the war against terrorism' but everything to do with transforming civil liberties.

Some of the changes introduced by the ATCSA 2001 are extremely significant. Citizens may be surprised to learn that the police and security services now have the right to access personal information held by any public authority. A public authority is required to disclose a citizen's information 'for the purpose of any criminal investigation whatever' and is defined in section 6 of the Human Rights Act 1998, and not only includes the police and the courts, but 'any person certain of whose functions are functions of a public nature'. As a consequence of this definition, a citizen's medical records, bank statements, school records and tax returns are all sources of information that can be accessed *even though* no crime has been committed or suspected. All that needs to occur is a criminal investigation to have commenced.

The ATCSA 2001 has also considerably extended the powers of the police. These additional powers allow the police to fingerprint a citizen without his or her consent and, once this data has been obtained by the police, it can be used not just for investigating any alleged terrorist activity, but for the investigation of any offence and the prevention or detection of any crime.

And there is more! A further extension to the powers of the police relates to the rights police now have to establish a citizen's identity. Any police constable in uniform can demand the removal of any item, such as a headscarf or a mask, which they believe is being worn to conceal a citizen's identity. Officers can now examine any citizen to discover if they have a 'mark' that could lead to identification. Any citizen can be photographed by a police officer without the citizen's consent; and what is a still further erosion of civil liberties is the fact that the photograph can be kept on file and can be disclosed to any party for any purpose related to the prevention and detection of crime.

The combination of the very broad nature of these powers and the fact that they have been generalised to all crime and not just terrorism, raises questions about the shift in the balance of power between state and citizen. Equally significant is the fact that the extension in the power to remove headgear and facial coverings could easily lead to discrimination against female Muslim citizens who could face unreasonable interference with their dignity.

Part 11 of the ATCSA 2001 concerns itself with the retention of communications data. Under the Act, all communication providers, such as internet providers and telephone companies, will be required to keep customer records and thus allow police access to a range of information that would include data about a citizen's emails, the websites a citizen has visited and a citizen's phone bills.

The ATCSA 2001 also introduces a series of new crimes. These include the crime of inciting religious hatred. There is a penalty of up to seven years for using 'threatening, abusive or insulting words or behaviour intended to stir up hatred against a group of people because of their religious (or lack of religious) belief'. They also include the criminalisation of citizens who publish details relating to the security of nuclear sites, transport of nuclear materials and sensitive nuclear technology. If a citizen withholds from any authority any information that could have been used to prevent a terrorist attack, they are also a criminal as well. The Act also allows for the immediate freezing of assets of overseas individuals and groups that support terrorism.

The most controversial part of the ATCSA 2001, however, lies in Part 4 which applies to foreign nationals. If the Home Secretary believes that the individual is a terrorist and believes that the individual is a threat to national security, the individual will be 'certified' and detained indefinitely if they cannot be deported. Once detained, the individual cannot appeal on any other grounds than points of law and his/her case will only be reviewed (within six months and thereafter every three months) by the Special Immigration and Appeals Commission (SIAC). SIAC's proceedings will be carried out in the absence of both the individual and the individual's legal representative and any evidence can be presented without the individual or the individual's legal representative being present. The reasons behind any decisions made by SIAC will be withheld from both the individual and the individual's legal representative.

The use of such a draconian power is clearly not compatible with Article 5 of the European Convention on Human Rights. However, under Article 15 of the Convention, a government can 'in time of war or other public emergency threatening the life of the nation' withdraw (derogate) from an article. This is what the UK government has done.

The use of detention without trial raises serious questions about a citizen's rights. In August 2002, evidence emerged from Gareth Pierce, the solicitor for many of those detained following the attack of 11 September 2001, that the detainees had been held in conditions of great oppression and were kept 'in solitary for 22 hours a day'. She also claimed that their access to benefits and bank accounts were frozen, they were not allowed to phone lawyers and for some, their families faced eviction and destitution. With the press prevented from printing the names of the detainees or establishing the reason for their internment, and their lawyers excluded from knowing the details of the charges made against them, the position of the detainees, who uniquely have to prove their innocence, rests with the Special Immigration Appeals Commission (SIAC). The balance between rights and responsibilities can be very problematic. Is it justifiable for a Home Secretary in preserving the rights of the majority of citizens to curtail the rights of a few? Alternatively, is the introduction of such sweeping powers apparently against a small minority actually a clever way of introducing such powers against all citizens? Probably the only certain thing is that detention without trial has never stopped terrorism; all that detention without trial has done is to create a deep sense of injustice that simply breeds more terrorism.

CCTV

Even at a day to day level, the balance between rights and responsibilities is still problematic. To illustrate this discussion, the issue of CCTV can be considered: when used responsibly, CCTV can enhance a citizen's protection from theft or violence, but if used irresponsibly it compromises a citizen's right to privacy, freedom of movement and freedom of association.

The following two newspaper articles illustrate this delicate balance between protecting the rights of a citizen and abusing the responsibility that accompanies the process of protection.

UK leads on cameras to fight crime

A bomb blast in Brixton, another in Brick Lane, and then a dawn police raid on a sleepy Hampshire village. All were linked by an image of the suspect, captured on camera.

Last night police investigating the Soho blast were poring over hours of footage from the 'large number' of cameras in the gay heart of London.

According to Clive Norris, an academic at Hull University and author of *The Maximum Surveillance Society*, there are now more than a million such cameras in the UK.

On an average day in London, or any other big city, 'an individual is filmed by more than 300 cameras, from 30 different CCTV networks', Norris said.

In London, a person is captured on a camera at least every five minutes and in central areas is likely to be watched by cameras at least half the time.

In several areas the police can take control of council cameras to track a suspect for several miles. Newham in east London has installed a computer system which can 'recognise' the faces of known criminals. The latest cameras are powerful enough to read a newspaper headline 100 yards away.

Police forces now see electronic surveillance as a vital supplement – or even alternative – to bobbies on the beat.

Civil liberties groups warned that more needed to be done to discriminate between the legitimate and unscrupulous use of footage.

John Wadham, director of Liberty, said: 'Most people tolerate the downside of being under surveillance because they believe it means people will be caught for terrible crimes like these.'

But in the absence of any regulation of CCTV use, he said, the there was a risk that the technology could be misused.

Friday's bomb was a good example. 'It could be that as part of a serious police

Thousands of new cameras filming street

The surveillance camera revolution continued apace yesterday with the announcement that 180 anti crime closed circuit television schemes had won government funding of £33m.

The projects include the installation of cameras on housing estates, in town and city centres, along beachfronts, in universities, outside pubs, and overlooking car parks and streets in England and Wales. The measures are part of a three year programme in which the Government is to award £170m to pay for thousands of CCTVs around Britain.

Crimes being targeted by yesterday's schemes include robbery, handbag snatches, business burglaries, thefts of and from cars, ram raiding and drink-fuelled violence.

The Home Secretary, Jack Straw, said: 'This Government is determined to reduce crime and the fear of crime. CCTV is playing a crucial role in helping the police combat crime and, importantly, reduce the fear of crime. Today's announcement is the largest single allocation of CCTV money to date and thousands of people across England and Wales will soon be able to benefit from CCTV in their communities, towns, villages and shopping centres.'

Recent research into operators of surveillance cameras found abuse by private-sector workers who used the CCTV to look at attractive women, watch people having sex in car parks and target a disproportionate number of young black people. There was also some evidence of police interference in surveillance when cameras captured wrong-doing by fellow officers.

However, the Police Complaints Authority has found CCTV footage extremely useful in catching out officers, as well as clearing them from malicious allegations.

Mr Straw added: 'As an extra set of eyes for the police, CCTV is always "on the beat" and able to provide an accurate and investigation, camera footage is used to catch a criminal. But in that area, cameras controlled by private security guards might use the images to blackmail people frequenting the area.'

'UK leads on cameras to fight crime',
The Observer, 25 May 1999

permanent record of what and who has been seen. The technology has proved its worth in reducing crime and making people feel safer.'

'Thousands of new cameras filming street',
Jason Bennetto,
The Independent, 18 January 2000

Between 1996 and 1998, 75% of the Home Office's crime prevention budget was spent on installing CCTV equipment. However, when the Home Office eventually evaluated the effectiveness of 24 CCTV schemes, they discovered that only 13 of the schemes had resulted in a significant reduction in crime, whilst in seven schemes the introduction of CCTV had no effect and in four schemes there was a significant increase in crime. For a success rate that is nearly equal to its failure rate some citizens have to pay a heavy price in terms of their right to privacy, freedom of movement and freedom of association.

The scheme referred to in the first newspaper extract in Newham in east London has been developed considerably and is referred to as a 'facial recognition system'. This system involves digital photographs of the faces of convicted local criminals and those who have been released from prison being fed into a computer. The computer then picks out a series of 'nodal points' and the distances between these points are converted into a string of numbers. Once a face has been programmed into the computer, the computer becomes the perfect unblinking, unsleeping, unrelenting observer that can compromise a citizen's right to privacy and freedom of movement and erode a citizen's civil liberties.

Explain the meaning of the following using a maximum of 75 words:

- A constitution
- Rights and responsibilities
- The 1688 Bill of Rights
- The ATCSA 2001
- The Human Rights Act 1998
- Civil liberties

Many politicians believe that there has to be a balance between a citizen's rights and a citizen's responsibilities. Complete the chart, outlining:

- the rights that you associate with the following issues; and
- what responsibilities you think should accompany the right.

Issue	What rights could be associated with the issues?	What responsibilities accompany this right?
Parenthood	Right to have one or more children Right to raise children according to your views	Care for child, teach the child right from wrong
The use of CCTV in public places		
Becoming an elected representative of your community		
Dissatisfaction with your working conditions and pay		
Interception and reading when emails are sent and received		
The testing of a suspect by the police for illegal drug use		

Some citizens take their rights and freedoms for granted. Others are unaware that many 'everyday' activities are examples of a citizen's rights and freedoms that could be compromised or removed. Many citizens in other states do not enjoy the same rights and freedoms that citizens in the UK enjoy.

For each of the following rights and freedoms:

- list the type of activities that could be included as an example of that right and freedom;
- list the ways that the right and freedom could be removed;
- list examples of when these rights and freedoms have been removed.

	Examples of behaviour which incorporate	Suggest **how** these rights could be removed	When **are** these rights removed?
Freedom of movement			
Freedom of speech			
Freedom of association			
Freedom of conscience			
Freedom of the person			
The right to be treated equally			
The right to privacy			
The right to a fair trial			
The right to own property			
The right to vote and to stand for public office			

To illustrate how citizens relate differently to their freedoms and rights:

- Rank the freedoms and rights in your personal order of importance and then compare your results to other members of your group.

- Why do you think each list is likely to be different?

It is only with the existence of a written constitution that the rights and freedoms of a citizen can be safeguarded.

CHAPTER 6

Freedom of Information, or the Right to Know versus the Right Not to Know

The aims of this chapter are to:

- Introduce debates and controversies surrounding a citizen's access to and restrictions on information
- Explore the relationship between citizens and the state
- Develop issues surrounding 'the public interest'
- Assess the social nature of information and its usefulness
- Introduce the idea of 'open government'

Thirty minutes' work that influenced 90 years

If Shakespeare had been a student of citizenship, he might have written the following:

> To know or not to know, that is the question ...

... for those who have knowledge or information are often faced with a dilemma. Should other citizens be informed or not informed? If the answer to the question is that they should be informed, are citizens to be informed about everything? At what point does information change from being a source of knowledge to a weapon that could have disastrous consequences if misused? As James Hacker, the fictitious government minister portrayed in the BBC's *Yes Minister* television series, 'Either they [the civil service] give you so little information that you don't know the facts, or so much information that you can't find them.'

There may be some agreement with the view that the state has a right, just like a parent when dealing with a child about a sensitive issue, not to divulge information that is of a particularly sensitive nature. However, who decides at what point information becomes 'particularly sensitive'? How can a citizen ask questions about an issue if there is no information about the issue or the issue does 'not officially exist' (meaning either that the 'issue' is not perceived as an issue, or that it is kept as an official secret)? Unless an event is in the public domain, how can questions be raised about that event?

'To know or not to know', to have information or to have access to information denied, is a crucial issue that serves as a starting point for discussions about the issue of whether information should be controlled by the state. If information is to be controlled by the state, does this mean that citizens in the UK are effectively denied access to information that they have a right to know? Alternatively, should citizens have free access to information which they can use to construct arguments and form opinions?

Official Secrets Act 1911

One possible starting point to this debate is the year 1911, when, within 30 minutes, the Official Secrets Act was passed. The significance of this Act is considerable.

First, the Act introduced new offences and laws. In section 1 of the Act, it became an offence to:

- disclose information which might be useful to an enemy of the state;
- undertake behaviour that would be 'prejudicial to the safety or interests of the state'.

In section 2 of the Act, it became an offence for anybody employed by the state (a Crown 'servant'!) to pass on any official information gained at work to anybody not authorised to receive such information. Thus, the colour of paint used on an office door or the number of paper clips used in that office became official secrets.

Although not a legal requirement, it is government/civil service practice to classify documents into four basic security categories:

- restricted: disclosure would be undesirable in the interests of the nation;
- confidential: disclosure would be prejudicial to the interests of the nation;
- secret: disclosure could cause serious injury to the interests of the nation;
- top secret: disclosure could cause exceptionally grave damage to the nation.

The wording in the first three categories uses the phrase 'the interests of the nation'. This immediately raises the question as to exactly whose interests these documents are protecting.

The relationship between citizens and the state

Secondly, and maybe more significantly, the Act reinforced the basis on which the relationship between citizen and state existed. This relationship has at its root a debate about the central focus of the political world. Does the political world consist of 'the *state's* citizens' who need to be ruled by a government that directs both what citizens can and cannot do and what citizens need or do not need to know? Politicians have a right to act in a way that limits the knowledge a citizen has because they 'know best' or limitation is in the 'public interest'. Alternatively, does the political world consist of 'the *citizen's* state' and the citizens are in control as they 'lease' their power to public servants in the form of politicians? Any information, therefore, is not the property of the government, but is the property of the citizens and it is the citizens who have the right to access this information. It is the citizens who will tell the government what it can and cannot do with any information it has and what secrets it can or cannot keep.

The Official Secrets Act clearly reflects the first of the two views outlined above and established a trend in the development of a culture of secrecy. This culture not only reinforces the imbalance of power between state and citizen, but also fundamentally influences and shapes that relationship. One way of illustrating this point is to argue that a politician is simply a citizen doing a particular type of job. What would happen if, at any time, there existed some confusion between the interests of the state and the self-interests of the politician? A culture of secrecy could allow the politician to withhold some or all of the information, not for the interests of the state, but as a result of his or her own self-interests or career advancement. This possible confusion between the self-interests of a politician and the interests of the state is not easy to solve, especially when compounded by the question of what exactly is understood as being in the 'public interest'.

Action in the 'public interest'?

It is possible to examine a range of actions that have all been carried out with the justification that the action was in the 'public interest'. In 1984, Sarah Tisdall was employed as a clerk at the Foreign Office and as a result of her employment she had information confirming that US cruise missiles had arrived in Britain; information that she felt, along with many others, was in the public interest. This concern led her to 'leak' the information to *The Guardian*. As a result of this action, Sarah Tisdall was charged under the Official Secrets Act. She pleaded guilty and subsequently received a six month jail sentence. For some citizens, the guilty verdict reinforced the view that the double standard was alive and well. When the state wants to withhold information on the grounds of 'public interest', that is part of the democratic process, but when a citizen discloses information on the grounds of 'public interest', it is a crime.

The imprisonment of Sarah Tisdall was to be the first in a series of high profile cases during the 1980s. One year later, a second 'leak' occurred when the civil servant, Clive Ponting, passed information concerning the sinking of the battleship *The General Belgrano* during the Falklands War. The significant difference to the earlier example was that, when the case went to court, Ponting did not plead guilty. He based his defence on the issue of 'public interest', claiming that knowledge about the deceit by Thatcher's Government was in the 'wider public interest'. Although Ponting was in effect guilty, as he did not have authorisation to release the information, he was acquitted by the jury, for reasons only known to the jurors themselves. Importantly, however, their acquittal did not establish a defence of 'in the public interest'.

David Shayler, Peter Wright and Naomi Campbell

The inability of citizens to defend their actions on the grounds that they were acting 'in the public interest' has serious implications and can be illustrated by reviewing the actions of David Shayler.

David Shayler, or spy G9A/1, was a former MI5 officer who, during 1997, made a number of allegations about the work of the security and intelligence agencies. These allegations fell into two groups. Some of the allegations suggested that MI5 and MI6 were involved in illegal activities and included the claim that the security services were involved in a plot to assassinate the Libyan leader Colonel Gaddafi. Shayler also claimed that MI5 was unlawfully tapping telephones and keeping files on various citizens that included future Labour ministers Jack Straw and Peter Mandelson and the ex-Beatle, John Lennon. The second series of allegations made by Shayler against MI5 and MI6 suggested that there was a 'drinking culture' which, when combined with the 'excessive bureaucracy' of the organisations, resulted in an incompetent and inefficient organisation that consequently had missed the opportunity to avert various terrorist actions.

Such incompetence and inefficiency, according to Shayler's interpretation, could only mean that MI5 was guilty of committing criminal acts. He chose to make his allegations and disclose classified documents to support his claim to the *Mail on Sunday* which published the information on 24 August 1997. This was a clear breach of the Official Secrets Act and the Government wanted to silence him and prosecute him. However, this was not possible as Shayler had fled to France 24 hours prior to the publication of his disclosures. The French courts ruled that his crimes were of a political nature which allowed him to remain free in France. Shayler eventually returned to the UK in late summer 2000 in the knowledge that he would be prosecuted under the Official Secrets Act 1989.

The Shayler case raises many issues surrounding freedom of information. Shayler believed he had evidence of malpractice, crime and incompetence on the part of the intelligence services and he believed that it was in the public interest that this information should be published. However, to publish this information was an illegal act. It was a crime to reveal a crime. Shayler's freedom of speech had been removed. But freedom of speech was a principle that had been enshrined in the Human Rights Act.

Shayler's right to freedom of speech and the knowledge he believed he had about criminal activities were in conflict, and raised questions as to whether the Official Secrets Act was incompatible with the Human Rights Act. This issue was one that the courts had to address before any trial of Shayler could commence.

During May 2001 in a pre-trial judgment, Mr Justice Moses stated that any unauthorised disclosures by a serving or former member of the security and intelligence services put national security at risk. He continued by stating that sections 1(1) and 4(1) of the Official Secrets Act did not permit a defendant to 'raise a defence in the public interest'. He ruled that the Official Secrets Act had taken into account the Human Rights Act and that members of the intelligence services had a duty of confidentiality that did not allow for unauthorised disclosure in any circumstances.

As a result of this judgment, when the case against Shayler was heard before an Old Bailey jury in November 2002, Shayler was prevented from presenting his public interest defence to the jury that the security services were involved in illegal activities. The prosecution, by contrast, only had to prove that he was guilty of passing documents to the *Mail on Sunday*. The outcome of the trial was that Shayler was found guilty of breaching the Official Secrets Act and was sentenced to six months' imprisonment. Perhaps the only surprise in the outcome was that it took the jury over three and a half hours to return a guilty verdict.

Another example of a one-sided relationship between the state and the citizen can be examined by looking at the controversies surrounding the publication of the memoirs of ex-MI5 agent Peter Wright in his book entitled *Spycatcher*.

The book was to be published in 1987 but its publication was banned by the Thatcher Government. The ban did not involve any prosecution under the 1911 Official Secrets Act but was obtained, and later upheld in part, by the European Court of Human Rights, based on a breach of confidence, even though the book could purchased and read abroad and, if an imported copy had been purchased, then it could be read in the UK. Enormous interest was generated by the attempted ban, so much interest in fact that public readings of the book took place. *Spycatcher* had become more than 'just a book'; it had become a symbol of both the problems of the 1911 Official Secrets Act and the justification for those who wished to achieve the changes that would lead to increases in the freedom of information.

By 1989, and as a direct result of the *Spycatcher* episode, it was apparent that the Official Secrets Act 1911 was ineffective and unworkable. Some citizens felt that, since the Act was unworkable, there would be progress away from a culture of secrecy and towards a more open government with freedom of information. The *Spycatcher* case divided attitudes towards the issue of official information and a citizen's right to have access to such information. All political opinion seemed united in the view that reform of the 1911 Act was necessary but divided between those, generally on the political Right, who felt that the Act needed strengthening and made more effective and those, generally on the Left, who felt that there needed to be much greater freedom of information.

As with the case involving the model Naomi Campbell, there is a conflict between Article 8 of the Human Rights Act, which requires respect for privacy, and Article 10, which protects freedom of expression. Naomi Campbell had denied that she had a drug problem. However, not only was she photographed by *Daily Mirror* journalists leaving a lunchtime meeting of Narcotics Anonymous, but a journalist had attending the meeting. The problem of how to balance the freedom of the press to inform and simultaneously preserve a citizen's right to privacy will be explored in the next chapter.

Official Secrets Act 1989

Change did occur, as the 1911 Official Secrets Act was replaced with the 1989 Official Secrets Act. In the context of the late 1980s, with the emphasis on the free market economy with its accompanying need for a strong state, the change from the 1911 Act to the 1989 Act was not accompanied in reality by any changes or developments towards greater freedom of information. In fact, in many respects the new Act created greater secrecy than the Act it replaced. The Official Secrets Act 1989 not only removed the discredited section 2 of the 1911 Act, but also removed the defence that the information being disclosed was either in the public interest or was already available in another country.

As a consequence of this case, a landmark judgment was delivered by Lord Justice Judge on 21 July 2000 when he declared that the press were right to resist police attempts to force them to hand over documents. His decision has considerable implications as many citizens may have documents or evidence that relate to a serious crime. If these are taken to the press, journalists will be able to resist demands for them to hand over their material.

The right of journalists to protect their sources lies in section 10 of the Contempt of Court Act 1981 which states that any journalist is protected from naming his or her sources unless it is necessary to disclose them in the interests of justice or national security or to prevent disorder and crime. The problem with the clause 'interests of justice' is that although it might have been originally included to protect defendants in criminal cases, its meaning has expanded to deny journalist protection and ultimately limit a citizen's freedom of expression.

During the first six months of 2002, a lengthy legal battle took place between the Belgian brewing company Interbrew and *The Financial Times, The Times, The Independent* and *The Guardian* newspapers. The newspapers had received from an anonymous source a document that suggested there was to be a takeover bid for the rival brewer, South African Brewers (SAB). As a result of the leak, Interbrew's share price fell by 7.5% whilst SAB's shares jumped by 8%. This made the takeover bid too expensive.

Not surprisingly, Interbrew were upset about this. They demanded all documentation from the various newspapers that would allow them to investigate the source of the leak. The newspapers refused and lost their case in both the High Court and the Court of Appeal. Because the document received by the newspapers was said by Interbrew to have been changed from the original, judgment rested upon the usage of the clause 'in the interests of justice' as there was, according to Lord Justice Sedley, no way that Interbrew could know the degree of change, so, in the interests of justice, the document should be returned. The issue, however, is that this defence has the potential to be easily used to remove the protection of a journalist's source. The newspapers involved believed that they had a duty to defend the identity of a source and thus the source's freedom of speech and on 12 July 2002, risking fines and other legal penalties, refused to hand over to Interbrew's solicitors any documentation. It is interesting to note that in the USA, Germany and Sweden, the right of a journalist to protect his or her sources is enshrined in law, and the newspapers involved in this case were prepared to go the European Court of Human Rights to win back their right until Interbrew withdrew their legal action.

Further restrictions on a citizen's access to information

The Official Secrets Act is not the only set of restrictions placed on a citizen's access to information. Another restriction placed on access to information is the 1958 Public Records Act. This Act places a restriction on the release of government papers either until 30 years have passed or after sufficient time for those papers no longer to be sensitive, after which the files can be read by citizens at the official archives, the public records office at Kew in London. There are, at present, 40 categories of papers which are automatically deemed to be too sensitive and which will be closed for 30, 50, 75, 100 years or indefinitely.

A further restriction to information can arise when a Public Interest Immunity Certificate is issued. These certificates prevent the release of documents and although they are infrequently employed, when they are used, they are very effective in preventing a citizen's access to information. At least four Public Interest Immunity Certificates were issued in the trial of David Shayler. A Public Interest Immunity Certificate was also issued during the trial of ex-royal butler, Paul Burrell. The use of these certificates tends to increase when the potential for government embarrassment is at its greatest. They were certainly employed, as Sir Richard Scott's February 1996 report into the 'arms for Iraq' scandal confirmed, by the government of the day in order to effectively prevent the release of papers and documents that were vitally important to the defendants in the Matrix-Churchill trial.

A citizen's right to information can also be restricted by the use of mechanisms that seem to exist for no other purpose. One such mechanism is the 'D-Notice'. (Officially speaking, these are now called DA-Notices, the DA standing for Defence Advisory.) The Defence Press and Broadcasting Advisory Committee issue a D-Notice. This D-Notice committee dates from the early part of the 20th century, and consists of representatives from the media, senior civil servants and a full time Secretary who is usually from the Ministry of Defence. Interestingly, when a D-Notice is issued, there is not a legal requirement to obey it as D-Notices do not have any legal force. A D-Notice is issued to serve as a guide to the media and they only work because the media let them. For a citizen, a D-Notice may sound like some form of censorship, but the view of Rear Admiral Nick Wilkinson, Secretary of the Defence Press and Broadcasting Advisory Committee, is that since a D-Notice is an informal and voluntary restriction, it is not official censorship. It is evidence of 'responsible journalism', journalists who balance their reporting duties towards citizens against their duties not to hand valuable information to those who could use it against UK citizens. D-notices work on a shared assumption between journalists and the state that some information and some events are just too sensitive to report.

An example of what essentially amounts to official censorship is summarised in the following article from *The Guardian* prior to the outbreak of the Gulf war in 1991.

Press and TV reports to be censored if war starts

Ministry of Defence censors in the Gulf will vet all broadcasts, pictures, and reports from journalists with the troops on the front line if war breaks out.

Any material that is considered to endanger human life, endanger operations, or disclose what are considered technical secrets is likely to be restricted as is media coverage of wounded servicemen.

Broadcasters in London, who have held fortnightly meetings with the MoD, have already agreed to the 'ground rules' for broadcast reporters and camera crews operating in the Gulf.

Journalists operating in the Gulf were briefed on how the MoD/British Army plan to organise coverage if war breaks out. Two 'media response teams' – consisting of one television crew, one radio reporter, two print journalists and one photographer each – will go to the front with the 4th and 7th armoured brigade.

All material will be pooled to all news organisations through a 'forward transmission unit' (an FTU in military jargon). The military censors will operate in the FTU, from where material will be sent directly to London.

G Henry, *The Guardian,* January 1991

Some citizens might argue that in exceptional times, exceptional measures need to be taken. However, the implications within the extract are far wider as they relate not just to the issue of freedom of information. Since all information would have to be pooled, the restrictions are effectively controlling the supply of information available to both citizens and the media. The restrictions on the supply of information were so great that in an image demanding world, UK citizens were denied any images for 54 out of the 74 days the war lasted. Indeed, the relationship between reporters and officials deteriorated to the point that when the ITV *News at Ten* introduced a bulletin with the words 'this bulletin is being censored', the censor removed them. As a consequence of this limited and controlled supply of news, the only point of view that is being represented is the official point of view which might lead some citizens to agree with the adage 'truth is the first casualty of war'.

The lobby system

A further way in which a citizen's access to information can be controlled or restricted is through the everyday management of news. One way in which this has been achieved in the UK is through the lobby system. The lobby system consists of secretive meetings between representatives of the government and selected journalists.

The journalists can report and publish the information, but only in the form of 'off the record' accounts that often take the form of 'Sources close to ...' or 'The view from Number 10 is ...'. If a journalist does not follow the 'rules', then he or she is no longer invited to future lobby briefings, and a journalist without a story is as useful as a bicycle without wheels. This system allows the representatives of the government to brief journalists and to feed the journalists their version of events, rather like feeding fish to penguins. To put it another way, the government can distribute and present (some) information that has been manipulated so that it conveys the message or paints the picture that is most favourable to the government. Information that has been subjected to such a reinterpretation is often referred to as having a 'spin' put on it. This control and management of information is now seen as being part of the work of a 'spin doctor'.

- Look through a range of newspapers and try to find examples of where you think journalists have obtained information through the lobby system.
- Look at some political news stories from a range of different sources. These could be newspapers, magazines, radio or television. How similar or how different are the stories?

Politicians as a source of information

There are many other ways in which information is controlled. The House of Commons has a list of taboo topics which ministers, when in the House, can refuse to answer questions about. Within the Cabinet there is the doctrine of collective responsibility. This means that no matter how much a minister may disagree with a decision or policy in private, in public all ministers must accept those collective decisions and policies and not disagree with them. The problem for a citizen, however, is that, when a minister states a point of view, it is impossible to know to what extent it is the view of the minister, or the view that has to be adopted due to collective cabinet responsibility.

As a source of information, politicians themselves can sometimes prove problematic. The sheer volume of information produced can prove a difficulty for citizens. The Labour Party, since its return to power in 1997, has, on average, produced a press release every four minutes.

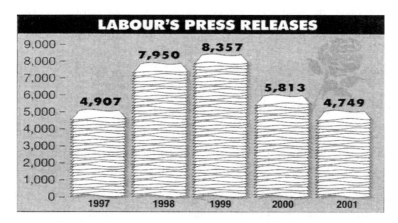

'It's spinful', *Daily Mirror*, 1 May 2002

With so much information being released, there is always an opportunity to abuse the situation. Evidence of this occurred when a memo from Jo Moore, a political adviser to the then Labour Transport Minister, dated 2.56 pm on 11 September 2001 (less than 30 minutes after the second tower of the World Trade Center was hit), was leaked. This memo stated that 'It's now a very good time to get out anything we want to bury'.

When being interviewed by the media, some politicians appear to be very keen to share information. Unfortunately for the citizen, the information that the politician is so keen to share has been decided prior to the interview. No matter what questions the interviewer actually asks, it is the pre-determined information that is going to be stated. It was as a result of an interview between the BBC's Jeremy Paxman and the then Conservative Home Secretary, Michael Howard, that won Paxman a Bafta for his January 1997 interview, in which he asked the question 'Did you threaten to overrule the director of the prison service?' 14 times without any direct response to the question. Such evasiveness seems to be part of a government minister's toolkit: the Chancellor of the Exchequer, Gordon Brown, in an interview with John Humphrys on BBC Radio 4's *Today* programme on 16 February 2001, refused 11 times to answer variations on the same question in a 13 minute interview. For the citizen who feels that they have a right to know, the information presented by the politician has often been moulded into a short, easy to remember phase or slogan, often referred to as a *soundbite*, and it is the soundbite that is most often reported in the media. The effect of this is that the soundbite becomes 'general knowledge'. The citizen's right to know, in effect, is changed from 'a right to know' to 'a right to know what the politician wants you to know'.

Politicians and stand-up comedians are two groups in society who have a reputation for being able to deal successfully with hecklers or awkward questions. The fictitious James Hacker, who is Prime Minister in the BBC *Yes Prime Minister* series, outlined eight ways to deal with questions that were 'difficult'.

How to answer the difficult question

1   *Attack the question.*   'That's a very silly question.'

2   *Attack the questioner.*   'How many years have you spent in government?'

3   *Compliment the question.*   'That's a very good question. I'd like to thank you for asking it. Let me reply by asking you one.'

4   *Unloading the question.*   Most questions are loaded. They are full of assumptions such as 'A lot of people have said that you consider yourself above the law'. There are two possible replies to such loaded questions:

    (a) 'Name ten.'
    (b) 'Surely in a nation of 56 million people you can find a few people who will say anything, no matter how irrelevant, misguided, or ill-informed.'

5   *Make it all appear an act.*   This approach only works for live TV interviews. 'You know, I've come to the conclusion that I don't agree with what you suggested I should answer when you asked me that question downstairs before the programme began. The *real* answer is . . .'

6   *Use the time factor.*   Most interviews are short of time, especially live 'on air' interviews. Reply: 'That's a very interesting question, and there are nine points that I should like to make in answer to it.' The interviewer will say: 'Perhaps you could make just two of them, briefly.' You say: 'No, it's far too important a question to answer superficially, and if I can't answer it properly I'd rather not trivialise it.'

7   *Invoke secrecy.*   'There's a very full answer to that question, but it involves matters that are being discussed in confidence. I'm sure you wouldn't want me to break a confidence. So I'm afraid I can't answer for another week or two.'

8   *Take refuge in a long pointless narrative.*   If you can ramble on for long enough, no one will remember the question and therefore no one can tell if you answered it or not.

I summed it up for him: if you have nothing to say, say nothing. But better, have something to say and say it, *no matter what they ask.* Pay no attention to the question, make your own statement. If they ask you the same question again, you just say, 'That's not the question' or 'I think the more *important* question is this:' Then you make another statement of your own. Easy-peasy.

Adapted from *Yes Prime Minister: The Diaries of the Rt Hon James Hacker* (Vol 2), by Lynn and Jay

---

Open government and freedom of information

The issue of open government is a crucial issue for any citizen living in any state. For a state to be able to justify itself as a democratic state, a citizen needs to have the right to access information. This could be the information that is recorded within a citizen's personal files. This is important because, without that information, how can a citizen know what is actually recorded in a file or, indeed, the accuracy of what is recorded, if access to that file is denied? Equally, if a citizen wants to monitor some element of the government's performance, if that citizen is denied access to information, how can any evaluation of performance take place?

There have been some recent developments relating to both open government and freedom of information; under the 'open government' code, some departments have released a large number of files that were previously classified as 'secret'. In a report updating progress towards more open government, published in December 2002, it was reported that the Ministry of Defence had released the greatest number of files, with some 83,000 files being declassified. The notion of open government seems to be slowly developing and there now exists the open.gov.uk website, which 'provides a first entry point to UK public sector information on the internet'.

At the start of this chapter, reference was made to James Hacker, that fictitious government minister from the BBC's *Yes Minister* series. The quote referred to the relationship between him and the civil service. The significance, however, of those words, 'Either they give you so little information that you don't know the facts, or so much information that you can't find them', could easily be related to the internet, where there is now so much information that what is significant and important is either simply 'unfindable' to the average citizen or, due to lack of access to the internet, just unobtainable.

The debate revolving around freedom of information is ongoing. The Freedom of Information Act was passed in November 2000, and according to the commencement timetable in the Act, it is due to be introduced in 2005. Many, however, feel that it could or should be introduced sooner.

There are over 300 secrecy clauses in existing Acts of Parliament that will have to be removed. Although implementation plans have not seemed to be high on the government's agenda, with training programmes being suspended, on 28 November 2002 the government promised to repeal or amend 97 laws and review a further 200 laws that ban the publication of information held by the civil service in Whitehall. The government also announced that from 1 December 2002, every government department and Whitehall agency will have a list on its website of all the types of publications that are available to citizens on demand. This represents the single biggest review of unnecessary secrecy for more than 20 years and appears to be the first stage towards the implementation of the Freedom of Information Act by 2005.

Potentially, the combination of the Data Protection Act 1998, implemented in great haste as a result of a European Union directive, which gives citizens the right to access files held on them, and the full implementation of the Freedom of Information Act, might, by 2005, afford to UK citizens a level of freedom of information that has been enjoyed by citizens in other societies for many years.

'Either they give you so little information that you don't know the facts, or so much information that you can't find them.'

The only way to test the significance of the quote by James Hacker above is to discover whether there is too much or too little information available to citizens. After referring to the *Code of Practice on Access to Government Information*:

- Access the open.gov.uk website and proceed with an enquiry relating to freedom of information. Would you expect about a quarter of a million 'hits' on this issue?

- Arrange to visit somewhere or someone in your local community. Examples could be the Town Hall, a local employer, even your place of study. The task is to discover:
  - What information will the organisation freely tell you?
  - What information will the organisation not tell you?

Information: it doesn't grow on trees!

For any citizen, however, the issue of freedom of information may not be as important as the issue of the reliability of that information. There is little point in a citizen having access to information if that information cannot be trusted. This point can be illustrated in a number of ways.

To understand the problem relating to information, it is useful to make a rather strange comparison between 'information' and the leaves on a tree. The leaves on a tree are entirely natural. They develop in size from sticky buds in spring until they fall in autumn. Leaves have a natural existence. Information, unlike the leaves on a tree, does not have a natural existence: information does not 'grow on trees', information is socially constructed. Information has to be gathered, decisions as to what is to be included and what left out have to be made. If a comparison is to be made, a decision must be taken as to which years will be compared. How the terms are defined, and the intended purpose of the information, may well influence how it is constructed, what is included or not included. Information is socially constructed, and any information that has been constructed by people in society is open to manipulation or reinterpretation. Although recently there seems to have been a rapid expansion in the amount of information available to citizens, the quantity of information is not the crucial issue. What is more important is to look at the quality of the information and assess its reliability and validity.

The reliability and validity of socially constructed information

To assess the reliability and validity of any information, the citizen should raise a number of important questions. These could be questions like: 'Who is doing the constructing of the information?' 'Why are they constructing that information in that way?' 'Why is it being presented in that format?' If it is being used to make comparisons: 'Why is it being compared to that group or that year?' Maybe most importantly: 'For what purpose is that information to be used?'

An issue that appears to be relatively straightforward is the 'number of ill people being treated by the NHS in hospital beds'. However, this seemingly innocent issue can illustrate how socially constructed information can become problematic.

The range of potential responses to this issue could involve, for example, establishing and then counting the number of hospital beds in the NHS. For many citizens, the answer to this question would result from adding together all those metal frames that support a mattress and are then covered with sheets and blankets in order to allow a patient to lie down. However, if a bed is used to treat two or three different patients in one day, does that metal frame become one bed, two beds or three beds? If a premature baby is being cared for in a specialist cot within a premature baby unit, is the baby using a hospital bed? If a patient is terminally ill and is receiving full time NHS care in their own home, is this a hospital bed? Since childbirth is not an illness, are the beds in a maternity unit to be counted as part of the answer to the original question?

The reason why there is such potential confusion around information is because any information is contaminated when it comes into contact with humans. To make information available to citizens, it has to be processed and packaged. It has to be put into a format that allows it to be understandable to citizens. It then has to be presented to citizens. The final product is processed, socially constructed information.

Freedom of information or quality of information?

To compound matters, in many cases there is only one source of information, which makes comparison between competing sources impossible. Without comparative data, effective evaluation is again impossible. For most UK citizens, the main source of information derives from the government, which raises an important issue relating to freedom of information. In many instances, the freedom of any information remains the secondary issue. The most important issue is how the information is constructed and presented to citizens. If it is only this information that a citizen has access to, then it is only this information that can be used to construct the meanings that allow the citizen to understand and make sense of his or her world.

To illustrate this point, consider the official number of people who were unemployed between 1979 and 1996. This information was freely available to citizens as the monthly figures were released by the government and were reported by the news media. However, what was less widely reported were the changes in the official definition of what exactly counted as 'being unemployed'. The official figures indicate that the trend in the rate of unemployment was decreasing. However, between the years 1979 and 1996, there were 32 changes made to the way the official unemployment figures were calculated. Each change in the definition had the effect of reducing the official figures.

The *Sunday Mirror* illustrated this point graphically.

4.5m

1979
Change from weekly to fortnightly attendance at benefit offices – total down 20,000.

1981
Effect of Government employment and training schemes – down 495,000.

Unemployed over-60s given option of higher benefits for not registering – down 30,000.

Adjustment of figures to compensate for the effects of Social Security department industrial action – down 20,000.

1982
Change from counting registered unemployed to only claimants – down 190,000.

Introduction of higher long-term rate of supplementary benefit for men aged over 60 already on supplementary benefit for one year – down 37,000.

1983
Men over 60 who considered themselves retired no longer have to register unemployed to get National Insurance paid – down 162,000.

Men over 60 no longer required to sign on to receive long-term rate supplementary benefit – down 54,000.

1984
No longer regarded unemployed if take up Community Programme places – down 29,000.

1985
Amalgamation of statistics in Ulster with the rest of the UK – down 5,000.

1986
Count put back two weeks to remove "over-recording of jobless" – down 50,000.

Abolition of reduced rate unemployment benefit for people with insufficient National Insurance contributions to qualify for full rate – down 30,000.

Extension of voluntary unemployment disqualification – down 9,000.

Introduction of Restart Programme and new availability for work tests for new claimants – down 300,000.

1988
Further extension of disqualification period for unemployment benefit – down 12,000.

16-to-17-year olds no longer entitled to unemployment related benefits – down 40,000.

Only those who had paid sufficient National Insurance contributions in the past two financial years entitled to unemployment benefit – down 38,000.

Abatement of benefit to occupational pensioners – down 30,000.

1989
Redundant miners receiving occupational pensions no longer have to sign on – down 26,000.

Introduction of Actively Seeking Work requirement – down 25,000.

Disqualification from benefit for refusal of unsuitable jobs – down 25,000.

Weekly earnings limit of £43 to qualify for benefit – down 30,000.

1996
Introduction of Jobseekers Allowance – down 137,000.

1.8m

Source:
Sunday Mirror,
16 March 1997

- Research some sources of official statistics. One good source is the annually published *Social Trends* (available as a book and CD ROM in most libraries).
- Take any area of social life on which there are official statistics. Do these statistics deliver a complete analysis of this area of social life?

This question can be approached by:

- trying to discover if there have been any changes in how the statistics have been collected from one year to another;
- trying to discover if there have been any changes in what categories of behaviour are being included as part of these statistics;
- trying to discover if there have been any changes in what categories of behaviour are being excluded as part of these statistics.

If the statistics are making a comparison, why is the comparison being made from that specific date?

Would the statistics read differently if an alternative comparison date had been selected?

Are there any other ways in which freely available official information is presented in such a way that its meaning changes?

Should the media take more care in how they present information to citizens?

Why do you think that the revelation about the official unemployment figures was published:

- by the *Sunday Mirror*?
- in March 1997?

The importance of freedom of information

Freedom of information remains a key issue in the study of Citizenship and, as with all key issues, there are ongoing changes and developments. The importance of this debate for students of citizenship is not just knowledge of the law, but appreciation of the underlying implications that this has for any citizen and the relationship between that citizen and the state.

This point can be illustrated by reference to the Disability Discrimination Act 1995. This Act requires that *all* information is accessible to people with disabilities. However, as the *Tunbridge Wells Borough News* confesses, information is not comprehensive for those with disabilities.

Disability Discrimination Act

Making information easily accessible to everyone

From this month a new act has come into force requiring organisations, such as ours, to ensure that all the information we produce is accessible to those with disabilities.

We hope that those of you who require information in another format are able to let us know so that we can be prepared to meet your needs. Whilst we have some information in this area it is not totally comprehensive and any help you can give us to help you would be appreciated.

This Borough Review has been produced on tape for those with a visual impairment. If you would like to get hold of a copy simply call the Public Relations Department on

There is an answerphone out of hours or you can e-mail us anytime at

Contact the Public Relations Department of your local council in order to establish how much information is available for those with some form of disability.

Another example of why freedom of information remains an important issue for any citizen, and should be a key concern for citizens in contemporary Britain, can be illustrated through contrasting two events that were to be found in one news report.

The first part of the news report, written by Nick Cohen and published in *The Observer*, 6 February 2000, refers to the proposed establishment of a national Criminal Records Bureau. This Criminal Records Bureau, run by the private sector, would allow any employer to be able to receive a copy of any potential employee's criminal records. This development has enormous implications for citizens living in the UK, especially when the Home Office is expecting to perform up to 10 million disclosure checks per year. However, it is only when the second part of the report is considered in conjunction with the first that the importance of freedom of information, and especially the proposed freedom to inspect files, becomes apparent. The second part of the news report refers to information provided through a 'mole' and highlights a random examination of criminal records in 16 London boroughs between January 1999 and April 1999. The Metropolitan Police's Security Inspection Unit discovered an 'overall error rate of 86%'.

A discussion relating to freedom of information would not be complete without reference to the workings of another state where there is a very different attitude toward the relative balance in importance between the citizen and the state. The US provides a very good comparison. An example of these differing attitudes can be illustrated by noting the form in which the government is addressed. Should politicians refer to '*the* government' or should it be referred to as '*your* government'? Is it '*Her Majesty's* opposition' or should it be '*The People's* opposition'? Why do politicians swear an oath of allegiance to the very person who cannot vote for them? Why not swear an oath of allegiance to the people who elected them? Is it 'the *state's* citizens' or 'the *citizen's* state'? A similar division in attitude between the US and the UK could also be said to exist towards freedom of information, and it could be argued that the attitude towards the relative importance of citizen and state is mirrored in the differing attitudes towards freedom of information between the two cultures.

The US has laws that ensure that information is freely available to citizens. The extent to which information is freely available can be illustrated by the tradition that the President will, on leaving office, establish a presidential library in his (her, one day) hometown that will enable citizens to have access to documents within five years. This contrasts with the UK where, in order for UK citizens to have access to the archive of Churchill's prime ministerial papers, they had to be purchased from Churchill's grandson using £12 million of lottery money. The final irony lies in the fact that, since the UK and the US pool an enormous amount of their information, very often information is available on one side of the Atlantic but that same information is unavailable on the other.

 How easy is it to research donations to political parties in the UK and the US? Try to discover who donates what to which political party in both the US and the UK. In which country is it easiest to find the answer to the question?

Jonathan Freedland graphically illustrates this point by citing how Professor Richard Brietman of Washington's American University was able to obtain 1.3 million pages of coded messages that had been intercepted by British code breakers. John Fox, history lecturer at the London School of Jewish Studies, had requested that the same documents be made available at the Public Records Office, only to be told that the papers were still classified, bearing the stamp: 'Most Secret. To be kept under lock and key: never to be removed from the office.' (*Bring Home the Revolution*, 1998, p 48.)

Freedom of information remains an important issue in the study of citizenship. Without freedom of information, citizens are denied the most important tool in their toolkit. Citizens cannot make an informed judgment and, in any balance of power, those who control information and knowledge control power. If freedom of information is to be achieved in the UK, changes in the culture of both UK citizens and government will be needed.

As a way of illustrating the contrasting attitudes towards freedom of information, the Regulation of Investigatory Power (RIP) Act, which become law in October 2000, can be considered. The justification for the introduction of this Act was the freedom of information needed by the security forces, but, as a result of this law, the state, police and security services will be able to monitor and intercept all emails and websites. The RIP Act allows all internet communications to be monitored without a warrant. As from October 2000, all citizens who use the net are subject to government surveillance. The Act will deny citizens the freedom and the privacy enjoyed by the majority of citizens in the world, as only Russia, Singapore and Malaysia have similar controls. RIP Act; RIP privacy.

 What do you understand by the following terms and concepts?

- Official Secrets Act
- The 'public interest'
- D-Notices
- Public Interest Immunity Certificates

- The lobby system
- Open government
- A 'spin doctor'

Spot and decode the soundbite

 During your Citizenship course, whenever you hear or read a soundbite, record it in a table like the one below.

Politician and issue	Source	soundbite

Now that you have recorded some soundbites, try to work out what the politician is really saying.

The soundbite	What it actually means

During your Citizenship course, whenever you hear or read about issues relating to freedom of information, dooido:

- whether they support the view that emphasises 'the *state's* citizens'; or
- whether they support the view that emphasises 'the *citizen's* state'.

Two nearly complete examples are included.

Source of quotation	Quotation	Position supported
John Grant, former Cabinet Minister for Government Information Services	Information is power. Confidentiality, allegedly in the public interest, is all too often used by those in authority to avoid discomfort, inconvenience, and any potential challenge to that power. The justification for secrecy should be subjected to rigorous testing, and openness should be the rule rather than the exception. *The Guardian* campaign for freedom of information	
Kenneth Clarke, as a member of the Cabinet, 1993	I am afraid that I think that [the proposed 'Right to Know' Bill] goes far too far. The so called freedom of information legislation in America has mainly benefited commercial competitors, private investigators and sections of the press.	

Freedom of information will never be achieved through changes in the law. It will only be achieved through changes in the culture of both UK citizens and government.

CHAPTER 7

The Citizen and the Legal System

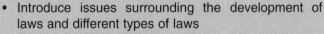

The aims of this chapter are to:

- Introduce issues surrounding the development of laws and different types of laws
- Introduce the different types of courts and encourage the student of citizenship to witness from the public gallery these courts in action
- Explore issues surrounding trials by jury
- Raise issues surrounding the cost of justice
- Develop concerns about the representativeness of the judiciary
- Explore potential links between a citizen's social characteristics and their ability to obtain justice

Imagine a set of athletes about to start a race without knowing how far they are going to have to run. Do they prepare starting blocks and launch themselves at the sound of the starting pistol at great speed, so that the leader disappears in a cloud of dust ahead of all the others, or do the athletes gently lean forward in order to pace themselves for a steady and prolonged jog around the track? The distance of the race will determine which option the athletes select. The speed of the athlete can only be understood in the context of the distance they have to run.

In discussions about citizens and the law, there also needs to be a starting point that will allow further discussion to develop. The most useful point from which to start, although it may well be based on an assumption, is that humans, people, citizens (the term at present is irrelevant), are, by definition and nature, social animals. As social animals, there is the desire for companionship and the necessity for co-operation, both of which can be achieved through the formation of groups. As society becomes increasingly complex, so the range and the diversity of the groups in which citizens are involved become larger and increasingly complex.

This complex network of interlocking groups – a plethora of individual relationships, institutional relationships and organisational relationships – is able to exist through socialisation, from which shared norms and values and social order derive. Citizens are able to lead ordered lives through the strength of the internalisation of shared ideas about the desirable and the undesirable, the appropriate and the inappropriate, the good and the bad, the right and the wrong.

Through the processes of custom and convention, the behaviour of individual citizens is limited; self-control exists, from which citizens voluntarily elect not to behave in a certain way. Pages of documentation do not govern these social rules; they are self-imposed with the threat of disapproval, ridicule or exclusion from the rest of the group being enough to control and modify behaviour. Behaviour is controlled and modified through informal sources of social control.

In some cases, though, the threat resulting from any informal source of social control is simply not enough to constrain the behaviour of some citizens, and a more formalised system of control is required. In some cases, in order to ensure obedience, it is necessary to introduce the idea of compulsion. Compulsion requires that citizens follow compulsory rules or compulsory codes that will limit or ban some forms of behaviour. As soon as compulsory rules or compulsory codes of behaviour are introduced, a citizen needs to know about the behaviour that is acceptable and the behaviour that will not be considered acceptable. When these rules of behaviour and conduct are formalised in writing and enforced on citizens, they become laws. Formal written laws are the rules of conduct for all citizens and are enforced on all citizens by the state.

The mere fact of having something written down will not change the behaviour of some citizens, who will continue to undertake activities that are not sanctioned or approved. This results in the need for some methods that enforce obedience to the law.

- In order to enforce obedience there is the need for some citizens whose role and function is to take responsibility for enforcement. There is the need for some citizens to be able to *police* other citizens.

- In order to achieve compliance there is the need for graded punishments and retribution. If punishment and retribution are required, there is also the need for certain citizens whose role and function is to take responsibility for the application of punishments on those citizens who break the law. There is the need for some citizens to *judge* other citizens.

The long arm of the law

 Keep a diary for one day describing the types of interactions that you have with other citizens or institutions. These could be:

- the milk or newspaper being delivered;
- catching a bus;
- going to school or college;
- buying goods from a shop;
- going to the cinema;
- watching television;
- helping around the house;
- a quick surf of the net;
- going to your part time employment.

Research whether the law is involved in any of these activities.

Each of the activities that you note indicates how you act as a citizen within the legal system. This could be as a consumer (a buyer of goods and services), or as an employee (with the corresponding role of the employer), or as a member of a family.

Each of the interactions involves both rights and duties, and when doing this activity, try to consider both sides – not just what you are allowed to do, but also what you are obliged to do.

Laws are meant to ensure that citizens are protected from harm, and in return for these laws, citizens give up some of their absolute freedom to act and behave as they please. This is a social contract, with the law providing the citizen with rights whilst imposing certain responsibilities.

Unlike many states, the UK has different legal systems in different regions. England and Wales have one legal system, Northern Ireland another and Scotland a third. If the existence of three different systems did not create enough complications when discussing the citizen and the law, there are also European courts – the European Court of Justice and the European Court of Human Rights – that play an important part in the legal system.

Civil law and criminal law

One common thread, however, among the legal systems of the UK is the distinction between civil law and criminal law.

Civil law

Civil law is concerned with the rights and duties of citizens towards each other and focuses on disputes that centre on:

- law of contract;
- law of tort;
- law of property;

- law of succession;
- family law.

These laws would cover disputes that could include issues like:

Contract   Promises. When is a promise legally enforceable and what might be the consequences of the promise?

Tort   Nuisance, negligence, defamation and trespass. (A tort is a private or civil wrong for which damages can be claimed.)

Property   Rights of ownership of land or issues concerning a lease.

Succession   The passing on of property after the death of its former owner.

Family   The rights, duties and status of all members of the household: wife, husband, child, parent, etc.

In civil law, individual citizens who wish to establish their rights initiate legal actions. For those citizens who lose a civil action, examples of what they can be required to do could include the paying of damages or giving another citizen the rights to custody of a child.

Criminal law

Criminal law is that part of the law which deems certain actions and activities to be offences against the state. Since the offence is against the state, it is generally the state that initiates legal action and, for those citizens who are found guilty, punishments can vary from fines and community service to lengthy imprisonment.

The life and death of 'Unfortunate Matilda'

Matilda was born in 1953. She went to school from the age of 5 until she was 16, when she left to start work in a local factory. She married Joshua in 1970, and they had two children. Matilda and Joshua divorced in 1988.

In 1990, Matilda was convicted of grievous bodily harm when she threw a glass ashtray at Joshua when he was late with her maintenance payment, and as a result spent 4 months in prison. Three years later, in 1993, Matilda's father died, leaving her £50,000 in his will. She used some of this money to buy a second hand car. This car turned out to be faulty and she was injured when the brakes failed. The hospital did not realise exactly how serious her injuries were, and she died two days later in hospital after extremely poor medical treatment.

Although Matilda's story may not be very happy, it does illustrate the extent to which her life has been influenced or controlled by the law. First, her birth had to be registered, and from that moment on her details become part of the system that governed the rest of life.

The law requires that every child and young person up to the age of 16 must undergo full time education, although this does not have to be in a school or college. Once Matilda left school and started work, the law provides strict guidelines as to the payment of taxation and National Insurance, as well as health and safety at work and protection against discrimination and unfair dismissal. There are restrictions up to the age of 18, so that she would not be able to buy cigarettes legally until she was 16, and alcohol until she was 18. When she married at 17, the law would have required her parents' consent.

The divorce, and *ancillary matters* (the children, property and money settlements) would have been dealt with by the civil law. The assault on Joshua was treated as a criminal matter and subject to different rules, although it could also have given rise to a civil action if he had chosen to sue her for compensation. The inheritance from her father would also be dealt with by the civil law, but the sale of the faulty car could be both civil (breach of contract) and criminal (selling an unroadworthy vehicle and, possibly, manslaughter). Similarly, the hospital would be liable to pay compensation in the tort of negligence, and perhaps those who treated her might be guilty of manslaughter if they were found to be 'grossly negligent'.

The courts

Very often, the legal system, with its responsibility for the application of punishments on those citizens who break the law, needs to have the significance and importance of this function visibly displayed to other citizens. As a result of this, the work and the activities of the legal system are undertaken in 'special buildings with special status', known as courts. It is quite usual for these buildings to be big, dark and solid in appearance, usually so that the look of the building reflects the importance attached to their purpose.

As a result of classifying different court buildings, it will become apparent that there are a number of different types of courts. The reason why there are different types is, first, the division in the legal system between the civil law and the criminal law and, secondly, the fact that the courts are organised in a hierarchical fashion. At the lower end of the hierarchy, civil and criminal courts are separate, but, towards the top of the hierarchy, courts combine and can pass judgment relating to both civil and criminal law.

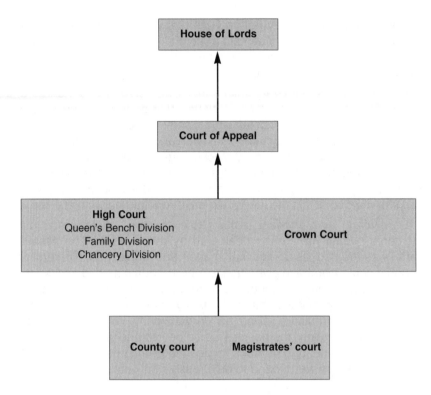

Magistrates' courts

These courts deal with the least serious criminal cases and account for over 95% of all criminal cases heard. Sentence is passed by a Justice of the Peace (JP). A JP is a 'normal' citizen who is not legally qualified but is trained to hear cases (though note that the number of professional (stipendiary) magistrates is now increasing).

There are about 700 magistrates' courts in England and Wales, and some 30,000 JPs. JPs sit as a team of three when there is a plea of innocence, and individually in the case of a guilty plea.

County courts

These courts deal with the least serious civil cases and would include most matrimonial disputes and divorces, disputes over contracts under £5,000, and so on.

There are about 270 county courts in England and Wales. These courts are presided over by either circuit judges or district judges, who number approximately 1,000 in total.

High Court

This court is essentially three courts dealing with separate areas of civil law. The work in this court is undertaken by High Court judges, of which there are usually around 96.

Chancery Division

This division has jurisdiction over issues of taxation and citizens' wills.

Family Division

This division has jurisdiction over matters relating to the family and a citizen's personal relationships.

Queen's Bench Division

This division hears cases referred from the county court either because there is a complex point of law involved or because the sums of money involved are very large. It is also responsible for reviewing any administrative decisions made by public bodies like government departments.

Crown Court

London's Central Crown Court, the Old Bailey, is the most well known of the 94 Crown Courts in England and Wales. All serious crimes are heard in a Crown Court where, with the plea of 'not guilty', a defendant is entitled to a trial by jury. This limits the role of the judge to advising the jury on points of law and providing a summing up of the evidence. There are 517 judges who hear the most serious cases. Part time judges called Recorders (around 900) deal with less serious cases. The Crown Court also hears appeals against any sentence or conviction made in the magistrates' court.

Court of Appeal

The Court of Appeal has a Civil Division and a Criminal Division. There are just over 30 Lords Justices of Appeal. The Civil Division does not hear witnesses. A judgment is arrived at by three judges who base their decision on the basis of the documents and the arguments by barristers. The Criminal Division hears appeals against any sentence or conviction made in the Crown Court.

House of Lords

Any case reaching the House of Lords will usually be heard by a panel of five 'Law Lords', or officially the Lords of Appeal in Ordinary. These 12 Lords are all senior judges who have received a life peerage.

European Court of Justice and the European Court of Human Rights

Added to these courts are the European Court of Justice and the European Court of Human Rights. The European Court of Justice is located in Luxembourg and is the highest court of the European Union. As the role and importance of the Union increases, so does the importance and impact of this Court. All UK courts must take notice of its decisions and its decisions can even override those made by the House of Lords.

The European Court of Human Rights is located in Strasbourg. Although the UK government ratified the European Convention on Human Rights, the Convention was not incorporated into the law of the UK until 2000. Its judgments must now be taken into account in applying domestic law.

Active citizenship

You can explore the issues surrounding the citizen and the law in a number of ways. Although one way is to break the law , this is not to be recommended! By far the best way to appreciate these issues is to view the administration of justice through the observation of the work of the courts in session.

- Arrange to visit a number of different types of court. These could be the local magistrates' court or the nearest Crown Court.

- Prepare a 'social characteristic' tally chart. Whilst observing the administration of justice, record as many of the social characteristics as possible of all the citizens taking part. Observe variables such as age, sex and ethnicity. Do any of the mannerisms of the citizens suggest certain attitudes? Do the way in which citizens speak, the words that they use or their accent suggest anything about their background?

- Combine your results with other students and reflect on the reliability of the results and whether it is possible to draw any conclusions.

Judging other citizens

Within the legal system, the process of passing judgment – innocence or guilt – on another citizen is undertaken by fellow citizens, either in the form of a jury or by those citizens who have had bestowed on them the 'special status' of being a judge.

One element of the legal system involves the need for special buildings (courts), which, although they may be large, dark and intimidating, are nothing more than objects and therefore do not have any feelings or values that favour some citizens or prejudice others.

The other element of the legal system involves the process in which citizens judge other citizens. Crucially, citizens are not buildings; they are human and, as humans, they have a personal history and past experiences of life in society with other citizens. Since all citizens, and that will range from the youngest juror to the most senior High Court judge, have some form of cultural baggage, how is it possible to achieve the impartial administration of justice?

Trial by jury

The system of trial by jury is a keystone in the rights of citizens. It is probably the most democratic element not only within the legal system, but also within the whole political system. The basic qualification to be a juror is that of citizenship, although there are some citizens who are excluded from jury service. The citizens who are excluded fall into three categories: those disqualified through criminal convictions; those who are ineligible, like lawyers, the police, the clergy and the mentally ill; and those entitled to be excused. The citizens who are entitled to be excused are doctors, MPs, members of the armed forces and many citizens in other occupations who can justify being excused on the grounds of work commitments. In an attempt to modernise the criminal justice system and to make the prospect of being a juror less traumatic, it is now possible for the 500,000 citizens a year who are called for jury service to get a realistic idea of what to expect by logging on to www.cjsonline.org. The site guides citizens through unfamiliar surroundings and procedures and helps to demystify the whole experience of serving on a jury.

The jury system involves 12 randomly selected citizens who will deliver verdicts that can even reject the directions of the most senior of judges. Such a rejection occurred in the trial of Clive Ponting, who was charged under section 2 of the Official Secrets Act for disclosing 'official information' relating to the sinking of the Argentinian cruiser *The General Belgrano*. He describes the summing up by Judge McCowan:

> The defence accept the evidence is all one way, that he [Clive Ponting] was not authorised to make the disclosures. There is only one ingredient in dispute: 'duty in the interests of the state'.
>
> Duty, I direct you, means official duty ...
>
> Interests, I direct you, means the policies of the state as they were then ...

Ponting did not deny that he had broken the law and, with the judge's summary and direction not to consider whether the decision was a wise one, Ponting himself was considering the best grounds to appeal.

However, on 11 February 1985, at 2 pm, the jury foreman delivered the verdict of not guilty. The decision was received with cheering and clapping. The jury of 'ordinary citizens' had delivered a handsome 'kick in the groin' to the high and lofty.

The sworn duty of a jury is to faithfully try the defendant and give a true verdict according to the evidence, and the system of trial by jury has the advantage of allowing all eligible citizens the opportunity to take an active part in the administration of justice. The jury system increases public confidence in the legal system, as it also allows for the voice of 'ordinary citizens' to be heard within the legal system whenever a judgment or verdict is made. One example of this occurred on 18 January 2001, when a Manchester jury brought in a verdict of not guilty on Keith Wright and Sylvia Boyes, two anti-nuclear protesters who had admitted their intention to damage a Trident submarine, as its nuclear weapons were 'immoral and illegal'. Lord Devlin regarded the jury's right to bring in a perverse acquittal as one of the great benefits of the jury system, as it gives citizens protection against laws that 'ordinary' citizens would regard as harsh or oppressive. Juries ensure that the criminal law will conform to the 'ordinary' citizen's idea of what is fair and just because, if it is not, the jury will not enforce any law felt to be harsh or oppressive.

Another advantage of the use of citizens in a jury is that it allows verdicts to be reached by a number of people as opposed to being left to a single citizen, and thus increases the transparency of the legal system, ensuring that it does not become associated with a small minority of citizens or the privilege of just one set of citizens. The jury system allows citizens to share in the responsibility for justice and in the process of government, and provides a vivid reminder of the duties that citizens have to their state. To quote Lord Devlin, the jury system is 'more than an instrument of justice … it is the lamp that shows that freedom lives'.

The jury system under attack

Since the election of the Labour Government in 1997, successive Home Secretaries have attacked jury trials for a variety of reasons. One reason why jury trials have become unpopular with successive Labour Home Secretaries is based on the claim that they are too expensive and too time consuming.

At present, all serious crimes, like murder, rape and offences involving violence, are automatically tried by a jury. Minor offences are heard in a magistrates' court. However, there are some offences that sit between the two extremes. These offences are known as 'either way' cases because the defendant can choose whether the case will be heard in a magistrates' court or a Crown Court. To determine whether a defendant can opt for the 'either way' route it is necessary to look at both the crime and the potential sentence. All crimes of theft have an 'either way' route and generally, if the offence carries a maximum prison sentence of more than six months, there is an 'either way' route. However, the offences of killing of another citizen by drink-driving and assaulting a police constable whilst they are on duty no longer allow the defendant an 'either way' option.

The problem with the 'either way' route is that although other crimes are divided into serious and minor, theft is not. As long ago as 1977, the James Commission on legal reform recommended that the right to a trial by jury be denied to minor charges of theft, with petty thieves being tried before a magistrate. For the 1977 James Commission the suggested dividing line was to be set at £20.

This issue can be illustrated by referring to the case of Steven Phillips who opted for a jury trial after being charged with the theft of a 92p can of spaghetti bolognaise. The case was heard at Newcastle Crown Court in June 2002 and

Phillips was found guilty by the jury. The whole case lasted for 32 minutes at a cost in excess of £10,000. The trial of Phillips, who had 30 similar convictions, illustrates the debate as to whether such a trial is too time consuming and too expensive and an abuse of civil rights, or is a fundamental right of all UK citizens. Are citizens' fundamental rights to access to justice being removed through administrative convenience?

The issue that trial by jury is too expensive and too slow, with Crown Courts getting clogged up with too many minor cases, is at the heart of the problem. The proposed reforms would speed up the process of justice and save an estimated £100 million in the process. They would also be a continuation of the reforms that started in the 1960s when the Criminal Justice Act 1967 removed the requirement for a unanimous verdict. However, one justification for change can no longer include the claim that the jury system was open to manipulation by lawyers, as the Criminal Justice Act 1988 removed the pre-emptory right of lawyers to challenge up to three jurors. This was an action that had been undertaken by Ponting, who took three middle-aged middle-class ladies off his jury because he feared they were of a 'similar type that would form a little social group and all vote the same way'.

The Labour Party's attack on the right to a trial by jury first became apparent when it introduced the Criminal Justice (Mode of Trial) Bill. Although this Bill was defeated, many of the same proposals have been reintroduced within the Criminal Justice Bill announced in the Queen's speech, November 2002. Although the Bill preserves the right of a defendant to elect his or her mode of trial in an 'either way' case, it proposes that trials of complex fraud and trials where there is the threat of (or evidence of) jury tampering will be held in judge only courts. This is in effect a further erosion of the right to a trial by jury because it adds to the present situation whereby judges in libel and slander cases can already decide to hear the case without a jury, if they feel it is likely to be excessively long or complicated. Two recent examples where a judge dispensed with a jury are the trial of Jonathan Aitken and the *McLibel* trial when McDonald's sued two environmental campaigners. The role of juries has also been curtailed when awarding damages, as they can now only award damages with reference to the parameters imposed by the judge.

The jury system is also under attack because there have always been some issues that have been seen as a weakness in the system. The foundation of these disadvantages often rests on questioning the ability of some citizens to undertake the role of juror. Questions are often raised on the grounds of:

- Age – is an 18 year old citizen old and mature enough with sufficient experience of life to serve on a jury?
- Intelligence – the fact that jurors do not have to have any knowledge about an issue or pass an intelligence test prior to being a juror.

- Corruption – will a juror accept bribes for their 'not guilty' verdict, or will they succumb to threats and intimidation?
- Advocacy skill – will some jurors be so influenced by the skill of experienced counsel that they judge upon this and not the facts of the case?
- Local issues – if the juror is local to the court, will they base their verdict on local prejudices that are irrational and not comprehensible to those citizens not from that community?
- Trial length – are some trials so long that they cause inconvenience and hardship to the jurors?
- Avoidance – as many professional people can escape jury service on the grounds of work commitments, there could be the tendency for juries not to be representative.

The issue of avoidance of jury service is particularly significant. At present, 60% of all citizens summoned to do jury service do not serve. One group that is about to lose its exemption from jury service are members of the 'royal household'. They had been exempt from jury service as their absence would have caused 'inconvenience to Her Majesty'. Equally significant is that members of the royal family, with the exception of the Queen and her immediate family, will now also lose their right to being exempted from jury service. The Criminal Justice Bill aims to redress the idea that some citizens are too grand, too clever or too important to serve on a jury. This is directly challenging the view held by many citizens that jury service, rather than being something to be seen as an important part of living in a democracy and a positive privilege, is something to be avoided. At present, it could be suggested that the typical jury is far from a being a cross-section of the population as by far the majority of citizens who are excused are much more likely to be employed, have professional qualifications and be proportionately better educated. This has led to the less charitable view that the typical jury is 'less intelligent' than a typical cross-section of the population. This 'middle class boycott' of the jury system is being addressed by the Criminal Justice Bill making its way through Parliament during 2003.

It could be argued that the continuation of ineligibility for some citizens and the possibility of some citizens being excused is another way to undermine the credibility of the whole jury system, and that what is in fact needed is a reappraisal of the system, with the removal of the concept of ineligible and excused citizens. This, combined with a greater knowledge and awareness about the work of juries, could help to reverse the culture of viewing jury service in negative terms.

Unfortunately, the work of juries is surrounded by mystery (unless of course you have served on one yourself) and, since the Contempt of Court

Act 1981 outlaws asking about or publishing details about 'statements made, opinions expressed, arguments advanced or votes cast' during the deliberations of a jury, it is hardly likely to become a major topic of debate; a fact that the *Mail on Sunday* discovered when it was found guilty for contempt of court and fined £75,000 for publishing interviews with jurors about how they reached a verdict in 1992.

France only uses juries for the most serious crimes; Holland relies on professional judges; Italy uses a tribunal of three judges; whilst Germany, Austria, Finland and Sweden try criminal cases with a combination of a professional judge and a number of lay citizens. In England and Wales, only about 1% of criminal cases end up in a trial by jury.

- As there is no knowledge about how juries reach their verdict,
- as there is no check on the behaviour of jurors whilst reaching a verdict,
- as there is no provision to ensure that a juror understands the case,
- and since some judges believe that juries get it wrong in 25% of cases,

how good is the jury system?

Some research has been undertaken on juries in New Zealand and, although there is not the same legal ban on questioning jurors, there is disapproval of any post-trial discussion. The New Zealand system, with the exception that a unanimous verdict is required, operates in a very similar way to the one in England and Wales and the question as to how reliable jury verdicts are has been openly discussed. Research by Young, Cameron and Tinsley, described on www.lawcom.govt.nz, suggests that some jurors had difficulty in distinguishing 'purpose' and 'intent', the burden and standard of proof. Some jurors felt intimidated by the counsel's stares whilst others were traumatised by the content of the evidence. One area of particular interest has been related to whether juries can remain unbiased when some cases attract high-profile media attention. Research by Victoria University of Wellington, in collaboration with the New Zealand Law Commission, pursued this issue and interviewed 312 jurors who had been chosen for 48 particularly high-profile trials. The research established that the input of the media both before and during the trial was minimal, with only 16 jurors remembering any detail that could have led to an element of bias. Jurors were far more likely to see themselves as being better informed and accurate in their own knowledge and would take little notice of the media coverage that they saw as partial and inaccurate. It would seem that citizens are able to reach a true verdict according to the evidence.

BobZ

Due to their very nature, juries have the potential to be representative of all citizens. The same, however, cannot be said about the process of judicial appointments. This process, in the view of some citizens, has resulted in the creation of such a socially unrepresentative group that legitimacy of the whole system has been called into question.

The social nature of the judiciary

Some of the problems associated with the socially unrepresentative nature of the judiciary can be traced to the issue of becoming a judge. It is not the type of employment we would find advertised in the local job centre. In fact, until 1994, the Lord Chancellor made all judicial appointments secretly. The Lord High Chancellor of Great Britain, the Lord Chancellor, is appointed by the monarch on the advice of the Prime Minister and is ranked as eighth in order of precedence after the Queen. The Lord Chancellor has a unique role in all three branches of government as a member of the Cabinet (the executive); as a member of the House of Lords (the legislature); and as the head of the judiciary.

To become a judge, a citizen needs to:

- be either a barrister or solicitor, with at least 10 years' experience, and who has rights of advocacy in the higher courts:
- pay a fee of £750, complete a self-assessment form and provide the names of up to six 'nominated referees' who are familiar with their work and will be able to comment on their suitability.

All application forms are sent to 300 automatic consultees made up of senior judges and other leading members of the legal profession who are asked to comment on suitability and to grade applicants A+ to D. Officials from the Lord

Chancellor's Department then meet with senior judges and the Bar Council to obtain their views. The information is then collated and an A list and a B list are constructed of the leading candidates according to levels of support. The Lord Chancellor is then briefed and after further discussions with senior judges, appointments are made. It is little wonder that with such a system the judiciary are overwhelmingly white, male and from a narrow educational background.

This appointments system is secretive, open to abuse and lacks the ability to be scrutinised or to have its decisions challenged by other citizens. The concern over the secretive nature of the system was to be addressed by Sir Colin Campbell who, on 15 October 2001, was appointed as head of the first Commission for Judicial Appointments. His task is to carry out a 'continuing independent audit of the appointment procedures'. The Lord Chancellor, Lord Irvine, stated that the Commission would be 'able to investigate every appointment, every piece of paper, every assessment, every opinion, and they will have the right to attend interviews for judicial appointments and meetings at which most senior appointments are discussed'.

The first report of the Commission was published in October 2002, and stated that they found that there was no clear 'audit trail' in the process of selection to show the reasons why candidates were selected or rejected. The comments by the nominated referees often did not follow guidelines to provide reasons for their assessments, with one referee describing an applicant as not being in 'in the normal silk mould'. The Commission discovered that 97% of the referees were male, white and from a narrow social group. It indicated that they felt that there were many other citizens who had the qualities to be a judge but would not be considered due to flaws in the processes of selection. The Commission is now to look at ways of diversifying the judiciary from citizens who are overwhelmingly white, male and from a narrow educational background.

One suggestion to widen the profile of those citizens who judge other citizens, being promoted by Harriet Harman, the Solicitor General, is to allow staff in the Crown Prosecution Service to be sponsored through law degrees, win promotion to crown prosecutor and eventually rise to become a judge.

Widening the social profile of those citizens who judge other citizens

The sight of black female judges in America is not unusual but the chances of a UK citizen who left school at 16, who has no post-school qualifications, who is black, female and from the inner city becoming a judge are minimal.

If you were 'Citizen in Chief', what would you do to change this situation in order to widen the social profile of those citizens who judge other citizens?

Magistrates

To some extent, a lay magistrate, also referred to as a JP (Justice of the Peace), is at the opposite extreme. For some, the very existence of magistrates, the unpaid citizens who give their time in order to dispense justice, is the most open and democratic element of the legal system. Lay magistrates are not trained as lawyers but are advised by clerks, who *are* trained lawyers. According to Home Office figures, in 2001 there were 30,400 lay magistrates in England and Wales, approximately 55% of whom were male and 45% female. The current percentage of magistrates from ethnic minorities is 4.5%, although ethnic minorities represented 7.6% of appointments in 1999.

A magistrate must ...	A magistrate cannot be ...
be of good character	anyone who is not of good character and personal standing
have personal integrity	an undischarged bankrupt
have sound common sense	
have the ability to weigh evidence and reach reasoned decisions	a serving member of Her Majesty's Forces
	a member of a police force
live or work in the area	a traffic warden or any other occupation which might be seen to conflict with the role of a magistrate
have good local knowledge and understanding of the local community	
	a close relative of a person who is already a magistrate on the same bench
be able to work as a member of a team	
	anyone who, because of a disability, cannot carry out all the duties of a magistrate

All citizens (other than those mentioned above) may put themselves forward for consideration to become a magistrate. Alternatively, a citizen or organisation may recommend another citizen for appointment. Magistrates are appointed by a Local Advisory Committee and application forms and information on the selection process are available from the Secretary of the Committee, whose name and address can be obtained from the office of the clerk to the justices in their local magistrates' court. Citizens must be personally suitable for appointment, possessing the range of qualities detailed above. The Lord Chancellor also requires that each bench should broadly reflect the community it serves in terms of gender, ethnic origin, geographical spread, occupation and political affiliation. The Lord Chancellor will not generally appoint a candidate under the age of 27 or over the age of 65.

Advisory Committees will seek to recommend for appointment candidates from a broad spectrum of occupations, with no more than 15% of magistrates on a bench being from the same occupational group. Advisory committees will also ensure that there are not too many magistrates on any one bench from the same village, neighbourhood or street. Advisory Committees also make efforts to recruit candidates from the ethnic minorities, with the aim that magistrates from an ethnic minority background reflect the ethnic composition of the area. It is essential that each bench should have a roughly equal number of men and women, as magistrates, when sitting in the family proceedings and youth courts, must be made up of three magistrates and include both genders.

The political views of a candidate are neither a qualification for nor a disqualification from appointment. However, in the interests of balance, the voting pattern for the area, as evidenced by the last two General Elections, should be broadly reflected in the composition of the bench. It is also important that there are not too many magistrates on the bench from the same clubs or organisations. In an attempt to remove the potential for some citizens to accuse magistrates of favouritism towards fellow Freemasons, candidates for the magistracy are now specifically asked on their application form if they are Freemasons, and citizens who are recommended for appointment will be required to inform the chairman of the bench or the clerk to the justices if they subsequently become a Freemason. There used to be requirement that benches should be balanced in terms of age. However, this has been temporarily suspended in favour of finding candidates with the appropriate social and political backgrounds in order to achieve a more balanced bench.

Duties and responsibilities of lay magistrates

Magistrates are required to sit a minimum of 26 half days a year. Training is almost always undertaken in the magistrate's own free time during evenings and at weekends. Magistrates receive no reward for their public duty, although travelling and subsistence allowances are claimable. Magistrates normally exercise their duties as part of a bench of three, and they have available to them at all times the advice of a qualified court clerk.

Magistrates' duties extend across both criminal and civil matters. Over 95% of all criminal cases are dealt with by magistrates, either in the adult court or in the youth court. This work involves, amongst other things, decisions about the guilt or innocence of a defendant, the passing of sentences as appropriate and decisions on applications for bail. Magistrates' sentencing powers include the imposition of fines of up to £5,000, community service orders, probation orders or, if the proposed extension to their powers outlined in the Criminal Justice Bill 2002 is passed by Parliament, a period of not more than a year in custody. In a further extension to their powers, magistrates will be able to use a formal system of sentence discounts. These discounts, however, may have more to do with economics than justice as their purpose is to encourage citizens to plead guilty in order to reduce the number of trials by jury. Magistrates may also sit in the Crown Court with a judge to hear appeals from magistrates' courts against conviction or sentence and proceedings on committal to the Crown Court for sentence.

In civil matters, a magistrate will make many decisions relating to family work. In the family court, panels deal with a wide range of matters, most of which arise from the breakdown of marriage, for example, making orders for the residence of and contact with children whilst in family proceedings courts; matters relating to the care and control of children are also dealt with. Some magistrates are members of specialist committees and are responsible for the administration of the liquor licensing system and for the granting or refusal of applications for licences and permits relating to betting and the registration of gaming clubs.

Although a very important component of the justice system, according to Professor Sanders (*Community Justice, Modernising the Magistracy in England and Wales*, 2001), 40% of the public are unaware that most magistrates are lay magistrates, and 50% are concerned that they have no legal training. In support of lay magistrates is the view that lay magistrates bring their local knowledge and social skills into the courtroom and are better judges of honesty. However, this view is not one that is shared by all citizens. Professor Sanders' research established that 71% of citizens do not think that lay magistrates do a good job, and 61% think they are out of touch.

There is another type of magistrate, known as a 'stipendiary' magistrate. These professionals are in effect district judges and at present number about 100, a doubling in number over the last 10 years. In some cities, stipendiary magistrates hear over one-third of all cases and research suggests that these stipendiary magistrates are not only more able to handle increasingly complex cases, but are also more efficient, hearing cases more quickly and making decisions more consistently.

At present, offenders do not know whether they are to be tried by an amateur or a professional. It is the view of Professor Sanders that all magistrates' courts should consist of one professional and two lay magistrates, with an offender's outcome being based on the combination of legal expertise and lay judgment.

The result of this development would be that lay magistrates, who would always be accompanied by a professional, would need less training and sit less often in court. This in turn could allow a greater involvement and contribution from a wider range of citizens. When coupled with a potential increase in confidence in the decisions made by the court and greater efficiency, there is clearly considerable potential in the proposal. The present system, with its lack of information about the process of becoming a magistrate, is associated with a lack of openness. In the opinion of many, although it is possible for any citizen to become a magistrate, the perceived reality is that appointments are more often than not associated with who is known to the citizen rather than what the citizen knows about justice.

Magistrates' courts

One of the great strengths that is often claimed for the magistrates' court is that the most open and democratic element of the legal system also represents local justice. Local citizens are judged by local citizens. This has advantages for both the magistrate and the defendant as each will know that they are being judged within the context of local knowledge. The local geography and social and economic environment will be understood by the magistrate who will be able to respond to local concerns with local sentiment. Not only will citizens be judged within the local context, but the local newspaper reporter will report local sentences passes at local magistrates' courts. The idea of local justice presided over by JPs has a history that dates back to 1361 and even today, government plans for 'market' towns – those towns with a population of between 10,000 and 25,000 citizens – demand that they have the facility of a magistrates' court.

Although the idea of local justice is over 600 years old, and the greatest strength of a magistrates' court is its locality, the problem faced by magistrates' courts is that in reality they are becoming increasingly less local for citizens. In January 2002, there were 435 magistrates' courts, yet 10 years earlier there were around 600 courts whilst in the 1960s there were around 800. Magistrates' courts are still closing at the rate of about 20 a year.

This reduction in the number of magistrates' courts effectively means that they are becoming less local and more regional. With a regional rather than a local structure, one of the main benefits of a local lay magistrate, the unpaid citizen, is removed. For many lay magistrates, there is the view that the removal of local courts and the gradual erosion of their total numbers is part of a creeping professionalisation of the magistrates' court with local lay magistrates being replaced with professional stipendiary magistrates. For those who are responsible for running the criminal justice system, a move from the unpaid citizen to the professional stipendiary would actually cut the cost of justice as stipendiary magistrates sit alone in a court and research has established that they are more efficient, judging a greater number of cases per day.

In May 2002, another move that challenged the idea of local magistrates serving the local community was introduced when Manchester City Magistrates' Court and Bow Street Magistrates' Court in London started to experiment with extended opening times. During the experiment, Manchester's court would open an hour earlier, at 9 am, and on two nights a week would remain open until 8 pm. Bow Street would operate two late night sessions from 6 pm to midnight on Fridays and Saturdays. This experiment in night courts was an attempt to enable the courts to dispense immediate justice. However, the official results of the pilot scheme resulted in night courts being declared a costly failure as justice became 'prohibitively expensive and not cost-effective'. During the trial, the Bow Street magistrates dealt with 368 defendants which cost an average of £3,257 per case compared to about £100 a case during a full conventionally timed day in a magistrates' court. The escalation in costs was a result of having to pay probation staff overtime and pay their taxi fares home. During the night court experiment, on some nights there were only three or four defendants who were dealt with, and overall a third of all defendants were beggars who only received a caution.

The Manchester early morning start was a little more successful with costs per case averaging £589, although there were often problems getting defendants to court for the 9 am start. The Government has decided to press ahead with early morning courts for adult cases even though it is felt that such an extension to the length of the court sittings, with the increased emphasis on dealing swiftly and effectively with offenders, means that the professional stipendiary magistrate will fit into the system much more easily than the lay magistrate.

Solicitors and barristers

The two branches of the legal profession, consisting of solicitors and barristers, are quite distinctive, both in how they are organised and in how they operate. Professional bodies control both branches, and each one has its own. The professional body that has control over solicitors is the Law Society, whilst the Bar Council controls barristers.

Solicitors, who normally practise in partnership, deal directly with their clients and provide assistance and representation on all legal matters. For many citizens, the most likely contact with a solicitor will arise when a solicitor undertakes work like conveyancing, the legal side of buying and selling houses, or work on divorces, wills or personal injury claims. In 1999, there were 100,957 solicitors on the Law Society's roll, although only 79,503 of those have a 'practising certificate'. Of this number, 27,906 are female – approximately 35%.

Since 31 July 2000, solicitors have been able to represent their clients in all courts. This major change occurred as a result of the Access to Justice Act 1999 introducing amendments to the Courts and Legal Services Act 1990 – before this, they could only appear in the lower courts, that is, a magistrates' or county court, and before tribunals by virtue of being an admitted solicitor. If a case proceeded to a higher court, a solicitor would prepare the case but barristers always undertook the advocacy. Consequently, now, if solicitors obtain the appropriate qualifications from the Law Society, it is possible for them to present cases in the higher courts – the Crown Court, High Court, Court of Appeal and the House of Lords. If a citizen feels that their solicitor has been negligent, they can sue their solicitor.

Barristers, however, practise on their own, as self-employed professionals. They work by referral; it is not normally possible for a citizen to go to a barrister directly and any approach has to be done through a solicitor. This is justified by barristers, who claim that they are not able to undertake the everyday tasks that solicitors do. In order to be cost-effective, they need the support that solicitors provide to isolate the issues on which they are really needed and do the administrative work required whilst conducting cases. Although this arrangement is very agreeable for those within the legal profession, for those citizens who have to use the system, many find that effective access is denied through the prohibitive costs associated with litigation inflated through a combination of fees, based on the heritage of monopolistic practices, and the dual nature of the system, made more expensive and complicated by the fact that a citizen's access to barristers is a legal cul-de-sac without the hiring of a solicitor.

Barristers are advocates, and are the experts who have the right to argue a case in court. Barristers have been providing expert advice and advocacy since the 13th century, and for centuries had the monopoly on the right to represent people in the higher courts. Barristers, unlike solicitors, cannot be sued for negligence for their advocacy in court. A citizen can only be a barrister if they have been 'called to the Bar' by an Inn of Court. Becoming a barrister and initially surviving as a barrister is an expensive process, a process that many citizens will be effectively excluded from. For a citizen to become a barrister involves successfully completing a law degree or a degree in another subject supplemented either by the Common Professional Examination (CPE) or an approved Post Graduate Diploma in Law (PgDL) course. This is followed by a vocational year. All prospective barristers are required to be admitted to an Inn of Court before registration on the Bar Vocational Course (BVC). This allows prospective barristers to acquire the skills, knowledge of procedure and evidence, attitudes and competence to prepare them for the more specialised training in the 12 months of 'pupillage' that follow.

All barristers who are called to the Bar on or after 1 January 2002 and who intend to practise as a barrister in independent or employed practice must complete 12 months' pupillage. This is the third and final stage of the route to qualification at the Bar. During this time, the 'pupil' gains practical training under the supervision of an experienced barrister. For the first six months, the pupils shadow their 'pupil master'. During the second practising six months, pupils, with their pupil master's permission, can undertake to supply legal services. Once called to the Bar, as the law becomes increasingly complex barristers tend to specialise in particular areas of work.

There are two levels of barrister, approximately 10% being QCs (Queen's Counsel), with the rest being juniors. It is the QCs who usually become judges. Significantly, becoming a barrister is also the route to becoming a senior judge and, since the employment background of senior judges lies in this field, the result is that judges are recruited from an unrepresentative pool of citizens. They are so unrepresentative that the Supreme Court Act 1981 lays down that appeal court judges are called 'Lords Justices of Appeal' and, when the first female appeal court judge was appointed in 1988, she was known as Lord Justice Butler-Sloss and was addressed as 'my Lord' in court until the title Lady Justice was adopted in 1999.

In March 2001, a report by the Office of Fair Trading was produced which some believe may result in the scrapping of the distinction between solicitors and barristers. The report stated that the continued distinction between solicitors and barristers has a 'significant adverse effect on competition'. The report also questioned why the mere fact of being a QC allowed fees to be increased by an extra 10%. This increases the cost to UK citizens of justice as it is most likely that QCs will be engaged in the small number of cases that last for more than 25 days. Even at 2001 prices, with the Bar Council's suggested reasonable hourly rate of £300+ for a defence QC, it is easy to understand how these cases rapidly consume public funds.

An unrepresentative elite?

According to a survey published by Labour Research (an independent research organisation) in 1997 and updated in 2002, the background of 690 senior judges revealed the extent of the unrepresentativeness of the group. Only 8.9% were female and 99.95% were white. The stereotype of an elderly white male with an accent that was indicative of an unrepresentative elite was largely confirmed when the findings revealed that the group were on average older than in previous research, that 82% had not attended a state school and 86% had attended either Oxford or Cambridge. This is a portrait that has remained unchanged for many years. By January 2001, Home Office figures revealed that there were only seven black QCs out of 1,074 in England and Wales (0.65%) and one black circuit judge out of 568 (0.17%).

There are occasions when the remoteness of this group of citizens becomes apparent. In 1960, Mervyn Griffiths QC addressed the jurors in the *Lady Chatterley's Lover* obscenity trial with the question: 'Would you approve of your young sons, young daughters – *because girls can read as well as boys* – reading this book? ... Is it a book you would let your *wife* or your *servants* read?' Nearly 40 years later, Nick Cohen reported in his 'Without Prejudice' column (*The Observer,* 16 July 2000) that Law Lord, Peter Millett, in response to a question about whether the Law Lords were in touch with the troubles and frustrations of their fellow citizens, said: 'When I was a young barrister, I had to struggle to pay the children's school fees like everyone else.'

With a shared educational background and a common experience of employment, the likelihood that judges will develop similar attitudes and principles raises the issue of impartiality.

The ability to dispense justice impartially, without fear or favour, is the backbone to the legitimacy of the legal system. When the administration of justice, however, becomes associated with an unrepresentative elite – a small minority of citizens that appear remote and out of touch with the majority of citizens – there are clear implications for all citizens. Can an unrepresentative cross-section of citizens ever be able to judge all citizens impartially?

According to Griffith in *The Politics of the Judiciary* (1991), it could be demonstrated that judges, for at least 30 years, had supported conventional, established and settled interests on issues concerning political protest, government secrecy, race relations and moral behaviour.

Although evidence of the lack of impartiality is impossible to substantiate, there are figures that could be used to raise questions about the role that social characteristics play in the receipt of justice – or in the receipt of rough justice.

The evidence that raises questions about the impartiality of the administration of justice ranges from simple issues concerning cultural codes of dress in which defendants are advised to 'wear something smart' to issues that suggest a systematic bias in the delivery of justice.

Not only are the detection and prosecution rates relatively low, the sanctions (punishments) delivered by the system tend to be more lenient in some types of crime compared to others. The difference in the numbers of prosecutions for tax fraud and for social security fraud is considerable and, although accurate figures are impossible to ascertain, the issue comes down to the fact that welfare benefits are much more likely to be a source of income for the less empowered citizens compared to the smaller number of more privileged citizens whose income is such as to be able to develop ways to evade paying tax. Not only do tax inspectors see prosecution as a last resort and negotiate 'a reasonable settlement by agreement', when a prosecution is successfully brought before the courts, the punishment, compared to other crimes, stretches the notion of equality before the law. Gerald Ronson, a man of considerable wealth, received a one year sentence in Ford Open Prison after being found guilty when, as a participant in the fraudulent disclosure of information known as the 'Guinness affair', he helped to increase the share price of the company, allowing it – and himself – to make a sizeable profit. With access to a telephone, and his wife's ability to continue to run the companies that he owned, when he was released on parole after about six months a sharp contrast could be observed with the crimes and punishments associated with the less powerful citizen.

Justice linked to social characteristics

Another area in which social characteristics may play a part in the receipt of justice has been described by barrister Helena Kennedy, who outlines instances of sexism in the legal system. One simple way in which she suggests that this occurs is the extent to which women receive harsher sentences compared to men; for example, 53% of women in prison have fewer than two convictions, compared with 22% of men. It would seem that being born female results in a greater likelihood of being imprisoned sooner for criminal activities. Add to this a range of sexist assumptions about traditional gender roles and the result is the criminalisation of behaviour in females that is socially approved of in males. Certain sexual behaviour and running away from home more often lead to greater institutionalisation amongst girls as compared to boys.

The question of whether the social characteristics of race play a part in a citizen's access to justice has been long disputed. The story told by one black barrister who, in response to the question 'which way', was directed by the court official to the defendants' waiting room, suggests the currency of the stereotypes that exist in this area. Although judges will maintain that impartiality exists, in a wide ranging study by Professor Jeremy Coid of the Royal School of Medicine, the conclusion is that black citizens are more harshly treated within the criminal justice system, with a far greater likelihood of receiving either a prison sentence or a longer prison sentence than white citizens. With black citizens accounting for 20% of the total prison population, the stark fact remains that if black citizens constituted a separate country, it would have the highest imprisonment rate in the world.

Being sentenced is only one of a variety of ways in which a citizen can interact with the criminal justice system. Other examples of interaction are when a citizen is accused of committing crime or when a citizen is the victim of crime. Another way in which the issue of race can enter the court is when the trial or lack of trial is connected to a racial incident.

There are thousands of cases dealt with by the courts every year in which the issue of race becomes irrelevant through the impartiality of the judges. However, there are times when it would appear that the issue of race *does* influence decisions. Two examples of cases that illustrate what can occur when things go wrong are the refusal by the Crown Prosecution Service to pursue charges against three youths alleged to have been involved in the attack on Stephen Lawrence, and the acquittal of an offence under the Race

Relations Act 1976 of the then chair of the extreme right wing National Front Party, Kingsley Read, who virtually celebrated the murder of an Asian citizen in a 1978 speech.

The treatment of minorities by the courts is seen as evidence of the lack of impartiality of the legal system. Home Office figures reveal one possible manifestation of this lack of impartiality – that black citizens, who represent about 6% of the population, constitute a little over 20% of the prison population.

A damning report from the inspectorate of the Crown Prosecution Service, published in May 2002, found that black citizens were far more likely to be charged with a more serious offence than warranted compared to white citizens, and that 11,000 cases that had a race element in them had been wrongly discontinued in 2001–02. The report also concluded that in 28% of a sample of race cases, charges had been reduced inappropriately. With the suggestion that there is a greater likelihood of using prison as the means of punishment, along with receiving longer sentences for the same crime, graphically illustrated in the differences in the length of sentence for Asian and white participants in the Bradford riots of July 2001, some citizens question the ability of the legal system to dispense justice without favour.

The issue of how 'good' or how 'bad' judges or the legal system appear to be is a question that is not often posed by some citizens, as their likelihood of needing to use the law is minimal. However, a legal system that does not allow equal access cannot serve the interests of all citizens. If the legal system becomes, in effect, an institution run by privileged citizens for the benefit of privileged citizens, the credibility of the system will be reduced.

Although there are no formal barriers to accessing and using the legal system, some citizens are considerably less likely to use the system as compared to others. For some citizens, there exists a chasm of class culture between themselves and those citizens who represent the legal profession. Without a bridge over the chasm, or adequate financial resources to be able to use an alternative method to cross the chasm, many citizens are left to ponder the mysteries of a system that could, in terms of its accessibility, be part of an alien universe.

For many citizens, the legal system has become rather like pondering whether to buy a Rolls-Royce; all citizens have the option to buy, but few citizens have the means to make this purchase.

In order to improve access to and wider usage of the legal system, the costs involved for citizens need to be reduced. There are a number of ways in which this reduction could be achieved, which include:

- a reduction in the cost of hiring professionals;
- an increase in any aid or benefits available to citizens;
- a greater use of information and communication technologies.

Although many monopolistic practices, like 'closed shop' agreements, in which all workers have to belong to a specific trade union, were outlawed under Conservative legislation, the monopoly of barristers appearing in court remained until June 1998. Without effective competition, there is little to control the amounts that a monopolistic service can charge. The reforms of June 1998 allowed the Crown Prosecution Service, an organisation created in 1986, to usurp the decision of whether to prosecute or not from the police, and allowed some salaried law firm lawyers to represent clients in court.

Whether the catalyst for the June 1998 reform was the desire to increase citizens' access or to decrease government costs is open to debate. However, the second way in which a citizen's costs for using the legal system could be reduced is through the provision of the subsidy known as 'legal aid', which is now officially known as public funding.

The system of public funding allows the costs of some citizens' use of the legal system to be paid by the government. By 1997 this had reached an annual cost of £1.47 billion. An annual bill of this magnitude was becoming increasingly unacceptable, both politically and economically. This resulted in the reform of the system, with the removal of the provision of legal aid for civil claims for damages. Personal injury cases, like claims for damages resulting from car accidents, must now be funded personally or on a 'no win no fee' basis. The Lord Chancellor did make an exception for claims relating to medical negligence, as these are usually extremely expensive.

Other suggested reforms of the legal system focus on its lack of accountability. At present, the Lord Chancellor is not elected and is not accountable to any committee in the House of Commons. It is an irony that one of the most powerful people in government is subject to some of the weakest levels of accountability. This could be reformed through the creation of a Secretary of State for Justice, a Cabinet post accountable to Parliament.

There are already over 3,000 centres with 30,000 volunteers and 6,000 professionals dealing with over 10 million enquiries a year: the system is not effective or efficient. At present, if a citizen wants legal advice, there are nearly 2,000 separate agencies involved with the delivery of that advice, ranging from the local Citizens Advice Bureaux to any number of independent advice centres. Each of these agencies is funded by different organisations, such as the local authority, the Legal Services Commission or the National Lottery Charities Board, each acting in isolation and each with its own rules as to the scope of advice that is available.

To solve the confusion, in which citizens often find themselves pushed from pillar to post, a single organisation, the Community Legal Service, could bring together the providers of legal and advice services into one properly co-ordinated network. The advantages of this system are as follows:

- communication can take place between those who provide the advice and those who fund them;
- people's access to justice will not depend on where they live as any gaps in provision can be identified;
- a network can be established so that citizens can be referred to another agency;
- funding can be targeted to where it is most needed;
- information technology can be used.

Another route to improving access to legal advice is through the application of information and communication technologies. The Community Legal Service website could offer a virtual advice arcade that provides a gateway to general information and more specialist services. This approach moved closer to reality in January 2001, when the consultative document *Modernising the Civil Courts*, issued by the Lord Chancellor's Department, outlined the aim to modernise the county court system. The proposed changes would involve the use of on-screen forms to be emailed in order to initiate small claims. The internet would also provide citizens with continuous information about the progress of their case and, when appropriate, it could effectively replace the courtroom in the early stages of a case, with a move towards a 'virtual' court.

At present, judges are experimenting with video conferencing at Leeds and Cardiff county courts and the Court of Appeal. At Preston county court, the need to attend court for an interim application – a decision before a case goes to trial – is being reduced through the use of emails to judges.

Although critics say that the move towards a system of e-justice will discriminate against those citizens who cannot afford their own computer or who are not linked to the internet, the Lord Chancellor's Department pointed out that citizens will have access to computers and the internet through Citizens Advice Bureaux or libraries, and the proposed changes would work in parallel with the existing forms of communication.

This approach to the provision of legal advice, however, might increase differences between citizens and not reduce them. This is because access to the internet differs considerably between different citizens and between regions. A Guardian/ICM poll in January 1999 established that 29% of citizens were online either at home or at work. However, there are considerable variations between citizens, with internet access for 33% of social classes A and B, compared to 16% of citizens in social class C1 and 2% of social classes D and E. More recent research undertaken by the Government, with its results published in July 2002, provides evidence of a growing divide, with citizens on high incomes being 800% more likely to have access to the internet than citizens on low incomes.

Access to information technology, by implication, is also an issue to be addressed in the study of citizenship. As Gordon Brown, in his 1999 budget speech, warned, 'anyone left out of the new knowledge revolution will be left behind in the new knowledge economy'. The issue relating to access to the internet has considerable implications as its importance grows. Professor Susskind, Information Technology Adviser to the Lord Chief Justice, believes that 'the world wide web will be the natural first port of call for information [and] guidance'.

If there is unequal access to the internet, there will be unequal access to legal advice. Although public and individual access could be improved, with greater access in buildings like public libraries, the attractiveness of using the internet in a *public* building automatically decreases, especially when compared to those citizens who can access the internet in the privacy of their own home at a time that is convenient and without pressure from other citizens who are awaiting their turn or who are reading the contents of the screen over the user's shoulder.

What do you understand by the following terms and concepts?

- Civil law
- Criminal law
- Trial by jury
- A court

- Crown Prosecution Service
- Public funding
- The judiciary
- Community Legal Service

- Jurors should not only be allowed to make written notes during a trial, but they should also be able to question witnesses and have access to a video tape of the trial in order to clarify issues and remind themselves of the proceedings.

- Far from being curtailed, a citizen's right to a trial by jury should be extended.

- University students are articulate, open minded and with few time pressures. This should mean that a university student would be an ideal candidate to become a lay magistrate. Should the rules be changed to encourage university students to become magistrates whilst still at university?

Interviewing a magistrate

 One way to meet a magistrate is to break the law, get arrested and go to court. This is not a good idea; a more sensible method is to interview a magistrate in order to understand their role in the criminal justice system.

You'll find a series of questions below that could be used as a basis for interviewing a local magistrate.

Where do you normally sit?

Are you an unpaid local volunteer?

Is it important that a magistrate acts in a professional manner?

When you arrive at your court, do you familiarise yourself with who is sitting with you and find out about the business of the day?

What is a 'bench'?

What is a 'winger'?

What is the clerk of the court responsible for?

What is a remand court?

I believe that in a Youth Court, defendants up to the age of 18 are addressed by their first name, whereas in an Adult Court, defendants are referred to by their surname. Do you think that it is good idea? Why?

Do you think it is a good idea to mix youths with adults?

What time are you supposed to start in court?

Is it common for a court to run late?

Which of the following is the most common excuse you have heard for delays?

1 'The defendant thought the case was being heard somewhere else.'

2 'The solicitor has not yet had time to talk to his or her client.'

3 'We are waiting for the papers to be faxed across to us'.

4 'The prison van has got stuck in traffic'.

A youth who is appearing before a magistrate for the first time, who has pleaded guilty and has no previous convictions, can be sentenced through a Referral Order. (Note: A Referral Order involves the young person appearing in front of a local panel consisting of people drawn from the area where the offence was committed. Parents/guardians are expected to attend and the victim of the offence is also invited. The young person enters into a contract – the object of which is to prevent him or her getting into trouble again. The problem for a magistrate is that the sentence is mandatory and does not allow him or her to use any discretion.)

Do you think this is a good idea?

What happens to young people who plead not guilty?

What type of crimes do you deal with?

What is your relationship to the Crown Court?

Can any case be quite funny or are they all tragic?

What is a remand case?

What is sentencing?

What punishments can you give somebody?

What is your view as to the purpose of punishment?

Do you consider it a success when you do not see offenders again?

How often do you send anyone to prison?

When does your day finish?

Don't forget to thank the magistrate for their time and when you say goodbye, tell them that you hope never to meet them again ... in their professional capacity.

Justice or rough justice?

- Research a number of different cases in which a citizen has supposedly received 'rough justice'.

  These could be local cases of a minor nature or major miscarriages of justice associated with groups of citizens, like the 'Birmingham Six'.

- Research examples where you think a citizen's race and/or sex has influenced the way in which that citizen has been treated by the court.

Does the punishment fit the crime?

There is an enormous mismatch between the number of citizens prosecuted for tax fraud compared to social security fraud. (In 1989, figures based on research by Dee Cook estimated the difference at 500 prosecutions for tax fraud compared to 8,000 for social security fraud.)

- Research the crime and punishment associated with the jockey Lester Piggott or any other citizen found guilty of tax fraud.

Tax fraud is not the only crime in which the balance between the crime and the punishment is disproportionate.

- Research the outcome of the court action involving the owners of the capsized ferry *The Herald of Free Enterprise*, resulting in 192 deaths.

- What conclusions can be drawn from your research?

CHAPTER 8

A Citizen's Ability to Redress Grievances

The aims of this chapter are to:

- Introduce issues surrounding tribunals and MPs resolving grievances
- Introduce the role, function and workings of ombudsmen in redressing citizens' grievances
- Introduce alternative methods for a citizen to resolve grievances
- Introduce issues surrounding service charters

The Ombudsman, or the Parliamentary Commissioner for Administration

It is highly unlikely that any citizen today could live their life without coming into contact with some element of government. This contact might take the form an interaction with a civil servant or with a government department.

What happens to the citizen if that civil servant is excessively rude or there is an excessive delay in responding to the citizen? What happens if the information supplied by the civil servant or the government department is incorrect? What happens if, as a result of a decision by a government department, a citizen's life will be in turmoil?

The common thread between these questions is that it is possible for an individual citizen to have a grievance, not against another citizen, but against the activities of a local council or a government department. If a citizen has a grievance against some element of the state, there needs to be a system in place for that dispute to be settled.

One means for a citizen to be able to resolve a dispute is through the use of a tribunal. With over 2,000 different tribunals in existence, it hardly constitutes an organised system; however, tribunals do offer a means to redress grievances in a way that is considered quick, cheap and informal. Some of the tribunals that exist are concerned with establishing a 'fair rent' for example, while the valuation tribunal will hear appeals from citizens who believe their property to be incorrectly banded in relation to the collection of council tax. Other tribunals exist to resolve disputes relating to, for example, social security, the NHS, housing, immigration and pensions.

An alternative way in which some citizens seek to find redress for a grievance against a government department is to take that grievance to their local constituency MP. If the MP believes that the citizen has a genuine grievance and the MP is willing, he or she can act on behalf of the citizen. (Sometimes, a local MP is will less willing to adopt the grievance of some citizens due to potential conflict with the government.) Initially, the MP can raise the issue through an exchange of letters with the source of the grievance and, If the grievance is still not resolved, the MP can question the appropriate government minister through either a written or an oral question. The minister is duty bound to answer these questions, although sometimes the answer is far from helpful. If either of these methods still does not produce a satisfactory outcome, the MP can request that the Parliamentary Commissioner for Administration, or as they are more usually referred to, the ombudsman, become involved in the investigation.

The present Parliamentary Ombudsman and Health Service Ombudsman is Ann Abraham, who took up her post on 5 November 2002. The Parliamentary Ombudsman undertakes independent investigations into complaints that an injustice has been caused by maladministration on the part of a government department or a public body. The role of the Health Service Ombudsman is basically the same, except that independent investigations are conducted into complaints caused by any failure of the NHS to provide a service, or a failure in service through maladministration. For many citizens living in modern Britain the ability to use the services of the Parliamentary Ombudsman to investigate complaints is limited. The Parliamentary Ombudsman fact file below outlines an extraordinarily complex and contradictory set of procedures that needs to be followed in the pursuit of justice.

Parliamentary Ombudsman fact file

- The Parliamentary Ombudsman is officially known as the Parliamentary Commissioner for Administration.

- The Parliamentary Ombudsman also holds the separate posts of Scottish Parliamentary Commissioner for Administration (the Scottish Commissioner) and Welsh Administration Ombudsman.

- The role of Parliamentary Ombudsman is to investigate complaints and possible injustices.

- Complaints to the Parliamentary Ombudsman must be referred by a Member of Parliament; complaints to the Scottish Commissioner must be referred by a Member of the Scottish Parliament; but complaints to the Welsh Administration Ombudsman may be put directly.

- The Parliamentary Ombudsman can investigate for members of the public – at no cost to the complainant – complaints about the actions (or inactions) of government departments and other public bodies which seem to have caused injustice which has not been put right.

- The Parliamentary Ombudsman can investigate complaints about failures to provide information contrary to the relevant Code of Practice on Access to Official Information.

- The Parliamentary Ombudsman also holds the post of Health Service Ombudsman for England, Scotland and Wales and will investigate complaints about failures in National Health Service (NHS) hospitals or community health services, about care and treatment, and about local NHS family doctor, dental, pharmacy or optical services. Any member of the public may refer a complaint direct, but usually only if a full investigation through the NHS complaints system has been carried out first.

- The Parliamentary Ombudsman cannot look at complaints about local government because the Local Government Ombudsmen deal with those. Nor can the Parliamentary Ombudsman look at complaints about the police, legal decisions, or government policy.

- The Parliamentary Ombudsman cannot help if the complaint is simply a disagreement with a decision. There needs to be some evidence that the decision was taken wrongly – for example, in the wrong way or on the basis of wrong information.

- The primary aim of the Parliamentary Ombudsman is to obtain a remedy for those who have suffered injustice.

- The secondary aim of the Parliamentary Ombudsman is to work to ensure good standards of public administration.

- If serious faults are found, recommendations will be made to the public body concerned as to what redress they should offer and the action they should take to ensure that such failures do not happen again.

- The Parliamentary Ombudsman's recommendations are nearly always adopted.

- The Parliamentary Ombudsman is wholly independent in any investigation of complaints.

- The Parliamentary Ombudsman reports to a Select Committee of the House of Commons, to the Scottish Parliament or to the National Assembly for Wales, as appropriate.

The origin of both the word and the concept of the ombudsman is Scandinavian. 'Ombudsman' means 'people's friend' and the concept has a quite considerable cultural heritage. The adoption of the concept of an ombudsman resulted from the lack of an even distribution of tribunals. Although many tribunals exist, there were some areas of government that had considerably fewer tribunals than others. To overcome this shortfall, there was a need for a general mechanism to investigate complaints of maladministration by government departments.

The role of the ombudsman to investigate complaints of maladministration by government departments was created in 1967 and has, since that date, steadily expanded its range of jurisdiction into bodies like the Sports Commission and the Equal Opportunities Commission.

Although the system of the ombudsman sounds attractive, there have been a number of criticisms levelled at it. Indeed, the use of the word 'ombudsman', the 'people's friend', is inappropriate, because 'people' (unless you are Welsh) cannot use it! The only way in which citizens can use the system is usually through their local MP or another MP.

What is maladministration?

Another major difficulty is establishing, if an office is set up to investigate complaints of maladministration, what counts as maladministration. According to the Central Office of Information for the PCA, 'maladministration means poor administration or the wrong application of rules'. Examples of maladministration are:

- Avoidable delay
- Unfairness, bias or prejudice
- Providing misleading advice
- Discourtesy
- Failure to answer reasonable questions
- Failure to inform about the right to appeal

- Failure to follow correct procedures
- Failure to handle a claim correctly
- Failure to apologise for errors
- Failure to provide an adequate remedy

It may well not be possible for all ombudsmen to use exactly the same criteria of maladministration. The 'failure to provide an adequate remedy' might lead to some unfortunate interpretation if applied directly to the Health Service Ombudsman. There are, however, some attempts by ombudsmen to state clearly and outline the scope of potential investigations. The website of the Health Service Ombudsman (www.parliament.ombudsman.org.uk) achieves this goal.

THE PARLIAMENTARY
AND HEALTH SERVICE
OMBUDSMAN

The Office of The Parliamentary Commissioner for Administration and The Health Service Commissioners

The Ombudsman can investigate complaints against hospitals or community health services which are about:

a   a poor service;

b   failure to purchase or provide a service you are entitled to receive;

c   maladministration – that is, administrative failure such as:

- avoidable delay
- not following proper procedures
- rudeness or discourtesy
- not explaining decisions
- not answering your complaint fully or promptly.

Where the matters you are complaining about happened after 31 March 1996, the Ombudsman may also investigate:

d   complaints about the care and treatment provided by a doctor, nurse or other trained professional;

e   other complaints about family doctors (GPs), or about dentists, pharmacists or opticians providing a NHS service locally.

Complaints about access to information

You have rights to information about how the NHS operates locally. These are set out in the government's *Code of Practice on Openness in the NHS*. Copies of the Code should be available in your local library or from your local hospital. If you ask your Health Authority (Health Board in Scotland) or Trust for information and are not content with the response you first receive, you should write to the chief executive of the Health Authority/Health Board or NHS Trust concerned. If you remain dissatisfied you can complain to the Ombudsman about such things as:

- refusal to provide the information – unless it something you do not have a right to see;
- a delay of over four weeks in getting the information requested;
- the level of any charge you are asked to pay for it.

Such information may be about services available locally, the standards set or achieved, or the details of important decisions or proposals.

Under the Code you can ask for information about the NHS services provided by your local general practitioner, dentist, pharmacist or optician. If you are not satisfied with the reply you receive you may complain to the Ombudsman.

The process of investigation

If the ombudsman does support a citizen's allegation of maladministration, then the citizen will be sent a statement of complaint. This sets out exactly the area that the ombudsman will investigate. The organisation that is being investigated will also be informed and will be asked to send to the ombudsman their comments and all relevant papers.

When the ombudsman receives the paperwork, the citizen may be asked to attend an interview at a convenient time and place and be accompanied by a friend of their choice. Interviews are carried out in private and, although they are usually informal, the ombudsman does have the same power as the civil courts to obtain evidence. This process, due to its thoroughness, can, according to the Health Service Ombudsman, take 'several months'.

At the end of the investigation, the citizen will be sent the ombudsman's report. A copy is also sent to the offending organisation. If the citizen's complaint is justified, the ombudsman will seek to gain either an apology for the citizen or another remedy. That may include getting a decision changed, or repayment of unnecessary out-of-pocket expenses. The ombudsman does not recommend damages. The ombudsman may also call for changes to be made, so that what has gone wrong cannot be repeated. If the organisation states that it is to make changes, the ombudsman checks that they have done so.

The report from the ombudsman is the final stage in the procedure for pursuing a complaint, so there is no appeal against the decision. If completely new information should ever be discovered, there is the very rare possibility that the ombudsman may start a new investigation.

However, for many citizens it is not maladministration that is the problem, nor is it the procedures used to reach the final decision; it is the final decision that is the problem – the decision might be biased, arbitrary or incompetent. Although it is the final decision that usually has the greatest impact on the life of a citizen, maladministration only refers to the procedures used to reach that decision.

Problems

There are two problems that some citizens feel raise questions about the effectiveness of the role of the ombudsman. Many citizens who use the ombudsman experience a very lengthy delay before a decision is reached. By the time the procedures have been followed and decisions made, many citizens feel little sense of justice. This feeling is not helped by the nature of those appointed as ombudsmen. Those most likely to be appointed are ex-civil servants; hardly the most neutral of appointments in a dispute between citizens and alleged maladministrators.

Finally, some claim that the ombudsman is a toothless animal, as there is no opportunity to initiate an investigation into alleged maladministration; they have to wait until a citizen raises evidence of maladministration. Also, an ombudsman cannot make an investigation if there is in existence a route through tribunals or the courts. This has led to the exclusion of investigation into areas like the armed services and the police. If and when a recommendation is made, the last problem for citizens is that the ombudsman's decisions are not enforceable. As some say, 'with a friend like this, who needs enemies?'.

Alternative methods of redressing grievances

With its anarchic nature, the internet provides a quick and relatively cheap means for a citizen to redress his or her grievance. The process is rather like the development of either, depending on point of view, a consumer terrorist movement or a consumer freedom fighter faction, in which dissatisfied citizens, consumers or customers can use websites to describe or show the nature of their grievance to a potentially worldwide audience. With the potential offered by this form of publicity, acting as your own personal ombudsman has a certain appeal. One such site, www.badcustomerservice. co.uk, can proudly boast 20,000 hits in a relatively short period of time. It must, however, be remembered that the laws of libel apply to the net so that, if an individual citizen is to use this method to seek redress over a grievance, then all alleged details must be accurate.

All citizens are consumers and all consumers have expectations about the level and quality of any service they are buying. In a restaurant, the customer

would not expect a hot meal to arrive tepid or cold; in a hotel, a guest would not expect to have to wait a couple of hours before they can check in. In shops, consumers have expectations about the level of cleanliness.

In all these examples, if the level of service does not meet the required standard, the consumer can easily identify to whom they should complain. They can take stronger action, by returning the meal, moving to another hotel or spending their money in a different shop. On the assumption that the providers of these services wish to retain customers and remain in business, the potential of these threats should be enough to raise or maintain standards to match the expectations of the consumer.

If, however, the providers of that service did not really care about the level or quality of that service, or the provider had a monopoly of that service, the power of the consumer and the options available to the consumer are drastically reduced.

The pattern of the relationship between the consumer and the service provider, when applied to public services, is most closely aligned to the model in which the consumer has considerably less power than the provider. These are large monopolistic providers, without a single clearly identifiable person as the manager, that are very often staffed by poorly paid workers whose commitment to their employment certainly would not continue if they won the lottery. In the balance of power between the citizen as a consumer and the government as service provider, the citizen is small fry to the sharks.

Citizen's Charter

In an attempt to try to redress this balance, John Major, in 1991, initiated the *Citizen's Charter* scheme and, in an attempt to emphasise this new-found importance being placed upon the provision of public services, the scheme's status was enhanced by being located in the Cabinet Office as the Office of Public Service and Science Unit.

The thrust of the *Citizen's Charter* scheme was to award a Charter Mark to those public services that had met various performance targets whilst allowing citizens the opportunity for some form of redress when a public service failed to perform to expectations. The various charters created under the *Citizen's Charter* also provided information and knowledge for citizens on various complaints procedures, although it was less specific as to any outcome from those complaints.

Service charters

As a result of the initiative, many service charters were created and the terms in which citizens were referred to changed. No longer were citizens 'railway passengers', they were transformed into 'railway customers'. Many citizens in the early 1990s felt that, if the money that had been spent on the introduction of the charters had been invested in the service, the need for a charter scheme would not exist. With public services being starved of investment, the scheme was regarded as a public relations exercise to mask the decline in standards.

To be more critical of the scheme, the use of the term 'charter' hardly seems appropriate. It is hardly a case of citizens demanding from their rulers certain rights. The scheme, as devised, was imposed on citizens, with public service providers setting their own targets. As all sensible students will be aware, the process of setting targets can take two forms:

- The target that reflects the *best possible service* for the consumer but is unreachable. Since this target is unreachable, that service would be defined as failing.
- The target that reflects the *worst possible service* that will not result in a complaint by the consumer. Since this target is reachable, that service would be defined as successful.

Patient's Charter

One effect of the introduction of targets can be to transform the impression of a service that is basically unsatisfactory into one that appears to be very successful. The *Patient's Charter* clearly indicated that a patient should be assessed immediately (defined as within five minutes) on arrival in an Accident and Emergency department. The West Kent Health Authority Report on the Patient's Charter (April 1994–March 1995) suggests a positive rate of success.

Kent and Sussex Weald NHS Trust	% of patients assessed immediately
April–June 1994	100%
July–September 1994	100%
October–December 1994	100%
January–March 1995	99%
Total patients seen	34,000

However, what the report does not indicate is the length of the wait after the initial assessment! The length of the wait after assessment was only addressed with the introduction in 1995 of a revised and improved version of the *Patient's Charter* that outlines 'a maximum three to four hour wait for emergency admission to hospital through Accident and Emergency departments'.

BobZ

Another example of how the *Patient's Charter* creates the impression of success, whilst revealing a greater interest in the achievability of targets than the concerns of citizens, is the pledge of 'A maximum 18 month waiting time guarantee for admission to hospital for inpatient treatment'. Most citizens would prefer a time limit measured in 18 days or even 18 weeks rather than 18 months.

By the time the Labour Government came to power in 1997, the idea of awarding Charter Marks had become established, and 911 Charter Marks had been awarded. However, the means for judging the quality of a service remains an issue. Should the quality of service be based on the speed of response to a telephone call, a measure made almost irrelevant by the introduction of automated switchboards that dictate that a citizen responds to a sequence of options, or should the quality of service be judged by the citizens who actually use the service?

The Service First Unit

In June 1998, the Citizen's Charter Unit in the Cabinet Office became the Service First Unit, which requires that the providers of public services should canvass opinion through the use of local focus groups, local public meetings, interviews or questionnaires, with the expectation that they will, as a result, become more responsive to the needs and demands of citizens.

With the same aims to monitor the quality of the provision of public services and offer a route towards improvement, Service First does little to change the criticisms originally applied to its predecessor.

What do you understand by the following terms and concepts?

- Parliamentary Commissioner for Administration
- Ombudsman
- A tribunal
- The *Citizen's Charter*
- The Service First Unit
- Maladministration

The main purpose and function of service charters is not to help empower citizens but to make a substandard service appear to be a very efficient one.

To complete this activity, a copy of a charter is required. These are available in the reference sections of local public libraries.

1 Select evidence from the Charter that would support the view that the Charter is:

- trivial and/or meaningless, for example:
  - ○ *Patient's Charter* states: '… ensuring that your privacy, dignity, religious and cultural beliefs are respected.'
  - ○ *Patient's Charter* states: 'Where access to any area is difficult for people with physical disabilities, please speak to any staff member, who should be able to help you.'

2 Select evidence from the Charter that would support the view that the Charter:

- will empower a citizen and help to improve the standards of service received, for example:
  - ○ *Patient's Charter*: 'If you wish to make a complaint to … please contact the Authority at the address below or telephone …'

3 What conclusions can be drawn from your analysis?

Community poster

The purpose of this activity is to produce publicity that will increase the awareness of the work of the ombudsman and information about the work of tribunals in order to encourage a greater understanding of the contribution that these bodies can make to the life of some citizens.

The role of the ombudsman is to investigate complaints of maladministration by government departments. It would seem that very few citizens have ever heard of an ombudsman.

Equally, there are many tribunals in existence but if a citizen does not know how to contact or use them, they are effectively invisible and of little use. This activity will address both of these issues.

- Design a poster that could be used in your local MP's surgery that would increase citizens' awareness about the work of the ombudsman.
- Design a poster that could be used in a public building that would increase citizens' awareness about the work of tribunals.

CHAPTER 9

The Citizen and the Police

The aims of this chapter are to:

- Introduce issues relating to the role of the police and different types of policing and the possible effects of these on citizens

- Explore implications relating to police discretion

- Introduce issues surrounding the existence and application of a specific police culture and its impact on citizens

- Introduce discussions relating to the powers of the police

Whenever a citizen interacts with another citizen, each citizen has to interpret the other's behaviour. A smile or the offer of an outstretched hand is only understandable as a form of greeting between citizens if they know and understand the cultural code. Within any interaction there exists a process of interpreting the meanings attached to behaviour. Not only do those involved in the interaction interpret the behaviour of others, they also make assumptions about the behaviour of others. The process of interpreting behaviour and making assumptions about behaviour also occurs when citizens are interacting with the police.

When the assumptions and interpretation by both parties are the same, it is most likely that each party will trust the other and there will be broad agreement between those two parties. When both parties have the same goal and seek the co-operation and assistance of each other, they could be described as pulling in the same direction, with the probability that each will achieve their goal.

When shared assumptions and interpretation about behaviour exist between citizens and police, the result is that either the honest citizen will co-operate with the honest police officer who seeks to prevent, solve or arrest illegal activity, or the dishonest citizen would recognise the legitimacy of the police and declare that 'It's a fair cop, guv'. Rather like an equation, both sides of the relationship know, understand and have expectations about the other. There is no ambiguity in this harmonious example.

An alternative model could exist, in which the assumptions and interpretation by both parties are not the same. With one party pulling in one direction and the other pulling in the opposite, without the same goal, the relationship is more likely to rest not on trust, but on suspicion. Without shared assumptions and interpretation about behaviour, the result will be attitudes of intolerance, mistrust and doubt; allegations of bias and prejudice and actions of violence.

The role of the police in society

One problem faced by the police is that there is a contradiction within their role and their relationships with other citizens. It would be generally agreed that the police have a responsibility towards other citizens. This responsibility consists of having some authority within society that is justified, as it is essential to the function of protecting citizens. However, those members of the community who do break the law are also citizens. Consequently, on the one hand the police could be viewed as 'the goodies', who are using their authority in order to protect innocent citizens from 'nasty thieving criminals'. Alternatively, the police could be viewed as 'the baddies', who use their authority to 'oppress' or 'persecute' either individual citizens or certain groups of citizens.

Consensus policing

This difference in emphasis is the basis for two fundamentally different interpretations of the role of the police in society. On the one hand, the role of the police can be seen in non-controversial terms. The police are doing a socially useful job protecting the community against crime. They are supported and trusted by the local community and, because of this trust, citizens will willingly inform the police about any criminal activity. With such a flow of information, the police are able to follow up leads and identify actual suspects and there is less need to make broad, generalised assumptions about groups of citizens. In effect, there is less need to develop and utilise stereotypes.

This model represents a consensus view of policing and is supported by many traditional images. These images include 'the bobby on the beat' or 'community policing', in which the police constable is integrated into the local community with an almost encyclopaedic personal knowledge of all the citizens who live 'on the patch'. In the media there have been many representations of consensual policing, none more memorable than the television series *Dixon of Dock Green* that ran from 1955–76, in which PC George Dixon cleared up petty crime through placid, plodding policing.

The image of the friendly 'village bobby' described above is a long way removed from the images associated with policing in Northern Ireland or the role of the police during protests by groups of citizens. Images associated with the police in action in Brixton and dealing with the miners and poll tax demonstrators during the 1980s will still be fresh in the minds of some citizens.

Military policing

On another view, the police are far more confrontational and there is more conflict. The police is more akin to a military force. This approach to the role of the police is at the opposite extreme to the consensus model of policing and is usually referred to as military policing. There is little consensus between the police and citizens. The police are not viewed as part of the community and citizens generally fear a police force that is seen as oppressive, particularly against some categories or groups of citizens. Due to the lack of consensus, there is little or no flow of information about crime from citizens to the police. Without a flow of information, the police have to initiate investigations that may result in the harassment of some citizens or groups of citizens, with the result that stereotypes develop, or they may resort to more intrusive methods of surveillance.

Discretion

No matter what style is adopted within the policing of a community, the police will have to use discretion in their interpretation of the activities of citizens.

The police are constantly making interpretations and assumptions about the role and behaviour of citizens, who are in turn constantly making interpretations and assumptions about the role and behaviour of the police. When both sides have the same interpretations and make the same assumptions, the result is harmony. Disharmony and disorder will result from two groups who do not have the same interpretations and make the same assumptions about each other.

Each side of this equation has a role: citizens to live their life within the law, and the police to ensure that citizens obey the law.

In order to achieve their role in ensuring that citizens obey the law, the police can caution or arrest another citizen. Before the police can proceed with a caution or arrest of another citizen, they first have to interpret whether that citizen is actually breaking the law. In some cases, very little interpretation is necessary. The case of a citizen who is stopped at a roundabout driving a stolen car needs very little interpretation. However, when do a group of citizens who are enthusiastically celebrating some event turn from being in 'high spirits' into being 'drunk and disorderly'? The answer to this question lies in the idea of discretion.

The police have to interpret the behaviour of the celebrating citizens and, using their discretion, make a decision about their behaviour. Is it good-natured high spirits or a case of being drunk and disorderly?

Understanding police discretion

The interpretation or discretion shown by the police as to whether the action of another citizen is appropriate or not will, on the one hand, be based on:

- who is involved in the activity – age, sex, appearance, race, ethnicity, and so on;
- when the activity takes place – time of day or time of year;
- where the activity takes place – location, for example, beach or town centre;
- what the activity is – for example drinking wine.

On the other hand are the discretion, interpretations and assumptions of those making the judgments. For those citizens interpreting the behaviour of others, the basis from which judgments are made is the culture of a citizen.

Even when a citizen has undertaken some unlawful behaviour and has been apprehended, the police still have to use their discretion as to how they should respond to that citizen's unlawful behaviour. The question that the

... At your discretion

The groups described below are equal in number and are all making the same amount of noise.

- Decide whether you think that the behaviour of the citizens would be most likely to be interpreted as being in 'high spirits' or 'drunk and disorderly'.
- What conclusions can be drawn from your findings?

Group of citizens	Time of celebration	Reason for celebration	Location of the disturbance	Interpretation – 'high spirits' or 'drunk and disorderly'
Football supporters	8 pm	Winning the championship	Outside football stadium	
Local Women's Institute	4.30 am	Winning first prize in competition	Residential housing estate	
Residents of a hostel for the homeless	Midday	Receipt of weekly Giro	Outside run-down pub	
Local Masonic Lodge	1 am	AGM	Outside expensive hotel	
Strangers	Midnight	New year's eve	Central London	
Year 11 students	11.30 am	Last day of school	Local shopping centre	

police have to answer is whether they are going to prosecute the citizen or issue the citizen with a caution. As the flow diagram overleaf demonstrates, any citizen who has been apprehended as a result of their unlawful behaviour can never be certain of their fate as every step of the path towards being cautioned or prosecuted is determined by the police having to use their discretion.

The issue of police discretion took on a wider importance from 12 August 2002 when a pilot project was introduced that gives police officers the power to hand out fixed penalty notices – these are instant fines of £40 or £80 for anti-social behaviour. One of the offences that qualifies for an instant fine is if a citizen is 'drunk and disorderly', but since the issue of being drunk and disorderly is hardly a cut and dried affair, the ability for the police officer to act as judge and jury might, in the long run, lead to further claims by some groups of citizens that their treatment by the police is unequal.

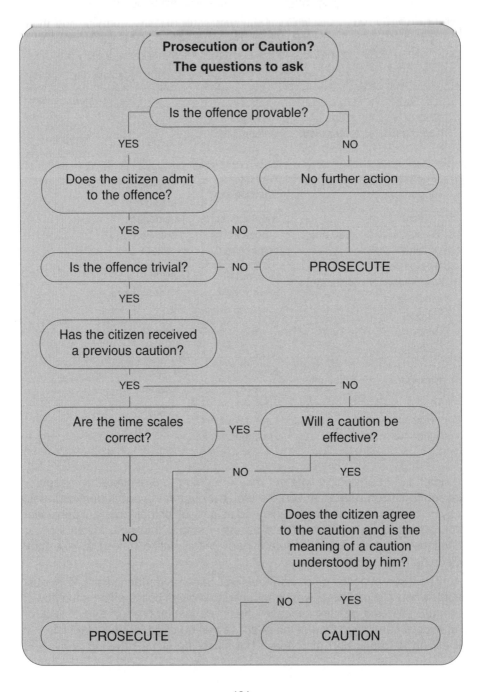

Police culture

Since culture forms an important base from which assumptions are made about other citizens, if there exists a specific 'police culture', this culture will determine the assumptions that the police have about other citizens and will be the base from which the behaviour of other citizens is interpreted. In *The Politics of the Police*, R Reiner outlines certain characteristic norms and values within the police service that, when combined, help to create a distinctive police culture.

According to Reiner, police discretion can be understood in conjunction with three variables. Some police officers will justify their actions in terms of their individual personality. These police officers will have their own individual reasons for showing discretion and it is impossible to generalise about why such discretion is shown.

A second way in which police discretion can be understood is to see any discretion exercised by the police in terms of the police culture. Police culture stresses the importance of working as a group whose members will support each other. There is also an emphasis on masculinity and the importance of physical power. Add to this the need for excitement and sensation, with elements of racism and sexism, and the role of the police culture could explain why some groups of citizens are treated differently from others.

One result of joining the police service for some citizens is the difficulty of continuing social relationships with other citizens due to the significance of the label 'police officer'. Future socialising is more likely to take place with other police officers who appreciate the stresses and demands of the occupation as well as sharing the same pattern of shifts. This, along with the importance of back-up and support from colleagues, can lead to both a reinforcement of any police culture and a degree of social isolation from other citizens. This degree of social isolation helps to perpetuate elements of police culture associated with ageism, sexism and racism.

The significance of the 'isms' lies in how they can help shape the nature of any relationship between citizens and the police service. At present, 85% of police officers are male and, if this is combined with an overtly masculine/macho culture, the result inside the service can lead to the experience of sex discrimination and sexual harassment of female officers; whilst outside the service, there is the increased potential that some female citizens will be reluctant to report certain crimes of which they have been a victim.

Even the National Crime Squad, which was formed to tackle organised crime, according to the inspectorate of constabulary, has failed to attract women and ethnic minority recruits because the organisation is perceived to be 'macho, elitist and sexist'. It has no senior women staff and only one middle ranking female officer. It is 88% male and there are only 16 black and Asian staff out of a force of 1,318 officers.

Figures in a report published by the National Association of Probation Officers in August 1996 revealed that the number of ethnic minority police officers in 1995 was 2,223, which represents 1.75% of the total 127,222 officers. The combination of two reluctances on the part of ethnic minorities – to apply and to remain employed – has created a police force that does not reflect wider society. One result of this structure in which over 97% of police officers are not from ethnic minorities is that police culture could continue to express attitudes and use language that in the wider culture could be defined as unacceptably racist.

The third element that could explain the reasons why police discretion takes the form that it does is the formal framework in which the police work. Changes introduced by the Criminal Justice and Public Order Act 1994 literally changed police powers overnight, allowing activities like the sabotaging of fox hunts, that had been outside the law and therefore previously ignored, to be redefined and, with discretion, acted on.

 Alison Halford was born in Norwich in 1940. She was educated at Notre Dame Convent Grammar School, Norwich. After leaving school she served for three years with the Women's Royal Air Force and came to London at the age of 22, where she joined the Metropolitan Police Force. A police officer for 30 years, she rose to the rank of Assistant Chief Constable in the Merseyside Police Authority by 1983. Alison was the first woman to reach the rank of Assistant Chief Constable in the British Police Force and became widely known as the most senior policewoman in Britain. No woman had ever achieved a higher rank. Yet after nine attempts, she failed to achieve the further promotion she most earnestly desired and believed she deserved. She came to national prominence when she fought a long-running and high profile sexual discrimination case against her employer. With the backing of the Equal Opportunities Commission, she took the police authorities to court. For two years she was vilified, humiliated and subjected to various forms of psychological pressure in an attempt to force her to relent and abandon her case. When the tribunal finally sat, Alison Halford was cross-examined for a gruelling fortnight in a case that was abandoned before any of her opponents were subjected to the same treatment. In the settlement (which, in effect, cost the taxpayer over a million pounds) Alison Halford received a well deserved pension and disability award. The justice of her case remained unchallenged, as did her own integrity. In 1997 she won a phone-tapping case against the Home Secretary and the British Government in the European Court of Human Rights that forced a review of UK legislation.

Source: www.alisonhalford.com

> - Why do you think the title of her book was *No Way Up the Greasy Pole?*
> - Do you agree with the view that while some members of an organisation still sexually discriminate against and harass fellow colleagues, it will not prevent the development of an environment that encourages those outside an organisation to report similar crimes in which they were victims?

Police powers

When considering the powers of the police, it is important to remember that the police do not have a different set of laws when compared to other citizens. All police officers must act within the law. However, since a lot of police work relies on the police officer using his or her discretion, the result is that some citizens may feel either that they have been treated unfairly or that the police officer's actions were simply not justified. The police officer cannot have unlimited power if there is to be a sense of balance between the police officer and the citizen. Unless there were some control over the behaviour of the police, it would be very difficult for a citizen who felt that they had been victimised to be able to redress this grievance.

One way to place a control on the power of the police officer is to make the police officer accountable for their actions. Accountability, in this case, means that the police officer would have to justify all their actions to their Chief Constable. In other words, the Chief Constable has some power and control over their police officers.

The balance of power between the citizen and the police officer will never be straightforward, due to issues surrounding police discretion and police culture, both of which make generalisations difficult. The police do have certain rights that accompany their position and these rights have been the subject of much debate and controversy in recent years. A citizen, for example, can be stopped if there is suspicion that they are carrying an offensive weapon, although the police cannot simply stop a citizen on the grounds that they have 'an offensive haircut' or because a citizen 'has previous form'.

The introduction of the Police and Criminal Evidence Act 1984 addressed some of the issues in the balance of power between citizen and police officer. One simple procedure that was introduced was the normalisation of the practice of recording all interviews, which, coupled with the citizen's right to have a solicitor present at the interview, effectively prevented police from being able to force a confession from a citizen.

The Police and Criminal Evidence Act 1984 also introduced the Police Complaints Authority. The PCA investigate police officers who have failed to perform their professional duties appropriately. Professional expectations of behaviour are outlined in the police's Codes of Practice and these codes give citizens some form of control over the powers of the police.

There are Codes of Practice that, for example, relate to the procedures that the police must follow when obtaining evidence or questioning a suspect. One example is the warning given to citizens prior to arrest. This has the clear purpose of providing the citizen with an indication that their status is about to change. This knowledge provides the citizen with an opportunity to amend and change their behaviour to the situation. Without such a warning, any evidence gained is not admissible in a court of law.

The police also have a disciplinary code that sets out clearly the limits between acceptable and unacceptable forms of behaviour. The police, according to their code:

- cannot, without good reason, neglect their duty;
- cannot make a false statement, either verbal or written;
- cannot abuse their authority through, for example, excessive force;
- should not be abusive to other citizens;
- should not behave in a discriminatory manner.

Many believe that the combination of the Police and Criminal Evidence Act and the PCA will remove the potential for repeating previous miscarriages of justice. In October 1989, the Court of Appeal overturned, on the basis of forced confessions, the conviction of the 'Guildford Four'. This was followed by so many other groups of citizens that, when referred to collectively, they began to sound more like a set of football results than citizens who had been victims of miscarriages of justice. By 1994, the 'Birmingham Six', the 'Broadwater Three', the 'Cardiff Three', the 'Swansea Two' and the 'East Ham Two' had all had murder convictions overturned. However, for others, the fact that the PCA, when it takes over a case, will place another police officer in charge puts a question mark over the objectivity of the procedures, as it effectively means that the police are investigating themselves.

Effects of police culture on citizens

There has been considerable research into examples of how police culture is applied to citizens in the day to day work of police officers and the possible consequences for citizens of the application of this element of police culture.

One example of this culture that has been widely researched is the way in which police officers refer to ethnic minority citizens. In a study conducted by Smith and Gray (*Police and People in London*, 1985), it was found that the use of racist language was common. This use of language could be seen to be one of the clearest examples of a racist police culture, although in the later study, *Talking Blues*, when the researcher, Graef, expressed disapproval at the use of language based on racial stereotypes, he was told that 'Policemen are insulting about everyone. It's not specifically the coons. You hear remarks about poofs, Pakis, lesbos, women, students, the Irish – you name it. We hate everybody'.

When a culture has at its root attitudes that are prejudiced against some citizens, the result of the application of that culture will be to make different assumptions about the behaviour of some citizens that will in turn lead to different interpretations of behaviour by those citizens. If police officers do have different assumptions and make different interpretations about the behaviour and activities of some citizens, the result will inevitably lead to:

• different attitudes towards the police by different sets of citizens; and
• different experiences of the police by different sets of citizens.

In a survey conducted by MORI from a sample of 902 people, of whom 129 were black and Asian (published in *The Sun* on 1 March 1999), the following results were gained:

	% of 'Yes' responses	
	All	Black & Asian
Do you feel that you can trust the police?	74	54
Do you think that most police officers are prejudiced against black and Asian people?	21	52
Thinking about the police in your area, do you think they are –		
Honest?	76	59
Racist?	15	40
Competent?	80	64

Although questions may be raised about the methodological processes involved, the significance of the differences between the percentages that replied positively could suggest that there are grounds to support the claim that attitudes towards the police differ between different groups of citizens.

There is considerable evidence from a wide range of sources which suggests that different groups of citizens have quite different experiences of the police. From the 1980s, the insensitive saturation policing of 'Operation Swamp' in Brixton was highlighted in the Scarman Report, which detailed the considerably increased involvement of black people in the criminal justice system, as both suspects and victims.

The issues relating to the different attitudes expressed and the different experiences of the police are sensitive and transient. It is not appropriate to divide ethnic minority citizens and police officers into two groups and assume that all the members of each group all have the same attitudes. However, the public inquiry undertaken by Sir William Macpherson into the death, in 1993, of the black teenager Stephen Lawrence, accused the Metropolitan Police of institutional racism, defining this as 'the collective failure of an organisation to provide an appropriate and professional service to people because of their colour, culture or ethnic origin'. Although many police officers stated that they were not racist, their actions and their language ('He is a white man; that is a coloured woman, he is a white man; that is a black man': Inspector Groves, quoted by Cathcart in 'Murder in the dark', *New Statesman*, 10 April 1998) could be interpreted differently.

In the wake of the damning Macpherson Report, the need to challenge and change police culture was seen to be a priority. One way the Home Office believes that this could be achieved is for each police force to develop strategies to achieve, within the next 10 years, an ethnic profile within the police force that reflects the ethnic profile of the local community. For the Metropolitan Police this means increasing the present proportion of ethnic minority police officers from 1 in 33 to 1 in 4.

One result of the Macpherson Report was a reduction in the use of the police's stop and search powers. Home Office figures reveal that the number of stop and searches fell by 21% in the year to April 2000 and a further 17% the subsequent year. However, for black citizens the number of stop and searches increased by 4% and now black citizens have an 800% greater chance of being stopped and searched compared to white citizens. Coupled with an arrest rate of 108 per thousand for black citizens compared to 14 per thousand for white citizens, the admission in October 1998 by the Chief Constable of Greater Manchester, David Wilmot, that institutional racism affected his force was not overly surprising.

Section 60 orders

Section 60 of the Criminal Justice and Public Order Act 1994 was intended to combat public disturbances, particularly at football grounds. It states:

> Where a police officer of or above the rank of superintendent reasonably believes that (a) incidents involving serious violence may take place in any locality in his area and (b) it is expedient to do so to prevent their occurrence, he may give an authorisation that the powers to stop and search persons and vehicles conferred by this section shall be exercisable at any place within that locality for a period not exceeding 24 hours.

Once a section 60 order has been invoked, it allows the police to stop any citizen and any vehicle and undertake a search whether or not the police have any grounds of suspecting the citizen of any crime. In effect, the police can stop and search for any reason whatsoever and although all citizens who are stopped and searched in the UK have the right to demand to go to a police station and be issued with a report, the number of reports actually issued is very small. This is either because citizens are unaware of their rights and there has been little publicity to inform citizens about their rights or because the citizen rather naturally feels the urge to remove themselves from the situation as soon as possible and not to the protract the interaction any longer than is necessary. The approach in Britain contrasts sharply to a recently passed law in Norway that attempts to combat racism under which all police officers are forced to issue an automatic on-the-spot 'receipt' to any citizen who has been stopped and searched or asked for their ID.

There are other ways to illustrate the differences in the ways that a citizen can experience police action. One approach is to look at figures that relate to the death of citizens in police custody as a result of arrest procedures such as the use of physical restraint or CS gas. In an *Observer* study between 1997 and 1999, these types of deaths accounted for 43% of black citizen deaths in custody compared to 8% of white citizen deaths. An alternative is to focus on a particular case. The case of Delroy Lindo can illustrate how some citizens' experience of the police differs from others' experiences. Mr Lindo, after 37 arrests, and 18 charges from which only one resulted in a conviction that was later overturned, felt that he was subjected to such police activity that it constituted harassment and decided that he was going to sue the police. As a result of this the Metropolitan Police launched an internal inquiry. The findings of the inquiry found evidence of harassment as a result of the 'negative stereotyping and frivolous comments' about the Lindo family. The inquiry also established that the family had been arrested unlawfully on three occasions and four of the charges had not been investigated to an acceptable standard.

From the same year as the Scarman Report, the Home Office issued figures that revealed that the likelihood of being a victim of crime was also not distributed evenly between citizens. South Asian citizens were 50 times and Afro-Caribbeans 36 times more likely to be the victim of a racially motivated attack. Many commentators believe firstly that these figures are a considerable underestimate and secondly that there is little difference today.

A further way in which citizens can experience differences in their relationship with the police is to look at issues inside the police. A study commissioned by the Home Office in April 1999, 'Career Progression of Ethnic Minority Police Officers', reported that ethnic minority officers take longer to be promoted, even though many Asian officers are better qualified than other groups, and that they were more likely to be disciplined. It was not until April 2001 that female Muslim recruits were to be given the option to wear a hijab, the traditional headscarf which is a symbol of belief and modesty. Although Sikh officers can wear a turban, there are still ongoing discussions as to whether Rastafarian recruits should be allowed to have dreadlocks.

What do you understand by the following terms and concepts?

- Consensus policing
- Military policing
- Police discretion
- Ageism

- Police culture
- Institutional racism
- Ethnicity
- Sexism

Research on the Macpherson Report

For this activity, reference to a copy of the Macpherson Report is necessary. If this is not possible, reference can be made to various newspaper archives which can be found on the internet.

- Compile evidence from the Report that would support the view that police culture helped to produce the behaviour and attitudes that resulted in the unsatisfactory nature of the police enquiry into the death of Stephen Lawrence.

- What suggestions and recommendations were made by the Report to change the assumptions about ethnic minorities that have had an influenced on police culture?

This activity relates to the representation of the police in television programmes and in the cinema, and can only be completed over a period of time. How are the police usually represented? In terms associated with consensus policing or in terms associated with military policing?

Using television programmes and films made in the UK, develop a list of programmes featuring the police that constitute evidence of the different forms of policing.

Can any conclusions be drawn from your results?

It is police discretion that creates the situation in which prisons become populated by the least empowered male citizens.

CHAPTER 10

The Role of the State in the Provision of Welfare

The aims of this chapter are to:

- Introduce issues relating to the subjective nature of citizens' 'needs'
- Introduce the impact of different ideologies on assumptions about the relationship between the state and the welfare of citizens
- Evaluate differing ideological assumptions

Debates surrounding the relationship between the state and the welfare of the citizen

In the debates about the relationship between the state and the provision of welfare to citizens, it is interesting to discover that there is a range of quite different approaches. Some of these approaches are more useful than others, but to commence the debate it is useful to start with what is probably the simplest and least fruitful approach to the relationship between the state and the welfare of the citizen.

The chronological approach

This approach adopts the principles of chronology and exists basically in the form of a list of dates that are associated with the delivery of welfare benefits. Some of these dates have become part of the culture of the UK and can often be recited by citizens or are held with reverence. One example of a date that is associated with the delivery of a welfare benefit would be 1944 and its close association with the Butler Education Act.

Date and event mix and match

1 Research a range of dates that are associated with some element of the introduction of the welfare state, for example 1944 and the Butler Education Act.

2 Divide the information into two sets. Write the dates in one column and in the other column what was associated with those dates. Make sure that you jumble each set.

3 Ask a small sample of people if they can correctly match the date and the associated event.

4 What is the percentage of correct responses?

The problem with this approach is that, once the date of an Act's introduction is known, there is little else that can be discussed. Does it really make that much difference if an Act becomes effective in 1944 or 1945? The date of the Act's introduction will not help to develop an understanding of why the Act was introduced, or what the intended consequences of the Act were. It will not help to develop any understanding of who was meant to benefit from the Act's introduction or whether the Act's introduction was linked to any other factors.

The reason why this approach is unsatisfactory is because it is not underpinned by any ideological discussion. Welfare benefits are not introduced into society without a reason, so, in order to understand why welfare benefits were introduced, the student of citizenship must look at the link between different ideologies and how those ideologies influence attitudes towards the introduction of welfare benefits. This essential link is missing both in a chronological list of dates and all other variations based around the development of some form of list.

The focus on issues

One variation in the list approach is to change the emphasis or focus of the list from a chronological list to one that takes as its main focus a range of recurrent issues that surround the provision of welfare benefits. These issues could include:

- the assumptions that determine the degree of intervention by the state in the promotion of individual welfare;
- the perception of need;
- the collection of funds to finance welfare benefits;
- the distribution of those funds to different sections or groups in society.

Lists based on issues have the advantage of moving away from a relatively meaningless list of dates, but they face another considerable handicap. If the main emphasis of the list is certain selected themes, in reality, this has nothing to do with the welfare of the citizen, but has everything to do with politics.

To illustrate this point, it is interesting to look in turn at those generally recurring issues and try to establish some of the political assumptions that have influenced them. As discussed previously, there is a relationship between the ideology of any government and how that government perceives the role of the state. As different governments have different priorities and different assumptions about how to promote a citizen's welfare, whenever there is a change in government, logically, changes should also occur in the priorities and assumptions about the promotion of a citizen's welfare. It is useful to look at the changes in the assumptions about the provision of housing as an illustration of this. The post-war assumption was based on the notion that, since housing in the private sector was unaffordable for many citizens, the government should provided 'enough dwellings of an acceptable standard and density for all households and at a price within the financial means of each household' (George and Wilding, *The Impact of Social Policy*, 1984). The perceived role of the state changed radically when, in the 1980s, Margaret Thatcher's ambition of a property owning democracy oversaw the effective privatisation and marketisation of council housing.

 Assumptions have always been made in areas concerning a citizen's welfare and the policies adopted to improve these areas. When these assumptions change, the policies have to follow.

- What were some of the historical assumptions made about the provision of welfare?
- What changes have occurred in these assumptions?
- How have these changes resulted in different policies?

	Assumption underlying policy when introduced	Change in assumption with corresponding changes in policy
Education		
Transport		
Housing		
Old age pensions		
Health care		

Another recurring issue relates to the perception of 'needs'. This debate is clearly influenced not only by the ideology of the government, but also by the performance of the economy.

Being in need

One of the questions that all governments face relates to the perception of 'need'. It is useful at this point to divide the category of being 'in need' into two types of need. Some citizens are defined as being 'in need' when certain conditions are met, conditions like reaching a certain age or becoming a parent. Other citizens, by contrast, are defined as being 'in need' when they are living at levels that have been declared to be unacceptable. Whereas the first category can be easily defined – for example, being over the age of 65 –

the second category is very problematic – for example, living in poverty. Both categories, however, result in a change in the definable status of a citizen. Not only are these definable statuses the result of government ideology, but so is the level of welfare provision for citizens within these new statuses. The implications relating to the changing perception of being 'in need' are clear and there are many examples that illustrate these changes. It is possible to take the issue of age and ask at what age does a citizen becomes a 'needy pensioner'; and, once they are a 'needy pensioner', what should the level of provision be for those within this category? The same is true for maternity welfare benefits. Another illustration of how those 'in need of support' can change is to review the financial support for the majority of Higher Education students. This has changed historically from the assumption that there was no discernible need and therefore no financial support, to the recognition of some need and therefore some support in the form of a grant, and then returning (coincidentally as student numbers grew) to the lack of need and effectively the lack of financial support. One final example is to focus on the structural changes that the policy of 'care in the community' introduced. Previous conditions that resulted in a citizen being defined as 'in need of being hospitalised' transformed, with the change in policy, to being 'in need but able to be looked after and cared for in the community'.

A much more complex and controversial debate relates to the problem of establishing the level at which material and physical conditions need to be in order for a citizen to be defined as 'living in need' or 'in need of care'. The reason why this debate is so problematic is because the judgments relating to need and care are subjective and any subjective criteria can result in some citizens experiencing discriminatory treatment.

Evidence of this discrimination is particularly striking in the field of mental health. Published in March 2000, the Mental Health Act Commission Report reconfirmed that a disproportionately high number of citizens who are compulsorily detained under the Mental Health Act are black and from the ethnic minorities.

On a single day in May 1999, 104 different types of mental health institutions were visited and within each visit there was an unannounced inspection of a randomly selected ward. Out of all the patients studied, 42% were classified as black Caribbean. Approximately one-quarter did not have English as their first language and 56 did not speak English at all. Only 31 patients were provided with an interpreter.

The problematic nature of 'being in need'

This new research only confirms previous findings and highlights the problematic nature of the subjective judgments needed to conclude whether a citizen is 'in need of care'. Littlewood and Lipsedge's research (*Aliens and Alienists, Ethnic Minorities and Psychiatry*, 1982) established that UK citizens of Afro-Caribbean origin were more likely not to be a voluntary patient, more likely to see a junior doctor and more likely to receive electro-convulsive therapy and powerful psychotropic drugs.

This well established link between certain types of citizens and the differences in hospital admission rates suggests that subjective judgments have a long and painful history for some citizens. These subjective judgments are illustrated in the following table:

Admission rates to hospitals per 100,000 people over 15 years of age, standardised to accommodate the different age structures of the different ethnic groups	Country of origin				
	England and Wales	Scotland	W Indies	India	Pakistan
Schizophrenia					
Male	87	90	290	141	158
Female	87	97	323	140	103
Manic depression					
Male	45	42	30	31	22
Female	92	99	31	57	38
Neuroses					
Male	48	56	19	33	36
Female	8	111	67	64	103
Personality disorders					
Male	43	100	27	36	18
Female	41	67	46	29	55

Adapted from R Cochrane, 'Mental illness in immigrants to England and Wales: an analysis of hospital admissions 1977', Social Psychiatry, 12, 24–35 – a comparative study of mental illness among immigrant and native people.

Quoted in *Sickness, Health and Medicine*, Ursula Dobraszczyc

The problem of establishing whether a citizen is 'in need of care' can also be discussed from the 'other side of the fence'. This involves shifting the focus of the discussion away from those citizens needing care to the providers of care and the facilities available for providing that care.

The reason why this is significant is because the provision of care rests on two elements. First, it is made up of those who are employed in a range of occupations that have some component in which the employee has a responsibility of care to other citizens. The second element consists of the facilities, the 'bricks and mortar', the buildings and institutions that exist in order to provide the care.

Due to financial constraints, both the number of people employed in the caring industry and the facilities are limited. Theoretically, if ever the situation arose where all the potential employees within the caring industries were fully employed and there were no vacancies in any of the caring facilities, the number of those citizens who could be defined as being 'in need of care' would be at its maximum. If more people are employed or more places created, then the system can cope with more citizens being 'in need of care'. If fewer people are employed or fewer facilities are in existence, the system can only cope if there are fewer citizens 'in need of care'. The supply and demand argument suggests that the number of citizens 'in need of care' rises and falls in direct proportion to the number of people employed in the caring services and the number of care facilities available for care to be delivered.

The third and fourth issues relate to the collection and distribution of money to finance welfare benefits, and to some extent these issues are linked to the previous point. It would generally be agreed that citizens who are in 'need of care' have to be supported and care facilities have to be paid for. The main source for this support would be through National Insurance contributions and tax revenues. Since the money to finance citizens in need of care and the caring industries is heavily dependent on revenues that have been collected, the level of welfare support for citizens is going to be influenced by a combination of the condition of the economy and decisions relating to what is perceived to be the appropriate role of the state. The result of these two points for the student of citizenship is the realisation that many of the decisions relating to both the level at which welfare benefits are to be paid and the conditions under which they are paid are to be considered, since these are political decisions.

The social administration approach

Another broad, traditional approach to issues surrounding welfare benefits is the social administration approach. The primary aim of this approach to the provision of welfare is that of demonstrating areas of need and suggesting solutions to those areas of need through changes and reforms in social policy.

The problems associated with this approach arise from a combination of the lack of a consistent ideological base, its dominant methodology and the rather optimistic outlook that it applies to society. These problems can be demonstrated by looking at an application of this approach. To begin with, a need or a needy group has to be identified. This need or needy group could be established through the use of a social survey and, once identified, there is the optimistic belief that it would be in the interest of all citizens if a solution to this area of need could be achieved through 'better' social services. Any solutions introduced would achieve success without generating any disagreement between citizens.

The fundamental problems at the root of this approach centre around the method used to identify areas of need. The social administrative approach tends to advocate the use of social surveys to establish need, but the problem with this is that the use of a social survey does not prove that any identifiable need actually exists. The reason for this is the circular nature of the argument.

To explain this point, imagine a conversation between a parent and their student offspring that takes the following pattern:

Parent: I want you back home by half past ten.

Student: Why do want you me back home by half past ten?

Parent: Because I said so.

What the student could say now is something along the lines of, 'Your reply does not prove why want you me back home by half past ten, or indeed anything. All you are doing is re-stating the original time, chosen and made up by yourself, and using it to justify your decision'.

The social administration approach faces the same problem:

Researcher: All those citizens who cannot afford a range of selected goods are living in a state of poverty.

Politician: How many citizens are living in a state of poverty?

Researcher: All those citizens who cannot afford that range of selected goods.

The researcher has identified a need, classified the conditions that are evidence of that need, counted the number of citizens who experience the conditions that make them in need and then used this as proof that the need actually exists.

Unfortunately, any critic of this approach will point out that there is no proof that the category of 'need' first identified actually exists. This is because it is the researcher who identified the need at the start of this process and then used that need to explain and justify the proposed solution.

Apart from this weak methodological position relating to the existence of social problems, discussions relating to solutions are equally problematic. Indeed, solutions are usually proposed in the form of uncritical welfare benefits. It is assumed that these new or improved welfare benefits would change and modify the old 'incorrect' welfare benefits and thus improve the conditions of those citizens who were living in a state of 'need'. This approach obviously ignores the ideological diversity and divisions related to the different perceptions of what is considered to be the appropriate role of the state. The social administration approach also ignores any conflict surrounding the introduction of welfare benefits and assumes that these welfare benefits will change and improve the situation of those citizens in 'need'.

A further criticism of this approach is that it tends towards an uncritical description of events instead of locating them within a theoretical framework. It was this criticism, along with a combination of developments in theories about the state and sociological analysis questioning the assumption that welfare benefits were 'a good thing', which ultimately led to a reappraisal of this approach.

Background	
	There have been many different approaches and suggestions as to how issues surrounding poverty could be tackled. From both history and sociology AS and A2 textbooks, or any appropriate books in the relevant sections of a library, research the contributions to the issue of poverty made by the following:
C Booth	
S Rowntree	
S & B Webb	
E Chadwick	
P Townsend	

The different relationships between the state and the welfare of the citizen

The following three quotes each represent a different approach towards the provision of welfare benefits. Each approach is influenced by a different ideology and it is the ideological differences which shape not only the way in which citizenship is understood, but also the role and the obligations of the state in terms of the welfare of its citizens.

Quote 1   'The idea that the state should pay welfare benefit to some citizens is good because:

- it is only the collective strength of the state that can overcome the problems of an unregulated free market, and

- some problems are so large that they are outside the control of individual citizens and consequently it is only the state that can organise a response to these problems.'

Quote 2   'The idea that the state should pay any welfare benefit to any citizen is not a good idea because these payments interfere with the functioning of the free market.'

Quote 3   'The only reason that the state pays any welfare benefits is to maintain the status quo which keeps those with power in power.'

The disadvantage of putting a name to each of these three quotes is that it is effectively grouping a broad range of ideas under a single umbrella heading. However, the approaches associated with these three quotes are usually referred to in terms of:

Social democratic or collectivist approaches   – – – – – - *Quote 1*

Market liberalist or anti-collectivist approaches   – – – – - - *Quote 2*

Marxist and feminist approaches   – - – – - - *Quote 3*

Social democratic or collectivist approaches

The starting point for this approach to the welfare of citizens is the belief that all citizens have some responsibility towards each other; a view based on the principles of collectivism. To achieve this collectivist ideal, it is necessary to use the organising powers of the state, as it is the state that is thought to be most effective in turning that responsibility into the active delivery of services.

This approach has a long history and it is the approach that is most often associated with the development of the modern welfare state. Essentially, this approach is reformist in nature. Reformists argue that society is essentially harmonious. A general consensus exists, as there is widespread agreement in citizens' norms and values. This general consensus could be threatened by the economic system because the economic system produces extremes of both poverty and wealth. The purpose of the introduction of any welfare benefits, consequently, is not to produce radical change in society, but to remove, through redistribution, those pockets of extreme deprivation in order to maintain consensus within society. Stability in society is important to achieve and change will only occur through evolution, not revolution. For Marshall, stability is achievable when 'citizenship rights' are achieved. Marshall argued that such citizenship rights, like the right to health care and the right to education, would encourage a citizen to be loyal to the state. The introduction of welfare benefits would not only maintain consensus, but ultimately help create a more ethical and just society. One of the assumptions within this approach is the belief that, if left unregulated, the economic system could threaten the stability of society. This approach also believes that the economic system is wasteful, inefficient and unjust, and these points need to be taken into consideration when discussing the collectivist assumptions about the relationship between the welfare of the citizen and the state.

An unregulated economic system would, according to this approach, be characterised by, and produce, uneven employment and an unequal division of wealth. This is because some groups of citizens would be less able to meet the challenge of the economic system. Those citizens that might be adversely affected are those who have a long term illness or disability, or those who are outside the acceptable age limits to be employed. Some might be adversely affected merely because of where they live. Due to the fact that these situations are likely to be outside the control of citizens, social democratic approaches suggest that the economic system must not be left unregulated and that some intervention is essential if problems like regional unemployment are to be tackled successfully. After all, unemployment for the individual citizen can also be seen as a wasted labour resource and loss of a tax revenue source for the state. Without intervention, unemployment will lead to both greater poverty and divisions within society that could threaten the consensus between citizens.

For some citizens, an unregulated economic system would be simply disastrous. This is because they are effectively outside the economic system and, without some form of intervention, they would be left to the ravages of the system with all its accompanying hardships. Citizens who are likely to be outside the system are those who fall into the categories of the elderly, the long term sick and the disabled.

Criticisms of the social democratic or collectivist approaches

This approach has been criticised in a number of ways. One criticism is that, when welfare benefits are introduced, it is not only those citizens who are effectively outside the economic system that benefit, but in some cases all citizens. This is especially true if the benefit is a universal rather than a selective benefit.

A universal benefit is a benefit that is paid to all citizens, regardless of wealth, if they fall into a particular category, whereas a selective benefit is means tested and is payable only to those citizens whose wealth is below a certain level.

If universal the welfare benefit is paid to all citizens and there are no differential tax rates. The welfare benefit will not reduce any divisions between citizens or 'close any gap' between citizens and thus, by definition, cannot be used as a tool towards the social engineering of a less divided and more just society achieved by the redistribution of wealth. Critics also ask why the state should provide benefits for those citizens who can adequately provide for themselves. Some go even further and argue that the state does not have the right to force citizens to make contributions towards the welfare of others. Some critics also argue that, by nature, a large state bureaucracy is not going to be the most efficient mechanism for the distribution of welfare benefits to citizens.

A further type of criticism that can be applied to this approach develops from questions about which citizens use and gain the most from these welfare benefits that have been introduced. There is compelling evidence that suggests an unequal use of and an unequal gain from welfare benefits when comparing different groups of citizens.

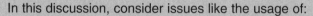

'It is the wealthiest sections of society that gain and benefit the most from the provision of welfare.'

In this discussion, consider issues like the usage of:

- Preventative medical services, like dental and eye check-ups.
- Higher education.
- The proportion of a citizen's total weekly income that is paid as:
  - income tax;
  - VAT.

The final criticism of this approach focuses on the issue of the level at which welfare benefits are set. The state, which is responsible for determining those levels, derives much of its income from National Insurance contributions and collection of taxes. The amount of money raised from these two sources is determined by, or very heavily influenced by, the performance of the economic system. Consequently, critics argue, it is not the level of need that determines the level at which welfare benefits are paid, but how much revenue has been raised and how much of that revenue is to be spent on welfare benefits.

Market liberalist or anti-collectivist approach

The belief that the state should not interfere with the economy is the assumption on which the anti-collectivist or individualistic approach to the provision of welfare benefit is based. The market liberal approach is often referred to as a *laissez faire* approach, which means 'to let things be'. The reasons why the economy should not be interfered with revolve around the view that any interference by the state in the economy would destroy natural market forces and, if the state did interfere and destroy these natural market forces, it would result in an economy that is not able to operate efficiently. If market forces, which refer to the increases and decreases in the supply and demand of goods, services and labour change, it can result in any possible combination of:

- too many or too few goods or commodities;
- too many or too few services;
- too many or too few employees.

The market can solve the 'too many or too few' (supply and demand) problem by either increasing or decreasing price. If there is not a sufficient supply of either a particular commodity or a particular service to meet the demand, an increase in the price of the commodity or service will reduce the demand until the demand and the supply are in balance. The pricing mechanism of the free market has efficiently reduced demand to match the supply.

For the market liberals, these principles of the free market also apply to citizens. If there is not enough of a particular set of skills to meet the demand for those skills, then those citizens who possess those skills will be able to achieve an increase in wages. As wages increase, demand will reduce until the demand and the supply are equal. Alternatively, if there is too much of a particular skill available to employers, then employers can reduce wages until citizens will transfer to other sources of employment until supply and demand are again in balance.

Market forces can work in two ways for citizens. They can, at times, produce wealth and employment, but at other times they can produce poverty and unemployment. Since the market liberal approach does not advocate that there should be any interference in the market, it would not see as appropriate the provision of welfare benefits by the state in a citizen's time of need because any provision of benefits would destroy the workings of the free market. If or when a citizen *does* face times of hardship, it is the citizen's responsibility to fall back on any arrangements made earlier for the provision of welfare or, alternatively, rely on those institutions that could be a source of welfare, like the family. Whatever the source, welfare benefits should not take the form of collectivist state benefits.

Although the market liberal or anti-collectivist approach in its purest form is more reminiscent of the 19th century during industrialisation and may seem out of date, it is, however, the ideology that lies behind a significant number of ideas which influenced the Conservative Government elected in 1979 and which ultimately developed into 'Thatcherism'. The modern market liberals face a dilemma, in that they cannot ignore the provision of welfare for citizens, and consequently have compromised the pure form of market liberalism to develop ideas and strategies for the delivery of welfare benefits.

This has resulted in the modern market liberal approach to the provision of welfare, adopting the strategy that, if a welfare service is to be provided, there should be some competition between the public and the private sectors. This competition between public and private sources will ensure that there is market competition and will help to generate both efficiency and economy in the delivery of welfare services. The second strategy adopted by the modern market liberals in their approach to the provision of welfare would be to place an emphasis on the importance of maintaining the incentive to work and develop new enterprises. For individual citizens, the incentive to work and create wealth would be enhanced by allowing them to keep as much as possible of the money that they earned. This aim could only be achieved by reducing the role of the state to a minimum, an approach summarised by the three 'M's: minimal public spending, minimal taxation, maximum incentive.

Marxist and feminist approaches

Marxists and feminists believe that the provision of welfare does not act in the interest of all citizens. It is through the provision of welfare that the state is able to maintain the status quo and keep those with power in power. For Marxists, the provision of welfare enables elite 'ruling class' groups to be maintained in a position of power, whilst feminists argue that it is the provision of welfare that provides one of the explanations for the continuation of male dominance.

For feminists, the view that male dominance, or patriarchy, can be linked to the provision of welfare has its root in the historical development of the welfare benefit system. To illustrate this point, it is necessary to remind the student of citizenship of the historical assumption that women were dependent on men. This assumption was built into many of the earliest welfare benefits and in some cases has only recently been removed. The notion of a 'family wage paid to men' is an example of one of the assumptions that was made at the turn of the last century, by both the trade unions and the providers of the earliest welfare benefits. For the idea of a family wage paid to men to work, an essential assumption is that a family consists of a male and a female, who are not going to separate or divorce, with children; and, since the wage earner would receive a 'family wage', only one of the two adults needs to be employed. In the norms and values of the time, there would only be work for the men, who would then support their family – thus creating female dependency. This assumption was still evident when married women were allowed to opt out of full National Insurance cover after the introduction of the Beveridge Report in 1942.

Although equal pay legislation has removed for ever the possibility of the family wage becoming a reality, feminists argue that the culture of lower pay and lower expectations associated with women's work still remains. Whenever it is stated that a woman is working for 'a little bit of pin money', the reality of the statement is that it is still seen, by some, to be justifiable to pay females lower wages compared to men because men are the breadwinners and women are economically dependent. Even though many benefits have been reformed, these views still have some resonance or impact, as there is a cultural legacy which influences the norms and values of citizens today.

Marxist and feminist approaches share the view that the provision of welfare does not act in the interest of all citizens. The difference between the two approaches centres on the citizens who do or do not benefit from the provision of welfare. Some writers use this issue as a starting point from which they develop the argument further and raise the question as to whether the provision of welfare is actually designed to benefit *any* citizens. These writers argue that the real purpose of the provision of welfare is not for the benefit of individual citizens, but is to provide benefits for the economic system, thus reinforcing the view that it is those citizens who are already in a position of power and privilege that benefit most from the system.

To understand how the provision of welfare benefits the economic system, it is necessary to look at what, according to this view, is considered to be a major contradiction within the economic system. This contradiction stems from the way in which the economic system creates two groups of citizens who have opposing interests. The chart below gives a simplistic version of some of these opposing interests.

Employee	Employer
Does not own any place of work	Owns and controls a place of work
Works for somebody else	People work for her or him
Receives wage or salary for working	Pays wages or salary
Ideal situation – to receive the greatest amount of pay for least amount of work	Ideal situation – to pay the minimum for the greatest amount of work
Consequently • Paid breaks and holidays are good • Health and safety provision is good	*Consequently* • Paid breaks and holidays are bad • Health and safety provision is bad
At the end of the week/month/year – wealth is based on the total amount of wages or salary paid minus essential costs	At the end of the week/month/year – wealth is based on the total amount of profit made from the sale of goods or services, less the sum of wages or salary paid plus essential costs

As a result of these differing interests, two groups of citizens emerge. There are those citizens whose wealth is based on their wages or salary, and those whose wealth is based on the profit from the sale of goods produced by the labour of other citizens. This contradiction, Marxists would argue, produces two unequally sized groups of differently empowered citizens. One relatively small group accumulates wealth and privilege, the other group does not. For those that accumulate wealth, there is also an accumulation of power, and the combination of wealth and power produces greater opportunities and improved life chances.

The result of a system that is unfair is usually quite predictable. The unfairness will generate resentment and anger and there will be direct and/or indirect pressure to change the system to make it fairer. Since it is only a relatively small number of citizens who accumulate wealth, power and privilege that benefit and gain from the system, why is the system not challenged and changed?

For some students of citizenship, the answer to the question is rather surprising, as it appears that the very thing that is supposed to help citizens is also responsible for making the situation for the majority of citizens worse. The answer lies in the purpose behind the provision of welfare benefits.

In order to understand why the provision of welfare benefits makes the situation worse for the majority of citizens, it is necessary to outline another contradiction within the system. This contradiction lies between the stress placed on the importance attached to the accumulation of wealth and the necessity for the wealth accumulators to give some of that wealth away. This contradiction seems more bizarre when it is realised that the wealth that is given away to the state, in the form of taxation, is then paid to those who only have the skills to accumulate limited wealth of their own. Why not just pay those citizens higher wages and stop an enormous amount of money going round in circles? The answer lies in the view that the economic system needs taxation and welfare benefits to make it all seem fair. The system needs to be legitimated.

'Legitimation' is a term used to describe the process of making a course of action or a policy appear to be fair and just for all citizens. As stated previously, the Marxist approach believes that the system exists to enable those with power and privilege to remain in positions of power and privilege, and that the system works to benefit some groups of citizens at the expense of others. Why is there not the anger and resentment amongst citizens that will lead to challenge and change? The answer to this question lies in the ability of the system to makes everything appear to be fair; the system individualises failure and legitimates inequalities. If it can be ensured that the apparent reason for failure in the accumulation of wealth, or any other life chances, is seen to be the fault of the individual, it cannot be the fault of the system. The system is not only above blame, but also the system will seem to be fair and just as it is providing a range of welfare benefits to some citizens when they are at a certain level of need.

An essential element of this approach is the view that the system requires a number of citizens who are living in poverty and/or experiencing ill health and/or unemployed or unemployable. The system needs a number of citizens who are seen as failing and who can be blamed for their fate. In this way, failure can be individualised and it allows the system to legitimise itself. With a small, almost permanent pool of citizens living in poverty, the system uses these citizens as:

- an incentive for other citizens to continue to work – the 'you don't want to be like them' argument;
- a way to personalise failure – the 'it must be in their genes' argument;
- a way to legitimise the system – the 'we are looking after your welfare' argument.

The purpose of the provision of welfare, for writers who have this point of view, is not to benefit citizens, but to work for the benefit of the economic system; and that is why the provision of welfare has not and will not remove poverty, has not and will not reduce inequalities in health, and has not and will not remove unemployment.

 What do you understand by the following terms and concepts?

- Ideology
- Social administration approach to welfare
- Being 'in need'
- Marxism
- Legitimation

- Care in the community
- Collectivist approaches to welfare
- Patriarchy
- Market liberalism
- Thatcherism

 The provision of welfare based on a modern market liberal approach will automatically lead to a 'two tier system', an expensive private system for the minority and a minimal state system for the rest.

Complete the chart to either support or refute the notion that some groups of citizens, through the accumulation of wealth, privilege and power, will always have greater opportunities than others.

Area of social life	Evidence	Who benefits
Private education	eg, Eton Shares, assets and property worth at least £131 million Annual spending over £27 million (10 times greater then most state schools) Over £2.3 million tax refund due to charitable status (This information only became public when the Charities Act removed the school's right to exemption)	1,270 boys
Health		
Housing		
Life expectancy		
Leisure		

CHAPTER 11

Attitudes Towards Citizens Receiving Welfare Benefits

The aims of this chapter are to:

- Develop a realisation that both positive and negative attitudes exist towards citizens' receipt of welfare benefits
- Develop an understanding of the different approaches to welfare benefits through the selective/universal debate
- Develop an appreciation of the importance of the welfare state to citizens
- Introduce issues surrounding welfare pluralism

The previous chapter developed discussions concerning different and contrasting approaches to the provision of welfare benefits for citizens. It is now necessary to change the focus of the debate from issues concerning the provision of welfare to the reactions and attitudes towards those citizens who are in receipt of welfare benefits.

Reactions to those in receipt of welfare benefits

These reactions and attitudes will tend to fall into two distinct groups. On the one hand there are those citizens who use a series of illogical statements to justify an opinion that is prejudiced against citizens receiving welfare benefits. These opinions can lead to anti-social and irresponsible behaviour and are often associated with the use of derogatory slang terms. Another source of such prejudice against citizens receiving welfare benefits can be located in some irresponsible elements within the mass media; an issue that is pursued in Part 3 of this book.

The alternative to those citizens whose views are only based on a narrow and prejudiced set of opinions are those whose attitudes develop from a reasoned and systematic set of opinions, ideas and views. These opinions, ideas and views, when combined, develop an ideological view towards the provision of welfare. The distinction between the two sets of reactions is an important one to make because the first, characterised by ignorance and bigotry, is impossible to discuss logically or provide arguments against. The second *does* provide a basis for an informed discussion towards those in receipt of welfare benefits.

To initiate this discussion, read the following extract from *Monty Python's Life of Brian*. It relates to the scene when Brian and his mother, Mandy, who are returning home, are approached by a very healthy Michael Palin playing the part of an 'ex-leper'.

As they (Mandy and Brian) pass through the city gate, they attract a rather muscular, fit and healthy young beggar, who pursues them relentlessly through the busy streets.

Ex-Leper	Spare a talent for an old ex-leper, sir!
Mandy (to ex-leper)	Buzz off.

The ex-leper has come round to Brian's side.

Ex-Leper (to Brian)	Spare a talent for an old ex-leper, sir!
Brian	Did you say ex-leper?
Ex-Leper	That's right, sir (he salutes) ... Sixteen years behind the bell and proud of it, thank you sir.
Brian	What happened?
Ex-Leper	I was cured, sir.
Brian	Cured?
Ex-Leper	Yes sir, a miracle, sir.
Brian	Who cured you?
Ex-Leper	Jesus did. I was hopping along, when suddenly he comes and cures me. One minute I'm a leper with a trade, next moment me livelihood's gone. Not so much as a by your leave. (Gestures in the manner of a conjurer.) 'You're cured mate.'
Mandy	Go away.
Ex-Leper	Look. I'm not saying that being a leper was a bowl of cherries. But it was a living. I mean, you try waving muscular sun-tanned limbs in people's faces demanding compassion. It's a disaster.
Mandy	You could go and get yourself a decent job, couldn't you?
Ex-Leper	Look, sir, my family has been in begging six generations. I'm not about to become a goat-herd, just because some long-haired conjuror starts mucking about. (Makes gesture again.) Just like that. 'You're cured.'

Brian	Well, why don't you go and tell him you want to be a leper again?
Ex-Leper	Ah yeah, I could do that, sir, yes, I suppose I could. What I was going to do was ask him if he could ... you know, just make me a bit lame in one leg during the week, you know, something beggable, but not leprosy.

They have reached Brian and Mandy's house.
Mandy goes in. Brian gives the beggar a coin.

Brian	There you are.
Ex-Leper	Thank you sir ... Half a denarii for my life story?
Brian	There's no pleasing some people.

Source: *Monty Python's Life of Brian.*

The extract illustrates some of the attitudes held by some citizens towards those who are receiving welfare benefits. Some of these negative attitudes are summarised on the left hand side of the chart below. The way that attitude is expressed in the *Life of Brian* extract is on the right.

Attitude towards citizens receiving welfare benefits	*Words from* Life of Brian
• It runs in the family	'My family has been in begging six generations'
• Lazy	'You could go and get yourself a decent job'
• Ungrateful	'There's no pleasing some people'
• Hostility	'Buzz off'
• Being a beggar is their occupation	'One minute I'm a leper with a trade, next moment me livelihood's gone'

However, there are two ways in which these negative attitudes can change dramatically. The first is when circumstances for some citizens change and they now find themselves in receipt of welfare benefits. This change in circumstances will often be accompanied by changes in attitude towards citizens who are receiving welfare benefits.

Negative attitudes towards citizens who are receiving welfare benefits can be replaced with either a neutral or a positive attitude. A simple test of this claim can be conducted using the activity below.

Attitudes towards citizens receiving welfare benefits	
Would citizens who are receiving the welfare benefits listed on the left experience a positive, negative or neutral attitude?	
Welfare benefit	Positive, negative or neutral?
• Child benefit • Retirement pension • Free eye examination for a citizen with glaucoma	

It would be very surprising if the majority of responses towards citizens receiving child benefit, a retirement pension or a free eye test were negative.

Universal and selective benefits

The reason why these three benefits are not likely to become associated with negative attitudes is because these benefits are universal benefits, rather than selective benefits. The difference between these two types of benefit is that a universal benefit is paid to all citizens who fit into a definable category, whilst a selective benefit is only paid to those citizens who can prove that they are in need. Child benefit and the retirement pension are universal benefits because they are paid, not according to need, but according to the category of being a parent or being over a certain age. To receive a selective benefit, a citizen has to be 'means tested'. This is a process in which officials use a range of techniques in order to establish how much money, disposable income or wealth a citizen possesses. This process is found by some to be a very humiliating experience, which is often cited as one of the main reasons why so many who are entitled to these selective benefits do not actually claim the benefit. The take-up rate of both child benefit and the retirement pension is, according to the DSS, virtually 100%. Selective benefits, however, generally have a much lower take-up rate compared to universal benefits.

According to official estimates from the DSS, figures for 1998–99 reveal that more than £4 billion of means tested welfare benefits were unclaimed with estimates that for some benefits, between 13% and 21% of eligible citizens were failing to claim their entitlement. The benefit with proportionately the greatest number of non-claimants was the working families' tax credit. Many other selective benefits were also unclaimed, with 1.5 million citizens failing to register for council tax benefit and an estimated 700,000 citizens failing to claim their entitlement to income support. The view held by some that selective benefits are a far less effective provider of welfare is endorsed by the fact that the DSS figures show that there has been very little change in citizens' take-up rates for these benefits for many years. Many believe that the lower take-up rate of these benefits is the direct result of means testing which continues to reinforce the negative status of selective benefits. Many would conclude that this approach to the provision of benefit is a far less effective provider of welfare to needy citizens.

There are many different welfare benefits available to citizens in the UK. The range can be located on the internet, in post offices, GP surgeries, local libraries and from Citizens Advice Bureaux.

- Find as many different welfare benefits as possible.
- Categorise the welfare benefits in the appropriate column.

Welfare benefit	Universal	Selective
	Yes / No	Yes / No
	Yes / No	Yes / No

Sometimes, the same welfare benefit can be both selective and universal, with the division between the two being based on the criterion of age. This can be illustrated by the changes in entitlement towards the preventative health strategy of routine dental and eye examinations. This is a universal benefit until a citizen reaches a certain age, and returns to being a universal benefit after a certain age. Between these two ages, the benefit is selective and is only free to those who have fulfilled the criteria of other means tested benefits.

The influence of society's norms and values

The attitude towards those citizens who do receive welfare benefits is further complicated because society's norms and values create certain overriding attitudes which have almost become part of culture. There is very little likelihood that negative attitudes would be applied to a citizen receiving an eye test, whereas some other benefits do generate negative attitudes. The historical attitude of dividing the poor into two groups, consisting of the deserving poor and the undeserving poor, could be argued to be still in existence – only expressed in different words.

A different attitude towards the provision of welfare benefits is argued by some citizens, who support the view that, whenever a category of need is defined and a specific welfare benefit becomes attached to that situation, what in fact is actually being created is a special status for some citizens in special categories or conditions. Once this special status has been accepted, it allows those citizens to use this status almost as an 'occupation' which causes (or forces) them to remain within this 'special status' category and thus allows them to be eligible to receive benefit. In the words of the Ex-Leper, 'One minute I'm a leper with a trade, next moment me livelihood's gone'.

A more contemporary illustration of this issue would apply to the sellers of *The Big Issue*, the magazine produced by and sold by the homeless. Being homeless provides the citizen with a 'special' status from which they can justify 'special' behaviour of street vendors. Logically, once the seller successfully returns to the 'norm', by having a home, they are no longer homeless and have thus lost their 'occupation'.

Once you have completed the task in the research box on the previous page, you will have a comprehensive list of different welfare benefits.

For each welfare benefit, the percentage of citizens who claim what they are entitled to differs. Complete the chart below by researching the estimated take-up rate as supplied by different organisations. An 'unofficial source' might be a charity, such as Shelter; an 'official' source is an official organisation such as the Department for Work and Pensions.

Welfare benefit	Estimated take-up rate from unofficial source	Estimated take-up rate from official source	Universal or selective

The universal/selective debate towards what is considered to be the most effective and efficient manner in the provision of welfare provides the student of citizenship with a classic debate. On the one hand there are advantages to the universal approach but, equally, the same approach has a range of disadvantages. The potential advantages and disadvantages are contrasted against a range of issues that have to be considered when judging the issue of effective and efficient distribution of welfare benefits.

Suggested responses relating to the debates about the provision of welfare		
	Universal	Selective
Costs resulting from provision of welfare	Higher costs	Lower costs
Stigmatisation resulting from receipt of welfare benefit	Lower stigmatisation	Higher stigmatisation
Size of bureaucracy to administer welfare benefit	Larger bureaucracy	Smaller bureaucracy
Take-up rate for welfare benefit	Higher take-up rate	Lower take-up rate
Influence on the incentive to work	Neutral influence	Reduces incentive
'Common sense' logic	Higher	Lower
Ability to redistribute wealth	Possible to achieve	Possible to achieve

When the responses to issues surrounding the provision of welfare benefits are compared, the universal and selective approaches produce opposing views in all of the categories, with the exception of the the the ability to redistribute wealth. The reason why the redistribution of wealth is possible to achieve with either the universal approach to the provision of welfare benefits or the selective approach is because of the role played by taxation. The table below illustrates this point.

The potential influence of taxation in the provision of welfare benefits							
Welfare system based on selective benefits				Welfare system based on universal benefits			
Weekly income	Tax	Benefits	Remaining income	Weekly income	Tax	Benefits	Remaining income
£500	£90	0	£410	£500	£250	£160	£410
£400	£70	0	£330	£400	£230	£160	£330
£300	£40	0	£260	£300	£200	£160	£260
£200	£30	£80	£250	£200	£110	£160	£250
£100	£10	£160	£250	£100	£10	£160	£250
Total distributed/ collected	£240	£240		Total distributed/ collected	£800	£800	

The amount of money in the 'Remaining income' column, after the deduction of tax and the addition of all benefits, is identical for all groups. There is, however, a very large variation in the amount of tax paid and benefits received by citizens, depending on approach. There is also a variation in the amount of money, made up from the combination of the citizens' taxes and state benefits, which flows through the state. The important conclusion to be drawn from the table, however, is that decisions relating to the style of benefits, whether selective or universal, are going to be influenced by political decisions relating to perceptions of the role of the state and what is acceptable to the electorate.

'Institutional benefits' and 'residual benefits'

Another division in the debate about welfare provision is the consideration of welfare benefits in terms of 'institutional benefits' and 'residual benefits'. An institutional benefit is one that is not only built into the system, but is part of the system, whereas a residual benefit is one that becomes active only when other institutions or structures, like the family, that could provide welfare have broken down. This 'institutional/residual' debate relates to the universal/selective approach because an 'institutional benefit' shares the assumption that a welfare benefit is a (universal) right for all citizens to receive, as it is built into the system, whereas a 'residual benefit' is a benefit that should be selectively available for some citizens, acting as form of safety net that comes into play when all other means of survival have been exhausted.

The debate relating to the effective and efficient provision of welfare can present the student of citizenship with impossible right/wrong choices. However, a more realistic basis to answers that relate to the provision of welfare does not lie in simple judgments; answers must be based on a careful consideration of all the underlying ideological assumptions; and it is these ideologies and ideological assumptions that must be used to justify your point of view.

From your study of Citizenship, what evidence can you find that will either support or reject the view expressed in the first column below? One way to complete this activity is to divide your discussion group into two and debate the views.

View	Evidence you believe supports this view	Evidence you believe does not support this view
State provision of welfare is too slow and bureaucratic to respond to the needs of citizens.		
At election time, the level of state welfare provision is manipulated in order to win votes.		
State provision of welfare removes a citizen's responsibility to look after him or herself.		
State provision of welfare removes a citizen's incentive to work.		
The state does not have the right to force citizens to pay compulsory contributions for welfare provision.		

Welfare pluralism

In society today, there is much discussion about the 'welfare state'. When citizens discuss the 'welfare state' there is a shared understanding of what the term actually means. This is rather surprising, as this term is a relatively recent arrival within our cultural terminology. In fact, according to DC March, the term 'welfare state' only started to be used in the 1930s and was not found in print until 1941 (*The Welfare State*, 1970). This development of a term to symbolise a system of government or a culture of government in which the state has assumed responsibility for the provision of benefits is significant for a number of reasons. Most significantly, when a single umbrella term is used to represent large and diverse areas of social policy, it can allow politicians to make many minor alterations, or substantial changes, whilst still being able to claim that the 'welfare state is safe'.

Although the claim that the 'welfare state is safe' may sound familiar, the reality is that the welfare state consists of a complex and constantly changing set of assumptions and relationships between the state and the citizen. By using a single term to describe the nature of these assumptions and relationships, it is possible for politicians to achieve the impossible – the ability to move in two opposing directions, simultaneously. This is achievable because the use of the singular term, 'welfare state' can act as a smokescreen. Whilst the totality of the welfare state might be safe, various sections and parts of the welfare state are not.

The 'welfare state' is not a useful term

The term 'welfare state' is, when critically analysed, not very useful. Many citizens' welfare is not provided for by the state, as their main source of welfare is provided by family, friends or neighbours. For other citizens, it is a commercial transaction between supplier and consumer. A good number of UK citizens choose not to use the state's provision of welfare at all and have made their own arrangements, very often based on unpaid full or part time carers. The welfare state has not narrowed the health gap between wealthy citizens and those citizens who are not so wealthy. The welfare state has not narrowed the educational divide in the success rates between children from different backgrounds. For some citizens, the welfare state has turned into a sort of 'banking service', as it is the provider of loans. Others believe that any statutory organisation that exists to provide welfare is going to be too big and bureaucratic to be efficient. Providers of welfare are more likely to develop policies that lack initiative, procedures that are cumbersome and slow to respond to the changing needs of citizens. The service is likely to become institutionalised, lack clear objectives and be subject to political interference.

So why is the 'welfare state' so important?

The answer to this question lies again in ideology. The welfare state, in a relatively short space of time, has become part of the culture of the citizens of the UK. However, in reality, the welfare state has never been totally responsible for the provision of welfare, as there is a long cultural tradition of welfare being provided by a combination of the informal sector, the voluntary sector and the commercial sector. The 'informal' sector refers to welfare provided by family, friends and neighbours. The 'voluntary' sector consists of those non-statutory organisations that usually focus on one area of welfare and develop expertise in that area. These organisations are usually charities, of which the NSPCC would be an example. The 'commercial' sector consists of those profit-making organisations that have developed in all areas of welfare provision, so long as they believe that there is a market that can be profitably exploited. These organisations are usually referred to in terms of a 'private hospital' or a 'private school'.

As a result of welfare being provided by a combination of four different types of provider, many commentators feel that it is a mistake to talk about *the* welfare state as *the provider* of welfare. Discussions about the provision of welfare for citizens should take into account the fact that there is a range of providers of welfare. This has led to the development of the term 'welfare pluralism', which many feel is a more realistic reflection of the reality of the provision of welfare in the UK, and there are some compelling arguments to suggest that the provision of welfare based on the principles of welfare pluralism is preferable to the reliance on a centralised welfare state.

The voluntary sector

To some extent, the voluntary sector can be seen to overcome some of the problems associated with the statutory sector. The voluntary sector has a heritage of involvement that is longer than the state's, as many of these voluntary organisations were established at a time when the state did not feel that it should be involved in the provision of welfare. Barnardo's and the Salvation Army are just two of the voluntary organisations that have their roots in Victorian England.

It is not a straightforward task to categorise the organisations within the voluntary sector because of the vast diversity in their aims and activities. The sheer size of the voluntary sector makes it preferable to make some division between these organisations. One possible division is to focus on the organisation's chosen role, which would allow the voluntary sector to be divided up according to whether the organisation is a provider of a service, is acting as a pressure group or is acting a source of self-help. These roles are not mutually exclusive and, just to complicate the issue, some voluntary organisations provide all of the roles whilst others develop a more specialist role and limit the range of their activities. The possible roles of the voluntary organisations are:

- As a provider of a service. In this capacity, voluntary organisations can provide those services for citizens that are not otherwise provided by the welfare state. Alternatively, they can supplement the services provided by the welfare state, or indeed they can do both. An example of a voluntary organisation that fits predominantly into this category would be Barnardo's.

- As a pressure group. In this capacity, voluntary organisations can become the 'experts' in a certain area and use this position as a method to champion the cause of a certain group of citizens, or protect the interests of citizens.

The voluntary organisation has in effect become a pressure group. Some voluntary organisations become so influential and well respected in this role that they are consulted by the state in considerations about the provision of welfare. An example of a voluntary organisation that fits predominantly into this category would be CPAG, the Child Poverty Action Group.

- As a source of self-help. In this capacity, voluntary organisations can help to encourage citizens to take a degree of personal responsibility for their own welfare and develop an organisation that enables the principles of self-help to be successfully applied. An example of a voluntary organisation that fits predominantly into this category would be Alcoholics Anonymous.

Decentralisation

The heart of welfare pluralism encompasses the principles of decentralisation and participation. Decentralisation can have a twin focus. It can initially revolve around the process of reducing the relative importance of the state in favour of voluntary organisations. Secondly, decentralisation can focus on the notion of developing welfare provision services at a local level. This means a movement in the responsibility for welfare away from central government to local government. The logic underlying this principle is that there are advantages to be gained from the provider being a relatively small organisation. With this in mind, some argue that the local authority is still too large for the efficient provision of welfare and that it, too, should be decentralised into small teams of social workers who have a responsibility for a neighbourhood. This decentralisation could allow greater participation by citizens in the process of welfare provision. This could be participation in the provision of welfare through voluntary work, or participation in the processes of decision making when in receipt of welfare.

Decentralisation would allow voluntary organisations to become increasingly active in the provision of welfare, and since, it is claimed, these organisations are neither handicapped with a large bureaucracy nor faced with excessive labour costs, as they can utilise the unpaid labour of volunteers, the provision of welfare by voluntary organisations is cheaper and more cost effective than the provision of welfare by the state.

Decentralisation from provision of welfare by the state to provision of welfare by voluntary organisations would be advantageous, it is claimed, because the internal organisation of the smaller voluntary organisations allows them to respond more quickly to changes. These changes could relate to developments in a condition that creates the need for some form of welfare provision, or in potential sources that could provide a solution to the perceived area of need. Equally important is the claim that decentralised welfare provision also enables voluntary organisations to organise the provision of welfare for those areas of need ignored by the state. The response of the voluntary organisations to the development of HIV/AIDS, particularly the work of the Terence Higgins Trust, compares favourably to centralised responses.

Another advantage for citizens that is often claimed when the provision of welfare is decentralised to voluntary organisations rests on the view that voluntary organisations have the capacity to respond quicker than the state in times of crisis and when there is a sudden and unforeseen increase in demand for services. This speedy response can also benefit citizens if, for some reason, there is inadequate provision. The voluntary organisation can supplement provision; a role that has been referred to as 'plugging the gaps'.

It is also important to consider decentralisation in the provision of welfare between citizens. It is the provision of welfare that gives the opportunity for some citizens to contribute towards either the welfare of other citizens or their community. This contribution can only be achieved through decentralisation, with the move away from state provision to provision based on small local or even neighbourhood units. The emphasis on the small and the neighbourhood is also an important consideration in assessing the effectiveness of 'self-help' groups.

Advantages when welfare is provided by the voluntary organisation

There can be no doubt that there are some definite advantages for citizens when welfare is provided by the work of a voluntary organisation. Many voluntary organisations are happy to continue with their present role and do not believe that their role should become official. This issue became topical during the Conservative years in the 1980s. These governments were set on a course to reduce the role of the state, and one of these reductions included recommendations in 1984 that local authorities contract out services for children, the elderly and the handicapped to voluntary organisations.

The problem for these organisations was the conflict between the desire to remain a voluntary organisation and the expectation from the government of the day. Voluntary organisations could not be expected to take over the role of local authorities without financial support, and once they received financial support they would have an official role. If voluntary organisations were to be funded by central government, they would no longer enjoy all the advantages that being an independent voluntary organisation allows. Voluntary organisations could become vulnerable as they became dependent on government funding. The funding could be provided with 'strings attached'. These strings could take the form of having to follow a particular set of policies. For some, the most likely outcome would be that they would develop bureaucracies and become less efficient. Another equally important factor to consider is the issue of accountability: if these voluntary organisations were to receive large sums of taxpayers' money, since they are not statutory bodies, it is difficult to establish to whom these organisations would be accountable. To put it simply, a voluntary organisation cannot have an official function.

Voluntary organisations do play a very important part in the provision of welfare for citizens. Whether they supplement the role of the state or provide an alternative is not really the main issue. The mere fact that they are there, which helps to create a form of welfare pluralism, is their single biggest contribution to the provision of welfare for the citizen.

The informal sector

Another essential element that constitutes a part of the pluralistic approach to welfare is the contribution made by the informal sector. This is the welfare provided by family, friends and neighbours which many believe was the main, or only, source of welfare prior to the introduction of the welfare state. For others, any assumption that welfare was ever provided by family, friends and neighbours represents an unjustifiably optimistic view of those groups.

Supporters of the view that questions whether family, friends and neighbours were ever the main providers of welfare suggest that a quick look through history will raise enough questions to support their point of view. The use of institutions like workhouses, orphanages and asylums would suggest that, historically, the source of welfare did not derive from family, friends and neighbours. Institutional welfare for most citizens would have been the norm.

For many citizens, however, the solution to the citizen's problem is located in the provision of some form of institutional welfare, and this institutional welfare transforms the solution into a new problem. There is considerable evidence to support the view that, once in an institution, a citizen becomes institutionalised.

The process of institutionalisation is described by Goffman (*Asylums*, 1968) as one in which those who enter an institution, since their behaviour is totally regulated by the institution, lose the ability to deal with life outside the institution.

By the 1980s, a large number of institutions were the source not only of welfare, but also of many problems for citizens. As discussed previously, the 1980s also saw fundamental ideological changes in the role of the state. The ideology demanded a reduction in public spending, especially public spending on welfare, whilst promoting the importance of the family, the community and adopting private provision. These aims could all be achieved simultaneously through a policy of de-institutionalisation.

The de-institutionalisation of welfare is based on welfare support from informal sources such as family, friends and neighbours. It is seen as having a range of advantages for citizens, including the view that it allows citizens to continue to experience 'a normal life' in their own community with their family and friends. Equally important is the view held by many citizens who are in need of care that they would much sooner be cared for by family or friends in their own home than an institution. Significantly, this form of welfare is also a lot cheaper. In 1989, an Equal Opportunities Commission survey estimated that the informal care provided by women saved the government £24 billion of public expenditure per year (Crowley, 1992).

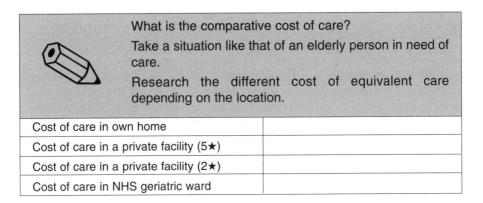

What is the comparative cost of care?

Take a situation like that of an elderly person in need of care.

Research the different cost of equivalent care depending on the location.

Cost of care in own home	
Cost of care in a private facility (5★)	
Cost of care in a private facility (2★)	
Cost of care in NHS geriatric ward	

Carers

One of the problems associated with any discussion of the informal approaches to welfare is that much of this welfare takes place within the home, behind closed doors and in private. This makes it very difficult to establish and analyse the range of care, the scope of care and the quality of that care. Indeed, it is very difficult to establish precise information about how many citizens play a role within the informal provision of welfare. The Department of Health, in their 'national strategy for carers' (see www.doh.gov.uk/carers.htm) puts the figure of carers providing more than 50 hours a week at 855,000. The Carers Association provide a figure of 2.7 million who combine work with the provision of care, whilst H Green, in the 1985 General Household Survey of Carers, puts the figure of adults who were caring for dependent relatives at 6 million.

For a non-institutional approach to the provision of welfare to be successful, it requires some citizens to take on the role of carer. Although some would relish this activity and see it as part of their responsibilities, others would not. For some, any policy that relies on the unpaid goodwill of other citizens or is based on some form of emotional blackmail is not acceptable; it is the role of the state to provide for the welfare of its citizens. Some citizens may wish to take on the role of carer but they find that the provision of welfare takes time and needs a range of skills which they do not possess. Even those citizens who become carers can face the problem of having missed many years in their contributions towards their own pension.

Taking on the role of carer can result in a range of problems for citizens. It is difficult to generalise about these problems, but they can be grouped into:

- the problems associated with being a carer;
- the problems associated with the conflict between the duty of care and the desire to undertake that duty;
- the problems associated with the situation when there is no longer any need to provide care.

Some examples of problems associated with caring		
Problems associated with being a carer	Problems associated with the conflict between the duty of care and the desire to provide care	Problems associated with the ending of the need to provide care
Providing a service without training	Desire to follow own career	Lack of pension contributions
Isolation	Desire to have a break from caring in the future	Finding another job

'A national strategy for carers' and the Carers and Disabled Children Act 2000

In February 1999, the deputy Prime Minister, John Prescott, recognised the importance that citizens who are carers play in the provision of welfare. The document 'Caring about Carers: A national strategy for carers' clearly outlines a wide range of issues that needed to be addressed concerning the well-being of citizens who are carers. The issues concerning citizens who care are clearly raised in the summary outlined in the 'Caring about Carers' document below.

Caring About Carers:
A national strategy for carers

We, the Government, are giving new support to carers – because we value what they do. Carers care for those in need of care. We now need to care about carers. So the Government is bringing forward for the first time **a new substantial policy package** about carers.

- Caring may affect every one of us.

- We may all need care, or need to provide care.

- Caring forms a vital part of the fabric and character of Britain.

- One in eight people in Britain is now a carer – close to **6 million people**.

- **Women** are more likely to be carers than men.

- Three-fifths of carers are looking after someone with a **disability**.

- 855,000 carers provide care for more than **50 hours a week**.

- Three-fifths of all carers receive **no regular visitor support services** at all.

- Carers' needs are currently only being **met patchily**.

What carers want

   - wellbeing of the person being cared for

   - freedom to have a life of their own

   - maintaining their own health

   - confidence in services

   - a say in service provision

- Two-thirds of working age carers are in **paid employment**.

- **Flexibility** is central to their employment.

- Clear **business case** for carer-friendly employment policies:

   - **cost:** reduced turnover of staff, absenteeism

   - **flexibility:** labour availability, matching of work

   - **motivation:** improved morale

   - **performance:** business success

Information:

- **new charter** on what people can expect from long-term care services: setting new standards
- consider how to **improve the consistency of charging** for services
- carers need good **health information**
- NHS Direct **helpline** for carer information
- Government information on the **internet**.

Support:

- carers need to be involved in **planning and providing** services
- local caring organisations should be **consulted**
- Comment cards, advice surgeries, carers' weeks are good ways to **involve carers**.

Care:

- carers' right to have **their own health needs** met
- **new powers** for local authorities to provide services for carers, as well as for those being cared for
- first focus of the new powers should be on helping carers **take a break**
- **new special grant** to help carers take a break
- on top of the £750 million for prevention and rehabilitation, there will be **£140 million** over the next three years to help carers take a break, to be used in a targeted way
- **financial support** for working carers to be kept under review.

There are special measures for carers in employment and young carers. The Government's carers' package also includes:

- **new legislation** to allow authorities to address carers' needs
- time spent caring will entitle carers to a **second pension**
- Government **consulting** on proposals, but by 2050, carers could receive an **extra £50 a week** in today's terms
- **reducing council tax** for more disabled people being cared for
- support for neighbourhood services, including **carers' centres**
- considering scope for extending help to carers to **return to work**
- new **census** question to tackle incomplete information about carers
- support for **young carers**, including help at school
- special funding for **breaks for carers**.

Department of Health

© Crown Copyright 1999

With such a clear policy commitment, it was not a surprise that when Tom Pendry MP won the Private Members' Ballot he received full government support to present the Carers and Disabled Children Bill to Parliament on 15 December 1999. The Bill not only fulfilled the pledges outlined in Prescott's national strategy for carers, but in some areas developed reforms even further. The Bill successfully passed through Parliament, becoming the Carers and Disabled Children Act on 28 July 2000.

The Act enables local authorities to offer new support to carers in three main ways:

- Those local authorities with social services functions will have a power to supply services directly to a carer, following an assessment, which will help the carer to care and to maintain their own health. Carers will have the right to an assessment even where the person cared for has refused an assessment for the provision of community care services.

- Local authorities will be enabled to make direct payments to:
  o carers (including 16 and 17 year old carers), for the services that meet their own assessed needs;
  o persons with parental responsibility for disabled children, for services for the family; and
  o 16 and 17 year old disabled children, for services that meet their own assessed needs.

- Local authority social services departments will be able to run short term break voucher schemes and have the power to charge carers for the services they receive.

The private commercial sector

The final component of a 'welfare pluralist' system is the contribution that the private sector makes towards the provision of welfare. Out of all the sectors that make a contribution to the provision of welfare, it is probably this sector that generates the strongest debate, although much of the debate usually has more to do with the role of the state than the provision of welfare.

When discussing the impact that the commercial sector has had on the provision of welfare, it is essential to divide the issues into two. The first issue relates to the scope of the services provided. This is of very little value to the student of citizenship, because the commercial sector's role is now so wide that it permeates every aspect within the provision of welfare. The second issue is, however, of considerable value in the study of citizenship, because it relates to the fact that, by its mere existence, the private sector creates debates about the appropriateness of certain organisations and their role in the provision of welfare.

In order to establish the exact nature of the private sector, it is useful to ascertain the range of organisations that constitute this sector. The one factor that would seem logical in uniting all organisations in the commercial sector would be the assumption that the provision of welfare is linked to the creation of some monetary profit. Indeed, for many organisations this is their sole motive, and profit can be generated from direct charges for services, the selling of insurance cover or the receipt of premiums.

An alternative view is to argue that all non-statutory providers of welfare are in the commercial sector. The problem with this view is that it would include all the previously discussed voluntary organisations. However, it does allow the point to be made that some voluntary organisations do charge for their services or for providing some facilities. If, for example, provision was made for a citizen to rent a sheltered home at a rate that was below the local market average, this could generate a profit for the renting organisation. The difference between this organisation and the organisations in the previous paragraph rests on the word 'motive'. If the motive and the reason for the organisation's existence is profit, it is a commercial organisation. If the organisation is essentially a charitable organisation, then it would fit better amongst the company of other voluntary organisations.

The growth in the commercial sector

The commercial sector has grown rapidly in recent years. The main reason for this can be understood by returning to previous discussions relating to the changes in the role of the state during the Conservative years from 1979. These policies, although designed to reduce the role of the state, would not automatically reduce the number of citizens who needed some form of welfare. The simple application of supply and demand would reveal the logical outcome that, as provision by the state decreased, the vacuum would be filled by a greater involvement by the private commercial sector.

In some cases, citizens were left without any choice and were forced to use private commercial services. Take the case of the provision of dental services, particularly in the south-east of England. The number of dentists who felt they were still able to provide a service within the framework of the NHS declined to the point where large areas of the country were without any state services. The result of this decline in state services was a rise in commercial provision either through the use of insurance schemes or the payment of fees. Although the figures suggest a growth in the provision of welfare through the private commercial sector, it is important to remember that this growth may not represent absolute agreement with the commercialisation of welfare. Many citizens were forced into a private arrangement against their will due to the lack of any other dental services, whilst other citizens reluctantly use the private commercial sector to bypass inefficiencies and waiting lists in the state system.

The arguments and debates that underpin discussions about the provision of welfare for citizens in the UK provide the foundations from which the student of citizenship can evaluate future changes in welfare provision.

Although the future is impossible to predict, it is possible to plan for it using projections and models. Likewise, the future in the provision of welfare is impossible to predict, but there are many plans in place based on various sources, such as demographic projections of changes in the age structure of the population.

The importance of the provision of welfare to issues of citizenship cannot be overstated, as it is only through the provision and support of policies concerning education, pensions, health and housing that citizens can become free to participate in the life of the community, which is the essence of citizenship.

 What do you understand by the following terms and concepts?

- Universal/selective benefits
- Institutional/residual benefits
- Decentralisation of provision
- Voluntary organisations
- Carers

- The welfare state
- Welfare pluralism
- Informal providers of welfare
- Private commercial sector
- Emotional blackmail

 If you had the opportunity to redesign the welfare benefit system, what type of benefits would you introduce: universal or selective? Completing the chart may help your decision.

Potential advantages of a welfare system based on *selective* benefits	Potential advantages of a welfare system based on *universal* benefits
• Smaller bureaucracy	• Less stigmatisation
•	•

Numerous Acts of Parliament have had an impact on the provision of welfare. Some are significant because they introduced provision for the very first time. Others are significant because they fundamentally changed assumptions of provision.

In this research activity there are listed a number of Acts that have had a significant influence on the provision of welfare.

Research:

- the changes introduced by the legislation;
- the impact that the changes had on the provision of welfare in the areas of:
  - housing;
  - provision for old age;
  - health care.

Legislation	Impact of legislation on		
	Housing	Provision for old age	Health care
Social Security Act 1988			
National Health Act 1946			
Housing (Homeless Persons) Act 1977			
Social Security Act 1980			
Chronically Sick and Disabled Persons Act 1970			
Housing Finance Act 1972			
Social Security Act 1986			
Social Security (Pensions) Act 1975			

The growth in the provision of welfare by a profitable private commercial sector will only lead to greater inequalities in the provision of welfare and can never be justified.

Part 2

The Citizen and the Political Process

INTRODUCTION

Participation in a political process is, believe it or not, a very common activity in the UK. It is an activity that a majority of citizens engage in throughout their life; often without fully realising they are actually involved in a political process. Think about the number of times children at school vote for a 'form captain', think about those occasions at school or college when a representative for the class has been chosen, who then, on behalf of the class, outlines a point of view at a school council meeting. Think about the number of citizens who have signed a petition, or have collected money for what they believe to be 'a good cause'. There are citizens who have put a poster on their bedroom wall or a sticker in the window of their car. There are those who will refuse to purchase goods from a certain supplier or country. How many meetings must take place in community centres, church halls or village halls in a year? Think about all the letters of support or complaint that are written to newspapers in a year. Citizens commonly undertake these activities at various times throughout their life. The irony is that, whilst many citizens will involve themselves in all or some of these activities, they simultaneously declare that they are 'not interested in politics', or that the political process is 'nothing to do with them'. The activities outlined above, however, would suggest the opposite, and indicate both the centrality of political processes in the everyday life of the UK citizen and the fact that one specific political process has come to dominate all others, to the extent that it has become part of the culture of the UK. It is from this base that it is possible to explore the wider relationship between the citizen and the political process.

CHAPTER 12

The Citizen's Choice: To Participate or Not to Participate within a Representative Democracy

The aims of this chapter are to:

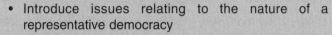

- Introduce issues relating to the nature of a representative democracy
- Assess the advantages and disadvantages of different voting systems
- Consider explanations as to why some citizens do not vote
- Consider issues concerning the role of candidates in elections
- Consider ways of modernising a representative democracy
- Consider ways of encouraging citizens to vote

When considering the issue of political participation, a number of key issues are central to the study of citizenship. Who are the citizens that are most likely to engage in some form of political activity? Why do some choose to become actively involved in a political process whilst others choose not to take any interest or any part? What influences a citizen when choosing whether or not to vote? For those citizens who do vote, why do they vote for that specific candidate or party? Is the degree to which a citizen participates in any political process linked to the citizen's social class, age, ethnicity, sex, religion or even their geographical region? These are all key questions in any discussion of citizenship and political participation.

Although citizens can vary in how much they participate and to what extent, the essence of political participation in a representative democracy involves the right to vote in free and fair elections. Some citizens could participate by standing for public office in an attempt to become the elected representative for other citizens. Some citizens participate through their ability to organise meetings to support or challenge a candidate or a course of action, whilst some citizens' participation would be to attend these meetings. The participation from some citizens would be through their campaigning or fundraising. Other citizens publicise their participation through displays of support or disapproval, whilst other citizens go further by engaging the media or organising activities like a demonstration in order to influence other citizens. Alternatively, other citizens opt not to involve themselves within any of these processes.

However, before developing issues concerning political participation, it is necessary to return to the suggestion that 'one specific political process has come to dominate all others, to the extent that it has become part of the culture of the UK'. That political system is referred to as a representative democracy.

A representative democracy

It is very likely that many students of citizenship will be able to recall times at infant/junior school when large groups needed to be divided into smaller groups. One example of this is when sports teams were needed for a match. When they were selected in the playground, this often involved two 'captains'. Typically, these two captains would have selected themselves, based on some criteria like their level of skill, for the role. The rest of the teams, too timid to object, would then wait to be picked by the captains, who based their selection on sporting prowess, friendship or other factors such as the ownership of an important part of the equipment like the bat or ball.

The procedure in the classroom, however, was usually different and often involved a discussion of the issue prior to any decision being made. In a small group, like a tutor group, it is possible for everyone to make a contribution to the discussion. Students can have a direct input. However, as the group gets larger, from tutor group to year group, to the whole school, to all the local schools, to all the schools in the area, culminating with all the schools in the country, it becomes harder and harder for all students to be able to have their say. The solution to this problem of numbers is instantly solved if each tutor group selects one or two students to express the views of the whole group; all further meetings are attended only by those students selected, as they represent the views of all the other students. This is the basis of a representative democracy.

A teacher can experience many problems when conducting a classroom debate. These may range from the students not wishing to discuss the topic in question to the class having one or two students who dominate the discussion with their views and opinions.

- List as many possible influences as you can that you think are important for a successful classroom debate.

- List as many possible causes as you can that you think are responsible for a classroom debate not being successful.

When a class elects a form captain or a school elects a head student, a number of factors are important and will influence who is elected.

- List the qualities that you think may make some students more electable than others.

- List the qualities that you think may make some students less electable than others.

- List the reasons why some students may not vote for the student who they know or feel is the best person for the job.

The process described in the imaginary school would probably sound not only familiar, but also quite 'normal' to most citizens in the UK. The process is, in fact, an example of a system known as a representative democracy, and it is this system that has become not only a part of the culture of the UK, but also forms the model for much of the participation in every type of political activity by UK citizens. It would be hard to imagine that a citizen of the UK, even the ones who claim to have no interest in politics or would never consider themselves to be politically active, had never, at some point in their life, taken part in procedures that are the essence of a representative democracy.

A representative democracy would, at first sight, seem to favour and empower the citizen who, after winning a vote, is entrusted to take the decisions for all the other citizens. And indeed, this would be the case if all the citizens who were the voters played no further part in the process. However, it is possible to control the citizen elected to represent the group, in theory, because there is the potential (or threat) that if the representative does not act in a way that is responsible or meets the approval of most of the electors, the same set of electors will call their fellow citizen to account and simply not re-elect him or her as their representative. In this way, the electors can control their representative who, being fearful of being called to account and not being re-elected, will at all times act in accordance with the instructions or wishes of the electors.

The system of a representative democracy has at its base two elements that must work in conjunction with each other if the system is to operate successfully. These elements are:

- first, the critical importance of the election process in which citizens vote;
- secondly, the fact that citizens are prepared to hand over to another citizen the responsibility for taking decisions.

The single ballot, simple majority electoral system

The electoral system that is most widely used in the UK takes the form of a single ballot, simple majority. Within the classroom, in the election of a form captain, it is usually the case that one round of voting (a single ballot) produces one student with more votes than any other candidate (a simple majority). The student who receives the most votes is declared the winner. It is quick, simple to understand and easy to operate. The margin of their victory is irrelevant and could range from receiving just one more vote than any other candidate to receiving all of the votes. The fact that the student simply has more votes – a simple majority – determines their success. It is similar to participating in a race. The winner, regardless of the distance between first and second place, is always the first athlete to break the tape. This accounts for the single ballot, simple majority electoral system also being referred to as the 'first past the post' system.

Although there are many who claim that this system is perfectly acceptable, others question both of its elements, casting doubt on the ability of a single ballot with a simple majority to achieve a result that is actually representative of the electorate.

To explain this point: the winner of an election with a simple majority is the candidate who receives the greatest number of votes. This can be illustrated by referring to the 2001 General Election results for the constituency of Liverpool Walton.

Liverpool Walton		
Candidates	Number of votes	% of votes
Kilfoyle, P (Lab)	22,143	77.81
Reid, K (Lib Dem)	4,147	14.57
Horgan, S (Con)	1,726	6.07
Forrest, P (UK Ind)	442	1.55

With such a large majority, there can be no doubt as to the legitimacy of the claim that the person with the most votes won that election. An overall majority was obtained because, if all the votes for the other candidates were added together, they would not be greater than 22,143.

Overall majorities are not always as easy to spot.

Did the candidate with the most votes for the constituency of Wakefield have an overall majority?

Wakefield		
Candidates	Number of votes	% of votes
Hinchcliffe, D (Lab)	20,592	
Karran, T (Con)	12,638	
Dale, D (Lib Dem)	5,097	
Greenwood, S (Green)	1,075	
All other candidates	1,852	

Did your local MP achieve an overall majority in the 2001 General Election?

The doubts surrounding whether the single ballot, simple majority electoral system can achieve a result that is actually representative of the electorate can be illustrated by referring to the fact that no government for the second half of the last century was elected with over 50% of the votes cast. Added to this, in the 1951 election, the Conservative Party polled 13.71 million votes. This was less than the 13.9 million polled by the Labour Party, yet it was the Conservative Party that 'won' the election. The same phenomenon occurred in the February 1974 General Election. Again, the political party that polled the most votes did not 'win' the election. The results for the 1974 General Election produced the following anomaly:

- the Conservative Party received 11,869,000 votes and won 297 seats in the House of Commons;
- the Labour Party received 11,639,000 votes and won 301 seats in the House of Commons.

Some further problems associated with a simple majority are illustrated by taking a closer look at some results from the 2001 General Election. In Liverpool Walton, it is evident that all those citizens who voted for the losing candidates had no effect on the result. There were 'only' 6,315 of them. A further question that can be raised when looking at any result in a constituency with such a large majority is the motivation for citizens to actually vote. In Liverpool Walton, 15,828 citizens could have stayed at home and that would have had no effect on the result. What is also unknown is how many citizens opposed to the winner actually did stay at home because they felt there was little or no point in voting. Many citizens in this type of constituency feel that they are effectively disenfranchised: that their vote is of no value; it is in effect a wasted vote. In this type of constituency, since the winner is as certain as anything of this nature possibly could be, the most influential citizens are those who actually select the candidate.

A different set of issues arises when looking at the constituency of Bristol West. Whilst 20,505 voting citizens wanted the 'winner', 35,160 voting citizens did not. How, then, is it possible to 'win' an election when 63% of those citizens who voted actually wanted somebody else?

Bristol West		
Candidates	Number of votes	% of votes
Davey, V (Lab)	20,505	36.84
Williams, S (Lib Dem)	16,079	28.89
Chesters, P (Con)	16,040	28.82
Devaney, J (Green)	1,961	3.52
All other candidates	1,080	1.93

These problems were also experienced in the constituency of Winchester in 1997. With such an even division between the first two candidates, the balance of power is effectively held by the views and attitudes of the smallest group of citizens.

Winchester (May 97)		
Candidates	Number of votes	% of votes
Oaten, M (Lib Dem)	26,100	42.06
Malone, G (Con)	26,098	42.06
Davies, P (Lab)	6,528	10.52

If the pattern of these constituencies were to be repeated across the whole of the UK, many citizens would feel that the resulting government would lack any form of legitimacy. This disparity between the percentage of votes cast and number of seats won has produced results that many citizens feel to be unfair. In the 2001 General Election, the Conservatives in Scotland polled 16% of the citizens' votes, yet only won a single seat. For the Liberal Democrat Party there was both good news and bad news. The good news was that they won 10 seats in Scotland from only 16% of citizens' votes. However, the bad news was that, in the whole of the UK, it took over 112,000 citizens' votes, on average, to elect a Liberal Democrat MP, compared to approximately 35,000 citizens' votes to elect a Labour MP.

Alternative voting systems

There are many different voting systems used in different states around the world, and many would fit into one of the following six voting systems:

The Alternative Vote

The Single Transferable Vote

The Additional Member System

The Supplementary Vote

The Party List System

The Regional List System

The best source for researching these different voting systems is in textbooks for AS/A2 politics courses. From your research, briefly describe:

• The characteristics of the way the system works.

• The main advantages for citizens using the system.

• The main disadvantages for citizens using the system.

• Whether any of the systems would benefit citizens in the UK.

Lack of electoral fairness

One of the most important elements, if not *the* most important, of a representative democracy is that the electoral system must be fair (or at least appear to be fair). Many citizens would feel that the process of voting is a pointless activity if their preferred candidate, or the candidate that actually reflects their true political opinion, has absolutely no chance of winning the seat. The losing candidate's votes are simply ignored. Equally, there is little incentive for a citizen to vote for the candidate who is certain to win, as once the candidate has achieved a majority, all extra votes are, in effect, meaningless. One consequence of this situation is that, for many citizens, the present electoral system acts as a disincentive for citizens to vote, as many feel that their vote can only be described as a wasted vote.

There have been citizens in the UK who, at times, have felt disquiet about the fairness of an electoral system that effectively ignores the wishes of so many citizens. This lack of fairness can be easily demonstrated by looking at the results achieved by the Liberal Democrats in the 1992 General Election: 17.9% of the vote, 3% of the seats.

Over the years there has been much discussion about the electoral system based on a single ballot with a simple majority, with its tendency to produce disproportionate representations of citizens. Many critics have suggested that a different electoral system will benefit not only citizens, but also the whole concept of a representative democracy.

191

One simple improvement, as claimed by some, is to change the concept of winning an election from being based on the simple majority, which is the present requirement, to an 'overall majority'. An overall majority exists when one candidate obtains a greater number of votes than all the other candidates combined. Mathematically, this occurs when one candidate acquires 50% + 1 of the total number of votes cast. Since it is not always likely that an overall majority will be achieved in a single ballot, there needs to be provision for subsequent ballots until one candidate achieves an overall majority.

Electoral systems that set out to achieve the objective of an accurate reflection of the wishes of voters in the final composition of any elected assembly are referred to collectively as majority systems, or proportional representation. There are many different systems that seek to achieve the ideal of an accurate reflection of the wishes of voters in the constituent members of an assembly. However, it does not matter how good or fair the electoral system is if citizens do not, for whatever reason, cast their vote. It is for this reason that some suggest that more attention should be given to getting citizens to vote rather than tinkering with electoral systems.

Two significant events ultimately occurred in the closing years of the last century. First, the then Labour leader John Smith spoke of the possibility of a referendum, a consideration that was supplanted when, in March 1997, Tony Blair stated that, once in power, an independent commission would be established to recommend one proportional electoral system that could, subject to approval from a referendum, replace the existing system.

When the Labour Party achieved power in May 1997, Lord Jenkins of Hillhead was set the task of recommending a system that fulfilled the criteria of:

- being broadly proportional;
- producing stable governments;
- being able to extend the choice of citizens;
- maintaining the link between an MP and his or her constituency.

Alternative vote plus

The report, published in October 1998, recommended the adoption of an electoral system that was known as 'alternative vote plus', or 'alternative vote top-up'. This proposal would involve a number of significant changes. The first change would be to reduce the number of constituencies from the present level of 659 to a total of between 530–60. The second major change would be that citizens would have two votes. A citizen would use their first vote to elect a constituency MP. These constituency MPs would account for about 80–85% of the elected chamber. The remaining 15–20% of the chamber would be decided by citizens' second votes. The second vote would elect additional members from a list put forward by political parties. It is claimed that this system not only fulfils the criteria given to the commission, but also creates an electoral system that is much more proportional than the present single ballot, simple majority system. Indeed, it was this system, on 4 May 2000, which was used in the election of the London Authority (see below).

For many citizens, the process of voting in an election has simply revolved around writing one 'X' against one name on one ballot paper, usually consisting of only three to four names. The larger, more complicated ballot papers used for the election of the London Assembly may have confused as many citizens as they pleased others. If two votes were not bad enough for some citizens, two elections using different systems was even more daunting. This occurred because, simultaneously, the second component of the election involved the first directly elected Mayor in the UK.

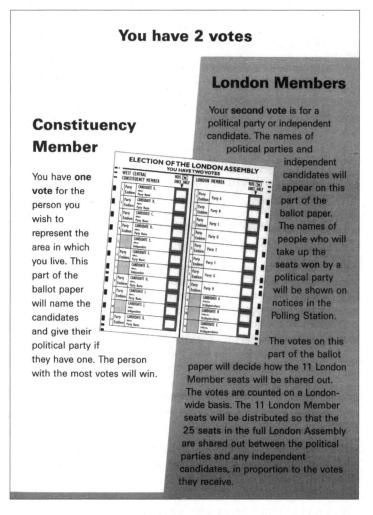

Source: Department of the Environment, Transport and the Regions booklet explaining the process of electing the London Authority, January 2000

The electoral process for choosing the Mayor differed in style to that used to elect the London Assembly, although both systems incorporated the principle of increasing the fairness of the electoral process. In the election, the Mayor of London would need to secure an absolute majority. The electoral process that was used is described below.

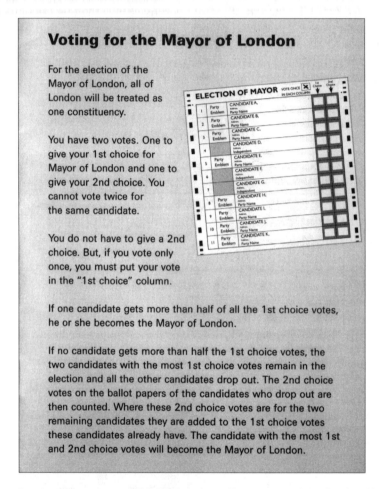

Voting for the Mayor of London

For the election of the Mayor of London, all of London will be treated as one constituency.

You have two votes. One to give your 1st choice for Mayor of London and one to give your 2nd choice. You cannot vote twice for the same candidate.

You do not have to give a 2nd choice. But, if you vote only once, you must put your vote in the "1st choice" column.

If one candidate gets more than half of all the 1st choice votes, he or she becomes the Mayor of London.

If no candidate gets more than half the 1st choice votes, the two candidates with the most 1st choice votes remain in the election and all the other candidates drop out. The 2nd choice votes on the ballot papers of the candidates who drop out are then counted. Where these 2nd choice votes are for the two remaining candidates they are added to the 1st choice votes these candidates already have. The candidate with the most 1st and 2nd choice votes will become the Mayor of London.

Source: Department of the Environment, Transport and the Regions booklet explaining the process in electing the London Authority, January 2000

The election of Mayor of London was the culmination of a process that started as a 1997 Labour Party manifesto pledge and proceeded through the stages of the nomination of candidates, to the election in which one victorious citizen was elected to represent the other citizens of London. This devolved form of government is one of many types within the UK.

Voting in the London Mayoral election does not have the honour of being the first proportional election in the UK, as proportional elections had previously occurred in the elections for the European Parliament, initially in Ulster and subsequently in the whole of the UK on 10 June 1999.

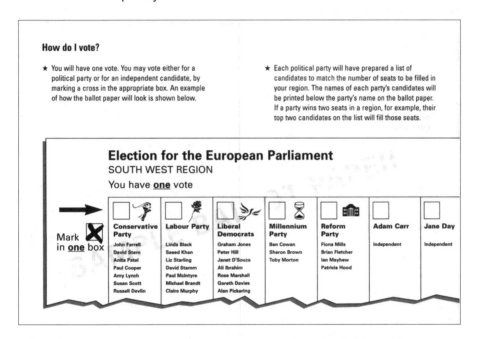

Source: Home Office Communication Directorate, *Voting in Elections for the European Parliament*

Problems with candidates

Within this chapter, the merits and demerits of different electoral systems have been discussed. However, some citizens feel that any issues raised in the discussion of voting systems are only a partial reflection of the debate. It does not matter how good or bad a voting system may be if there are no candidates or only 'identikit' candidates from which to select.

'Identikit' candidates are those who, as a result of 'grooming' by their party, are all so similar that there is little point in trying to distinguish between them. The voting system also becomes irrelevant if all the candidates are only pursuing their own self-interest, or merely want to 'line their own pockets'. What if all the candidates are so convinced that their way is the right way that they will not listen to any arguments about alternatives and change? The voting system is only as good or as bad as the citizens who are elected.

Voting systems allow citizens to vote; they allow for a representative to be elected. They will produce winners and losers. They can be fair or unfair. What a voting system cannot do is to provide the citizens who are going to use that system either as a voter or as a candidate. To put it quite simply, a voting system represents only half of the equation. *Voting systems need voters and candidates as much as voters and candidates need a voting system.*

Non-voting in elections

In both local and general elections, candidates often receive comments like 'You're all the same ... nothing ever changes no matter who wins ... we've heard it all before ... none of you listens to what we think ... none of you ever answers any questions ...'. For many citizens who stand to fight an election, their biggest foe is not the opposition but non-voting election apathy. Whilst some citizens will always vote in every election, there are others who do not vote. However, before non-voting is condemned, it is important to divide non-voters into two groups. Some non-voters are actively involved within the political process but choose not to vote because their political preference is not being represented. This could be illustrated by the constituency of Tatton in the 1997 General Election. In this constituency there was neither a Labour nor Liberal Democrat opponent to the sitting Conservative MP, Neil Hamilton. Both the Labour and the Liberal Democrat Parties withdrew their candidates allowing the Independent, Martin Bell, to stand successfully on an 'anti-sleaze' ticket. Some citizens, however, took the view that there was not a 'proper candidate'. Without a 'proper candidate', these citizens' parties were not represented with the consequence that there was 'nobody to vote for'. The only possible action would be to abstain. One suggestion to tackle the issue of positive abstention is to allow citizens to cast their vote in a box labelled 'none of the above'. This suggestion, when used seriously, could address the issue of low turnout as it would effectively allow the politically aware citizen to declare that they really wanted to vote but their political perspective was not available or the candidate of their party did not match their ideals. However, there is also the risk that some citizens will just select this option as an easy route and when the votes of both the serious and the sceptical citizens are combined, there exists the potential that the 'none of the above' candidate receives the most votes and is elected!

If this idea was applied to local council elections, where the lack of candidates that represent a specific ideology is a much more common occurrence, the potential results could create chaos. To illustrate the extent to which some local elections lack the full range of political ideologies, in the Tunbridge Wells Borough Council election held on 4 May 2000, out of 14 wards, the following eight all lacked a candidate from one of the larger political parties.

Ward	Candidates' party		Ward	Candidates' party	
St James	Con	Lib Dem	St Marks	Con	Lib Dem
Capel	Con	Lib Dem	Park	Con	Lib Dem
Pantiles	Con	Lib Dem	Sherwood	Labour	Con
Pembury	Con	Lib Dem	Sandhurst	Labour	Con

Although some citizens are non-voters through voluntary absence caused by this lack of choice, other citizens fall into the same category as a result of many factors, of which illness is just a single example. For other citizens, however, non-voting is not the result of a rational or reasoned choice, but a result of apathy or disillusionment with politicians, political processes or both. These citizens are the non-voluntary absent and would appear to be growing in number. In fact, the turnout – the percentage of citizens who actually voted – at the last General Election was just 59.4% of citizens and was by far the lowest percentage turnout in any General Election since 1945. Although the 2001 General Election turnout was low, it has quite a way to go to better the citizens of Melrose Ward in Liverpool who preferred to cross their fingers rather than cross their ballot paper in December 1997 when just 6.2% of the total electorate voted in a council by-election.

The General Election turnout of 59.4% is a little misleading as it disguises considerable variations in electoral activity. One major variation is to be found when comparing specific constituencies. Although there were 68 constituencies in which turnout was under 50%, there were many others where turnout was in line with previous elections. Two extremes of turnout can be illustrated by reference to two results from the 2001 General Election:

- Liverpool Riverside: Electorate   74,827
                          Total vote   15,503
                          Turnout   34.08%

- Winchester   Electorate   81,852
                          Total vote   59,158
                          Turnout   72.27%

Another major variation is to be found when comparing citizens as there are considerable differences between the percentages of citizens who voted in the 2001 General Election. The table below summarises some of the variations in citizens' turnout at the General Election.

197

Voting patterns in the 2001 General Election					
Citizen's age	% of citizens who votod	Citizen's educational qualification	% of citizens who votod	Citizen's income	% of citizens who votod
18–24	34	None	63	Lowest third	56
25–34	40	Key stage 4	53	Middle third	59
35–44	53	A-level	61	Highest third	62
45–54	64	Degree	70		
55–64	67				
65+	76			Source: BES cross-section survey 2001	

The problem for any representative democracy when an election attracts minimal political participation, with such a small percentage turnout of those entitled to vote, is that the whole legitimacy of the electoral process is put in question. The disinclination of some citizens to vote in elections has long been a concern to those who seek to promote and protect the rights of all citizens. With their considerably smaller electorates, one potential outcome of such low levels of voting in local elections is that some wards could be vulnerable to being targeted by extreme groups or individual extremists who, with a little organisation, could generate sufficient votes to win the ward.

The low level of voting by citizens, with all its implications, can be illustrated by the results of the Tunbridge Wells Borough Council election on 4 May 2000.

Ward	Electorate	Turnout	Ward	Electorate	Turnout
St James	4333	25.8%	Speldhurst & Bidborough	4505	31.05%
Capel	1646	34%	Sandhurst	1018	34.08%
Pantiles	3658	30.65%	Culverden	3783	25.93%
Pembury	4376	34.94%	St Johns	4721	23.32%
St Marks	3969	31.9%	Hawkhurst	3248	36.2%
Park	4114	31.11%	Lamberhurst	1116	27.62%
Sherwood	4752	20.54%	Rusthall	4278	26.93%

One example of the implications of what could happen when so many citizens do not vote occurred in the first round of the French Presidential election in April 2002 when the right wing extremist, Monsieur Le Pen, was elected ahead of the mainstream left of centre candidate to leave French citizens with a second round choice between a centre right candidate and a far right candidate.

Low levels of political participation or just low rates of voting?

Much of the previous discussion has focused on whether a citizen does not vote in elections. However, voting is only one form of political participation that is available to a citizen during an election. Research from the British Electoral Study 2001 suggests that citizens can participate in the electoral process in quite different ways. To illustrate the differences between citizens' level of participation during an election, the British Electoral Study suggested that citizens fell into one of seven possible groups, each with a differing level of participation.

 Listed below are the names and descriptions of the British Electoral Study's division of citizens according to their level of participation in an election.

1 Take a sample of people over 18 and ask them to decide which of the seven descriptions they believe best fits their level of participation in a recent election.

2 Record your results and calculate the percentage for each level of participation.

3 Compare your results to the findings from the British Electoral Study (see the table later in this chapter).

4 How difficult did your sample find it to select only one name to describe their level of participation in that election?

5 From your research, how useful is the British Electoral Study's division of citizens into categories according to their level of participation in an election? Justify your answer.

| Gladiators | Citizens who are loyal party supporters strongly committed to the party, who are active throughout the election campaign. | |
| Helpers | Citizens who are willing to help a candidate or a party throughout the election campaign through some actions like giving their time or money. | |

Proselytisers	To proselytise means to convert. Proselytisers are those citizens who have strong views and will try to convert other citizens to change their support and change their vote.	
Talkers	Citizens who talk and discuss election issues with other citizens.	
Spectators	Citizens who follow an election campaign from their armchair as a spectator of the media's election coverage.	
Minimalists	Citizens who say that they have some interest in the election but do not follow the election campaign.	
Apathetics	Citizens who say that they have no interest in the election and do not follow the election campaign.	

The citizens of the UK are not afraid to vote. Indeed, nearly 625,000 votes were cast in one week to eject a member of the *Big Brother* household. It would also seem that many of those citizens who did vote to evict a housemate from the *Big Brother* house fell into the 18–24 age group, 66% of whom did not vote in the General Election. Why is it that the *Big Brother* programme attracted so many votes from exactly the age group that virtually ignored the General Election?

Two possible answers to this question exist. The first suggestion lies within the world of politics and the nature of the political parties. If the policies of the political parties become so similar that the difference between the parties is negligible, then logically, it does not really matter who wins the election; and if it does not matter who wins the election, what is the point in voting?

For some citizens, who is ejected from the *Big Brother* house is a matter of real concern, and the house will be different depending on who is in the house and who is out. The perceptions about the other house, the House of Commons, are that it never really changes. It still consists of a few citizens who behave in a strange manner. If it is perceived as an outdated and irrelevant body that looks and sounds identical before and after an election, then it should not be too much of a surprise to discover that some citizens cannot see the point of casting their vote.

Another possible explanation for the low turnout at the 2001 General Election lays the blame on the media. Both the coverage of the General

Election by the media and the politicians' use of the media have been cited as contributing towards the low turnout.

According to research for the ITC (Independent Television Commission), 40% of viewers regularly switched channels in order to avoid the election whilst many other citizens perceived, as a consequence of the election coverage, that the result was a foregone conclusion that would make voting irrelevant.

Politicians' use of the media has also been cited as contributing towards the low turnout at the 2001 General Election. Research from the British Election Survey 2001 reveals that the largest category of citizens view themselves as 'spectators' and follow the election through the media. Interestingly, research from a MORI poll a month after the 2001 General Election discovered that there was a good level of political interest amongst citizens: specifically within the 18–24 age group, there was quite a degree of political activity, with 24% of that age group stating that they had either written to an MP or taken part in a protest march. If the findings suggest that political interest and activity exist, what influenced citizens to abstain from voting? The poll suggests that it was the poor election campaigns run by the political parties that contributed towards the low turnout at the election. Indeed, in the areas where a candidate did engage the electorate, either through positive or negative issues, the number of citizens who voted at the 2001 General Election increased. This can be best illustrated by looking at the election success of Dr Richard Taylor who, standing as an Independent candidate for Wyre Forest, pledged to save the local hospital. Turnout increased by 5% from the 1997 election, and was 8.6% above the national average.

	Percentage turnout of citizens within each category at 2001 General Election by self-description	Estimated percentage of citizens in each category
Gladiators	91	2
Helpers	73	8
Proselytisers	71	7
Talkers	68	27
Spectators	62	37
Minimalists	54	8
Apathetics	29	12

Adapted from British Election Survey 2001

Alienation or apathy?

Alternative explanations for the low turnout in elections have been that this represents an expression, by some citizens, of alienation from political processes and even society in general, and a widespread cynicism towards all forms of participation.

Citizens with the greatest sense of alienation and cynicism towards political participation, who are more likely to become the non-voluntary absent voter, have become associated, according to Johnston and Pattie (in *A Nation Dividing?*, 1988), with the most deprived sections of society. It is the citizens who are the most marginalised in society and who tend to view any political activity as being largely irrelevant that have by far the lowest rates of political participation. This view was confirmed when Margaret Hodge, the Labour MP for Barking, the 24th most deprived area in the UK with the lowest average take-home earnings in London, interviewed citizens who had either voted in 1997 but not in 2001 or never voted. Her research found that citizens were not apathetic or disengaged from political issues but believed their concerns were not seen as important to politicians. For many of these citizens, the decision not to vote was their only way of expressing their alienation. As one citizen said in her interview, 'If enough people don't vote, they may start thinking – hang on, maybe we ought to change the way we've been doing things'.

Reports from the British Election Study discovered that the level of non-voting has changed significantly over the years and is very uneven between different communities. The study revealed that approximately 15% of black Caribbean citizens were not registered to vote for the 2001 General Election. This is a vast improvement when compared to the 1970s when nearly a third of black Caribbean citizens, with only 6% of white citizens, were not registered to vote. These figures contrast sharply with the figures relating to Asian citizens. During the 1960s, only about 13% of this group of citizens voted compared to 2001 when these citizens were the most likely group to cast their vote.

This lack of political participation has, in some communities, a long history, a point discovered by Salford MP, Hazel Blears, who in an interview in the *Manchester Evening News* (2 December 1998) stated that not only is 'a large section of the community we are supposed to represent in the Commons completely disengaged from the political process', but also that 'generations have not voted, they do not know what happens at the ballot box'.

Although some citizens are alienated from the political process, others are simply apathetic and literally can't be bothered to vote. The degree of voter apathy is difficult to establish. This became evident in a survey conducted by the London Borough of Barking and Dagenham and reported in January 1999. The survey, designed to encourage more citizens to vote, found that in some wards, when the number of citizens who claimed to have voted was compared to the actual number of votes cast, 12.5% of citizens simply gave the incorrect answer, claiming to have voted when they had not. The main reason why some citizens did not vote was that they 'simply could not be bothered due to pure lack of interest'.

Encouraging citizens to vote

The lack of interest among some citizens in voting has, over the years, been tackled in a number of different ways. During the 1990s the 'Red Wedge' tour and the 'Rock the Vote' campaign were both attempts to mobilise some specific groups of citizens. The 'Red' and the 'Rock' would suggest that it was potential younger supporters of the Labour Party who were being encouraged to vote at concerts. Another faster and more fashionable attempt to reach and encourage younger citizens to vote was adopted by the Labour Party during the 2001 election campaign when it endorsed text messaging, sending messages along the lines of 'X LBR IF UR UP 4 IT' to its supporters.

R Txts OvR8d?

Using a maximum of 160 characters, devise a text message along the lines of 'VOTE 4US 2MORO' that a political party could use to encourage maximum political participation in the next General Election.

The 'Operation Black Vote' campaign is another attempt to encourage one group of citizens to vote, whilst other campaigns have their focus on age-related issues with the 'Take your parents to vote' campaign aimed at mobilising the more mature citizen. Other campaigns focus on a specific community. One example here was the Manchester based 'Register to Vote' campaign which adopted the strategy of employing well-known Mancunians to encourage citizens through traditional publicity and dedicated websites to 'get out there and vote'. A further example is the 'Vote Smart' website which is dedicated to encouraging Muslim citizens to vote.

'Dont 4get2 vote': e-democracy?

'Voting is the cornerstone of our democratic system. Yet the way we vote has hardly changed for 100 years,' declared Jack Straw in 1999 whilst introducing a new Representation of the People Bill into Parliament. His intention was quite explicitly stated when he said he wanted to make it easier for citizens to vote in order to ensure that as many people as possible participate in the democratic process.

To help achieve this goal, the Representation of the People Act 2000 extended the vote to the homeless, who previously could not vote as they had no address from which to register, and allowed those citizens who are not convicted but who are held on remand in prison to vote. The Act also allowed for some quite innovative changes to occur, with variations in the times and places that citizens can vote and the possibility of voting in supermarkets, railway stations and other locations not in a voter's neighbourhood. Provision was made to allow experiments with e-voting and voting by telephone.

With ever-increasing improvements in information and communication technologies (ICT), the concept of digital democracy has been developed. Hague and Loader, in *Digital Democracy: Discourse and Decision Making in the Information Age*, explain the possibility of national and local governments 'interacting with citizens via websites, e-mail addresses and public information kiosks' with the possibility of electronic voting and citizen juries. As a concept, e-democracy holds the attraction that through the use of ICT, there will be broader political participation, as the technology allows citizens to connect with elected representatives and with each other irrespective of space or mobility. Such developments could at a stroke promote a more effective parliamentary democracy, tackle voter apathy and remove the perceived remoteness of Parliament from the life of many. Such is the Government's enthusiasm for e-voting that a Cabinet Office report stated that 'a programme to achieve successful implementation of e-voting is under way to ensure that robust systems can be in place for an e-enabled General Election after 2006'.

The move away from traditional voting methods was experimented with in a small number of areas in the May 2002 local elections, and in one Liverpool ward where voting by text message was allowed, about 350 votes were cast in this manner, representing some 17% of votes cast. In Swindon, however, only approximately 5% of citizens elected to vote by telephone. Swindon was also a local authority that was selected to allow e-voting across all wards, and turnout increased from 27.7% in 2000 to 31.2% in 2002. This small increase was in line with increases across the whole country. There were, however, some councillors who achieved significant results. After a particularly strong online campaign, one councillor received 28% of his votes via the internet. One problem with internet voting is that if a citizen does not have access, they are disadvantaged in this respect. Figures from Swindon after the 2000 election revealed that the Liberal Democrats received 13.3% of their votes online, compared to the Conservatives' 11.4% and Labour's 8.7%. Since it would seem that not all citizens gained equally from the convenience of online voting, there should be a way of ensuring that all citizens are in future given a way of accessing e-democracy.

The May 2003 local council elections witnessed further experiments with e-voting, with 18 councils piloting various systems which enabled citizens to vote electronically. Citizens in Swindon had a wide range of options: they were able to cast their vote not only via the internet, but also using an automated telephone system, or by using the town's information web-kiosks or through the luxury of using their NTL digital television service.

Drawing conclusions relating to the impact and success of the e-democracy experiment is very difficult. The small increase in turnout could be directly related to the success in the previous month of far right M Le Pen in France whilst the geographical variations could be related to local issues. The only conclusion at present that can perhaps be drawn is that younger citizens are more likely to take advantage of democracy's flirtation with new technology and some wards are more likely to embrace change than others.

For many citizens, however, the main issue surrounding e-democracy is not that it will encourage some citizens to vote, but that it introduces a voting system that provides less accountability, poorer reliability and greater opportunity for electoral fraud compared to traditional voting methods. E-voting does not offer citizens the reassurance that the votes declared at an election are really the votes cast and that all votes can be traced back to an original ballot paper. Citizens who vote electronically have no proof that the vote they cast actually corresponds to the vote that is transmitted. The insecurity of the internet, in which websites can be spoofed and identities stolen, is potentially an expensive price to pay for a relatively small increase in the total number of citizens who vote in an election.

The Representation of the People Act also made provision for postal voting being available on demand and all-postal ballots. In one all-postal ballot in the 2002 local elections in the Hertfordshire town of Stevenage, there was a response rate of over 53% voting compared to 29% who voted in 2000, the last borough polls, and in Chorley, Lancashire, turnout jumped from 32% to 61%. In the London Borough of Havering, the all-postal election increased the vote from 34% at the last local elections in 1998 to 45% in 2002, the highest in London. Some citizens did express concerns about the confidentiality of their votes and 1,794 citizens' votes were rejected as the completion of the 'Declaration of Identity' was incorrect. Such was the success of the 13 experimental all-postal ballots that it is proposed to replace traditional voting methods for the 2004 European elections with all-postal ballots. This is in stark contrast to the Home Office's 1994 declaration that 'Voting in person at the local poling station in general provides the least opportunity for impersonation or electoral fraud'.

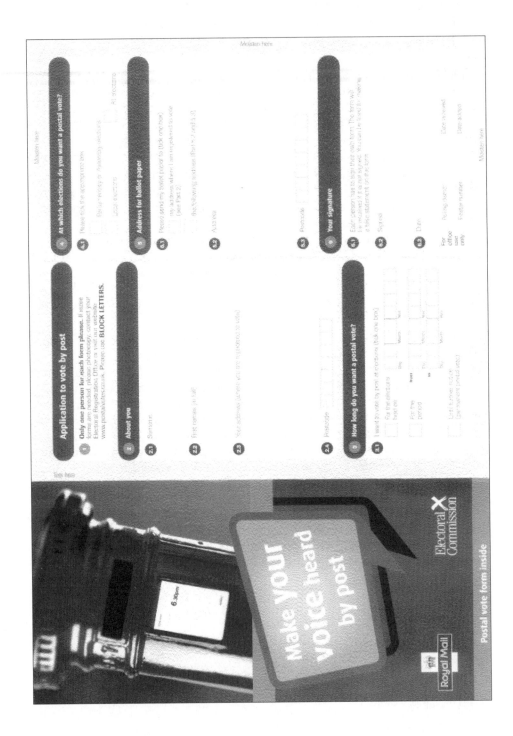

The Representation of the People Act eased the rules relating to voting by post and in the 2001 General Election over 2 million citizens voted in this way. However, inquiries after the 2001 election revealed that in some areas, it was believed that some politically motivated groups had made multiple applications for postal votes, the so-called 'ghost voters'. For many citizens, the balance between increasing a citizen's opportunity to vote whilst maintaining the confidentiality of that citizen's vote is an area of concern, and the Electoral Reform Society believes that more safeguards are needed in order to remove 'ghost voters' from the system.

Practical changes

An alternative view suggests that wholesale changes in the process of running an election are not necessary and that minor tinkering could produce the desired outcome of increasing the level of voting in elections. One suggestion is to change the traditional day for voting from a Thursday to a Sunday. There are no laws or reasons, apart from relatively recent custom, that force the UK to hold its elections on a Thursday. Indeed until 1910, General Elections could last for several days, and since this practice was discontinued, General Elections have been held on various days of the week. The 1918 General Election was held on a Saturday, whilst the 1922 and 1924 elections were held on Tuesdays and the 1931 election held on a Wednesday. Thursdays were only established as 'the norm' in 1935. The potential Sunday voting may afford many citizens, as a result of its smaller range of alternative distractions or commitments, an increased opportunity to vote, with an increased likelihood of political participation.

Another change that aims to increase the level of participation in both voting and the judicial system through availability for jury service is the change to the October construction of the electoral roll that becomes operational in the springtime, replacing it with a 'rolling' system of registration. Equally important is the introduction of a second official electoral register. One will be a full and complete version that is only available to official users of the register whilst the second, from which citizens can remove themselves, is an online version.

Apathy and marginalisation

Voting apathy is of concern to those involved with the process of democracy. Democracy needs participating citizens, and non-voting devalues the democratic process. Although voter apathy is most often associated with the marginalised and the socially excluded it is clear that voting apathy extends to and cuts across many sections of society.

With such a breadth of voter apathy, the point made earlier by Johnston and Pattie, that voter apathy is associated with those citizens who are the most marginalised in society and who tend to view any political activity as being largely irrelevant, needs to be re-examined. The statement has two component parts. Voter apathy is associated with:

- marginalisation; *and*
- relevance,

These two components need to be seen as independent of each other – as two different coins and not two sides of the same coin. Consequently, it is important to look at a range of election results before blame is attached to those citizens from the most deprived sections of society, who are already blamed for many social problems, and who are also blamed for the decline in effective representative democracy. It is possible to suggest that the issue of electoral relevance is also a cause of voter apathy and may be just as significant as those of marginalisation and social exclusion, if not more significant.

Imagine that you are employed in an advertising agency and you are contracted to develop a campaign to decrease voter apathy in all sections of society and for all types of elections. What strategies would you and your departmental colleagues develop in order to increase the number of citizens who vote in elections?

Make sure you justify all your suggestions.

Sometimes, there is a sharp contrast in turnout within the same area or parliamentary constituency. The following two results for the constituency of Tottenham in London are separated by just 37 months.

Tottenham General Election, May 1997	Tottenham By-Election, June 2000
Electorate 66,173	Electorate 64,554
Total vote 37,704	Total vote 16,417
Turnout 56.98%	Turnout 25.43%

Does this result show that there is a sudden and dramatic rise in the number of citizens who are deprived and marginalised? The answer is clearly 'no'. It is evident that the percentage of citizens that turn out for an election is subject to much wider influences.

Research the voting behaviour by citizens at the following General Elections.

Election	% turnout	% support for successful party	Election	% turnout	% support for successful party
1945			1974 (Feb)		
1950			1974 (Oct)		
1951			1979		
1955			1983		
1959			1987		
1964			1992		
1966			1997		
1970			2001		

Present your results in the form of a graph, showing:
- the changes in the turnout at General Elections;
- the changes in the support for each political party.

What conclusions relating to political participation can be drawn from the evidence of voting in General Elections?

Concern for democracy

There is so far within the discussion of political participation an assumption that needs to be addressed. This assumption is that there is an automatic link between the two elements of voting in an election and political participation. Some commentators have expressed concern for democracy, suggesting a decrease in political participation as a result of the decline in the percentage of citizens who choose to vote. The argument assumes that, in a representative democracy, it is the elected representatives who make decisions on behalf of other citizens. They have, after all, been elected for exactly that function – to make decisions on behalf of others – and since these elected representatives have 'specialised skills and access to greater information' it stands to reason that they should be in a far better position to make decisions than other citizens.

A low level of political participation for citizens is all that is required, because other citizens have specialised in the role of representing. This approach would suggest that a low level of political participation is acceptable because citizens do not need to have any involvement in political processes other than to vote in elections. Voting in elections, on this view, is an extremely important element of a representative democracy and any long term decline in the percentage of citizens who vote in elections is a cause for extreme concern.

It is, however, important not to equate democracy with simply the percentage of citizens who vote in an election. The 2002 Presidential election in Iraq had a very high turnout of nearly 100%. However, when this resulted in Saddam Hussein receiving 99.9% of all the votes, there might be a question mark over correlating a high turnout of electors and a state being democratic. An alternative view is to suggest that a high level of political participation is far more important in a representative democracy because it ensures that any elected representative is kept under check and that they really represent their constituents. Political participation in this context involves more than just voting every few years in an election. In this context, participation involves activities like organising or attending meetings or demonstrations, lobbying, signing petitions, or attending rallies and marches; joining and campaigning through the membership of a pressure group; engaging the media to get your point of view broadcast to as wide an audience as possible. All these activities have one thing in common, which is that they all act as a control on elected representatives. This involves a much higher level of political participation than just voting, and for some citizens it will only mean the occasional bout of activity, while for others it can be a full time occupation. When there is a considerably higher level of political participation by citizens, the decline in the percentage of voters who turn out at elections may be seen as being less significant.

Political participation by citizens can, as discussed, take many different forms. There are some who debate the question as to what is the most important form of political participation that a citizen can undertake. For others, however, the response to this question is not an issue, as they feel that voting in an election is the most significant and crucial element of any representative democracy. Politicians need votes in order to claim a democratic mandate to fulfil promises. A representative democracy needs voters, otherwise it can be hijacked by anti-democratic organisations or anti-democratic ideologies. So, although it is important to question whether political participation in its widest possible sense is related to variables such as social class, ethnicity, sex, age, religion and region, it is also important to look independently at the issue of voting behaviour.

It is evident that different elections are supported by very different levels of political participation from citizens. Why is it that citizens' voting behaviour is so fickle? One explanation for the vastly contrasting turnout percentages in elections is that a citizen's attitude to voting in any election is influenced by a potentially wide range of factors. These factors will include the individual citizen's level of cynicism and apathy, but cynicism and apathy are not solely responsible for a decline in the percentage turnout. Other factors are equally significant and include issues relating to the personal qualities and characteristics of those candidates to be elected. Other factors, like the social class, the age, the sex, the religion and even the geographical region of the election can all influence the likelihood of voting. To complicate the issue even further, citizens tend to respond differently to different types of elections, and all of these factors can be changed and influenced by the media.

What is the level of political participation among your fellow citizens?

In order to complete this research, you will need to select a sample of citizens and ask them the following questions:

- Have you ever written to an MP?
- Have you ever telephoned an MP?
- Have you ever attended your local MP's surgery?
- Have you ever written to or telephoned your local councillor?
- Have you ever been involved with a formal group in order to raise an issue?
- Have you ever been involved with an informal group in order to raise an issue?
- Have you ever attended a meeting of a political party?
- Have you ever helped in a political campaign?
- Have you ever been a candidate in a political election?
- Have you ever not voted in a General Election?
- Have you ever not voted in a European election?
- Have you ever not voted in a local election?

Collate your results.

What conclusions can be made about levels of political participation among your fellow citizens?

Your task is to encourage local community participation in a future event. This could be a local election, fund raising for a local charity or supporting a local community event.

Devise a text message, using a maximum of 160 characters, that will assist your local event towards a successful conclusion.

The following constituencies are significant because of the high or low turnout at the last General Election.

Birmingham Ladywood 54.24%	Ulster Mid 81.3%
Glasgow Maryhill 40.11%	Winchester 72.3%
Tyne Bridge 57.08%	Devon West and Torridge 70.51%
Liverpool Riverside 34.1%	Manchester Central 39.13%

- Try to draw some comparison between these constituencies. It could be in terms of factors like the geographical location, the socio-economic make-up of the constituency, the nature of the main form of employment, the main type of housing, or any other considerations, like the role of religion within the constituency.
- Is it possible to make any generalisations to explain the differences in the number of citizens who decide whether or not to vote?

What do you understand by the following terms and concepts?

- A single ballot, simple majority electoral system
- Overall majority
- Voter apathy
- Simple majority
- Proportional representation
- Alienation
- E-democracy

The disadvantages associated with the single ballot, simple majority electoral system are so great that it should be replaced with some form of proportional representation.

CHAPTER 13

Why Differing Levels of Citizen Participation in a Representative Democracy?

The aims of this chapter are to:

- Consider a broad range of explanations for citizens' voting behaviour
- Introduce issues surrounding tactical voting
- Consider the influence of internet sites on tactical voting
- Raise issues relating to wider political participation
- Outline arguments for and against the issue of compulsory voting

Psephological health warning!

Psephology (the study of voting behaviour) has a long and interesting history. Studies in this field aim to provide explanations for voting behaviour that can be applied to the majority of citizens over a period of time. Some claim that research in this field has produced models that provide explanations of the voting habits of the UK citizen. Others argue that much of this work is full of contradictions and does not stand up to critical scrutiny. Perhaps of even more concern to the student of citizenship is that some believe that a consequence of work in this field is the production of very broad generalisations or stereotypes of voting patterns that have subsequently become part of UK culture. Students of citizenship should realise that the work in this field, which has produced models and knowledge about voting behaviour, must be seen as temporary, not permanent. Since nobody knows the result of the next election, there is a strong possibility that models of voting behaviour and conclusions about voting behaviour are destined to be irrelevant on the declaration of the result.

Michigan model of voting

Explanations of citizens' voting behaviour can be traced to the Michigan model of voting, in which the key element was partisan alignment. Partisan alignment suggests that there exists a clear identification between voters and a specific political party. This link between voter and party was researched initially by Butler and Stokes, who suggested that the identifiable link between a citizen and the political party that gained the citizen's vote was based on the citizen's social class. Thus was born the phenomenon of social class alignment, which has established itself as part of the culture of the UK. The working class citizen was associated with a different voting preference from the middle class citizen. Put in its most simplistic form, the link was established that working class citizens voted for the Labour Party whilst middle class citizens voted for the Conservative Party.

Although the link between class and party has a foundation and has been used widely to explain patterns of voting behaviour, particularly between 1945 and 1970, the link between class and party was never absolute, as there was always a large percentage of citizens who simply did not vote in the direction indicated by the partisan alignment model of voting.

Partisan alignment

There are a variety of reasons why the assertion of the link between social class and voting behaviour can be seen as too simplistic. The first is that the notion of class alignment does not allow easily for the existence of third parties. The 9.1% of citizens who voted for the Liberal Party in the 1950 General Election do not fit easily into a model that essentially views elections as a game between two sides. Equally significant is the issue that, if the link between social class and voting behaviour was essentially correct, the Labour Party would have won significantly more, if not all, elections, as the working class was the larger of the two social classes.

Questions were also raised about the suitability of the class alignment model when applied to different regions of the UK. Cornwall, Wales and Scotland all displayed quite different patterns of voting behaviour, whilst Northern Ireland suggested a completely different set of assumptions about voting behaviour.

These issues do not take into account more complex criticisms revolving around how social class is defined or measured. If social class is to be linked solely to the occupation of a citizen, into what social class are citizens without an occupation to be put? If social class is to be defined by household, what outcome is there for those households that consist of citizens who are in different social classes?

Another issue that needs to be explored is akin to the age old dilemma of trying to establish which came first: the chicken or the egg. Is a citizen's voting behaviour determined by their social class identification (egg), or does their social class identification determine their voting behaviour? There is no answer to the egg/chicken conundrum; we could argue about it until the cows (or chickens) come home. Similarly, it is not possible to determine an answer to the question of which factor – a citizen's voting behaviour or their social class identification – has the primary influence on the other.   This is expressed in the following table.

> **Voting behaviour is determined by social class**   **Social class determines voting behaviour**
>
> 'I am voting for the Labour Party because I am working class'   **?**   'I am voting for the Conservative Party because I am middle class'
>
> **or**   **or**
>
> 'I am working class, therefore I must vote for the Labour Party'   ⟷   'I am middle class, therefore I must vote for the Conservative Party'

Taking either the Conservative or the Labour example, both are subject to the same criticism that the model in this instance is subject to a citizen's own class identification. What could quite easily happen can be exemplified by the infamous comic creation of Alf Garnett, featured initially in the BBC series *Till Death Us Do Part*, who would have turned the statements above into either of the following:

> 'I am voting for the Conservative Party because I think I am middle class'
>
> **or**
>
> 'I think I am middle class, therefore I must vote for the Conservative Party'

The implication of the above is that voting behaviour could easily be related to a citizen's self-assigned social class, as opposed to their actual social class. If voting behaviour is the result of a citizen's self-assigned social class, it could be claimed that the model is based on fantasy and not reality.

Although some commentators believe that partisan alignment still provides an explanation for the voting behaviour of citizens in the UK, the results of many elections increasingly challenge the basic assumption of partisan alignment that there exists a clear identification between the social class of citizens and a specific political party. This can be illustrated with reference to the percentage of citizens who voted for what is now called the Liberal Democrat Party. Between the 1970 and 1983 General Elections, the percentage of Liberal Democrat voters increased from 7.5% (1970) to 25.4% (1983). The fact that the Labour Party received only 2.2% more of the vote than the Liberal Democrats, a total of 27.6%, in the 1983 General Election, made explanations based around the link between voting behaviour and social class untenable. Many citizens in the Liberal Democrat Party have never accepted the suggested link and refer researchers to local councils and local elections where support for the Liberal Democrat Party is much higher.

Embourgeoisement

Embourgeoisement is a theory that suggests that citizens from the working class are adopting the lifestyles and behaviour patterns previously associated with the middle class and are as a consequence changing voting allegiance to the Conservative Party.

Although there have been some attempts, like the idea of embourgeoisement, to claim that there are grounds for evolutionary changes in the link between social class and voting behaviour, the general conclusion is one of two points of view. For some, it is necessary to reverse previous assumptions and now focus on 'partisan de-alignment' or the ending of the link between social class and political party. Others have adopted an alternative point of view and would argue that it is inappropriate to talk about partisan de-alignment, since much of the evidence relating to the link between social class and voting behaviour was only an assumed link in the first place, as it was never fully established.

Tactical voting

If social class is considered to have a dwindling influence on a citizen's voting behaviour, what are the alternatives that exist to explain the voting behaviour of UK citizens? The first suggestion is directly linked to growth in the success of the Liberal Democrat Party in recent elections, and also the growing strength of Nationalist parties. These parties can now be seen as a genuine third force that generates its own impetus and attracts support either from a latent pool of supporters or through the use of tactical voting. Tactical voting occurs when a citizen opts to support a candidate who is not their first choice in order to prevent the worst possible candidate from winning.

The General Election of 1997 saw the first real development of organised tactical voting when, either as a result of greater citizen sophistication or greater publicity in the media, some newspapers launched a GROT (Get Rid Of the Tories) campaign, publishing lists of vulnerable Conservative seats. However, by 2001, the organisation of tactical voting had reached a new degree of sophistication with dedicated websites explaining and introducing citizens to the wonders of the tactical vote. With money from the Joseph Rowntree Reform Trust, Jason Buckley, a supporter of voting reform, developed www.tacticalvoter.net which received well over 50,000 hits prior to the 2001 General Election. The site develops informed tactical voting and, according to the Electoral Reform Society, was 'just on the right side of the law'. Whether the real purpose of the site is not just to stop citizens feeling that their vote is wasted but to bring about a change in the voting system, or to stop the Conservative Party from returning to power, or both, is very much down to a citizen's own interpretation of the site. What, however, cannot be denied is that there exists the potential for an electoral earthquake as vote swapping allows people to vote for their least bad option in the knowledge that another citizen is doing the same, thus achieving simultaneously a vote *for* a citizen's political preference (in a different constituency) and a vote *against* their worst political option (in their own constituency).

What is "vote swapping?"

There are 659 seats in the UK Parliament. Only 38 saw Labour and Lib Dems running head-to-head in first and second place. The vast majority of seats are either Tory vs Labour or Tory vs Lib Dem contests.

For instance, in Wimbledon in SW London, Labour beat the Tories in 1997. The Lib Dems were way behind in third place. If you are a Lib Dem supporter living in Wimbledon, a vote for your own party is a wasted vote. To make sure of keeping the Tories out, you need to vote Labour.

Just next door in Kingston & Surbiton, the opposite applies. The Lib Dems beat the Tories in 1997 with a majority of just 56. Labour were way behind in third place. Here, a Labour vote is a wasted vote and it makes sense for all anti-Tory voters to support the Lib Dem candidate.

Vote swapping allows people in this awkward situation to pair up and vote tactically for each other's parties.

Result: instead of two wasted votes made out of misplaced party loyalty for candidates with no hope of winning, you and your pair end up casting two useful votes for candidates with a real chance. Both parties benefit – only the Tories lose out.

Using www.tacticalvoter.net, you can register that you intend to vote tactically. We can then pair you up by email with someone who is returning the favour by voting tactically for the party you support.

For legal reasons, all we can do is pair you up. You can't physically exchange votes, so there's an element of trust involved. But why should either of you welch on what you've said you'll do? You have nothing to lose but a Tory MP!

If you don't want someone else to receive your email address, you can still register that you intend to vote tactically – we'll be keeping a tally of how many voters register from each party.

The site was inspired by nadertrader.org and votetrader.org in the US presidential elections. Over 1,500 Green voters pledged to vote Democrat in Florida. If the sites had started a few weeks earlier, they might have gathered the small number of extra swappers needed to keep George Bush out of the White House.

There are dozens of UK seats with majorities of under 2,000 that could very easily be swung by vote swappers – contributing to a historic Tory meltdown that might bring them to their senses and stop the party dragging British politics towards the right.

We might even end up with a better electoral system, which would do tacticalvoter.net out of a job. Recycle your wasted vote!

What may surprise citizens is that tactical voting has the potential to radically change the outcome of a General Election. Although the 1997 General Election provided a landslide victory for the Labour Party, if only 168,000 citizens in 90 key constituencies had not voted Labour, the Labour Party would not have won the General Election.

In 2001, some areas of the country developed their own tactical voting sites. One such area was Dorset. Dorset's four constituencies are all marginal seats between different political parties and the 2001 General Election produced the following results:

	Dorset Mid and North	Dorset North Poole	Dorset South	Dorset West
2001 General Election results	Liberal Democrat majority over Conservative 384	Conservative majority over Liberal Democrat 3,797	Labour majority over Conservative 153	Conservative majority over Liberal Democrat 1,414
Changes from 1997 General Election	Liberal Democrat gain	Conservative hold	Labour gain	Conservative hold

The results in Dorset reveal that it would only take a handful of citizens to change their votes in order for the Conservative Party to either win or lose all four seats. The musician and Labour supporter, Billy Bragg, realised that the county would be particularly suitable for tactical voting and developed the votedorset.net site with the expressed aim of removing the Conservative Party from Dorset. It is impossible to draw any conclusions as to the importance of the vote swapping service provided by this site but whatever impact it had on the 2001 General Election, with growing citizen awareness and greater numbers of citizens going online, the only real conclusion that can be drawn is that future elections may be decided as a result of organised tactical voting.

votedorset.net
recycle your wasted vote

In 1997, two Conservative MPs were elected to represent the West Dorset and South Dorset constituencies, despite the fact that the majority voted against them. To avoid this happening again, Labour supporters in West Dorset could make a tactical vote for the Liberal Democrats, whilst in South Dorset, LibDem supporters could reciprocate by voting for the Labour candidate.

In order that votes cast might better reflect the democratic will of voters in our area, we are providing an online voter matching service which seeks to pair Labour supporters in West Dorset with Liberal Democrat supporters in South Dorset to facilitate dialogue about tactical voting in the forthcoming general election.

Due to attacks by Tory activists, we have been forced to change our format to make it more secure. Click on <u>forum</u> to access the new page. Leave a message seeking a voter valentine or make a connection with someone already there. As vote-swapping is based on trust, we suggest that you strike up an e-mail dialogue with your partner and build confidence in your ability to oust the Tories from your area by working together on election day.

For those who do not have access to the web, votedorset.net is providing a postal vote-swapping service. Simply send a postcard with your details to:

Tactical voting posters and bumper stickers for the West Dorset and South Dorset constituencies are available to download free from <u>tacticalvoter.net</u>

votedorset.net is not affiliated to nor funded by any political party.

Another factor that is now considered by some to be important is what has come to be seen as a move towards the 'presidentialisation' of General Election campaigns, with a greater and greater emphasis being placed by the media on the leader of each political party.

Other potential factors include the role of a specific event, or the prolonged effect of an event between elections that comes to be seen as representative of that party's time in office. The event, depending on whether it is positive or negative, can either increase or decrease support. Thus, the 'Falklands factor' was seen to be significant in increasing Conservative support in 1983, whilst the prolonged 'cash for questions' and general sleaze resulted in a haemorrhage of Conservative support in 1997.

Some have linked this idea to more general factors and developed the idea of a 'feelgood factor'. The essence of this factor in explaining citizens' voting behaviour is that there is no long term loyalty to any party. What matters is the citizen's individual psychological experience of the party in power – whether it has produced the economic or general conditions which are beneficial to the citizen. When a citizen perceives him or herself to be benefiting, they 'feel good'.

Consumer model of voting

Other models of voting have been developed to explain the voting behaviour of citizens. One of these, associated with Himmelweit *et al* (in *How Votes Decide*, 1985) moves away from explaining the voting behaviour of a citizen based on social class, and towards an explanation based on a consumer model of voting. This makes the comparison between 'shoppers in a supermarket' and 'voters in a political supermarket'. A shopper's selection of goods can be influenced by a wide range of considerations: price, past experience, brand name, packaging, loyalty, as well as the totally unpredictable 'impulse buys' that so many come to regret.

If the scene is changed from the supermarket to voting in an election, the same could also be true. Some voters will read and get to know all the issues and policies of a political party and will cast their vote accordingly. Others will cast their vote on the basis of the party's name. Some voters will cast their vote as a direct result of previous experiences of that party, whilst others might just like the appearance of the leader of that party. Some voters will never change their support from a specific party and others might 'shut their eyes and take pot luck'.

Listed below are 10 factors that have been used to explain voting behaviour:

- The influence of social class
- The importance of making rational choices
- The importance of the issues
- The role of dominant ideology
- The importance of a citizen's perceptions of party competence
- The importance of a citizen's perceptions of the party leader
- The influence of the mass media
- The influence of advertising
- The influence of opinion polls
- The importance of the electoral campaign

Ask a number of other citizens to rank the 10 factors in order of importance.

Score your results – 10 points for being considered the most important to 1 point for the least important.

Present your results in a chart or graph.

Compare your results with other students' results.

What conclusions can be drawn from your results?

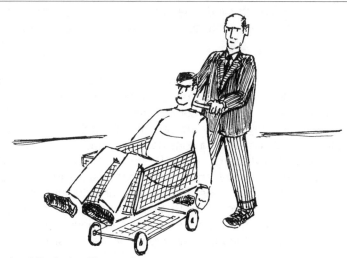

Question: 'What's the difference between a supermarket trolley and a politician?'
Answer: 'Nothing, they both take you where they want you to go.'　　　BobZ

Although there are many influences on a citizen's voting behaviour, some are considerably more significant than others. Some factors that were significant at different times in history have become considerably less significant. Three of these less significant factors are the age of a citizen, the sex of a citizen and, for most of the UK, the citizen's religion.

Another factor that some believe to be a significant influence on the voting behaviour of a citizen is that of a citizen's race. The problem, however, is that when this factor is placed under scrutiny, the evidence is so contradictory that it is impossible to draw a conclusion about any alleged link between the factor of race, or indeed ethnicity, and voting behaviour.

A further factor that is often believed to be a significant influence on a citizen's voting behaviour relates to the geographical regions of the UK. There are some regions, as previously discussed, in which there are different sets of assumptions about the direction that a citizen will cast his or her vote. Northern Ireland, Wales and Scotland are examples of these regions. The debate relating to the influence that a geographical region can have on a citizen's voting behaviour has developed since the early part of the last century and is often expressed in terms of a 'north/south' divide.

To divide the UK into a 'north' and a 'south' requires an imaginary horizontal division to be placed across the UK. If a citizen's voting behaviour is influenced by a 'north/south' divide, there should be visible evidence in terms of the results from General Elections.

Using the election results from the last General Election, is it possible to place a single horizontal line across the UK and conclude that there is a significant difference in voting behaviour between 'the north' and 'the south'?

To complicate the issue relating to a geographical influence in voting in the UK, there is the fact that there could be grounds to argue that a 'west/east' divide also exists. There is a further complicating factor when this division is discussed because of many citizens' perceptions about the geography of the UK. This point can be illustrated by a consideration of the geographic position of two cities, Bristol and Edinburgh. Since Bristol lies towards the west coast and Edinburgh the east, many citizens assume that Bristol is further west than Edinburgh. Although this may seem logical, it is unfortunately not correct; Edinburgh is actually further west than Bristol. The implication of this point is that, if a 'west/east' division in citizens' voting behaviour exists, it is very difficult to find a line of longitude that will support a 'west/east' divide.

Using the results from the last General Election, try to place a single vertical line down the UK that would support the conclusion that there is a significant difference in voting behaviour between 'the west' and 'the east'.

If there were any justification for the division of the voting behaviour of citizens by region, after the 2001 General Election the most appropriate division would be an arc from the constituencies around Bristol to the constituency of Scarborough and Whitby. Even this line would need to be clarified with the provision to exclude not only Greater London, but also the celtic fringe of North Devon and Cornwall.

The range of political participation

The discussion so far has mainly focused on the issue of voting and, although voting is often seen as the most important single form of political participation, it is not the only way in which citizens can participate in the political process. In a study in 1993, Parry and Moyser identified a range of quite different forms of political participation in which a citizen could become involved. With the exclusion of voting, a citizen's political participation could include:

• Raising funds for a political party
• Canvassing support for a political party
• Providing clerical assistance for a political party
• Attending rallies organised by a political party
• Informally joining a protest group
• Becoming the organiser of a group
• Raising issues on behalf of a group
• Participating in protest meetings
• Organising a petition
• Signing a petition
• Participating in a protest march
• Participating in a political strike
• Participating in a political boycott
• Using physical force
• Making contact with an MP
• Making contact with a civil servant
• Making contact with a local councillor
• Making contact with the town hall
• Making contact with the media

Parry and Moyser identified a range of 23 different forms of political participation. They then asked citizens how many of the listed activities they had actually taken part in during the previous five years. Their results showed that only 23% of respondents had taken part in four or more forms of political participation, which led them to conclude that the level of political participation by citizens in the UK was very low.

Theories of political participation

A range of theories have been offered to help explain differing levels of political participation by citizens. Broadly, these explanations suggest that differing levels can be explained through:

- a citizen's social resources;
- a citizen's socialisation;
- a citizen's rational choice; or
- a citizen's individual personality.

As with most theories, they are best treated as a guide to understanding and may well make more sense if combined rather than being seen as four independent ways of explaining the likelihood of a citizen participating in political processes.

In order to try to explain differing levels of political participation, the 2001 British Election Study compared two groups of citizens. These groups consisted of 'apathetic' citizens on the one hand and 'participants' on the other. The 'participants' were made up of 'gladiators', 'helpers' and 'proselytisers', the three categories of citizen with the greatest levels of political participation, as discussed in Chapter 12. It is, however, important to note at this stage that political participation in the British Election Study refers only to voting in the 2001 election and does not take into account all other forms of political participation.

The first explanation suggests that differing levels of voting result from citizens' differing social resources. Different groups of citizens have different social characteristics, such as their level of education, which will allow them to participate more effectively in any political process. Results from the 2001 British Election Study suggest that a citizen's occupation, education and income do influence levels of voting. Citizens who are educated to degree level or higher form the smallest percentage of apathetics (3%) and the largest percentage of participants (25%) compared to all other groups. Middle class, higher income citizens are, when compared to all other groups, considerably less likely to be classified as 'apathetic'. Although there is no significant difference in rates of voting between men and women, there is a significant difference related to a citizen's age, with a steady increase in voting from a low of 35% for 18–24 year olds to a high of 76% for those over 65.

Closely related to the explanation based on a citizen's social resources is the explanation that different levels of voting can be explained through a citizen's socialisation. Although there is no significant difference in rates of voting between men and women, the British Election Study does suggest that slightly more men than women are interested in politics, which has been explained in terms of traditional patterns of socialisation producing a stereotypical division between public and private spheres of influence between men and women. Although this conclusion is weakly supported, the British Election Study does support the notion that some citizens are influenced by family and friends. There was a considerably lower rate of voting among those citizens who agreed with the statement that 'most of my friends and family think that voting is a waste of time', compared to citizens who disagreed with the statement. The problem with this conclusion, however, is that it is impossible from the data provided by the British Election Study to determine whether it is the process of socialisation that influences voting levels or whether it is a citizen's social resources that influences their socialisation which in turn influences their likelihood to vote in an election.

An alternative interpretation of explanations based on socialisation, however, is possible. To appreciate this interpretation, it is necessary to accept the view that voting is considered to be 'culturally normal' and that voting in elections is viewed as being part of modern Britain's culture. If a citizen rejects the idea of voting they are effectively rejecting an element of British culture, which could only have occurred through a problem with their socialisation. If a citizen has experienced an unsuccessful process of socialisation, this will reflect itself in the rejection of dominant cultural values that will in turn lead to a reduction in the likelihood of participating in legitimate political activity.

A further explanation suggests that a citizen's level of voting is simply a matter of each and every citizen making a rational choice in their decision to vote or not to vote. Again it is difficult to use the British Election Study to provide conclusive proof. The study does, however, suggest that some citizens do make a rational choice. It is suggested that those citizens who identify strongly with a political party make a rational choice to support that party and turn that support into a vote for that party. Of those citizens who did identify very strongly with a political party, 38% were identified as 'participants' whilst only 4% were identified as 'apathetics' in the 2001 election.

The final explanation, based around an individual citizen's personality, locates explanations away from social or group influences and within the psychological make-up of the citizen. This explanation, by definition, makes it impossible to generalise about influences on levels of political participation.

Eliminating non-voting: make all citizens vote

When any comparison is made between citizens of Australia, Luxembourg, Brazil or Belgium and British citizens, it would appear that British citizens are considerably less interested in using their democratic right to vote. However, the comparison is not quite that straightforward. Students of citizenship need to ask the question as to what Australia, Luxembourg, Brazil and Belgium have in common. The answer is that these four countries require by law that *all* citizens must vote in elections. The idea of compulsory voting has been seen by some in modern Britain as a means of reducing voter apathy and reinforcing a balance between a citizen's rights and their responsibilities. All citizens have the right to elect their representatives, but for this right to be meaningful, enough citizens have to act responsibly and cast their vote. At present, UK citizens are required by law to enter their names on the electoral register but there is no compulsion to make a citizen vote. For those who support the notion of compulsory voting, there is the belief that citizenship not only gives a citizen rights, but demands certain responsibilities and obligations from them. One such responsibility and obligation is to judge other citizens and perform jury service when called. If compulsory jury service is culturally acceptable to British citizens, then logically the responsibility to preserve those democratic traditions that shape British culture and citizenship should be equally acceptable. Compulsory voting would appear to be a small price to pay for citizens to preserve a democratic system that provides peaceful social change and protects citizens' human rights. Some would go further and argue that the democratic system that shapes British culture needs to be not only preserved, but also strengthened, and this is something that all citizens have a responsibility towards achieving. Since all citizens should share this responsibility, all citizens should vote. Compulsory voting would provide a major contribution towards supporting the democratic system that could be achieved with minimal inconvenience for citizens.

There is also the belief that if compulsory voting was introduced, citizens, knowing that they had to vote, would take much greater interest in political matters. This would in turn lead to an improvement in levels of political literacy which, it is believed, would enhance and enrich British democracy and encourage further political participation.

At present, one characteristic of voting behaviour is that there is a link between the likelihood of a citizen voting and their socio-economic status. The poorer the citizen the less likely that citizen is to vote in an election. If these citizens are less likely to vote, many politicians will feel that there is little point in addressing the issues that directly concern them and concentrate on the issues that are more directly related to the concerns of the group that are most likely to vote. If this happens, politicians will increasingly focus campaigns on the richer, more affluent voter whilst the poorer citizen will become increasingly excluded and marginalised from political processes.

When there is an unequal turnout between citizens at elections, then some groups of citizens do not have an equal voice. Compulsory voting would, it is believed, be a simple way to ensure that all citizens' views are recorded at elections and would force political parties to address all issues that are of concern to all citizens rather than the issues of those most likely to vote.

At a more practical level, supporters of compulsory voting argue that it will, at a stroke, address the issues of increasing voter apathy and decreasing voter turnout. If compulsory voting is to address these two issues through changes in the law, political parties will not have to spend many millions of pounds trying to persuade citizens to cast their vote, and this would decrease the significance of a political party's wealth. Although compulsory voting might remove the need for political parties to persuade citizens to cast their vote, it would not remove the role of money in trying to persuade a citizen *how* to cast their vote.

The whole issue of voter apathy and the declining electoral turnout is complex and has been raised earlier. Many believe that compulsory voting will do little to change voter apathy and decreasing voter turnout and might actually devalue and damage the political process. Damage could be caused through politically ignorant and unaware citizens making ill-considered choices at the election, and the whole political process could be devalued if compulsory voting demands that some citizens have to be rounded up and marched to the ballot box. This image raises the question of who would enforce compulsory voting, and the prospect of the 'voting police' could greatly increase discontent with political processes rather than increase support.

The issue of implementation would also have to be addressed. The administrative costs of tracing non-voters could be enormous and determining the appropriate punishment would raise further moral and political questions. The mere fact that a non-voting citizen could be traced could also raise questions surrounding the confidentiality of a citizen's secret vote.

Critics of compulsory voting also raise the issue of whether compulsory voting can sit alongside a citizen's human rights. At present citizens have the right to vote, which also means they have the right not to vote. Compulsory voting would change this right to a duty which some believe would infringe an individual's liberty. If compulsory voting was introduced, very similar arguments could be made for 'compulsory membership of a political party', 'compulsory attendance at political meetings' or 'compulsory viewing of election broadcasts'. If forced participation is used as an argument to defend a citizen's freedoms, then the element of compulsion does not strengthen human rights but effectively weakens them.

Ultimately, critics of compulsory voting argue that the real reason as to why political participation has declined is increasing alienation and dissatisfaction with the whole political system, including politicians, by some citizens. Compulsory voting would not effectively address this problem; it would only address the result of the problem, and it would be far better to address the cause.

What do you understand by the following terms and concepts?

- Partisan alignment
- Tactical voting
- Psephology
- The 'feelgood factor'

Listed below are three different types of democracies. The most profitable source to research these democracies will be from AS and A2 politics textbooks. From one or more such texts, write a 50-word description for each of the following:

- Direct democracy
- Liberal democracy
- Parliamentary democracy

In some countries, voting is not an optional activity as the law requires all citizens to vote. Greater political participation in the UK could be achieved with the introduction of compulsory voting.

The age, sex and religion of a citizen are no longer an influence on their voting behaviour.

CHAPTER 14

Putting the Representatives into a Representative Democracy ... at all Levels

The aims of this chapter are to:

- Introduce the importance of making informed choices
- Raise issues relating to manifestos
- Discuss issues relating to the power and responsibilities of elected representatives
- Raise issues relating to the ability to control elected representatives

Some of the key elements of a representative democracy have by now been discussed. However, a representative democracy will only be successful if citizens are prepared to participate. It is essential in a representative democracy to have some citizens who are prepared to represent other citizens. A representative democracy needs citizens who are not only prepared to represent other citizens, but who will also be prepared to openly state and communicate their ideas, attitudes and aspirations to all other citizens in order for those citizens to be able to make an informed choice in a free and fair election.

'Career politicians'

There are some citizens who enjoy politics and want to be elected representatives. This can be seen with the development of the concept of the 'career politician'. This trend was first identified in an article published by Anthony King in 1981. He highlighted the trend for some citizens to enter Parliament at a relatively young age with the intention of remaining in Parliament throughout their working lives. This trend can be identified to a greater extent after the 2001 General Election, with 66 MPs describing themselves as 'politician' and 35 MPs having previous experience in local government or the civil service.

Although there is a growth in 'career politicians', they are still a small minority of the many thousands of citizens who decide to be a candidate in an election. The reasons why any citizen would want to stand as a candidate are very diverse and could range from an entirely personal reason to the ambitious long term career opportunity described above. The answer to the question as to why a citizen should decide to be a candidate in an election will often differ between those citizens who are standing in an election and those who decide not to stand. For those who are standing, the response often takes the form of a desire to serve or to achieve some particular course of action, or because they feel their view is the correct view and they want to get this view adopted and acted upon.

From chocolate box lottery to making an informed choice

Although a box of chocolates may seem irrelevant to any discussion of the topic of a representative democracy, it can provide a very useful analogy. A large box of chocolates, when opened, will be very tempting, with a range of chocolates that are more than likely all to be the same colour, although there might be one or two that are a different shade and one or two that are outrageously coloured in bright foil. They will all be roughly the same size. All exist for the same purpose – being enjoyably eaten. However, each piece of confectionery, under the chocolate walls, hides a different interior and, although they all look similar, it is evident that they are not because everybody has different favourites and, in many households, it is always the same chocolates that are unwanted and get left in the box until an unsuspecting guest arrives.

LIFE IS LIKE A BOX OF CHOCOLATES......

BobZ

When a citizen receives or buys a box of chocolates and looks inside, how do they know which chocolate to select? Some might simply refrain, saying that they are all bad for the waistline. Others might say that they are as bad or as good as each other, so they close their eyes and pick at random. Some might be tempted by the attractive bright foil wrappers; whilst others may select on the basis of size. Another set of consumers may have made a previous purchase so they have already decided on their favourite and automatically select it from past experience. Then there are those consumers who may try something new, only to discover that the 'old ones are the best'.

For some, the ability to distinguish the 'coffee cream' from the 'nutty surprise' might be a very serious issue if they have an allergy to nuts. In this case, a decision needs to be made based on accurate and detailed information that can be obtained by first identifying each chocolate and then establishing its contents. Some consumers will simply want to know what is inside each chocolate. Their answer lies printed in the lid with a key allowing each chocolate to be identified. Once each chocolate has been identified, an important choice can be made on the basis of an informed decision. The chocolate is finally eaten.

From the chocolate box to parliamentary elections

A large box of chocolates, when opened, will be very tempting, with a range of chocolates that are more than likely all to be the same colour, although there might be one or two that are a different shade and one or two that are outrageously coloured in bright foil.

In a parliamentary election, the candidates are likely to be very similar types of people, usually from a narrow section of society, with relatively few from the ethnic minorities. There are likely to be some fringe candidates.

They will all be roughly the same size. All exist for the same purpose of being enjoyably eaten. However, each piece of confectionery, under the chocolate walls, hides a different interior and, although they all look the same, everybody has different favourites and, in many households, it is always the same chocolates that are rejected and get left in the box.

The candidate's aim is to win votes and although all candidates are human, no two humans are identical. Some will be winners, others rejected.

When a citizen receives or buys a box of chocolates and looks inside, how do they know which chocolate to select? Some might simply refrain, saying that they are as bad or as good as each other, so they close their eyes and pick at random. Some might be tempted by the attractive bright foil wrappers; whilst others may select on the basis of size.

How does an elector know who to vote for? Some might abstain, some might pick at random, some might be persuaded by the candidate's 'packaging' that has been designed to create a candidate who looks good.

Another set of consumers may have previously purchased a box so they have already have made up their mind which is their favourite, and automatically select it. Alternatively, from past experience, some consumers may have tried something new only to discover that the 'old ones are the best'.

Some electors have pre-determined their vote whilst others float from candidate to candidate at each election.

The ability to distinguish the 'coffee cream' from the 'nutty surprise' might be a very serious issue for those consumers who have an allergy to nuts. In this case a decision needs to be made based on accurate and detailed information obtained by first identifying each chocolate and then establishing its contents. Some consumers will simply want to know what is inside each chocolate. Their answer lies printed in the lid with a key allowing each chocolate to be identified. Once the differences are identified, that important choice can be made on the basis of an informed decision. The chocolate is finally eaten.

For some, elections are a serious business and they want to know what each candidate stands for, what are they promising to do, and what their policies are. These electors will read each candidate's manifesto (set of election promises) and on the basis of this knowledge a vote is finally cast.

A manifesto

Although classroom elections may not necessitate each candidate writing a declaration of what they hope to achieve if elected, at the time of a General Election, citizens need information from each political party that outlines what that party intends to achieve if elected. These descriptions of a party's intended policies describe possible changes in laws or potential changes in the emphasis of existing policies, and are contained in a document referred to as a manifesto. The manifesto is a set of election promises made by the political party and is published whenever a General Election is called. The document is presented, usually with a great fanfare, to the electorate and should make a clear and unambiguous declaration of that party's policies and promises for the next Parliament. Candidates at an election can also produce their own manifesto, consisting of their declarations of what they would do for the community. Manifestos are exceedingly important because they should help citizens to decide which political party or which candidate will receive their vote. Various committees within the party organisation painstakingly develop manifestos during the years prior to an election, although sometimes a policy suddenly 'appears' due to a political gaffe. Equally, and more alarmingly, some policies are introduced that were never previously published in a manifesto.

Mix and match manifesto game

- The following promises are all taken from the manifestos published prior to the 2001 General Election. Clue: there are an equal number of manifesto promises from the Conservative Party, the Labour Party and the Liberal Democrat Party (don't forget that more than one party might have made the same promise). Circle the party you think made the promise.

- Using the internet, check your answers from the broadsheet archive editions published for the week ending 19 May 2001. The answers are also given at the end of this chapter.

Manifesto promise	Political party
• Provide 10,000 more hospital beds	C / Lab / Lib Dem
• Recruit 10,000 more doctors and 25,000 more nurses	C / Lab / Lib Dem
• Recruit 10,000 more teachers	C / Lab / Lib Dem
• Allow patients to choose hospital for their treatment	C / Lab / Lib Dem
• Cut primary school classes to an average size of 25	C / Lab / Lib Dem
• Reduce road tax on environmentally friendly vehicles	C / Lab / Lib Dem
• Send every taxpayer an account of how their taxes were spent by the Government	C / Lab / Lib Dem
• Raise the speed limit on motorways to 80 mph	C / Lab / Lib Dem
• Establish stock market linked endowment funds to pay for universities	C / Lab / Lib Dem
• Abolish charges for dental and eye check ups	C / Lab / Lib Dem
• Recruit 6,000 more police officers	C / Lab / Lib Dem

There is considerable debate as to how useful political party manifestos are to voting citizens. Many citizens do not read them, believing them to be of limited reliability as they are only promises; and promises can always be broken. Some citizens feel that the language is vague or ambiguous. One Conservative manifesto promised that 'child benefit would continue to be paid as it is now'. When the child benefit allowance was not subsequently increased, the ambiguity of the words 'as it is now' became apparent. Also, the lack of any manifesto pledge to abolish the Inner London Education Authority casts doubt on the usefulness of some manifestos.

The one thing that unites both candidates who are prepared to represent others and the electorate who wish to select a representative is the need for some electoral system that is going to allow both of these desires to be achieved simultaneously and satisfactorily. The only reason why voting systems exist is to elect representatives. Is it the voting system that allows a greater proportion of certain types of citizens to be elected, or are some types of citizens just going to be more electable than others?

The reason why some are critical when the debate only centres on the role of voting systems in electing representatives is because systems of voting represent only half the issue. When the debate only focuses on voting systems, it is not only too one-sided, but also many feel that it is not the most important side of the debate. This is because while the citizens will have the power to make choices about a representative on *one day* every four or five years, elected representative will have the power to make choices about citizens *every day* for four or five years, and it is the issue of the power of an elected representative that should be the most important consideration in a representative democracy.

The power and responsibilities associated with citizens who become elected representatives

For any elected representative, once in office, it is true to say that there are invariably clear limits to the amount of power attached to the post. It is equally true that some elected representatives, in the same post, appear to be or actually are more powerful than similarly elected representatives. How is it possible that, when the amount of power entrusted to a specific office does not change, it is possible for some elected representatives to be far more powerful than others?

The answer to this question lies in the combination of two factors:

• First, the social characteristics and the personality of the elected representative. Since each citizen is unique and has a unique history, all elected representatives bring something different to the office for which they have been elected.

- Secondly, how that elected representative interprets their role and responsibilities.

The role of a representative

Once elected, a representative has the potential to develop quite different interpretations of his or her role. Some elected representatives will feel that they can only act according to how they have been instructed by the electors, or, to put it another way, they can only act according to their mandate. Other elected representatives argue that, since it would be impossible to know what all the citizens individually believe to be the correct course of action, once elected, the representative has the right to act on his or her conscience and to take decisions accordingly, regardless of the views, wishes or instructions of the electors.

This conflict facing citizens who become elected representatives is summarised below.

'I am your representative. I was elected to represent you and speak on your behalf. In order to do this, I will need to consider what I think is in your best interests. This will mean that I will sometimes have to make a decision or make a judgment based on my conscience.'

'I am your delegate. I was elected by you for the purpose of expressing your views and feelings on any issue. This is my role: to express your views directly and as accurately as I possibly can.'

© Crocodile Photos

How the elected representative citizen perceives their role is significant. Do they, as a delegate, proceed to express the views of the electorate as accurately as possible, or do they consider what they think is in the best interests of all citizens and then make a decision based on their own conscience? The main problem associated with the first option is the difficulty, or impossibility, of expressing the views of all the electorate. When the second approach is chosen, it presents to the elected representative both powers and responsibilities.

Powers and responsibilities of elected representatives

The issue relating to the power and responsibility of an elected representative is a complex one. The difficulty of the role faced by elected representatives can be illustrated by raising this question: who does the elected representative support when there are areas of conflict amongst the voters?

Should the largest group of citizens be supported or the loudest group? Should support go to the most loyal supporters or those citizens who can organise the best demonstrations? Should support be given to your favourite group of citizens or to those who pay your salary? These are all questions of power, responsibility and integrity and are faced daily by MPs elected by the voting citizens within a constituency. (Issues of integrity are discussed in Chapter 15.)

As an occupation, being an MP is different from many other occupations. At work, there are two things that most citizens will have, which are useful even if they may not always like them: a job description and a 'boss'. The job description is useful, as it outlines the employee's duties, commitments, and what is expected of the employee at work. 'Bosses' are also useful, as they are the ones who should direct and, when things go wrong, be there to take the blame!

Job descriptions for MPs

To complete this activity, first of all establish, from as many different sources as possible, what is involved in being an MP.

Once you have done this, try to write a job description for an MP.

If possible, send your job description to your local MP and ask him or her whether it bears any resemblance to the realities of being an MP.

The occupation of an MP, apart from the prospect of being judged at least every five years with the possibility of being removed from employment, lacks a definitive job description but, more importantly, has an ambiguity around the issue of who is 'the boss'.

For an MP, the ambiguity about who is 'the boss' results from a conflict of loyalties between, on the one hand, the interests of all the citizens in the constituency, even the ones who did not vote for the MP, and, on the other hand, the political party that expects the support of its MPs. This debate is not unique to MPs and applies to many different types of elected representatives. It revolves around the conflict Edmund Burke aired in 1774, when he said: 'Your representative owes you not his industry only but his judgments; and he betrays, instead of serving you, if he sacrifices to your opinion.'

There are measures to control the power of elected representatives. In the House of Commons there is the Register of Members' Interests.

Research the following:
- What is the Register of Members' Interests?
- What are the advantages of the existence of such a register?
- What are the weaknesses in the present system?
- Does such a register exist for:
  - The House of Lords?
  - Your local Council?

Controlling the power of the elected representatives

Being an elected representative will lead to greater empowerment, and some elected representatives will use this power appropriately and be fully accountable for all their actions and decisions. However, 'the power of power' for others will lead to temptation and corruption. If humans are by nature selfish, how is it possible for an elected representative not to take his or her own self-interest into account? In order to ensure that the empowerment of those citizens who become elected representatives does not lead to the situation in which they are the ones that benefit from their decisions, there need to be ways and means to ensure that the power entrusted *to* the elected representative does not become power *for* the elected representative. Controlling the power of the elected representative is a key function for those citizens who decided not to stand in the election. It is always worth remembering that all elected representatives are only in a position of power because other citizens have put them there.

The power of elected representative can become a source of concern when it seems to become excessive. This can be illustrated by looking at the head of the executive in the House of Commons: the Prime Minister.

The powers of the Prime Minister, according to an article written by Tony Benn in 1979, 'are so great as to encroach on the legitimate rights of the electorate ... the present centralisation of power into the hands of one person amounts to a system of personal rule in the very heart of our democracy'. Two years previously, Lord Hailsham equated the post of Prime Minister to that of an 'elected dictator'.

To illustrate this point, the declaration by Mrs Thatcher, quoted in February 1979 when interviewed in *The Observer*, that 'as Prime Minister, I could not waste time having any internal arguments', should have been a clear indication of the personal qualities that she was to bring to the post of Prime Minister. Coupled with a specific interpretation of her role as the elected representative, this combination of personality and interpretation developed into a style of leadership that came to be more associated with a 'handbagging dictator' than with Cabinet democracy.

The reason why the post allows the holder so much power is based on the ability of the Prime Minister to appoint and control. This ability has developed through royal prerogative, when the task of forming an administration was entrusted to an individual, and was institutionalised through precedent. It is the Prime Minister who is responsible for appointing the members of the Cabinet, chairing Cabinet meetings, dismissing Ministers, creating peers and effectively deciding the fate of the Parliament with either a threat of resignation or, with shrewd cunning and opportune timing, the dissolution of Parliament at the most advantageous time in order to help secure another election victory.

Levels of government

Another aspect of a representative democracy can be illustrated by reference to the different levels of government. In the UK, citizens can, at different times, vote for their local councillor. Within their constituencies, they can vote for MPs and MEPs and, in some areas, citizens can vote directly for their mayor.

At every level of government, there is the necessity that rules or laws are made. Even returning to the idea of the school classroom, there are rules about many activities. Sometimes, rules are made about which students can use the lockers at eye level, rather than those at floor level or hidden behind stacked chairs. Whenever rules or laws are discussed, so is the issue of power. Because all rules or laws need to be made, administered and enforced for them to be effective, there are essentially three different types of political power. These powers are usually referred to in terms of:

* legislative power;   * executive power;   * judicial power.

Each of these involves quite different tasks. Legislative power refers to the task of making new laws or substantially changing existing ones. Executive power refers to the task of policy making. This involves not only suggesting new laws, but also implementing laws by ensuring that the requirements demanded by specific laws are carried out. The third element is judicial power, and this involves interpreting the law and making decisions as to whether the law has or has not been broken. Judicial power rests with the courts, ranging from the Law Lords in the House of Lords to the local magistrates' court.

It is important to remember that, although the terms 'legislative' and 'executive ' are most often associated with national government, the terms are applicable to all levels of government because, at every level of government, there is still the need for a legislature, entrusted with the task of making new laws or substantially changing existing ones, and an executive with the responsibility for policy making.

Difference in power of elected representatives according to the level of government

There is, however, one important respect in which being an elected representative varies according to the level of government, and that lies in the scope or degree of power that the elected representative is able to exercise. If, as a result of a decision made by an elected representative, the lives of many millions of citizens are going to be directly influenced, it is legitimate to argue that these elected representatives have more power and influence than the elected representative whose decision only affects 10 or 20 citizens in one small community.

Local, regional, sub-national, devolved government; what's in a name?

Local government, regional government, sub-national government and devolved government are essentially all in the same subordinate position, as all their powers have been granted to them by central government, and what is given can be taken away. The UK is a unitary state. A unitary state is one in which the powers associated with government are held by a central authority and, although this central authority may transfer or devolve some of its powers to other forms of government, there is no removal of the central authority's sovereignty. A state in which regional government is guaranteed its own powers is called a federal state. Canada and the US are examples of federal states. For the UK citizen, the idea of having different sets of laws for different states, as they have in Canada and the US, is quite alien, the equivalent of having different VAT rates in different UK counties.

This existence of non-central governments will, however, have some impact on citizens in the UK. The extent of this impact will vary according to where in the UK the citizens live. Over the last 25 years, there have been numerous changes in the links between non-central and central government that have now created a confused and complex set of relationships between the two.

Local government

Local government can be considered the layer of government that is the most subordinate to central government. The reality of the position of local government is that it is constitutionally very weak. It gains all its powers from Parliament and, if it is felt that the local government has acted beyond its powers, as in the case of the old Greater London Council's (GLC) 'fares fair' campaign to reduce the cost of using public transport, the courts can declare the council's action illegal. If this was not sufficient power, central government can also control, through a variety of mechanisms, the spending of local governments.

Those citizens who are elected to be part of local government are known as local councillors. Their role is different from that of an MP, in that local councillors do not have a major legislative function. They cannot make or change the laws of the state. The only legislative role they have relates to local bylaws. Citizens do not pay different VAT rates as they move from one local authority to another, although they could face different fines if their dog fouled the footpath.

The shape of local government has been determined by a series of Acts of Parliament. One of these was the Local Government Act 1972, which introduced amongst its tiers of government the GLC and eight metropolitan county councils. Although these were introduced with the intention of improving life for citizens, when a clash of ideology and policy occurred between central and local government, local government always came second. In the case of the GLC and the metropolitan county councils, the ideological chasm between them and the Thatcher Government resulted in their abolition.

The dilemma faced by central government in its judgment over local authorities is that there exist two fundamentally irreconcilable aims within local government. It has to be small enough to be able to respond to the needs of the individual citizen and large enough to organise, efficiently and economically, services such as the fire service and the police force. This is the justification for a tiered service. Rather like a wedding cake, each tier is responsible for smaller, more intimate services; from major roads to local roads to footpaths.

By the start of the 21st century, a citizen's local government might resemble one of the following forms, depending entirely upon where the citizen lives.

TIER 1	TIER 2	TIER 3
England		
Greater London Authority	33 London Borough Councils	
36 Metropolitan District Councils		
34 Non Metropolitan County Councils	238 Non Metropolitan District Councils	Parish Councils
46 Unitary Authorities	Parish Councils	
Scotland		
32 Unitary Authorities	Community Councils	
Wales		
22 Unitary Authorities	Community and Parish Councils	
Northern Ireland		
9 Area Boards	26 District Councils	

Devolution

Devolution is the process of transferring some powers and responsibilities from central government to a regional government. A regional government can be likened to 'big local government' and may be based on a geographical region or area. The victory of the Labour Party in the 1997 General Election produced referendums in Scotland and Wales which both led to the establishment of devolved regional authorities. There have subsequently been further discussions of varying intensity relating to the question of devolution. However, at the start of 2003, issues relating to devolution began to be more seriously debated when the Government launched a widespread consultation exercise to test citizens' attitudes towards regional devolution. Citizens are, at the time of writing, being encouraged to send their views to a new Whitehall website at www.local-regions.odpm.gov.uk/consult/assembly-bill/index.htm which is the first stage in a process that could see local referendums in October 2004. Depending on the outcome of these consultations, there is a possibility that eight regional assemblies could be created. These regional assemblies would take into account the 'identities and interests of local communities' whilst achieving 'effective and convenient local government'. Although the Government does not envisage these regional authorities replacing local county councils, they would have tax-varying powers and some would have a degree of responsibility for planning, transport, waste, housing and tourism. They would be funded by a direct grant from government and would consist of between 25 and 35 directly elected members.

How local is local?

Two of the claimed advantages of localising government are that local government can serve citizens better and more efficiently. Implicit in this type of assessment is the notion that the link between a citizen and their local representative will be closer than their links with other representatives. The following activity sets out to test whether citizens do have greater knowledge about their local representative in their smallest constituency compared to their 'local' representative in their largest constituency.

One claimed advantage of local government is that it brings the process of government closer to citizens. One way to test this claim is to complete the following activity.

Ask the following questions to a number of other citizens.

From your results, what conclusions can be drawn about your fellow citizens' knowledge about their local councillor? How much does this differ from their knowledge relating to their MEP?

Knowledge about local councillors

- What is the name of one of your local councillors?
- What level of local government does this councillor represent: parish, district, county or unitary?
- What political party does he or she represent?
- What are the details of your local ward?
  - Name
  - Number of voters
  - What percentage of citizens voted in the last local election?
- What committee does your local councillor sit on?

Knowledge about MEPs

- What is the name of your MEP?
- What political party does he or she represent?
- What are the details of your European parliamentary constituency?
  - Name
  - Number of voters
  - What percentage of citizens voted in the last election?
- What role does your MEP play in the European Parliament?

From the smallest wards, each with maybe only a couple of thousand citizens entitled to vote, to one of the 87 European constituencies with a six-figure electorate, how local is local?

MPs are not the only representatives that citizens elect. They are, however, sometimes seen as the most important and, in terms of media coverage, there is much greater emphasis on General Elections, and the role of elected representatives in national politics, than on local or European politics and elections.

The office rules

There are usually rules that elected representatives have to observe. In the House of Commons the way in which one MP addresses another MP, what they are allowed to say, how they are allowed to refer to others, and how they are allowed to dress are all controlled. Do these conventions or rules exist amongst meetings of other elected representatives?

Try to attend some meetings like your school or college council or your local assembly/Town Hall, or research the House of Commons in order to:

- Find similar sets of rules.
- Do these rules serve any purpose?
  - Do the rules help to maintain order?
  - Do the rules help in the organisation of the discussion?
  - Do the rules mystify the procedures so that only those in the 'club' know what is going on, which helps to deter outsiders?

What do you understand by the following terms and concepts?

- Manifesto
- Delegate
- Career politician
- Devolution

- Legislative power
- Executive power
- Unitary authority
- Elected representative

1 Try to find as many examples as possible of the extent of the Prime Minister's power, listing each element in the appropriate column.

2 This account of the Prime Minister's power will be very one sided. Research all the ways in which the power of the Prime Minister is constrained, listing each element in the appropriate column.

Ability to appoint	Ability to control
• *Permanent secretaries in the civil service*	• *Circulation of Cabinet papers*
•	•
•	•

Constraints on power from inside Parliament	Constraints on power from outside Parliament
•	•
•	•
•	•
•	•

Answers to the mix and match manifesto game (p 233)

Manifesto promise	Political party
• Provide 10,000 more hospital beds	Lib Dem
• Recruit 10,000 more doctors and 25,000 more nurses	Lab
• Recruit 10,000 more teachers	Lab
• Allow patients to choose hospital for their treatment	C
• Cut primary school classes to an average size of 25	Lib Dem
• Reduce road tax on environmentally friendly vehicles	Lab
• Send every taxpayer an account of how their taxes were spent by Government	C
• Raise the speed limit on motorways to 80 mph	C
• Establish stock market linked endowment funds to pay for universities	C
• Abolish charges for dental and eye check ups	Lib Dem
• Recruit 6,000 more police officers	Lab and Lib Dem

The Social Characteristics of a Good Representative – or a Representative that Just Looks and Sounds Good?

The aims of this chapter are to:

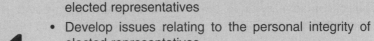

- Develop issues relating to the social characteristics of elected representatives
- Develop issues relating to the personal integrity of elected representatives
- Raise questions about the influence of the styles of leadership
- Introduce issues relating to the ability to communicate effectively
- Question the representativeness of elected representatives

Whenever one citizen has the opportunity to vote for another citizen to be their representative, it is always going to be a very subjective process. No matter how well prepared, how good the political address or how logical the arguments, if the voter does not like their face, their laugh or the colour of their socks, the potential representative might not receive that vote. How and why do some qualities associated with elected representatives come to be approved of whilst others are frowned on? What role does the media play in establishing the qualities that are associated with being a good elected representative?

Personality

One starting point for this discussion is the issue of an elected representative's personality. Like many concepts, the concept of personality is not easy to define. It is, however, something that is often discussed without the lack of definition creating a problem. There is a shared understanding of the concept between citizens; and this implicit understanding of the concept allows it to be used without a problem.

When the concept of personality is used in discussions relating to elected representatives, it is very often used with the implicit understanding that 'everybody knows what everybody else is talking about'; the concept is usable, as it has a shared meaning. When a concept is as generalised as this, however, it can be argued to be of little value in extending any understanding about, in this case, elected representatives. This can be illustrated by applying the concept to any group of citizens. It would not be incorrect to hypothesise that in any group of citizens there is going to be a wide range of different personalities. If that hypothesis is accepted, then in a group of elected representatives there is also going to be a wide range of different personalities. This makes the group of elected representatives essentially no different from any other group of citizens. Consequently, if the concept of personality is to be used in a discussion related to elected representatives, it needs to be used with precision and with caution. It is not satisfactory just to lump all elected representatives together and suggest that there is a specific type of personality that goes hand in hand with being an elected representative.

Since the concept of personality is often seen to be one of the factors that influence the effectiveness of different elected representatives, there needs to be some attempt to refine this concept. One approach to personality would take, as its central focus, the issue of consistency of behaviour over time. In this approach, personality is equated to the predictability of a citizen in their attitudes, responses and general behaviour.

Another approach to personality is based on the issue of 'personality traits'. A personality trait refers to the stable and enduring elements of a citizen's personality and relates to elements like 'sense of humour' or 'being quick tempered'. The problem when discussing personality based around traits is that opinion is divided between those who believe that some personality traits are present, at different levels, in all citizens, whilst others believe that personality traits are unique to every citizen.

The question relating to the issue of elected representatives and personality can be of particular interest when discussed as a comparative concept. In order to be able to describe a citizen as being 'tall' or 'short', it is necessary to compare either one citizen against another or one citizen against the cultural norm. To be 'tall', it is necessary to compare against another: it is a comparative concept. In terms of personality, a citizen can only be described as 'having a jolly personality' if there exists another less jolly or miserable citizen to compare him or her against. One elected representative can only appear to be 'a good leader' by comparing the elected representative with one that does not appear to 'be a good leader', or by using the cultural norms associated with being 'a good leader'.

It is in this context that personality becomes an issue for both the voting citizen and the elected representative. It is not in effect personality that is important, but it is those perceptions about an elected representative's personality, made by all voting citizens, that are of particular importance and often hold the key to the electability of an elected representative, their success or failure in office, and their potential re-electability.

Public perceptions of elected representatives

 To undertake this activity, you need to take an 'opportunity sample'. An opportunity sample is selected from those people who 'happen to be in the way when the researcher is approaching'. The easy availability of the sample is an advantage for you, the researcher, as you do not have to worry about getting a representative sample. However, the lack of representativeness does not allow for reliable conclusions to be drawn easily.

- Select an opportunity sample and ask the following questions:
  - If you had to select five words that you think were descriptive of MPs, what are the first five words that enter your mind?
  - If you had to select five words that described your local MP, what are the first five words that enter your mind?
  - If you had to select five words that described your local councillor, what are the first five words that enter your mind?
  - With regards to any other election in which you have been involved, if you had to select five words that described that elected representative from that election, what are the first five words that enter your mind?
- Once you have your results, they need to be analysed. One way to do this is to divide the descriptions into those words that suggest a positive image and those that suggest a negative one.
  - From this, a montage of the images of other citizens' perceptions of elected representatives can be constructed.
- You will then need to draw conclusions from your results and present them to a wider audience.

Charisma

One term that has come to be widely used to describe some elected representatives is that of 'charisma'. The charismatic leadership of one elected representative is often seen as the key to the success of a particular campaign. Charisma refers to those special features of an elected representative's personality that other citizens consider to be significantly important. There is no logical explanation of the role that charisma plays in the success or failure of an elected representative. The very thing that may appear to be a source of strength in one elected representative is perceived as a source of weakness in another. Before a closer examination of the role of charisma as a source of success or failure, it is important to remember that the media has a role in helping to develop and sustain some elements of an elected representative's personality, or a specific image of an elected representative that helps in the wider construction of how they are perceived by other citizens.

To illustrate how inconsistent perceptions of personality potentially are, it is possible to cite the instance of Tina. Tina is not a reference to an ageing rock star, but the acronym that became associated with Margaret Thatcher. 'There is no alternative' was the strident justification for a series of radical and, for some, questionable policies. However, rather than being viewed negatively as a leader who was too autocratic, this quality came to be perceived as a sign of strength. In comparison, John Major's less confrontational and more diplomatic style of leadership came to be seen as a source of weakness, with accusations of dithering and incompetence. If a politician's charisma is thought to be a significant source of their success and electability, John Major was an exception to this rule, being described as 'a ventriloquist's dummy' by fellow Party MP Sir George Gardiner.

The role of the media in developing or destroying the charisma, personality and credibility of an elected representative can be illustrated with reference to a single night in Sheffield. In 1992, with polling day imminent, and a significant chance of victory, a huge Labour Party rally was held at the Sheffield Arena. For those present, the whole event was an uplifting experience and reinforced the opinion that the then leader of the Labour Party, Neil Kinnock, would be the next Prime Minister. Unfortunately, the edited image repeatedly played on the news programmes was of a fist-waving, smiling Neil Kinnock who, not once but three times, jubilantly and elatedly declared (or asked) 'Are we all right?!'. Neil Kinnock, who described himself in a Radio 4 interview as being 'overcome by the occasion', concedes that the reporting of the rally was a turning point in the 1992 election campaign. As a result of the image, there was a change in voting citizens' perceptions of both the social characteristics and the personality of the leader of the Labour Party, with the ultimate result that Labour lost the General Election to John Major's Conservative Party.

Leadership styles

It is evident that no two elected representatives will have the same personalities. It is equally evident that different elected representatives have or create quite different leadership styles. What is much harder to ascertain is whether it is the personality of the elected representative that determines their leadership style or whether voting citizens prefer one style of leadership to another and, as a result, those candidates whose leadership style is more in tune with cultural expectations, by definition, make themselves considerably more electable than others.

Research the role of the following party leaders and the success or lack of success associated with their party whilst they were its leader:

- Neil Kinnock
- Margaret Thatcher
- Michael Foot
- Paddy Ashdown
- Lord David Sutch
- John Major

There are no hard or fast rules about the social characteristics and qualities that are needed in order to be a 'good' elected representative. For every generalisation that a citizen can produce about the desirable social characteristics and qualities of elected representatives, another will be able to provide evidence that questions the assumption.

The social characteristics and qualities of electability

1 Are these the social characteristics and qualities that make some citizens more electable than others?

- Having a stable home life
- Having good local knowledge
- Having lots of energy
- Having previous experience of public life
- Having a professional background

- Being a good speaker
- Being a local citizen
- Being a graduate
- Being wealthy
- Being from a public school background

- Their appearance
- Their age
- Their sex
- Their religion
- Their ethnicity
- Their sexuality

2 Consider the social characteristics above that are believed to influence electability. Is it possible to rank the characteristics in their importance from 1–16?

Social characteristics or personal qualities?

One issue that is worth brief discussion is the nature of social characteristics and personal qualities. So far, these two component parts to the debate have been treated as a singular item. However, are these two elements different sides of the same coin or are they in fact two quite different coins?

Social characteristics or personal qualities?

 What is the difference between the social characteristics of an elected representative and the personal qualities of an elected representative?

One way to determine the difference between social characteristics and personal qualities is to consider how easy they are to change.

Social characteristics or personal qualities	Relatively easy to change	Relatively difficult or impossible to change
Having a stable home life		
Having good local knowledge		
Having lots of energy		
Having previous experience of public life		
Having a professional background		
Being from a public school background		
Being a good speaker		
Being a local citizen		
Being a graduate		
Being wealthy		
Appearance		
Age		
Sex		
Religion		
Ethnicity		
Sexuality		

Consider the changeability factor for each of the above, and from your considerations decide whether social characteristics are going to be less changeable than personal qualities.

One way in which these two elements can be distinguished is by the possibility of change. An elected representative's social characteristics are going to be less changeable than their personal qualities. No matter how hard any citizen or elected representative may try, they are never going to be able to alter their age.

Donkey jacket and baseball cap

On the other hand, elected representatives have a degree of choice over some of their qualities. Some elected representatives change and some do not. There are even those who did change and then regretted the change! It was at the Cenotaph Remembrance Service in 1982 that Michael Foot, then leader of the Labour Party, wore what was in his view a 'perfectly good jacket' over his Sunday suit to keep himself warm. The dark green suit, purchased on Jermyn Street, was transformed by some tabloids into a 'donkey jacket' and it was said that wearing it was an insult to the memory of the war dead. No political leader in the UK has since been seen in public in a duffle coat! Likewise, William Hague received press attention when he (unwisely) donned a reversed baseball cap during one Notting Hill Carnival, and he has subsequently raised comment when discussing his excessive drinking habits in his youth.

Some political leaders have clearly taken a different view and either have changed or have presented a different image in order to achieve the illusion of change. Unlike the Labour Party leader of the 1960s, Harold Wilson, who was rarely seen without his pipe and was at one stage 'pipe smoker of the year', Mr Kinnock was never on public display smoking his pipe. Another feature that changed about Neil Kinnock was the length of his hair. His red hair progressively got shorter and shorter so that he could avoid any comparison or confusion with the similarly coloured, but longer haired Arthur Scargill. Equally, Mrs Thatcher also altered her hairstyle. With Harold Wilson, there was a remarkably improved appearance to his teeth between the time he became Prime Minister and the time he left the post. Mrs Thatcher also altered her appearance in terms of both her clothes and her expression, and ultimately altered the pitch of her voice.

Public speaking

Ability to speak in the blaze of media attention has long been seen as a desirable quality in elected representatives and although many nationally elected representatives can enjoy the luxury of employing professional speech writers, this is not a possibility for many locally elected representatives or the thousands of citizens who are representatives for a community group in their neighbourhood. Regardless of whose keyboard produced the speech, it still has to be delivered to its audience.

The art of public speaking involves the ability to deliver a message that is audible and understandable; this usually means a slower and a more deliberate style of communication than in everyday speech. Making an impression on an audience is beneficial, but to be able to get that audience to remember the key points of the speech is essential if it is to have a long term impact.

Claptrap

The art of achieving lasting impact from a speech has a long tradition, and any trick that is used in order to make a part of a speech more memorable than another is known as 'claptrap'. Claptrap is literally a device used in public speaking to trick the audience into showing approval through clapping. The meaning of the word has, over time, changed and is now more equated with talking spurious nonsense or rubbish. The case could be made that the word could now be replaced with the term 'soundbite'.

Some claptrap devices are considerably more powerful in getting a message across than ordinary speech. For example, to achieve success, it is best to personalise issues. Elected representatives will tend not talk about 'your choice' or 'your child's education' but will talk about 'our children' and 'the choices we have to make'.

One claptrap device is the use of a three part list or the repetition of a word or phrase, which has been found to be three to four times more successful in getting a point across than an 'ordinary' sentence. Probably the best remembered quotation from the 1997 General Election was the declaration by Tony Blair that the election was all about 'Education, Education, Education'.

Another way in which a representative can make his or her message more memorable is to construct a contrast between him or herself and other representatives. This simple device, which involves juxtaposing two opposites, can make a representative's sentence far more memorable than an ordinary sentence. Just as in a game of tenpin bowling, the skittles need to be set up before they can be felled. To achieve some contrasts, a speaker will need to outline some element of the opposition's policy in order for them to be linguistically felled, a process of 'set 'em up to knock 'em down'. Research has suggested that this device can be 12 times more effective in making a memorable point than an ordinary sentence.

The following extracts from Blair's Labour Party speech, delivered at Bournemouth on 28 September 1999, show a range of claptraps in use:

> People are born with talent and everywhere it is in chains ... For how do you develop the talent of all, unless in a society that treats us all equally, where the closed doors of snobbery and prejudice, ignorance and poverty, fear and injustice no longer bar our way to fulfilment ...

Arrayed against us [are] the forces of conservatism, the cynics, the elites, the establishment. On our side, the forces of modernity and justice. Those who believe in a Britain for all the people. Those who fight social injustice. Those who believe in a society of equality, of opportunity and responsibility.

---

1 How many examples of claptrap can be identified in Blair's speech?

2 Write two different, short speeches on a 'complex subject' of your choice. In one of the speeches use as many of the claptrap mechanisms as you possibly can.

- Read your speeches to the rest of your group, or any other suitable audience, or allow a number of people to read your speeches.

- Apply a distractor to your audience, for example saying a nursery rhyme in reverse (such as full bags three sir yes sir yes).

- Ask your audience how much of your first speech and how much of your second speech they can remember, for example:

  ○ What were the topics you spoke about?

  ○ What were the key points?

  ○ How many of the words can be remembered?

  ○ How many phrases can be remembered?

- Was there a difference between the speech with the claptraps and the speech without?

Making a monkey out of the research

In recent years, a lot of research has been undertaken to try to explain the relative importance of a candidate's social characteristics in helping or hindering their chances of being elected. None of this research has yet assessed the advantages of wearing a monkey costume. The citizens of Hartlepool, however, were presented with this option when H'Angus the Monkey became a candidate for Hartlepool's first elected mayor. Campaigning with the slogan 'Vote H'Angus, he gives a monkey's' and promising little else except free daily bananas for all local school children, the success of H'Angus the Monkey in becoming the first elected executive mayor of Hartlepool, with a salary of £54,000 a year, will confound academic research.

Seven principles of public life

For the Neill Committee, the issue as to what makes a 'good elected representative' can be answered with reference to the seven principles of public life that were outlined in their consultative document. These principles can be summarised as:

Selflessness	Elected representatives should act solely in terms of the public interest. They should not seek to gain financial benefits or other rewards for themselves, their family or their friends.
Integrity	Elected representatives should not place themselves under any financial or other obligation to individuals or organisations that might seek to influence them in the performance of their official duties.
Objectivity	Elected representatives should base any appointments or recommendations on merit.
Accountability	Elected representatives are accountable for their decisions and actions to other citizens and must submit themselves to the scrutiny of other citizens.
Openness	Elected representatives should be as open as possible about all decisions and actions they take.
Honesty	Elected representatives must declare any private interests relating to their public duties.
Leadership	Elected representatives should promote these principles through example.

In order for a citizen to make a decision about their elected representative, the one thing they need is knowledge. Without any knowledge about the activities of the elected representative, how can a citizen decide whether an elected representative is acting solely in the public interest? Information is required in order for a citizen to make judgments about the integrity, objectivity and honesty of elected representatives.

The mechanism that has been employed in order to help a citizen to judge whether an MP fulfils the seven principles of public life is the requirement that all MPs publicly declare their interests. Since November 1997, as a result of the Nolan Report, all MPs have had to make an annual declaration in the Register of Members' Interests of all income generated and will, in the future, have to declare the amount of money received in expenses. The Register reveals that some MPs can inflate their salary substantially through speaking engagements and book deals. In 2002, William Hague, ex-leader of the Conservative Party, declared an income of £200,000 from speaking tours and book rights. Other MPs enjoy gifts or 'freebies'. Theresa May, in 2002, declared that she received three pairs of Hot2Trot shoes from the Russell and Bromley shoe shop. May 2002 saw the development of the Register of Members' Interests when the previously voluntary code of the House of Lords was abolished, forcing all the peers in the UK to declare publicly for the first time their wealth and influence.

Are elected representatives representative?

Are elected representatives different from other citizens? In terms of an elected representative's social characteristics, the question as to whether they differ widely from the general population is, in some respects, impossible to answer. This is because, in reality, nobody actually knows how many citizens are elected to represent other citizens. Even in political circles, the amount of information available differs widely, according to the level of government. There is considerably less information easily available relating to locally elected representatives working in Town Halls up and down the country compared to MPs in the House of Commons.

Age

Within any specific Parliament, there will always be extremes of age between MPs. The minimum age at which a citizen can be elected as a political representative remains at 21, a feat achieved both in 1969 when Bernadette Devlin became an MP and in 1999 when Matt Dixon became the Liberal Democrat local councillor for the Sheffield seat of Netherthorpe.

Matt Dixon became the Liberal Democrat local councillor
for the Sheffield seat of Netherthorpe

When collectively MPs have a wide range of ages, it does allow the claim to be made that a cross-section of citizens has been elected to be representatives. However, upon closer scrutiny any such claim is of limited reliability because within the extremes of age, there is a considerable over-representation of MPs between the ages of 40 and 59. At the 2001 General Election 317 Labour MPs out of 402 were aged between 40 and 59. This represents 79% of Labour MPs, a figure that is similar to the Conservatives' 73% and the Liberal Democrats' 71%. At the other extreme, with only 5 MPs from all parties being under the age of 30, the median age of the 2001 House of Commons increased to 50. Should the fact that MPs have a median age of 50 be a matter of concern to voting citizens? There is no single correct answer to this question. Some citizens would view the age of 50 without due concern, feeling that it is necessary to be 'of a certain age' in order to develop the skills and experience appropriate to the role of representing the varied interests of other citizens. Equally, in the process of selecting candidates for constituencies, the selection committee would need to have some evidence of a degree of maturity and success in a previous career, in order to make a meaningful judgment. These qualities arrive, for some, with age. An alternative view is that the typical MP is too old, too remote and too out of touch with the younger citizen; a view that has been used to explain lower rates of voting amongst younger citizens.

Occupational background

The occupational background of the elected representatives in the House of Commons is particularly unrepresentative of the voting citizens of the UK. Approximately 55% of Conservative MPs after the 2001 election have either a legal or business background, while approximately 23% of Labour MPs have a background in education. Representatives from middle class, professional backgrounds dominate the House of Commons. This, by definition, creates the situation in which working class citizens are very poorly represented, with only 12% of Labour Party MPs coming from a working class background. Percentages for the other parties are too low to be meaningful, with the Conservatives and Liberal Democrats each having only one MP with a working class background. The decline in elected representatives from a working class background is quite dramatic. In 1945, over 40% of Labour Party MPs could claim to be from such a background (figures based on Criddle, B in Butler and Kavanagh, 2002).

	Labour	Conservative	Liberal
Law	31	31	6
Education	98	7	12
Journalism and publishing	32	14	4
Civil Service and Local Govt	30	2	3
Armed services	1	11	0
Other professions	10	11	6
Company directors	5	18	6
Other business	28	42	8
Other white collar	73	2	1
Manual	51	1	1
Other	53	24	3
Total	412	166	52

Adapted from *The General Election of 2001* by Butler and Kavanagh, 2002

The extent of this imbalance becomes clear when figures from the three largest political parties are combined. For these parties, the MPs from 'solid middle class occupations' number 630 and constitute 91.7% of their MPs. This compares, according to the Registrar General's classification of social class, with approximately 34% of all citizens in the UK being from 'solidly middle class occupations'.

The overriding conclusion that can be drawn from these figures is that the body of elected representatives that constitute the House of Commons is not a representative cross-section of all citizens. This is a situation that has been used by some as an explanation for the increasing alienation between politicians and other groups of citizens and a cause of the lack of motivation for some citizens to vote in elections.

Educational background

Educationally, the MPs elected in 2001 are not a typical cross-section of citizens of the UK. This can be illustrated by comparing the educational experience of MPs to that of all UK citizens. However, before this can really be achieved, it is necessary to look closely at each type of school. The three terms most often associated with educational establishments are those of:

- state schools;   • private schools; and   • public schools.

Although some critics feel that 'state schools' derive their name from their poor maintenance, the school's appearance has nothing to do with the term. State schools are essentially the norm; they are the free primary and comprehensives that exist in communities throughout the UK. State schools are required to teach the National Curriculum and are financed, through the redistribution of taxes, by a combination of local and central government funds. State schools are responsible for the education of between 92% and 93% of all citizens.

Private schools differ from the schools previously described in the fact that they are institutions that are essentially financed from the fees that they charge. There are about 2,250 registered private schools in England and Wales. These schools are responsible for the education of between 7 and 8% of the school population.

Although all public schools are private schools, not all private schools are public schools. Public schools are a subgroup of the private school category. To be a public school, membership of the Headmasters' and Headmistresses' Conference (HMC) is required.

There are about 235 members of the HMC, including educational establishments like Eton, Rugby and Harrow. Although public schools are responsible for the education of less than 1% of the school population, it is noticeable that this type of school is most often associated with the process of educating an elite. Two simple examples are that, first, the three public schools cited earlier, Eton, Rugby and Harrow, alone produced 51 Conservative MPs in the 1992 General Election; and, secondly, Eton, in 2001 alone, produced 14 Conservative MPs, 8% of the total, and 18 MPs altogether. In the view of some citizens, however, there is one thing at least to cheer, and this is the fact that the percentage of MPs from Eton is at its lowest ever, indicating a considerable change from the situation of 1945, when 29% of all Conservative MPs shared Eton as their 'old school'.

Due to the fact that the division between private schools and public schools is not always easy to ascertain, many commentators combine the two types and simply refer to all non-state schools as part of the 'independent sector'.

The 2001 General Election produced a set of elected representatives who were, in terms of their education, also unrepresentative of the electorate. The independent sector supplied:

- 106 Conservative MPs from a total of 166, approximately 64%.
- 18 Liberal Democrat MPs from a total of 52, approximately 35%.
- 68 Labour MPs from a total of 412, approximately 17%.

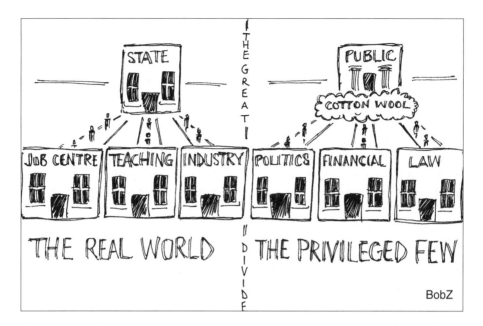

These are percentages that are very different from the electorate as a whole. The unrepresentative nature of MPs' educational background can be further illustrated with reference to their education after the age of 18. Approximately 74% of the three main parties' MPs are graduates, a substantially higher figure, especially when analysed in conjunction with the age profile, than for the electorate. Not only is there a disproportionate percentage of graduates amongst MPs, there is also an over-representation from the universities of Oxford and Cambridge. Amongst Conservative MPs, approximately 79 (or 48%) attended either Oxford or Cambridge. This percentage decreases to approximately 27% of Liberal Democrats and approximately 16% of Labour MPs (figures based on Butler and Kavanagh, 2002).

There are a number of other ways in which elected representatives are often unrepresentative of citizens. Again these can be illustrated through the results of the 1997 General Election. One noticeably unrepresentative feature of the House of Commons is the low percentage of female MPs. Until 1983, the percentage of female MPs stubbornly remained around 3–4% with relatively small increases in both 1987 and 1992. However, since more than 50% of all UK citizens are female, even the election of 118 female MPs in 2001 still meant that only a little under 18% of MPs are female.

Under-representation of women in the House of Commons

This under-representation of women as elected representatives in the House of Commons is more pronounced in some parties than others. Out of the 120 female MPs elected in 1997, there were only three female Liberal Democrats, 13 female Conservatives and two for the Scottish National Party.

Another noticeably unrepresentative feature of the House of Commons is the low percentage of black MPs. This group, making up approximately 6% of all UK citizens, is considerably under-represented amongst MPs. The 1997 General Election produced nine black MPs, all for the Labour Party, which constituted approximately 1.3% of all MPs.

The issue of sexuality is a considerably harder figure to establish, but within a community of 659 there should statistically be a number of gay and lesbian MPs. However, with homophobic attitudes (especially in some areas of the press) making rational debate difficult, only two Labour MPs are openly gay.

Payment for representation

One issue that divides many is the question of whether the citizen who, once elected, is paid to represent other citizens, will be more responsible than one who is not paid. Should any elected representative who undertakes the role of representing other citizens do so out of a sense of civic duty, with the mere fact of being the representative being the reward; or should they be paid? If they are to be paid, the questions arise of 'how much?' and 'who decides?'.

Different levels of pay for different levels of government

There is a startling difference in approach to this subject, with different levels of government justifying different responses. At one extreme, the emphasis with local councillors is that the role provides its own rewards, and there is little or no remuneration. Since the Widdecombe Report in 1986 revealed that the average local councillor spent 74 hours per month on council business, it does not seem too surprising that there are there problems in the recruitment of potential councillors to represent their fellow citizens. With an ever increasing workload and the lack of pay, there is an over-representation of local councillors who are self-employed, retired or not in any form of paid employment.

Although local councillors can claim a basic allowance and their travelling expenses for attendance at council meetings, a study by the Audit Commission established that the rates claimed were very small – just under £2,000 per year. In 1995, the ceiling on the allowance was removed, allowing some councils to pay their local councillors an allowance that reflected the time and the responsibility associated with being a local councillor.

The issue of payments to councillors is difficult to generalise about as these representatives do not have a central authority that regulates payments. However, for some councillors, there have been changes in their workload with new local authority cabinets increasing substantially the workload of a select group of local politicians. These local politicians have a heavy responsibility for local services and attract a payment that is almost on a par with an MP's basic salary. The highest paid councillor was found to be the leader of Kent County Council who was paid £47,000 per year.

Prior to 1911, the job of being an MP was not paid, and until 1964 MPs only received a part time salary. Those citizens who did not have another private source of income were effectively denied the opportunity to put themselves forward to be a potential MP. It is clear that it is only possible to achieve effective representation if the role is accessible to all citizens. If wealthy MPs oppose higher salaries they reduce the scope for representation by the less wealthy. The issue of 'an appropriate rate of pay' for MPs will always be a contentious issue, especially on occasions such as that when, following a successful vote in the House of Commons on 10 July 1996, MPs awarded themselves a pay increase of nearly 30%. In an attempt to avoid similar future embarrassments, as from April 1997 MPs' pay was linked to the pay of senior civil servants and updated annually. MPs voted themselves two further increases on 5 July 2001 which, when combined with their annual increase, brought the basic pay for an MP up to £55,118. This date also saw the introduction of a new allowance called an 'Incidental Expenses Allowance'. This allowance was set at £18,234 and serves to meet MPs' expenditure incurred in the course of discharging their duties. MPs can also employ up to three full time secretarial and support staff for whom they can claim various staffing allowances up to a maximum of £72,310 per year. MPs benefit from free stationery, free inland telephone calls and free postal services from Parliament. MPs also benefit from centrally provided IT equipment worth around £3,000, travel warrants for journeys within a triangle of home, constituency and Westminster, and a car mileage allowance for travel on parliamentary business of 54.4p for the first 20,000 miles and 25.1p for all subsequent miles. Alternatively, an MP can claim a bicycle allowance of 7p per mile.

MEPs are paid at the same rates as their country's MPs. Not only are MEPs paid (some would say handsomely paid) but they can also claim allowances for research and secretarial assistance (£6,400 per month) and an annual amount of £2,100 to travel the world to investigate 'relevant problems'. It is also possible to legally increase their income by claiming the agreed cost of travelling regardless of actual costs incurred, and they can claim a daily attendance allowance of £159 provided they sign in. Remaining in the chamber is not a condition for receipt of the allowance. It is estimated that, with these allowances, an MEP can boost his or her income by up to £100,000 year (*The Guardian*, 17 June 1998).

Easy work?

Although some citizens might think that being an elected representative is an easy occupation, there are many who would disagree. Certainly the dangers were vividly exposed in two very different events which occurred within four days of each other. The then Agriculture Minister, Nick Brown, was attacked at the National Farmers' Union conference – a chocolate éclair was pushed in his face. This followed an attack on the Liberal Democrat MP, Nigel Jones, who needed surgery to repair tendon damage, and over 50 stitches in his hands, having survived a sword attack by a local man in his constituency office. His personal aide, Andy Pennington, however, was not so fortunate, as he died from multiple stab wounds.

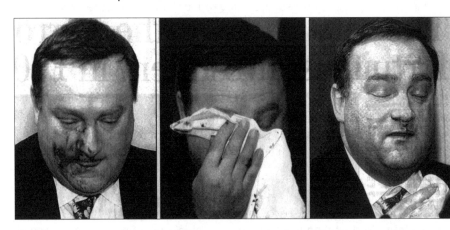

Being an elected representative brings with it a degree of danger

With an average constituency of 150 square miles, the potential for any of the approximately 65,000 constituents to make contact, the time needed to travel to and from Westminster in order to participate in the work of Parliament, and the sheer volume of routine tasks to perform, the work of an MP is not suited to all citizens. The workload is considerable. However, it is not considerable enough to prevent some MPs from taking second, third or even more jobs: a process referred to as 'moonlighting'. When Peter Bradley, MP for The Wrekin, Shropshire, tried to introduce legislation to ban MPs from moonlighting, he discovered that 154 MPs would have to give up their extra jobs. For Conservative MP Andrew Coldfield, this would mean giving up his nine directorships, and for Conservative MP Tony Baldry, it would mean an end to his 2001 income of £1 million. In percentage terms, 66% of Conservative MPs, 28% of Liberal Democrats and 8% of Labour MPs would be affected. Mr Bradley stated his belief that a 'quarter of MPs are not doing the job their constituents are paying them for ... Regrettably for many [MPs] self-service holds more attraction than public service'. He justified this view by looking at the voting records of MPs and discovered that MPs with outside interests had an average voting record of 65%, significantly less than the 91% voting record of MPs with no outside interests. It would appear that some citizens are not being represented as as effectively as they deserve.

One view of what makes 'a good representative' places the emphasis on the citizen's ability to work within a political party, with the 'good representative' being the citizen who will adopt and obey the collective view even at the expense of his or her own views. Others feel that it is simply impossible to teach or train a citizen to be a 'good representative'; they are just born with the desirable qualities. This reduces the debate to a simple question of nature versus nurture. Although some are born to be great, others will learn what is needed to achieve greatness.

To summarise the qualities required to be a 'good' elected representative is an impossible task. To illustrate how difficult it is to try to categorise the qualities needed, look at some elected representatives and try to establish what makes each of them, in some citizens' opinions, a good representative.

What do you understand by the following terms and concepts?

- Personality
- Charisma
- Claptrap

- Public school
- Private school
- Soundbite

Researching locally elected representatives

Try to research the following:

- the educational profile
- the occupational profile
- the age profile

of all your locally elected representatives. Try to get the information for all levels of government – your local councillor, your MP and your MEP.

Question – How much is an elected representative worth?

Answer – They are never worth as much as they get paid.

Do you agree?

Is a 'good' representative hard to find?

In his book, *If Voting Changed Anything, They'd Abolish It* (1987), Ken Livingstone described his joining the Labour Party (in March 1969) in terms of 'a rat climbing on board a sinking ship'. He goes on to outline how, at the small meetings he first attended, he was drawn into the organisation with a series of roles that delivered his first 'taste of unsupervised responsibility'. He describes early election campaigns in which a school hall with 1,200 seats attracted a crowd of two! He continues, describing a sense of excitement at the prospect of becoming a councillor, especially 'for the area in which I had spent my whole life. Now, at last, I could improve the things that I had wanted to change when I was growing up'. He felt he was appropriately qualified: 'After 25 years, I knew the area in detail,' and he was a good candidate: 'My local knowledge gave me a distinct advantage over other [candidates].'

By May 1971, he had become a local councillor in Lambeth and, between 1971 and 1981, he served on a series of committees, until May 1981 when he became leader of the Greater London Council. He remained in this office until the Conservative Party abolished the GLC in March 1986. In 1987, he became MP for the London constituency of Brent East.

March 1998 saw the publication of the White Paper for a London Mayor and Assembly, after which, in August, Livingstone published his first manifesto. In January 1999, he promised to be a loyal mayor and accept the party manifesto and, on 7 September, he officially launched his campaign for the Labour nomination, a position he did not achieve as, on 20 February 2000, Frank Dobson won the Labour nomination. Events moved quickly now: on 6 March, Livingstone declared that he would stand as an independent, leading to his expulsion from the Labour Party on 4 April. By 4 May 2000, Livingstone won the election to be London's first directly elected Mayor by a landslide.

- What evidence would you use to support the view that Ken Livingstone is a 'good' representative?

- What evidence would you use to challenge the view that Ken Livingstone is a 'good' representative?

- Select another elected representative, for example your local MP. Research their biography and present the evidence that would either support or challenge the view that he or she is a 'good' representative.

CHAPTER 16

Parties, Ideologies and Citizens

The aims of this chapter are to:

- Introduce issues surrounding the organisation of political parties
- Develop issues concerning the membership of political parties
- Raise questions concerning the funding of political parties
- Distinguish political parties from other organisations
- Introduce issues relating to political ideologies

At some point in a discussion about politics, you will probably hear the comment that 'all the political parties are the same'. It is important for the student of citizenship to realise that all political parties are not the same. To illustrate this, some citizens believe that all large supermarkets are the same. They all have silver chariots and sell the same or the same types of goods. The layout of the stores is remarkably similar, with the fresh produce at the entrance and the 'daily loaf' requiring a complete circumnavigation of the aisles, thus simultaneously giving the impression of freshness and offering the opportunity to acquire other purchases through temptation or memory. The subtext of the messages is the same, 'high quality' with 'low price', with even the checkouts looking the same. Undoubtedly there are similarities in style, image and organisation.

Although the supermarkets may look the same to the outsider, those in the supermarket trade would be able to point to substantial areas of difference, perhaps including the use or non-use of reward cards, the policy towards employment of part time workers, the development of e-shopping or the provision or non-provision of other financial services. They might also argue that the supermarket's present market position is based on a long history of planning and development. The characteristics of today are the result of a slow evolution. They might argue that they have created their own ambience, or have a greater focus on cleanliness and hygiene, or have developed ways to create a greater impression of value for money. The insiders would vehemently claim that the supermarkets were not 'all the same', a view that could well be endorsed by the serious and experienced shopper.

Just as some citizens claim that all supermarkets are the same, there are those citizens who think all the political parties are the same. However, as both the student of citizenship and those on the inside of politics will appreciate, although there are some similarities between political parties in terms of style, image and organisation, the ideas, characteristics and ideology of each political party are all part of a long, slow evolution which has come to shape the attitudes, concerns, issues and ideas of each political party.

The organisation of political parties

The way in which the three largest political parties are organised is very similar. Since the purpose and function of each political party is the same, it is not really surprising that they should share similarities within their organisational structure. They can all be divided into three sections:

Parliamentary nucleus or core of MPs

Centralised professional bureaucracy

The grass roots of the party:
individual members and constituency associations

One section consists of the parliamentary nucleus, or core, of MPs. These are often the most well known nationally and include all MPs, from the party leader to the most junior backbencher. The role of MEPs is a little less clear. At present, Labour MEPs can attend backbench meetings in Westminster and participate in the voting arrangements for the selection of the leader of the Labour Party. The position of MEPs, by definition, becomes less clear, even a little embarrassing, when, as was the case under the leadership of Mrs Thatcher, there was a degree of Euroscepticism within the Government.

Centralised professional bureaucracies

Another tier consists of the centralised professional bureaucracies, which are sometimes referred to by the name of the building in which the bureaucracies reside:

- Conservative Party – 'Central Office' based on Central Office, Smith Square, London.
- Labour Party – Old Queen Street, Westminster, London.
- Liberal Democrat Party – Cowley Street, London.

These bureaucracies have a very important function within the political party and are responsible for a wide range of activities. Some of these activities are internal activities that each party undertakes. This would include, for example, organising the annual party conference and providing services, like background research, for their MPs. Party finances and fundraising would also be part of this type of work.

A different aspect of the work of these bureaucracies involves their role in public relations. This includes the production of party information, party literature and party advertising. Liaising with the national media is another extremely important function of these bureaucracies.

The bureaucracies also have an important role to play in managing the third and largest section of political parties, as well as providing the link between this section and the Parliamentarians. To be a part of these bureaucracies, however, does not automatically mean that a citizen will be politically active. Not all citizens who are employed within a political party's bureaucracy will participate, as for some it is literally just their form of employment and the employer happens to be a political party.

Grass roots

The final section in the organisation of a political party is the grass roots of the party. This section consists of all the individual party members. Locally, there exist organisations for the individual party members, and these are usually referred to as local or constituency associations. These associations will have their own organisational structure of a chair and executive committee, annually elected at an annual general meeting (AGM). They provide a very important structure in order to fight local and national elections through a wide range of activities that could range from the writing of local newsletters, organising local fund raising, liaising with the local media, all with the common aim of raising the profile of the local candidate, to the more mundane, such as addressing envelopes or telephoning other citizens on polling day to remind them to vote. However, by far the most important function of any local association is its role in selecting candidates for local and national elections. Since, as referred to earlier, some constituencies never change and many constituencies are most unlikely to change in the way they vote, those citizens who are involved in the selection of a candidate have a particularly influential position.

Another function of the local association is to provide a forum for 'like minded' citizens to meet and socialise. Sometimes, however, the need to socialise is greater than the need to be with 'like minded' citizens, with the result that, in some cases, quite vehemently anti-Conservative citizens have cast aside their political allegiance in order to enjoy 'a cheap pint'. Whiteley's 1994 research discovered that some members of the Conservative Party do not attend meetings or participate in political activity; they joined in order to use the social facilities.

Divided loyalties

'Nice beer, hic, shame about the politics'

or

'Nice politics, shame about the beer ... hic'

One problem that arises from Whiteley's research is the difficulty in trying to measure political participation amongst citizens in the UK. The size of the membership of a political party will provide little in the way of evidence as to the extent of political participation amongst citizens, simply because not every citizen who is politically active will belong to a political party and there are those citizens who do belong to a political party who are not politically active.

Size of membership

Even the political parties are less than certain about the size of their membership. According to data from Pinto-Duschinsky's *British Elections and Parties Yearbook 1997,* the Conservative Party, from a high of three million in the mid-1950s, estimated its membership at 750,000 in 1996. Unfortunately, when many of these members were contacted by post in September 1997, a large number of letters were returned as the members had died.

The Conservative Party now claims a membership of 330,000, which is only slightly lower than Pinto-Duschinsky's alternative estimate which put the party membership at between 350,000 and 400,000 members. Membership of the Liberal Democrat Party also declined, from a peak of 98,611 in 1996 to a low of 71,000 in 2000. Membership has since climbed to an estimated 76,000 in 2002. The source of the frankest discussion of a political party's membership figures has to be David Triesman, the Labour Party General Secretary who, in January 2002, conceded that the Labour Party's membership had fallen to a total of 280,000. This is a considerable decline from the 400,465 members of the party in 1996 but is an increase from 1991 when the lowest ever total of members, 261,000, was recorded. These global numbers mask considerable differences in the age profile of those members.

Altogether, only approximately 1.4% of UK citizens are members of a political party, a figure that contrasts quite sharply with Italy's 7.4% and Sweden's 14.5%.

How easy is it to join a political party and is it worth it?

1 Research the addresses, telephone numbers and websites of as many political parties as possible.

2 Compare how easy or difficult it was to find the necessary information.

3 Compare the costs of membership between different political parties.

4 Compare the benefits gained by a citizen from their membership of each political party.

One result of the decline in the number of citizens who are members of a political party has been a decrease in the subscriptions that form an important source of income for all political parties. With the 2001 General Election expenses costing the Conservative Party £12.7 million, the Labour Party £11.1 million and the Liberal Democrats £1.3 million, it can be seen that running a political campaign requires vast sums of money.

Party funds

The whole issue of political party funding has created considerable debate for many years. Until quite recently, it was impossible to know exactly the financial details of the Conservative Party. No accounts were published until 1968. This could lead to the situation in which some citizens became unwitting donors to a political party to which they were ideological adversaries. This situation could arise through donations made to a political party by corporations. One of the largest donors to the Conservative Party was United Biscuits with a corporate donation of £1,004,500 between 1979 and 1993. All companies must declare any political donation over £200 in their annual accounts, and one independent trade union organisation, the Labour Research Department, checks the accounts of nearly 3,000 companies for evidence of political donations. In its latest survey of accounts, the Labour Research Department established that the Conservative Party had received a total of £1.74 million since the 2001 General Election, with the cereal group Weetabix donating £200,000.

By contrast, the Labour Research Department could only trace 12 corporate donations to the Labour Party, with one single donation of £100,000 representing over half of the £191,500 total for all corporate donations. Although often perceived as the poor relation of the main political parties, the Liberal Democrats did receive £1,063,000 from a single source, the Joseph Rowntree Reform Trust.

Another cause for concern expressed by some is the role played by a small number of very wealthy individual citizens who provide financial support for a political party. Although until 16 February 2001 there was no obligation for any political party to disclose either the name of a donor or the size of their donation, the debate about the funding of political parties has recently become more prominent both as the scale of donations has increased and as the source of the donation has become more controversial. For many citizens, the issue is simple. Do large donations to a political party buy influence at the heart of power?

In January 2001, Paul Hamlyn, of the publishing family, disclosed that he had donated £2 million to the Labour Party. He justified his donation when he stated:

> [I make] no apology for supporting the Labour Party in this way. Our democracy depends on vibrant political parties and, for years, the Conservatives had a virtual monopoly on large donations from individuals. I'm glad that has changed and I'm proud of the role I have played in helping the Labour Party.

This donation was followed by equally large donations from the writer and publisher Christopher Ondaatje and the Science Minister and former supermarket boss Lord Sainsbury.

For a political party to rely on donations from individual citizens raises many problems. The first relates to the party's ability to plan. Donations to the Labour Party in the three months to June, according to the Electoral Commission, varied from £3,379,641 in 2001 to £591,052 in 2002. The resultant cash crisis forced the Labour Party to ask the trade union movement for an emergency donation of £100,000 just to pay routine bills.

A second problem faced by political parties accepting donations from individual citizens relates to the character of the donor and how their wealth was generated. Questions have been asked about the donation of £100,000 by Richard Desmond, owner on the one hand of various magazines with a content that would make your teacher blush, and Express Newspapers, publishing the *Daily Express* and *OK!*, on the other.

When such donations are received, the question has to be raised as to whether decisions, taken on behalf of other citizens, might be influenced one way or another by the source of the funds. Indeed, the purchase of Express Newspapers was not referred to the Competition Commission; and after a £125,000 donation from Lakshmi Mittal, his bid to buy a Romanian steel plant was personally endorsed by Tony Blair. These cases reinforce the 1997 controversy surrounding the timing between the donation to the Labour Party of £1 million by Formula One boss, Bernie Ecclestone, and its exemption from a ban on the advertising of tobacco. Ultimately, the only way the party could make it explicit that the two events were not linked was to return the donation.

Such has been the embarrassment relating to donations that the Labour Party in 2002 set up an ethics committee that would vet all big donations. They also require new donors to declare that they support Labour values like the 'promotion of equality of opportunity and the fight against the tyranny of poverty'. The committee also demands that future donors will have to agree to sign a statement that declares they were not making the donation 'for commercial advancement or advantage for themselves or others'.

This form of funding for the Labour Party contrasts sharply with its traditional sources of funding. The traditional source, since the Trade Union Act 1913, was through a political levy paid by members of affiliated trade unions. Although a significant source of funding, this provided opposition parties with a claim that as a result of the source of the funds, certain decisions might be influenced. Indeed the British Election Study estimated that 77% of citizens thought that the trade unions were too powerful in 1979; a figure that decreased to 30% in 1992. A combination of Conservative legislation in 1984 requiring the declining numbers of trade union members to opt in to the levy rather than opting out, and the continuing and undermining claims that the party was 'in the pocket of the Unions', resulted in 'The Business Plan'.

This plan was part of the modernisation of the Labour Party and aimed to widen its financial base through contact with the business world, wealthy individuals and a system of 'blind trusts'. A blind trust was a mechanism that allowed donors to remain anonymous. However, in an attempt to ensure openness and honesty in party funding, new rules were introduced stating that all donations over £1,000 had to be registered and could only be made by a citizen registered to vote in UK elections or a company that operates in the UK and is registered either in the UK or Europe.

The Conservative Party is not without its multi-millionaire supporters. For many years, Irvine Laidlaw and Lord Ashcroft supported the party with substantial donations and on 18 January 2001, the party received the largest ever single donation of £5 million from Stuart Wheeler, chair of IG Index, the UK's largest spread betting firm. Interestingly, by April 2001, there were demands from senior Conservative MPs to amend the Budget in such a way as to reduce the amount of tax paid by spread betting firms. On the eve of the 2001 General Election, another £5 million donation was made to the Conservative Party by John Paul Getty Jr with the message that he hoped his donation would 'enable a new leader to deliver a Conservative victory at the next election'.

The role of Lord Ashcroft is of particular interest, as many citizens express concern at the idea that political parties could be financed by non-UK citizens with the possibility that foreign policy could be compromised. In an article written by D Harrison (*The Observer*, 20 June 1993), it is suggested that prior to the 1992 General Election, the Conservative Party had received £7 million from foreign backers. Under the new rules, these donations would no longer be allowed, and indeed the Electoral Commission forced Conservative MP Andrew Lansley to return a £10,000 donation as the donor was no longer on the electoral roll.

Although both the Labour and Conservative Parties seem to benefit from sizeable personal donations, many citizens are uneasy about the situation as they feel smaller political parties have effectively been squeezed out, and receive considerably less compared to the two big parties. The extent of this difference in donations can be illustrated by referring to donations for the last quarter of 2001 when the Labour Party received £1.49 million, the Conservative Party £1.58 million and the Liberal Democrat Party only £265,000. The extent to which substantial personal donations can lead to suspicion was voiced by the chair of the Liberal Democrat Party, Malcolm Bruce, who expressed the view that the 'reality is that they [the donors] must in one way or another be trying to buy influence'. The Liberal Democrat Party, not surprisingly, has expressed the strongest views in favour of state funding of political parties.

State funding of political parties

The issue as to whether some of the taxes paid by citizens should be used to fund political parties is one that has divided politicians as well as citizens. Many citizens feel that the idea of the state funding political parties is unacceptable. Not all citizens want to participate in any form of politics and do not see why some of their money should go to organisations they disapprove of. Even those citizens who are politically active might find unacceptable the idea of some of their taxes being used to support the activities of extreme right or left wing parties, or parties that want to persecute minorities, or undermine the whole system of representative democracy. The weakness, however, of this argument is that at present, without hypothecated taxes (those spent on a specific cause or project as opposed to going into a general fund), considerable sums of money paid by citizens to the government are already spent on research or activities of which they would not approve. At present the Labour, Liberal Democrat and Conservative Parties each receive £437,500 of citizens' taxes to develop policy. The opposition parties combined receive a total approaching some £5 million in state funding, which includes a sum of over £500,000 for the leader of the opposition.

The debate surrounding the state funding of political parties is an ongoing one, with both the Electoral Commission and the Institute of Public Policy research preparing reports on the issue.

The argument that all individual donations to a political party should be banned, and that citizens should fund political parties through taxation, is seen by some as the only way to ensure that political parties remain independent and protected from media allegations of sleaze.

If such state support were to be introduced it would not be without potential problems. One problem that would immediately be raised is the question as to what constitutes a political party. It could be the case that a minor party is developed with the sole purpose of receiving state funding that it then uses to support another larger party. Alternatively a wealthy citizen could use his or her wealth to found and finance an organisation that qualifies for state funding as a political party even though many citizens would not see it as a political party but as a single issue pressure group. This was the case in 1995 when James Goldsmith founded and financed the Referendum Party with the single issue related to holding a referendum on the UK's future membership of the European Union. With the pledge to disband once a referendum had been held, the £20 million backing from its founder helped the party to put up 547 candidates in the 1997 General Election and achieve an average of 3.1% of the vote in those constituencies (Curtice and Steed, 1997).

Would political parties like the Monster Raving Loony Party ('Vote for Insanity – You Know it Makes Sense') also receive state funding? If it did, what about the 'Fancy Dress Party', which also has a heritage of contesting a number of General Elections, unlike the 'Ronnie the Rhino Party'?

One way to distinguish between these fringe parties and 'proper' political parties is to locate each within an ideological framework. At the core of each of the mainstream political parties is an ideology which, returning to the supermarket comparison, allows those with a more intimate knowledge of the trade to focus on characteristics that make each one quite distinctive from its competitor. These ideologies are explored later in the chapter. State funding of political parties is an ongoing issue, with a House of Commons select committee taking evidence at present. The accepted position currently remains the conclusion on page 93 of the Nolan Report that 'No new system should be introduced whereby the state is obliged for the indefinite future to provide financial support for political parties'.

For many citizens, state funding of political parties would provide a solution to the present inequalities and simultaneously provide an ethical solution to the issue of how political parties raise their funds. Citizens who support the idea of state funded political parties focus on other representative democracies like Canada where political parties are funded by the state, and argue that their representative democracy has not been harmed by such funding. Other citizens point to the example of Italy where the problems experienced in the prevention of political parties overspending their limits led to the abandonment of the system in 1993. Other citizens argue that some state funding already exists in the form of free political broadcasts and the free postal delivery of one election leaflet, along with the funding received by opposition parties and indirect state aid associated with the costs of some research: so why not put political parties at the heart of the democratic process, and let the money from those citizens who have no objection fund political parties whilst for those who do object, a donation could be made to a range of 'good causes'? If citizens then realise that the political parties are spending their money, they may take more interest in how that money is being spent, and any increase in the accountability of the political parties is good not only for all citizens, but also for representative democracy. Both the 1976 Houghton Committee and Charter 88 argue that the only solution to the impression that money will secure influence is to radically change the rules and allow for political parties to be funded by the state.

'It's my party and I'll pay if I want to'

- What are the arguments for the Referendum Party being classified as a political party?
- What are the arguments against the Referendum Party being classified as a political party?
- If state funding of political parties was adopted, should parties like the 'Fancy Dress Party' also be funded?

Issues concerning money go further than just the financing of political parties, and can best be summarised with the description given by Professor Crewe in his evidence for Lord Nolan when he stated that: 'Whenever surveys have asked people to compare various occupations for honesty, trustworthiness or a moral example, Members of Parliament have been at or near the bottom of the league competing with journalists and estate agents to avoid the wooden spoon.' This reputation was enhanced when the Major Government was blighted with a series of incidents that suggested that the motivation for some MPs in public life was not always in tune with the ethics of being an elected representative. By 1997, it was revealed that two Conservative MPs had accepted payments of £1,000 to ask questions and, although this was not illegal (providing, within one month, a declaration had been made in the Register of Members' Interests), it hardly elevated the MPs up the integrity ladder. When this was coupled with allegations surrounding Jonathan Aitken, Neil Hamilton and Tim Smith, many citizens sensed that for some elected representatives, the acceptable standards associated with public life were no longer being adhered to. With both the media and citizens now equating public life with 'sleaze', such an erosion of confidence in the holders of public office had to be seen as a serious cause for concern to all citizens.

As a result of the allegations of 'sleaze', Lord Nolan was asked to set up a committee 'to examine current concerns about the standards of conduct of all holders of public office, including arrangements relating to financial and commercial activities'. Lord Nolan's request to inquire into the area of political party funding, however, was refused by the then Prime Minister John Major. To reverse this refusal became a manifesto pledge of the Labour Party, who stated that they would extend the grounds of the inquiry to include party funding.

Lord Neill (who succeeded Lord Nolan as chair of the committee) produced the Neill Report in October 1998. This report (also referred to as the Nolan reforms) called for an end to the culture of secrecy and made over 100 recommendations. Ten significant recommendations were as follows:

- Ban foreign donations.
- National donations over £5,000 and local donations over £1,000 to be declared in an open register.
- Ban anonymous donations over £50.
- Limit General Election spending to £20 million per party.
- Place a limit on spending for future provincial assemblies.
- Ban blind trusts.
- Campaigning by any other group on behalf of a political party to be limited to £1 million.
- Non-cash benefits (like the loan of a car, computer or office) to be declared.
- Shareholders should approve all donations and sponsorships made by a corporation.
- In any future referendum, there should be equal state funding for both sides of the question.

The reforms also introduced a new post of 'Parliamentary Commissioner for Standards' in order to administer the Register of Members' Interests, advise MPs as to their conduct and investigate complaints. Previously, any misconduct by an MP was judged by a committee of other MPs, who tended to make their judgment along party lines rather than dealing with issues of innocence or guilt. The Parliamentary Commissioner for Standards was to be an independent appointee with powers not only to investigate allegations of misconduct, but also to report all conclusions of the investigation to the Standards and Privileges Committee who would then accept or reject those conclusions. The first holder of this post, Sir Gordon Downey, argued in 'The Commons is not full of sleaze' (*The Guardian*, December 2001) that for the Commissioner to be effective, there must be 'a reasonable harmony of approach between the commissioner and the standards and privileges committee [which] requires a certain amount of give and take'. It would appear that the second holder of this post (from February 1999 to February 2002), Elizabeth Filkin, did not have the 'right' degree of give and take as she was not re-appointed at the end of her contract.

Her departure from the post, however, was not without controversy. During her time in the post, Filkin had investigated a series of complaints, some trivial, others much more substantive. Some MPs fully co-operated with the enquiries; others, however, went to unprecedented lengths to hinder enquiries.

Using the archive section of a broadsheet newspaper, research the allegations of misconduct against the following MPs between 1999 and 2002.

- Keith Vaz
- John Reid
- John Maxton
- Teresa Gorman

- Geoffrey Robinson
- Peter Mandelson
- John Major

An opinion poll conducted by ICM in December 2001 found that 66% of citizens strongly backed Filkin and believed that she was doing a 'very good job'. Political commentators like Hugo Young declared that she had been a brilliant success at her job. However, there exists evidence that she was subject to prolonged pressure through rumour and allegation and her employer, the secretive House of Commons commission, chaired by the Speaker, refused to provide her with adequate resources to conduct her job successfully. Filkin herself writes in her letter to the Speaker that 'the degree of pressure applied has been quite remarkable. In some cases this has been directly applied by members, some holding high office. In others it has been applied indirectly by unchecked whispering campaigns and hostile press briefings'. This conflict ultimately led to Filkin's job being advertised, a move that was tantamount to sacking her. Citizens who are concerned about the treatment of the only independent watchdog that can investigate allegations of sleaze and corruption will be disappointed that the House of Commons commission, which does not keep minutes of its meetings, has decided to downgrade the post. Future commissioners, although having an increase in their power to call witnesses and demand papers, will be part time with a lower salary and fewer staff and facilities to investigate the same number of (increasingly complex) complaints.

Although many citizens felt that the Neill Report went a considerable way towards ending the culture of secrecy and removing many of the problems of sleaze and corruption that existed, others argue that citizens' ability to shape, bend or break the rules still increases in direct proportion to their grip on power or their wealth.

From ideology to political ideology

The notion of ideology, first introduced in Chapter 3, revolves around those ideas and assumptions held by citizens which are used to classify, order, understand and ultimately judge the actions of others. All citizens judge the attitudes and actions of others and, from this, some groups of citizens will simultaneously be in agreement with some and in disagreement with others. The role of ideology is crucial in this process.

If similarly minded citizens form groups sharing the same basic ideas or ideology, this is the base from which political parties can develop. Since political parties represent citizens who share a broadly similar viewpoint, the role of ideology in this process is significant, and it is these ideological differences between the political parties that explain why political policies differ, why there will always be more than one solution to any social problem, why there are different views of human nature, and why there are different emphases on the importance of law, order and liberty. It is as a result of, and within the context of, ideology that all the issues surrounding the link between political parties and citizenship need to be judged and analysed.

Political ideologies develop with a range of interlocking ideas and concerns. These could include discussions surrounding the role of the state and the rule of law, and debates on liberty and human nature. However, since each concern is linked to another, it is not always straightforward to map the route from the philosophical foundations of the ideology to modern day practice of the ideology. The route is further complicated as, in some cases, the same ideology has influenced more than one political party or, alternatively, some politicians of one party, ideologically, might sit more happily with another party. There are many who believe that the former Conservative Prime Minister, Mrs Thatcher, was ideologically a 19th century Liberal.

Liberalism

The ideas associated with the development of liberalism underpin a considerable degree of Western political thought. At the heart of liberalism is the belief in the freedom of the individual. The French philosopher, Descartes, introduced the notion of the individual into philosophy. With the idea of 'I think, therefore I am', Descartes argued that the basis of knowledge must be different for each citizen, since each citizen's starting point was their own individual existence and not the community or other citizens.

The English philosopher, John Locke, developed this emphasis on the individual, as he argued that it was as rational individuals that citizens decided whether or not to make themselves members of a political society. Locke argues that decisions are not made on the basis of emotion, but rationally, using analysis, evidence and proof. Locke also argued that there should not be a state of war between citizens because, as rational citizens, each would be able to see that other citizens should be treated as equals. Locke also argued that natural rights, like the right to life, liberty and property, exist, and these can only be removed by the consent of citizens. The word 'consent' is important. Since citizens are rational individuals, they are capable of making their own decisions. If it is possible to make decisions, why is a government necessary? For Locke, the pursuit of happiness was the greatest good and a government could help to achieve this state of affairs. If the greatest happiness for the greatest number of citizens could be best achieved through a government, the citizens could, on the basis of equals, decide to group together and agree to transfer some of their own ability to take decisions to the government, which would also help to preserve their natural rights and freedoms.

The rights and freedoms associated with this ideology are a citizen's political, economic and legal rights, which include voting rights, the right to form political parties, rights to private property and the right to be treated equally before the law. This last point, he believed, is best achieved when the judiciary is not subject to any government interference. All these elements should sound quite familiar, as they are essential parts of any description of the UK's representative democracy. If citizens are rational individuals, they must have the means to express their individuality. Consequently, another essential element of this ideology is that of freedom. John Stuart Mill, in his essay *On Liberty*, wrote that 'it is imperative that human beings should be free to form opinions and to express their opinions without reserve ... Without making a nuisance to other people'. This, when combined with the economic philosophy of Adam Smith, who believed in the free market, with citizens pursuing their own best interests, became the recipe for minimum government. Citizens should be allowed to do whatever they liked, free from government interference, provided that it did not impinge on the freedoms of others.

Locke's influence on the development of liberalism can also be seen through his opinion that any rational citizen will always hold their opinions 'with some measure of doubt'. Fittingly, liberal ideology does not claim to be the only ideology, or even the true ideology. However, it can seek to justify its ideological stance through open debate. If opinions are always to be held in doubt, then free debate and discussion are essential pathways towards the truth. Consequently, it is essential for freedom of speech and freedom of information, without any form of censorship, to exist. Although Locke believed in equal rights, he also accepted that inequalities in wealth are quite natural. Consequently, liberals tend to see equality in terms of opportunity rather than outcome.

The reality of industrialisation in Victorian Britain, however, challenged elements of classical liberal ideology. It was of little value to argue that citizens had the right to make choices about their lives and the right to do whatever they liked if the reality of extreme poverty made any basic freedoms ineffective and self-help impossible. As a result of this situation, progressive liberals argued that some state intervention should exist to counteract the effects of poverty, thus allowing citizens a realistic option to pursue their freedoms.

As a consequence of this approach, the Liberal Government between 1906 and 1914 involved itself in areas of a citizen's life that had previously remained untouched. Old age pensions and insurance schemes for health and unemployment were introduced at this time. Interference by the state was to increase greatly when this progressive liberal ideology influenced the thinking of William Beveridge and the economics of Keynes.

For a period of approximately 30 years after the Second World War, both the Labour Party and the Conservative Party were partly influenced by progressive liberal ideology. The famous Beveridge Report, published in 1942, provided the plan for the 'welfare state', outlining the role of the state in the provision of health and education services and its role in overcoming problems associated with unemployment and poverty. Keynesian economics required the state to be active in the economy. Keynes advocated that governments should manipulate taxing and spending in order to manage the economy. Progressive liberal ideology was, however, to lose its influence when 'new liberalism', hijacked by the Conservative 'New Right', questioned and abandoned the ideology of the progressive liberals and returned to elements of the classical liberal approach, with its corresponding decline in the role and influence of the state in a citizen's life.

Conservatism

Conservatism is linked to the ideas of politicians rather than those of philosophers. It is associated with figures like Burke, Peel, Butler and Joseph. Like all other ideologies, conservatism has a view about humans and human nature. The conservative view of human nature is seen in the not very flattering terms of being flawed, corruptible and imperfect. Logically, since human nature is flawed, problems in society can simply be blamed on individuals. Human talent, within the ideology, is distributed unequally. As a consequence of this natural unequal distribution of talent within society, there is no point in pursuing policies that set out to achieve equality. The unequal distribution of talent is 'natural' and will therefore always re-emerge.

This view holds that, since citizens will be motivated by past experience, their behaviour will be inconsistent and irrational. When coupled with this ideology's notion of a flawed human nature, this means that it would not be sensible to base any political decisions on the assumption that citizens could be rational and could regulate themselves. Consequently, it is an essential requirement that some organisation created by the state exists so as to maintain peace and order in society.

Peace and social order would not only be maintained by political organisations. Since, in this ideology, human nature is seen as being flawed, corruptible and imperfect, other institutions, like the family, the church and the education system, would be required and would be seen as essential to help maintain social control. There would also be a need to emphasise the power of the institutions of law and order to control a human nature that is flawed.

Another way in which a stable society can be developed is through the ownership of property. Since citizens can only be sure of keeping their possessions in a stable, ordered society, the ownership of property has the important function of inculcating a resistance to change and a respect for the rule of law; which is the basis of all freedoms. Property also has another important purpose, as it is seen as the most important means of creating wealth and distributing power within a society. Property must be defended, as any attack on property is also an attack on the stability of society, the rule of law and also the state.

With its view that human talent is distributed unequally, this ideology argues that those citizens with the talents and skills that are essential for leadership will only be found within a small section of society. There would exist a natural hierarchy of all these citizens, headed by a traditional ruling elite. With such an elite, however, there would always exist the threat that the masses would be alienated by social inequalities, which could result in violent uprisings. To resolve this potential problem, Disraeli, in the mid-19th century, developed the idea of 'One Nation' conservatism. The logic behind this strand of conservatism was that the common threads that unite the citizens of the UK were stronger than the divisions. Although there existed a traditional ruling elite, this elite, with its tradition of public service, had a responsibility and an obligation to protect all those citizens who were less fortunate than themselves. The elite's leadership qualities would enable them to command respect from the masses without creating hostility and, thus, citizens would be united into 'one nation'. These leadership qualities would need to be developed and honed, so there would be the need for a small set of institutions that would help in the preparation of the leadership role for these citizens, a role associated with the traditional public schools and the ancient Oxbridge universities.

An alternative strand of conservatism is 'liberal conservatism'. This approach has the same basic philosophy, but believes that the role of the government in the economy should be minimised. Free market economics without state intervention, with a strong state to maintain traditional values, are the key elements of this approach. Indeed, it was this strand of conservatism that informed Conservative policies after the election of Thatcher as party leader in 1975. In 1975, however, the approach adopted by Thatcher was different from previous Conservative administrations. It was both 'new' and to the right politically, and was subsequently referred to as the 'New Right'.

The different strands of conservative ideology have the common thread of an emphasis on traditional qualities, a society characterised by its emphasis on the past, and slow evolutionary change, if any. The lack of a permanent, formalised, written constitution is not a problem, as an unwritten constitution can slowly evolve, bend and change as circumstances demand. Institutions are important in society, as it is these institutions that help to reinforce the sense of shared norms and values between citizens that in turn help to create harmony. Patriotism and the nation are important, as these allow citizens to unite in their ability to celebrate past successes and glories. If there are not enough successes and glories, defeats and disasters can be transformed into successes and glories in order to be celebrated.

Socialism

It could be claimed that the ideologies of liberalism and conservatism have a longer heritage than the ideology of socialism, because the roots of the socialist ideology emerge from the transformation in British society caused by the Industrial Revolution. The Industrial Revolution allowed for the development of capitalism, an economic system based on the division of citizens into either the owners of factories and land or the workers in the factories and on the land. Socialist thinkers attacked this system, as they believed that it was responsible for:

- inequalities – in the wealth of different groups of citizens;
- exploitation – of those citizens who were working in the factories by those who owned the factories;
- selfishness – through the encouragement and positive support of personal gain and profit;
- competition – which set citizen against citizen;
- alienation – whereby a citizen was removed from the support of the wider community or their family;
- wage labour – in which wages became the reward for working, thus removing any other obligations of the employer towards the workers;

- automation – which removed workers' traditional skills, turning them into 'slaves of the machine'.

In short, socialist thinkers believed that capitalism was responsible for encouraging and developing the worst characteristics of humans.

However, if one system can encourage and develop the worst characteristics of humans, another system could encourage and develop the best characteristics of humans. One consequence of this position is the implication it has for views of human nature. Human nature, within a socialist ideology, is essentially sound and good, but is changed and distorted by society. All citizens are born equal but it is the workings of society that creates differences. Humans are essentially social beings and have the capacity in their nature to live and work collectively and harmoniously with other humans. Human happiness, for example, would not revolve around the competitive accumulation of goods. Competition would only create divisions and be a hindrance to the desire to co-operate. It would be through co-operation that citizens would be able to achieve the greatest good for the greatest number.

If it is society that is responsible for developing the worst characteristics in citizens, a different type of society would create different types of citizens. Consequently, in this ideology there is an emphasis on change that would allow for the development of the more favourable characteristics in citizens. Changes would include an emphasis on greater economic efficiency through long term planning, which would remove the problems associated with the reliance on market forces. Other changes would lead to greater co-operation and the promotion of greater equality. These could be achieved on the one hand through policies associated with redistribution, and on the other through the development of essential caring services.

With the emphasis on the goodness of human nature, how can behaviour that does not benefit the community be accounted for? Within a socialist ideology, anti-social behaviour is caused by economic, social and material (or lack of material) factors like unemployment or poverty, not through flawed human nature. Consequently, if these factors can be addressed, many of society's problems would also be addressed. However, establishing the most appropriate way to achieve change, just as with any broad ideology, has created a range of different interpretations of socialism.

Revolutionary socialists believe that class conflict will ultimately lead to the revolutionary removal of the capitalist system, whereas reformist socialists believe that change is best achieved from inside the system, and advocate the path of being elected to form the government in order to introduce reforms that will gradually change society. Democratic socialists, on the other hand, combine the aim of revolutionary socialists with the means of reformist socialists. For democratic socialists, the aim is the removal of the capitalist system achieved by the introduction of radical reforms after forming the government.

Social democrats believe that it is unrealistic to expect to change society and, as a consequence, believe that reforms should be introduced that will benefit the majority of citizens; whereas Christian socialism places an ethical dimension on the ideology. Rather than placing the emphasis on revolution or class conflict, the emphasis is placed on shared values, values of fraternity and co-operation.

With regard to the Labour Party today, there has been an ideological shift since the election of Tony Blair as its leader in 1994. Prior to his election, the broad ideological base of the Labour Party would have been generally associated with social democratic traditions. Under the leadership of Blair, however, the ideological position of the Labour Party shifted. To highlight and signify this change, there was the increasing use of the term 'New Labour'.

Christian socialism, with its emphasis on ethics and shared values, communitarianism, with its emphasis on the idea of 'community', and stakeholding, with the desire to give the dispossessed a stake in society, have combined to create an ideology for 'New Labour'.

One common link between the varieties of socialism is that, if a desired aim is the transformation of society, the ability to control the state is an essential goal. It is only with state power that policies can be followed that will help to achieve essential goals. One means to help achieve the transformation of society would be some form of redistribution of wealth between citizens, a process that can be achieved through the taxation system ensuring that the more wealthy citizens contribute a greater proportion of their income than citizens who are less wealthy. The state is then able to provide measures like health care, education and social security, that not only allow all citizens to benefit from the wealth of the state, but also work towards the removal of poverty and disadvantage.

A second potential method of achieving the transformation of society so that it would benefit the greatest number of citizens would be to ensure that the economy is planned for the good of citizens rather than for the good of 'the market'. In order to achieve this, control of the economy would be essential and this could only be achieved if important sections of the economy were owned and controlled by the state. In order to achieve state control, industries and services could be nationalised and brought from private ownership to public ownership. Apart from the advantages attached to economic planning, public ownership legitimises subsidy when industries are required to take social factors into account and secures a return for citizens when subsidised industries become profitable.

Indeed, clause 4 of the 1918 constitution of the British Labour Party was committed to socialist goals through 'common ownership of the means of production, distribution and exchange'. This clause was, however, replaced in 1994, when Tony Blair replaced the 'old socialist clause' with a 'new socialist clause'. There can be no doubt that the 1994 clause 4 is considerably more communitarian, but some have raised the question as to whether it is actually socialist.

Paragraph 1 of the new clause 4 states that the Labour Party believes that more is achieved through shared rather than individual endeavour, which will create a 'community in which power, wealth and opportunity are in the hands of the many and not the few, where the rights we enjoy reflect the duties we owe and where we live together, freely, in a spirit of solidarity, tolerance and respect' (National Rules of the Labour Party, Constitutional Rules, Aims and Values, 2001).

From classical ideology to post-ideology

Although the previous discussion will give the student of citizenship a glimpse of the dominant ideological strands, it is worth stating two things. First, there is an enormous amount of discussion and disagreement about the development, roots and focus of these ideologies. Whole libraries exist within the world of political science that focus only on these ideologies.

The second point is that, when the student of citizenship comes to apply these classical ideologies, there is something of a problem. In some cases, there are easy fits between party and ideology: the Conservative lack of support for the devolution of government or for the Euro could be examples. However, there are many cases in which ideology and policy do not match.

Margaret Thatcher, far from preferring evolutionary change, had quite distinct aims and, with her emphasis on individualism, competition and choice, she hardly seems to fit into the classical conservative mould. The policies of the privatisation of state monopolies, the selling of council houses and the creation of schools that were allowed to opt out of local authority control would fit very comfortably with classical liberalism's view that the role of the state should be limited. Meanwhile, the Liberal Democrats' election pledge to increase taxation in order to fund improvements in education would seem to suggest an increase in the role of the state.

The ideological shift in the Labour Party would also question the usefulness of the classical ideologies in relation to the policies of political parties today. Some would argue that a single ideology called 'socialism' is too vague to be able to incorporate all the strands that exist. It could be suggested that the early Labour Party was representative of revolutionary socialism, only to transform into a democratic socialist movement. The outcome of this is to see ideologies as changing and evolving, almost in the classical conservative tradition. The move, then, from Labour to New Labour should not be a surprise. Ideology is not the jailer of ideas, keeping them locked in a specific format. Ideology is the set of plans which the prisoner can read and research and, as a result, go on to select the best escape route.

What do you understand by the following terms and concepts?

- Grass roots
- Sleaze
- Constituency
- Neill Report
- Blind trust

- Political ideology
- Liberalism
- Conservatism
- Socialism

Using, for example, the internet, information provided by political parties, or other sources, such as autobiographies, research the following:

- Which showbiz celebrities have, in the last 10 years, made a substantial donation to a political party?
- Which other wealthy individuals have, in the last 10 years, made a substantial donation to a political party?
- Research the events of November 1997 surrounding Bernie Ecclestone's donation of £1 million to the Labour Party. How could some citizens interpret these events?
- Research the claim that there was a link between financial donations to the Conservative Party in the 1980s and the receipt of a knighthood or peerage.

It is never acceptable for a UK political party to receive a substantial donation from a foreign citizen.

Classical ideologies are of only limited usefulness as a way of understanding the policies of political parties today.

Pick up-p-p-pa donation

- Research the range of products made by United Biscuits.
- Ask a sample of other citizens:
  - If they had ever purchased any products made by United Biscuits between 1979 and 1993.
  - Did they realise that as a result of these purchases they could have been making a contribution to the Conservative Party?
  - Do they approve of corporate donations to the funds of a political party?
- The Companies Act of 1985 obliged all companies to declare any political donation over £200. How useful is this Act in enabling an individual citizen to discover if the corporation for which they work has made a political donation?
- Do you think that political parties should be obliged to publish accounts outlining the source of all donations? Justify your answer.

CHAPTER 17

Popular Political Involvement

The aims of this chapter are to:

- Question the nature of pressure groups and how they differ from new social movements
- Develop issues concerning the role, function and tactics of these groups
- Question the legitimacy of pressure groups in a representative democracy
- Develop issues relating to increases in political participation

One common thread throughout the previous chapter was the central role that political parties play in allowing citizens to participate within the political process. However, there are times within a representative democracy when some politicians get 'carried away' with a sense of their own importance and decide upon a course of action that is not part of any manifesto. Sometimes, a course of action may be technically correct, but for the majority of citizens is basically unjust. Sometimes, the elected representatives follow the rules and procedures but their application is not popular with either the majority or a minority of citizens. At other times, the elected representatives may need to be reminded about their role and, when there is no possibility of expressing disapproval through the ballot box, other forms of political participation become necessary.

Political parties exist to control public affairs and in achieving this control some actions are approved and others rejected. Some citizens may feel that politicians need reminding about what they think is the most appropriate course of action, and set out to promote an alternative view in order to achieve a change in the views of the elected representatives.

The need to exert pressure on and influence elected representatives

In the desire to achieve control of public affairs, elected representatives will sometimes set about a course of action that could have an adverse effect on the lives of some citizens. These citizens may feel that they need to protect their interests and highlight their plight by bringing the implications of the proposed change directly to the attention of the elected representatives.

The only common thread so far is that these citizens have no desire to take control of the policy making process; however, they do wish to exert pressure on and influence over those elected representatives who control it. Groups that exist to exert pressure or influence on elected representatives, commonly referred to as 'pressure groups', are different from political parties in the respect that they only wish to influence public affairs, unlike the political parties, which wish to achieve the control of public affairs. Not only do these groups provide a wide range of alternative views to those expressed by political parties, but most importantly they create a means for many citizens to fully participate in the political process.

 Using a small sample, ask the following questions.

1 What do the following sets of initials stand for?
- NSPCC
- CND
- TUC
- CAMRA
- NASUWT
- WWF
- CBI
- NACRO
- BMA
- UNICEF
- NUS
- CPRE

2 What do the following organisations seek to achieve?
- Shelter
- Countryside Alliance
- Charter 88
- Greenpeace
- Animal Liberation Front
- Adam Smith Institute
- Liberty

3 All these organisations seek to exert pressure on and influence over elected representatives. In what ways do these groups differ when attempting to successfully achieve their objectives?

Questions 1 and 2 above may not prove to be too long or complicated to respond to. However, the last question should prove very taxing, even if the sample includes the odd professor. The reason why this question is so difficult lies at the heart of the difficulty in discussing pressure groups. Thousands of different national groups and countless different and diverse local organisations, each with different and diverse aims, have been referred to by the same name: 'pressure group'.

The somewhat confusing situation exists where the same term is used for a diverse set of organisations that:

- are very well known or not known at all;
- will take either direct or indirect action;
- will consult with elected representatives or will be hostile to elected representatives;
- will be permanent with a full time bureaucracy or temporary without any administrative assistance.

A week is a long time in political research

 Since a week was famously described as being 'a long time in politics', for the duration of a week, select any local or national newspaper and:

- Record all the reports of groups (not political parties) promoting an alternative view to that expressed by elected representatives.
- Record all the reports of groups that are seeking to protect an interest or the interests of their members.
- For each of the above categories, list the differences between the groups under the following headings:

Size of group	Tactics of group	Wealth of group

It is important, before any discussion, to evaluate the role of these groups. Although, for some, these groups can be linked by the claim that they all allow citizens to participate in the political process, for others, these groups not only perpetuate inequalities, but also undermine the fundamental principles of a representative democracy.

Winners as well as losers

In order to explore some of these issues, it is necessary to return to the theme that in any conflict or dispute there must be, by definition, at least two different sets of views, and there will be losers as well as winners. For some citizens, the threat of a course of action by elected representatives will promote frenzied activity to protect their interests (often by promoting some alternative that will directly threaten the interests of another group of citizens) and form a pressure group. If this process is repeated, very quickly citizens form a number of different pressure groups with conflicting aims, interests and purposes.

Since these pressure groups are in conflict with each other, there will be winners and losers and, although the existence of these pressure groups has allowed citizens to participate in the political process, do they allow citizens to participate equally or are they another expression of the inequalities in access and privilege?

Should a representative democracy in which citizens have entrusted elected representatives to take decisions allow those elected representatives to be hijacked by unelected and unequally empowered groups of citizens through the formation of pressure groups? To consider these points, it is necessary to look in a little more detail at some elements of pressure groups.

Classifying pressure groups

As indicated, this is a difficult activity with only limited benefits, the main being that, if it is possible to classify a pressure group as a particular type, it is sometimes then possible to see more clearly the role of the pressure group, understand its tactics and account for its relative success or failure.

Traditionally, pressure groups were classifies into two types. These consist of:

- 'protective' or 'sectional' groups that exist in order to protect the interests of a section of society; and
- 'promotional' or 'cause' groups that exist in order to promote a specific cause, a specific attitude, a specific point of view or a specific policy.

This division immediately runs into a problem because, for many pressure groups, the way to protect the interests of its members is to promote a cause.

Another attempt to classify pressure groups is based on the pressure group's relationship with elected representatives. If a trusting relationship has been developed between a pressure group and elected representatives, the group could easily be in a situation in which elected representatives regularly consult them. These pressure groups are essentially working 'inside' the system and are classified as 'insider' groups.

The opposite of 'insider' groups is, logically, 'outsider' groups. However, nothing is quite that straightforward, as 'outsider' groups can be subdivided into those pressure groups which are outside and want to be 'inside' and those outsider groups that want to remain outside.

The trade union movement can illustrate the changes that some pressure groups have encountered. For much of the time prior to 1979, when Margaret Thatcher became Prime Minister, they would have enjoyed 'insider' status. However, with a different set of values within the government, their status became 'outsider', but trying to get in. This example also illustrates one of the problems of classifying pressure groups in this way. Very often, pressure groups have little choice as to whether they are inside or outside; the owner of the 'keys to the door' determines their position. Equally, as a criticism developed by Dudley and Richardson (1989) suggests, the distinction between some insider and some outsider groups is becoming less clear as the politics of influence can be best achieved when undertaken at different levels.

On the other hand, other groups, like J18 or Reclaim the Streets, not only seek to remain outside, but also adopt strategies and undertake activities that will always exclude them from insider status. It is difficult to imagine many elected representatives endorsing the conflictual activities undertaken by some citizens attached to these pressure groups. Some pressure groups are much more likely to attract citizens who contest hierarchies and flout the cultural codes of dress and behaviour; and, since they are considerably less likely to achieve success, it raises the question of whether pressure groups are just another means of empowering some citizens at the expense of others.

Those pressure groups that are constituted by citizens who are empowered with cultural capital – those whose culture, norms and values coincide with those of the elected representatives – are effectively going to be empowered at the expense of other pressure groups.

👉	Using the pressure groups below, list the ways in which the groups could be classified as *both* a 'protective' or 'sectional' group *and* a 'promotional' or 'cause' group.

NSPCC	CND	Shelter
BMA	WWF	Greenpeace
NASUWT	UNICEF	Countryside Alliance
TUC	CAMRA	Animal Liberation Front
CBI	NACRO	Charter 88
NUS	CPRE	Adam Smith Institute

The role and function of pressure groups

To some extent, the role and function of a pressure group will vary according to whether it is a permanent group or a temporary group. There are many groups that have a limited life span simply because their cause is either won or lost. With the closure of a local railway link, the pressure group TWERPS, the Tunbridge Wells Eridge Railway Preservation Society, was initially formed in order to preserve the rail track between Tunbridge Wells and Eridge. This pressure group would have a limited life span, as the rail track could either be removed or preserved. If the rail track were removed, the pressure group would cease to have a function. The significance in the formation of the pressure group lies in the fact that it allowed all those citizens who wanted the rail link to be preserved to get involved with the project and participate in the preservation. Such an organisation allows citizens to work as group, which helps to further empower them, as elected representatives often take more notice of the collective opinion of a group of citizens than that of an individual citizen.

Sometimes, it is necessary for a pressure group to reinvent itself after its cause has been achieved. This occurred when the rail link was successfully preserved. TWERPS no longer had a reason to exist. However, since the rail link needed further development, TWERPS reinvented itself, which resulted in the birth of the Spa Valley Railway.

The belly button approach to classifying pressure groups

- Select two pressure groups, one that you consider to be an 'insider' group and one that you would consider to be an 'outsider' group
- Find as many images as possible, either publicity images provided by the pressure group or examples of advertising by the pressure group; or develop some images yourself.
- Make a presentation to a wider audience illustrating the difference between insider and outsider pressure groups.

Thousands of pressure groups develop and dissolve, merge or mutate throughout the course of a year, whilst others have become institutions that have a long and distinguished history. These groups have often developed considerable expertise within their specific area of concern and, in an attempt to influence elected representatives, are willing to share such expertise. Elected representatives who need information from a wide range of sources often make use of this expertise when making decisions. Other citizens who use the expertise developed by some pressure groups are students undertaking coursework for their examinations.

Increased political participation

Pressure groups have a very important function for citizens, as they can remedy some of the problems associated with the system of a representative democracy. For the citizen with only the possibility of voting every four or five years, the system raises questions about the nature and extent of participation. With such a limited degree of activity, can a citizen ever really view him or herself as deeply or fully involved in the system? For the citizen, once the election has passed, there are not many ways of influencing any elected representatives. This may account for the view, one that is widely supported by many citizens regardless of its accuracy, that manifesto promises after an election are quickly forgotten, or broken, or simply ignored. Another problem associated with the system of a representative democracy is that, as a result of the basic principle that the elected representative is chosen according to the wishes of the majority, what happens to any minority view? The situation in which minority opinion does not have an effective voice through elected representatives could arise.

Pressure groups can provide a solution to these issues at a stroke. If a citizen joins a pressure group, then membership of that group allows them to participate in the political process not only between elections, but, if the strength of feeling so demands, 365 days a year. The fact that the pressure group might be supporting a minority view becomes irrelevant as, simply through the formation of the pressure group, these citizens will be able to share their views with a wider audience and will hopefully be able to influence elected representatives.

For some citizens, pressure groups allow for wider participation in the political process. This could arise when a citizen who is generally opposed to the policies and principles of a particular political party supports one of its manifesto promises. The citizen may not wish to vote for that political party, but after the election may want to show support for the specific manifesto promise.

Another way in which pressure groups can increase political participation occurs when a specific manifesto promise that many citizens never expected to be activated turns into potential legislation.

The ongoing controversy surrounding rural issues and blood sports can illustrate these points. Many citizens who do not share the views of the present Government, but who would seldom describe themselves as being politically active, have been mobilised to support challenges to the Government's attitudes towards the countryside and hunting. The extent of this mobilisation emerged when, according to numbers provided by the Countryside Alliance, 400,000 citizens protested in London in 2002 as part of the 'Liberty and Livelihood March' to support the 'battle to preserve the rural way of life' which includes the traditional hunting of foxes. Many of these citizens had probably never expected any greater political participation than placing the electoral cross on the ballot paper.

However, the 'Liberty and Livelihood March', organised by the Countryside Alliance, can be used to criticise the view that merely having a lot of different pressure groups automatically solves the problems associated with representative democracy. Where did this group suddenly emerge from? There is not a hundred-year history of commitment to a specific cause as with many pressure groups. Where did it get its money from to be able to contact, organise and mobilise so many citizens so quickly? Who are the leaders of the group? Were they elected? Will they be re-elected? What is the purpose of the group? Were all the 250,000 who 'protested' in London in 1998 consulted, and did they all share the official views of the group?

The reproduction of existing inequalities

With so many questions to answer, it could be claimed that pressure groups do not solve one of the fundamental problems associated with a representative democracy. This problem is that in a representative democracy, citizens cannot actually make policy; they have to make a selection, at election time, from differently empowered elite groups that intend to make policies on behalf of citizens.

Since society contains differently empowered elite groups, pressure groups are also going to reflect these differences in power. Consequently, those pressure groups with the greatest amount of cultural capital and those that represent the rich and powerful are more likely to be successful in achieving their aim than the pressure groups that represent the marginalised, the less powerful, the underprivileged or minority opinions.

Pressure groups, although appearing to increase citizens' ability to participate in the political process, merely serve to disguise the unequal ability that different citizens have when participating in political activity. They create the impression of fairness that allows elite groups to continue to wrap themselves in a poncho of power.

The tactics of pressure groups

The tactics of pressure groups are wide and varied, and there are no hard or fast rules to answering the question as to what are the most appropriate tactics for a pressure group to adopt.

To a certain extent, the tactics that are deemed to be the most appropriate will vary according to the classification or the status of the pressure group. Tactics adopted by insider and outsider pressure groups will differ dramatically.

One tactic that is often seen to be particularly effective in reaching decision makers and raising their awareness about an issue is achieved when an organisation provides postcards that simply require a stamp and the citizen's name.

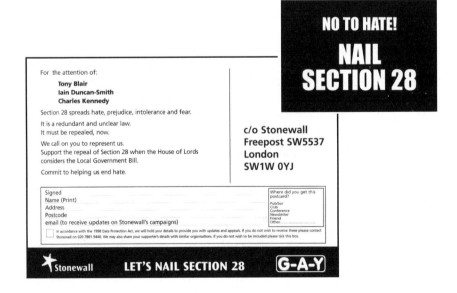

Listed below is a range of tactics that could be adopted by pressure groups.

- Rank the tactics according to how likely you think it is that they will enable a pressure group to achieve its aim.
- Compare your rank order with the rank order of other students. How is it possible to account for differences?

- Publishing a regular newsletter
- Regularly updating a website
- Obstructing the lives of other citizens
- Direct mailing
- Advertising on the radio
- Publishing polemics
- Establishing direct contact with ministers
- Establishing direct contact with civil servants
- Selling 'flags' or other emblems
- Developing and sharing expertise
- The long term enculturation of the aim and objectives

- Writing to local councillors
- Holding public meetings
- Organising processions and rallies
- Causing physical harm to other citizens
- Advertising in the press
- Writing to MEPs
- Involving politicians directly in the campaign
- Advertising on the television
- Causing damage to property
- Writing to MPs
- Taking the government to court
- Developing educational materials for use in schools

A tactic that is particularly effective for insider groups is to reach to the heart of government through contact either with ministers or with those civil servants who are involved with the formation of policy. This arrangement can benefit both the pressure group and the process of government, as it provides valuable detailed expertise to a civil service that is based on generalised ability.

These tactics, all of which are commonly associated with the work of insider groups, are also evidence of the difficulties that some citizens encounter in trying to achieve effective participation in the political process. Those citizens who wish to participate may well find that their ability to do so varies according to the degree to which their ideological aims and objectives match those of the decision makers – or those with access to the decision makers.

Access to decision makers does not only depend on the ideological aims of the pressure group; it also helps if the norms and values of the majority of the membership coincide with those of decision makers. Access can be made easier if a citizen has the right contacts or if the citizens in a pressure group not only talk the same language, but talk it with the same accent.

Inequality of access can result from many different factors. One important factor is the wealth of the pressure group. Some pressure groups are able to 'buy' access through the process of 'wining and dining' decision makers, whilst others will be able to provide an expensive and important piece of equipment that will have, coincidentally, the name of the pressure group quite clearly displayed. These pressure groups may well contrast with those groups that are only able to afford the donation of pens, mugs or the ubiquitous uni-size T-shirt that swallows some wearers, or creates embarrassing stretch lines when pulled over the generous stomachs of others.

Influence of wealth

The differing wealth of pressure groups is further evidence of the difficulties that some citizens encounter when trying to participate in the political process; the wealth of pressure groups often reflects the wealth of the members of that group. One illustration of this inequality is the rise of the professional lobbyist. Professional lobbyists have been likened to the 'English breakfast in continental holiday resorts', as they are expensive, located too frequently in an inappropriate environment, blessed with an excess of grease, and always seem destined to return at some point in the future. The role of these lobbyists, who charge for their services, is to make contact with decision makers and provide them with information about the pressure group. They hope to influence decision makers and then persuade them to support the particular aims and objectives of the pressure group.

The ability to 'buy' access, which is the logical interpretation of the work of such lobbyists, means that the greater the wealth of a pressure group, the greater is its potential to access those key citizens who shape opinions and take decisions. Such lobbyists do not increase the ability of some citizens to take an active part in the political process but actively work against it, due to the costs involved in the employment of such a lobbyist.

The relationship between many elected representatives and pressure groups is so cosy that, for many citizens, it would be virtually impossible to identify any form of opposition between them. Although this might be true for many established pressure groups, the same cannot be said, however, for many outsider pressure groups. Some of these outsider pressure groups are so far outside that to describe them as a 'pressure group' stretches the usage of the term beyond acceptable limits; these groups are often referred to as a 'social movement'.

New social movements

A 'social movement' is defined by Giddens (*Sociology*, 2002) as 'a collective attempt to further a common interest, or secure a common goal, through collective action outside the sphere of established institutions'. Social movements have their own history, and organisations such as Greenpeace, Friends of the Earth and CND could initially have been regarded as social movements. However, as these organisations become increasingly a part of the political mainstream, other social movements are developing with new agendas and new tactics, making it necessary to talk in terms of 'new social movements'.

These new social movements can be very small, with relatively few members, or essentially multi-national operations. They can operate either within the law or outside the law. They have diverse aims and methods, seeking to achieve either long term and far reaching structural change or partial change for individual citizens. New social movements are not easy to classify.

One way to distinguish new social movements from pressure groups is to focus on three potential differences. These are the profile of the potential membership, the use of direct action and the lack of the conventionally defined characteristics of an organisation.

In terms of the profile of the membership, activists within a new social movement are often characterised by their ability to contest the cultural codes of appearance. This counter-culture, or DIY culture, provides a high-profile means of visibly separating the activist from other citizens.

- Ask a small sample of people to describe the appearance of a 'typical eco warrior'.

- Select a range of pictures that have been published of members of a new social movement. Do they conflict with the stereotype constructed from your sample?

The desire or opportunity to contest cultural codes of appearance is not evenly spread amongst citizens. One approach towards explaining this unevenness is suggested by I Welsh (*New Social Movements*, *Developments in Sociology,* Vol 17, 2000), who contrasts those citizens who are 'bound to the treadmill of paid employment, pursuing either basic economic survival or career advancement' with those who possess 'the vital spark of youth [with] its wilful capacity to act now in the pursuit of the seemingly impossible'. His suggestion, clearly, is that, through either a biological lack of years or a cultural concept of youthfulness, some citizens are in a position to contest cultural codes of appearance more easily; and that the same citizens are more likely to be predisposed to direct or non-parliamentary action as their means of political participation.

Direct action

Direct action consists of those activities that citizens undertake in order to demonstrate or obstruct and thereby realise maximise publicity. Direct action is associated with individual citizens like 'Swampy', whose fame rests on his involvement in tunnelling at various road-building sites. Direct action can also be linked to larger protests that appear to be spontaneous. This spontaneity is largely achieved through the employment of modern technology. Through the internet, groups are able to access and share information instantly whilst mobile phones allow instant deployment to maximise effectiveness. One illustration of this effectiveness can be seen in the way that an extremely small number of seemingly unorganised citizens were able to disrupt the movement of fuel during September 2000 through the blockading of fuel depots and refineries and the disruption of traffic. The result of their action was considerable, with the supply chain almost breaking. In this case direct action worked as a means to gain publicity, and although those taking part in the fuel protests would claim not to be breaking any laws, there will, however, also be a smaller core of citizens who are prepared to go further and seek to achieve greater publicity through the use of illegal or violent action.

Lack of a formal structure

Another difference between new social movements and pressure groups relates to the differences in the formal structure of the group. Whereas many pressure groups have all the components of an organisation, with an executive, a bureaucracy and a mass membership, many new social movements lack the conventions of an organisation and appear to be 'non-' or 'dis-' organised.

The possibility of mobilising a 'non-' or 'dis-' organised group that lacks a leader, that lacks a bureaucracy but does have a mass membership, is achievable as the result of the increasing ability to communicate through electronic equipment coupled with the internet. With the potential, through globalisation, for a vast pool of participatory UK citizens and non-UK citizens, new social movements provide a very different stage on which to allow citizens to participate in the politics of protest.

In terms of effectiveness, 'non-' or 'dis-' organised groups provide many advantages to their activists. The non-structure emphasises the anarchic, anti-hierarchical approach and, without a recognisable Headquarters or a membership list, both infiltration and policing become more difficult.

The tactics listed below are some of the ways in which a group can achieve its aims. From the list, select the tactics that are most likely to be described as either direct or extra-Parliamentary action.

- Direct mailing
- Advertising on the radio
- Publishing polemics
- Establishing direct contact with ministers
- Establishing direct contact with civil servants
- Selling 'flags' or other emblems
- Developing and sharing expertise
- The long term enculturation of the aim and objectives
- Taking the government to court
- Developing educational materials for use in schools

- Publishing a regular newsletter
- Regularly updating a website
- Obstructing the life of other citizens
- Causing physical harm to other citizens
- Advertising in the press
- Writing to MEPs
- Involving politicians directly in the campaign
- Advertising on television
- Causing damage to property
- Writing to MPs
- Writing to local councillors
- Holding public meetings
- Organising processions and rallies

- Research the events that took place in the City of London on 18 June 1999.
- Research the events that took place in Seattle during November 1999.
- Can any comparisons be drawn between these sets of events?

From Friday 18 June 1999 to May Day demonstrations

For those who were employed in the City of London, it was common knowledge that there was to be, on 18 June 1999, a 'Carnival Against Capitalism' throughout the day. Many offices, either as a means of participation or as a form of disguise, advised office staff to 'dress down' and to leave the three-piece suits or twin sets in the wardrobe, replacing them with a 'smart casual' look.

What very few citizens predicted was that, by time the 'carnival' was over, there would be many arrests, 150 injuries, considerable damage and the fiercest riots for nearly a decade.

June 18 was said to represent a new form of protest, consisting of carefully planned and co-ordinated direct action by hundreds of protest groups who, through the use of internet websites, bulletin boards and discussion groups, were able to deliver the 'stealth protest'.

Even the tactics adopted on the day differed from those generally used by pressure groups. Originating from just one internet site, www.j18.org, a cellular approach was adopted in which one cell does not know what the other cells are doing. This creates an appearance of unorganised spontaneity, with the reality being the opposite. Highly planned, highly organised and global in context, new social movements, without identifiable structures or organisers, provide an alternative way for some citizens to participate within political processes.

To some extent, this approach to protest has become formularised as there have been repeated May Day anti-capitalist protests, especially in London. Recently these demonstrations have culminated in conflict between police and demonstrators and, in 2001, considerable damage to property. Both sides have developed tactics, the protesters suggesting that protest will be fluid and spontaneous with events happening everywhere at once, without a fixed starting point or finish. On the other hand, police dressed in riot gear encircle groups of protesters to contain movement, and use their power under the Criminal Justice and Public Order Act 1994 to demand that citizens remove any facial coverings.

Can popular political participation ever be successful?

The good news is that any citizen or group of citizens involved with any form of popular political participation has the potential to be successful. The bad news, however, is that some citizens or groups of citizens are much more likely to experience success than others.

Before the reasons for the differences in the likelihood of success can be drawn together, it necessary to consider the issue of 'success'. At what point is a citizen's participation deemed successful? The answer to this question lies in the aims of the individual citizen. With reference to the construction of the road intended to bypass the town of Newbury, citizens' participation took a number of different forms. Some 5,000 citizens, on 11 February 1996, peacefully walked the proposed route, a visible sign of disapproval for the authorities and a visible sign of support to those protesters living in tree houses. By January 1997, however, just over 900 citizens had been arrested at the site on the grounds of aggravated trespass or obstructing the Sheriff in his duties.

Since it is now possible, on some occasions, for some citizens to drive the length of the bypass (although on other occasions citizens will still be subjected to a queue and may contemplate the need for a bypass to the bypass), were those citizens who were participants in any of the different forms of activity successful?

For those citizens who campaigned for the bypass, the answer will be positive: the bypass now exists. For those citizens who campaigned against the building of the road, if their objective was to stop the building of the road, the answer is obviously that the campaign was not successful. However, since in reality there was only a very slim chance of stopping the construction of the road, for many participants, the objective was to raise awareness about environmental issues, the loss of woodland, heath and water meadow, or to raise awareness of the long term implications of continual road building. The active participation by citizens was extremely successful in this context, elevating the issue from a local to a national stage and helping, through national news coverage, to place all the issues on the national agenda. Success, then, is not only dependent on the outcome of any form of participation, but can also lie in the aims and objectives of the group or the individual participants involved in the activity.

For some, the question as to whether popular political participation can ever be successful is not the correct question to ask, as any form of political participation by any number of citizens is a success for democracy. This is especially true when used as evidence that citizens are actively interested in politics. Although participation in the conventional forms of political activity like voting may be declining, the increase in less conventional forms of popular political participation may actually represent a change in culture and indicate one way in which interest in politics and democracy might be revitalised.

'Would Ma'm agree that one's small number of "subjecti horribiles" do not deserve an equal chance of success?'

For those citizens who are members of MA'M, the Movement Against the Monarchy, the Queen's Golden Jubilee celebrations provided an ideal time for political participation. However, those citizens who took the opportunity to actively participate in the group's activities may well question both the democratic nature of modern Britain and the likelihood of a successful outcome to a citizen's political participation. Many citizens would question whether the chances of success are evenly distributed between citizens. This can be illustrated by looking at MA'M, whose members were arrested and held for five hours during the Queen's Jubilee celebrations in June 2002. The members of MA'M had held a peaceful 'Execute the Queen' street party and were, according to their spokesperson, Mr Brandon, 'sitting in the pub having a drink' when they were arrested, held for five hours and then released. One conclusion that the student of citizenship can draw from this example is that although considerations like the size of the membership, whether the organisation occupies a monopoly in the field and the organisational skill of the group are important, the likelihood of success is conditional on two overriding considerations: culture and wealth.

The closer the correspondence between the aims and values of the group and those of the rest of society, the media and the decision makers, the greater the likelihood of a sympathetic response and successful outcome of any political participation.

If the inequalities associated with the distribution of wealth are added to these cultural factors, it becomes clear that some pressure groups and some forms of political participation are considerably less likely to succeed than others.

What do you understand by the following terms and concepts?

- Pressure group
- Groups to promote
- New social movement
- Groups to protect
- Counter culture
- Insider/outsider groups
- Direct action

Elected representatives that have been entrusted to take decisions by citizens should never be allowed to be influenced by unelected and unequally empowered pressure groups.

The inevitable combination of cultural differences and other inequalities will always result in some citizens being less able to participate successfully in political processes.

1 Research some local pressure groups and try to group them in terms of:

- local pressure groups that were successful but no longer exist;
- local pressure groups that were not successful and no longer exist;
- groups that were successful and have had to change as a result of their success.

2 Do the pressure groups that were successful represent the interests of a majority of citizens or a minority of citizens?

3 Select a well known pressure group and apply the following questions to that group:

- What is the history of the group?
- When was the group founded?
- Who founded the group?
- Why was the group founded?
- Where was the group founded?

4 What is the purpose of the group?

- Does it have a constitution?
- Does it have a set of aims and objectives?

5 How affluent is the group?

- What is its main source of income?
- Does it have an investment portfolio?
- Does it have an ethical investment policy?
- Who are the leaders of the group?

6 Who has ultimate responsibility for decisions about the group?

- Are the leaders elected?
- Will they be re-elected?
- How many members voted in the election of the leaders?

7 What is the percentage of members that vote in decisions about policy?

8 How does the group communicate with its membership?

9 How can the members communicate with the leaders of the group?

From your results, what can you conclude? (Apart from the issue of how easy or difficult was it to find the answers to these questions.)

Part 3

The Citizen, Society and the Community

INTRODUCTION

The underlying context of Part 3 is the debate that has as its central focus the issue of empowerment. Empowerment of citizens is a key issue within the study of citizenship, and one issue that needs to be discussed is why some citizens have more power and influence than others. What is the role of socialisation, the process of learning society's norms, values and culture, in the creation of differently empowered citizens? Do the media influence the degree of empowerment enjoyed by some citizens, or is it all a process of natural selection? These are the essential questions that form the backbone of Part 3.

CHAPTER 18

Social Influences on the Creation of Differently Empowered Citizens

The aims of this chapter are to:

- Raise questions surrounding elitism
- Assess the importance of socialisation in the creation of differently empowered citizens
- Explore links between empowerment and a citizen's identity

The 'old boy network'

In his illuminating article, 'Power, glory and the advance of the Old School Tie' (*The Times*, 24 April 1997), Jason Cowley provides an account in which he outlines the influence that a citizen's upbringing and socialisation can have on their ability to participate equally in society. Cowley suggests that the ability to participate equally is compromised by the informal 'old boy network'. The 'old boy network' refers to the combination of family connections, the 'right' school and the 'exclusive' university that combine to give some citizens 'cultural capital'. Cultural capital is a concept developed by the contemporary French sociologist Pierre Bourdieu and applies to those citizens who are more integrated into the dominant value system and the dominant culture. As a result of this integration, they are more successful, not only in education, but in all life chances; a point made previously by Walter Ellis, in his book *The Oxbridge Conspiracy* (1994), when he suggested that Oxbridge students 'are still apprenticed rigorously to the establishment'. Cowley develops the issue of cultural capital in his article, and quotes a 'City headhunter' who graphically describes the way in which the process of socialisation within the family can still play a significant part in developing cultural capital, with all its influence on a citizen's ability to participate equally:

> Although we recruit outside what we call the establishment, we prefer public school types, not because they are cleverer, though they often are, but because their background offers them so many natural advantages. Their education is rounded. They can talk, they know how to conduct themselves at dinner, they can choose a good bottle of wine, they have sophisticated interests, they have been to interesting and unusual places.

Their families have usually been successful for several generations and so they are used to mixing with top people. They are not fazed by wealth or privilege. At least 85% of the people we place are of this ilk. It takes a special person to have none of their advantages and still break into the inner circle that runs the country.

Are some citizens born with privileges?

© Crocodile Photos

In order to put this argument into context, it is worth trying to establish the extent to which the combination of family, school and university can create citizens who are more able to participate effectively in society. To take two examples, at the start of 2001 in the House of Commons there were more MPs from the same school (43), Eton, than female MPs (42). In numerical terms, a single school for approximately 1,290 boys produced more MPs than a population of approximately 32 million females. This does, however, represent some progress from the days of the Macmillan Government, which managed to achieve a Cabinet consisting of over 90% 'Old Etonians'.

Elitism

The debate surrounding elitism moved to the top of the news agenda after a speech made by Gordon Brown on 25 May 2000 blamed the 'old boy network' for Oxford University's refusal to award a place to a state-educated student from Tyneside, Laura Spence. This debate was intensified when the Sutton Trust, a philanthropic educational body, published a report on 5 June 2000 concluding that even when equal grades have been achieved, students from independent schools are 25 times more likely to gain a place at the so-called 'top' 13 universities. The report suggested that future members of the elite were drawn from an 'extraordinarily narrow field', stating that 40% of the entry to Oxbridge came from the 7% of students who attended independent schools.

The debate surrounding the 'cosy elitism' within education surfaced again in March 2002 when Tony Blair claimed that snobbery lay behind the criticism of his Government's target that by 2010, half of all citizens under 30 would receive higher education. He also stated that he believed that since there was 'no proper vocational route and no proper educational opportunities', the majority of young citizens today receive only a second class education whilst a small minority receive the best academic education.

The 'drop out society'

In contrast to the elite described above, the National Youth Agency produced a report entitled *The Drop Out Society* (1995), which focused on those citizens it describes as 'aimlessly drifting, with no apparent purpose in life, no sense of attachment to mainstream society, with ever diminishing prospects of employment, and likely to be involved in criminal activity'. It went on to conclude that many of the opportunities that the majority of citizens would regard as essential, opportunities that include education, qualifications, training, work, career prospects, and a secure future, are 'irrelevant' to them.

The 250 children in the study lived on three estates in the North East of England and mostly attended the same secondary school. The school, with 70% of its pupils receiving free school dinners, has a truancy rate five times the national average. Twenty per cent of pupils leave without any qualifications and its GCSE results are amongst the worst in the country. Every year, when the children first enter the school, reading tests reveal that over 50% have reading ages of two or more years below their chronological age. It is important to point out that the school is *not* described by Ofsted as a failing school; it is doing a good job.

Effective participation linked to socialisation

Why is it that this school, unlike the establishments discussed earlier, appears to be producing not the next generation of MPs but the next generation of the underclass? The answer again lies in the importance of the process of socialisation, as it is this process that influences a citizen's upbringing and will ultimately have an influence on their ability to participate in society.

The combination of material and cultural factors during the process of socialisation play a significant role in the creation of a citizen's identity. These factors have an influence on a citizen's ability to participate in society. Complete the following table, suggesting, with reasons, how material factors and cultural factors can have an influence during the process of socialisation.

	Material factors	Cultural factors
Positive influences on the process of socialisation		
Negative influences on the process of socialisation		

The debate suggests that the impact of socialisation is of fundamental importance in influencing the citizen's ability to participate effectively in both the local community and wider society. The focus of this discussion so far has been on the impact of socialisation within families, and the weight of evidence would indicate that families are arguably crucial in the creation of a citizen's identity. However, a citizen's identity is constructed around a complex web of attitudes towards their social class, sex, sexuality, ethnicity and age, all of which help to create differently empowered citizens. These attitudes derive not only from the influence of a citizen's family, but also from wider society and in particular the influence of the mass media. In fact, many feel that it is the mass media that helps to create the labels and stereotypes that have a direct influence on the citizen's ability to participate effectively in the local community and wider society. These influences ultimately result in the creation of differently empowered citizens. However, before continuing the discussion, it will be useful to answer the following question.

Does the citizen's social class, sex, sexuality, ethnicity and age have any influence on his or her ability to participate successfully in society?

To draw a conclusion from this activity it is necessary to complete the grid for the people listed below. Describe in simple terms the characteristics of the following:

	Sex	Social class	Sexuality (assumed)	Ethnicity	Age (approx)
Prime Minister					
Leader of the Opposition					
Governor of the Bank of England					
Governor of the BBC					
Any of the Law Lords					
General Secretary of the TUC					
An Editor of a national broadsheet newspaper					
Lord Chancellor					
Archbishop of Canterbury					

What conclusion can be drawn from the findings?

Empowerment linked to class, sex/gender, sexuality, ethnicity and age

This activity provides the student of citizenship with an opportunity to look at a number of successful participants in society and plot some of their characteristics against a range of different criteria. One question that might be raised is, 'why those characteristics?'. Why not a characteristic like whether they are left or right handed? The reason why the characteristics in the question box have been chosen is because they are felt to be fundamentally important in their ability to influence a citizen's life chances. (If the research had been related to sport, the issue of whether somebody was left or right handed would be very relevant, because of the disproportionate percentage of successful left handed sports people in those sports like cricket that need hand/eye co-ordination.) Not only are those characteristics felt to be of fundamental importance in influencing a citizen's life chances, but there is considerable evidence to support the view that social class, sex/gender, sexuality, ethnicity and age have an influence on a citizen's ability to participate successfully in society. Before taking the debate forward, it is necessary to establish some degree of clarity regarding these categories.

Social class

This term is widely used to divide society into different sections. These divisions are usually based on economic considerations like income or wealth, because it is these that influence a citizen's lifestyle and life chances. Citizens may be categorised as being either 'middle class' or 'working class', or may be divided into groups that are then given a label. These labels usually take the form of letters and numbers (A, B, C1, C2, D or E) or just numbers (1, 2, 3, 4 or 5).

There is enormous variation in approaches to social class. In response to the first approach above, some would argue that the division into just the two groups of 'middle class' and 'working class' excludes citizens at the extremes and should include the two 'u' groups, the 'underclass' and the 'upper class'. Many critics would demand that citizens should be divided into nine groups. Others would argue that social class is an ideology, not just a matter of economics, and can only be approached through the study of the writing of people like Marx or Weber.

Sex/gender

Sex and gender are two words that are often used as alternatives to each other. However, the two words do have quite distinct and different meanings. Many do not realise this, which results in the frequent misuse of the word 'gender'.

- 'Sex' refers to the unchanging, universal, biological division of people into either male or female based on an individual's reproductive capacity.
- 'Gender' refers to the changing, socially constructed, cultural behaviour that is described as either masculine or feminine.

There is no logical reason why a citizen's sex should have an influence on their ability to participate successfully in society. However, due to a combination of factors, there exists a cultural legacy within society that still influences the decisions and assumptions that many citizens make about the appropriateness of their participation or the appropriateness of their ambitions.

Sexuality

The term 'sexuality' can be used in the context of how a citizen feels personally, in terms of their desires and emotions. Alternatively, it can relate to the nature of the attraction between citizens. This attraction can take the form of either mixed sex attraction or same sex attraction. It is in this latter context that the term is significant, because the attitude towards those citizens who favour same sex relationships often has an influence on those citizens' ability to participate successfully in society.

Ethnicity

Ethnicity refers to a common cultural identity shared by particular citizens. This could be because they belong to a particular community or because they share common cultural traditions. The key feature of ethnicity is that of the learned, shared behaviour that defines culture. Again, this term is often incorrectly used, as it is often applied exclusively to those citizens who are differentiated by skin colour. The term that correctly applies to the biological differences based on skin colour is 'race'.

The elements of common culture that would create an ethnic group could include one of, or a combination of, the following: common language, common religion, common social norms and values and common dress. There are numerous ethnic groups living in the UK that have long established communities. Some of these communities would include the Irish, the Italians, the Greek Cypriots, the Jamaicans, the Pakistanis, the Australians and the French. Although ethnicity should not be an influence on a citizen's ability to participate successfully in society, the reality for some ethnic groups is very different.

If the rights and opportunities that are available to other citizens are effectively denied to an ethnic group, this discrimination can result in those citizens feeling rejected, increasingly isolated and apathetic. These conditions will have an influence on those citizens' ability to participate successfully in society.

Age

At last, a term that is not complicated. Age refers to a citizen's chronological years, although to describe somebody as 'old' or as 'elderly' is making a subjective statement. The only context in which age can directly influence a citizen's ability to participate in society is where some citizens are excluded from certain roles on the grounds that they are too young or too old.

There is evidence to suggest that opportunities that are open to some citizens are effectively being denied to others of a certain age. At present, age discrimination is still legal, but can result in some citizens feeling rejected when employment opportunities are substantially reduced.

What do you understand by the following terms and concepts?

- 'Old boy network'
- Socialisation
- Elitism
- Cultural capital
- Underclass

It's not what you know but who you know that really counts.

The discussion relating to the issue of the influence of social class, sex/gender, sexuality, ethnicity and age on a citizen's ability to participate successfully in society still produces considerable disagreement and confusion.

To appreciate some of these debates, complete the following.

Social class

Research the following approaches to defining the term 'social class'.

- the Registrar General's definition;
- the standard occupational classification;
- the Surrey occupational class scheme.

Gender

Gender refers to behaviour that is described as either masculine or feminine. Research examples of behaviour described as feminine and masculine:

- that has changed in the last 30 years;
- that has changed in the last 100 years;
- that is different in another culture.

Sexuality

Research the following:

- the ruling by the Law Lords on 28 October 1999 establishing that a homosexual couple in a stable relationship can be defined as a family;
- the history of 'clause 28'.

Ethnicity

- take a range of textbooks which discuss social issues and try to find examples of where the term 'ethnicity' has been used instead of the term 'race';
- repeat the exercise using newspapers as the source of error.

Age

Research the following:

- the age limits associated with a citizen being able to become an elected representative of other citizens;
- the age limits associated with a citizen being deemed to be 'too old to be competent';
- the unemployment and re-employment rates for citizens under the age of 40 and for citizens over the age of 40.

To what extent do some citizens, or groups of citizens, share the following characteristics?

The information for this activity can be found in political and sociological textbooks.

Citizens/groups of citizens	Family	Type of school	Particular school	University
Conservative MPs				
Labour MPs				
Liberal Democrat MPs				
High Court judges				
Civil Service permanent secretaries				
Chairs of major clearing banks				

CHAPTER 19

Role of the Media in Creating and Maintaining a Citizen's Identity

The aims of this chapter are to:

- Develop an understanding of the relativity of knowledge
- Assess strengths and weaknesses of different models used to understand the influence of the media on the empowerment of citizens
- Understand the significance of agenda setting and the role of 'gatekeepers'
- Develop the use of content analysis and semiology to assess the power of the media to construct identity

'Ignorance is strength.' This quotation is taken from the novel *Nineteen Eighty-Four*, written by George Orwell in 1949. This motto was used by the Ministry of Truth to ensure that Big Brother remained in control; the citizen's ignorance was Big Brother's strength. The same quotation could have been used at the start of Chapter 6, as many of the issues and debates relating to freedom of information raised in that chapter are relevant to this one. The purpose of this chapter, however, is not to repeat those debates, but to take the issue forward and focus on the role of the media in the creation and maintenance of a citizen's identity.

Hegemony

The quotation 'ignorance is strength' is a very useful starting point, because it implicitly raises questions about the balance of power between the 'ordinary citizen' and those who have some form of power and control. One form of power and control is the ability of some groups of citizens to get their view of the world adopted as being 'correct', which by definition means that opposing and different views are 'wrong'. If a dominant group of citizens can impose their view of the world and it is that view that becomes 'reality', it is this group of citizens who will be able to influence, dominate and effectively control the cultural and political perceptions of other citizens. This dominance is sometimes referred to as 'hegemony'.

What is knowledge?

The mass media are those organisations that are designed to reach a mass audience and include the press, television, radio, the cinema and the range of games for machines like PCs, Nintendo or PlayStations. Much of a citizen's knowledge comes as a result of interacting with the media through the activities of looking, listening or reading. A lot more knowledge is gained in this way than by direct experience. This, however, does raise some questions. Although rather basic, there is an issue relating to the use of the word 'knowledge'. What is 'knowledge'? If knowledge is taken to mean all those events, situations and things that a citizen knows about, then a citizen gains knowledge through the media. However, it is extremely important to stress that there are very many different versions of, and explanations for, the same event. Each of these different versions and explanations would also count as 'knowledge'. So, how does a citizen select and decide which version and explanation is correct? There are two possible answers to this question.

(a) Focus on the citizen

The first response is to focus on the citizen. Many citizens effectively filter the range of possible explanations and only read about, look at or listen to those explanations that confirm what they already believe to be correct. This response assumes that other agencies of socialisation have already influenced the norms, values and culture of the citizen, so the media will simply reinforce the citizen's views.

(b) Focus on the media

The second response is to focus on the media and argue that, in reality, the citizen only receives one version and explanation of an event from the many different and competing versions that could be presented. It is from this single explanation, selected and presented by the media, that the citizen constructs not only their knowledge, but also their norms, values and culture. Since the mass media could conspire to function in such a way as to manipulate a citizen's norms, values and culture, the mass media, by implication, becomes extremely influential in the construction and distribution of social knowledge. This makes the mass media a very important agency for socialisation and social control.

The different views expressed on the influence of the media on a citizen's ability to participate successfully in society can be divided into a number of models or approaches:

- the hegemonic or neo-Marxist model;
- the manipulative or orthodox Marxist model;
- the feminist approaches;
- the pluralist model and New Right approaches.

The hegemonic or neo-Marxist model

The hegemonic or neo-Marxist model of the media places its emphasis on ideological control. The idea of ideological control sounds complicated, but in reality it is something faced every day. Imagine the situation in which a small group of citizens (for example, teachers or lecturers) wish to get a larger group of citizens (students) to undertake an activity that they feel is important and want them to complete (homework). The problem for the smaller group is that there is a different point of view and resistance from the larger group. One solution would be for the smaller group of citizens (teachers or lecturers) to use force in order to get this task completed. However, this solution is not acceptable or effective. An alternative solution is to convince the larger group not only that they actually want to do the activity, but also that it is in their best interests. (Teacher: 'I am not setting this homework for my benefit,' or 'If you want to stand a chance of passing your exam, you need to research some of the activities.') There is, when expressed in this way, every likelihood that the larger group will comply with the request from the smaller group and complete the homework. In terms of control, the larger group are both giving their consent and actively participating in their own control. If power can be achieved by consent, it is much more effective than power achieved through coercion. If some groups of citizens can get their view of the world adopted as being 'correct' by consent, this is much more effective than trying to coerce citizens to adopt those views.

The relevance of this argument to the study of citizenship is that, if the media can be described as hegemonic, it will create differently empowered citizens because it is selecting only one point of view or ideology, the dominant ideology, and reporting, interpreting and analysing events within the context of that dominant ideology. Any citizen who steps outside that dominant ideology becomes redefined as an 'oddity' and will be less able to contribute to or participate equally in society.

Is the news hegemonic? This activity is best completed in groups on the same day. Each group selects a different but comparable news broadcast, for example, the 10 o'clock news on BBC 1 or the ITV news, or the six o'clock news on Radio 4 or a commercial radio station.

For each broadcast, record:

- the running order of the stories;
- the length of each story;
- within each story:
  - the factual content,
  - the degree of speculation and conjecture,
  - the use of any subjective labels like 'terrorist'.
- For the television news, were any images used with the story? Were they essential in understanding that story?
- Was the story attributed to a source?
- The tenor of the report: was it very serious, serious or trivial?

Most importantly, compare your findings with another group, which will enable you to complete the following chart.

Story	Source 1	Source 2

The manipulative or orthodox Marxist model

The manipulative or orthodox Marxist model suggests that the mass media are owned and controlled by a small, influential and powerful group who are effectively using the media to maintain the status quo. Since this group is one of the most influential and powerful in society, they would suffer the most if there were any changes that affected their position. Consequently, they wish to avoid change and maintain the present arrangements. To achieve this they provide 'entertainment' in order that citizens can escape from the realities of their existence. A citizen, in their day to day life, could be faced with the realities of, for example, poverty, boredom, frustration, danger and stress, to list just a few. If these citizens are drip fed a diet of trivia in the form of millionaire quizzes, celebrity news or gossip and soaps (all of which, some believe, can be achieved simultaneously with uncritical coverage of the royal family), attention is directed away from the power and influence of the small and powerful group. The content of the media is effectively used to manipulate the views and attitudes of citizens. The system does not produce thinking, critical citizens who are going to question the position of the small and powerful group who own and control the mental means of production. When viewed in these terms, the media has a significant influence on a citizen's ability to participate successfully in society.

 Within a single four-week period during 2002:

- The most popular television programme was *Who Wants to be a Millionaire?*
- There were television programmes about television programmes and television programmes about television celebrities: *Your 100 Top TV Moments* and *I'm a Celebrity – Get Me Out of Here!*
- David Beckham became a father again, which made him front page news.

Choose a short period of time and research evidence which supports or does not support the manipulative or orthodox Marxist model of the media.

Evidence to support the manipulative or orthodox Marxist model		
Quizzes	Celebrity news/gossip	Soap news/gossip
Evidence that does not support the manipulative or orthodox Marxist model		

Feminist approaches

The feminist analysis of the media shares many of the assumptions of the previous two approaches, in that the media is seen to have a significant influence on a citizen's ideology and is a major contributor to a citizen's socialisation. Although the feminist approach shares these assumptions, it does have a significantly different emphasis. Writers taking the feminist approach argue that the chances for a female citizen to participate successfully in society are compromised and effectively reduced as a direct result of the influence of the media. The reason for this lies in the belief that the media is still essentially patriarchal. Patriarchy is a term that is generally used to describe the dominance of men over women. Any system that perpetuates this dominance can be described as patriarchal. The media are still a major influence in the process of socialisation, which for many women is a process that creates subordinate citizens through:

- the creation and continuation of both male and female stereotypes;
- the creation and continuation of an ideology of 'femininity';
- the continuation in the use of sexist language;
- the portrayal of women in a narrow range of roles; and
- the fact that women are given access to a narrow range of activities and occupations in advertisements.

Writers taking this approach claim that the media is guilty of gender apartheid, creating and maintaining a culture of subordination, inequality and invisibility. It is this apartheid that creates the conditions that result in many female citizens being unable to participate equally and fully within society.

Although some students of Citizenship would look at the television and be able to cite examples that may initially question the validity of the term 'gender apartheid', there are many issues to consider. Remaining with television, with developments in digitisation, cable networks and the continuation of satellite broadcasting, there is now a far greater range of channels available to citizens. One type of channel that is now available is a 'gold' channel. This is a channel, like UK Gold, that is dedicated to the broadcasting of a back catalogue, the polite term for 'old programmes'. Old programmes reflect old cultural norms, that is, the cultural norms and values of their day, so, although there has been some progress, many citizens who watch these programmes could be living in a media time warp and, by implication, a cultural time warp. It also has to be remembered that television is only one part of the media.

Newspapers, magazines, radio and the cinema are all examples of mass media, and some of these media have a very long way to go in order to be able to claim that their treatment of women is fair and equal. So, although there may be developments to challenge and successfully overturn gender apartheid, the evidence still does not support the view that women are treated equally and fairly within the media. The media not only have an impact on the creation and maintenance of a citizen's social identity, but also influence some citizens' ability to participate successfully in society.

Content analysis and semiology

One way in which the student of citizenship can test the claims about the presentation of groups of citizens by the media is to undertake some form of content analysis. Content analysis is a process of research that literally analyses content. The process, however, is not quite as simple as it may sound, as it often requires the ability to deconstruct the message through decoding and semiology.

'Deconstruction' means breaking down images so that the assumptions on which they are based are exposed.

The media, in order to present news, views and stories, use a wide range of images, signs and symbols. These can include an enormous range of possibilities from the presenter's clothes, tone of voice, the set, the lighting and the theme music to the pitch, speed and accent of the actual words used.

Media watch: spot how we do it one way, but they do it another

 The following words and expressions were all used by the British press during one week in 1991. The significance of this particular week is that the first Gulf War was being fought.

Some of the words and expressions were used to describe the activities of the allies whilst some were used to describe the enemy.

If you are working individually, your task is to write a news report, using all of the words and expressions below, describing the activities of both the allies and the enemy.

If you are working in a pair you must remember that you are both on the same side. Your first task is to select who is to describe the allies and who is to describe the enemy. Each of you must then produce a news report using whichever words and expressions you think are appropriate, one of you describing the activities of the allies and the other describing the activities of the enemy.

Defiant	Blindly obedient	First strike
Evil tyrant	Destroy	Civilian casualties
Censorship	Assured	Zapped *PTO*

Kill	Statesmanlike	War Machine
Confident	Demented	Dare-devils
Boys	Resolute	Propaganda
Cannon fodder	Cautious	Fear of Saddam
Loyal	Brainwashed	Cowardly
Professional	Hordes	Heroes
Troops	Take out	Eliminate
Precision bomb	Desperate	Press briefings
Lads	Collateral damage	An old fashioned sense of duty
Without provocation		Reporting guidelines
Failed to return from a mission		Army, Navy and Air Force

The reason why all the elements of the list can be used in different ways is because they are, in effect, images, signs and symbols that have been selected and chosen in order to create the meaning or atmosphere that the director strives to achieve. Semiology is the study of these images, signs and symbols that are used in order to construct and maintain meanings within the media.

Supporters of this approach believe that the media contribute towards:

* the creation and continuation of stereotypes;
* the creation and continuation of ideologies of both 'femininity' and 'masculinity';
* the use of sexist language;
* the creation of gender specific roles.

The application of the principles of semiology to the content of the media makes it possible to quantify the impact of the media on the creation of social identity. It can also explain the media's influence on citizens' ability to participate successfully in society and on different levels of empowerment within society.

Gender based content analysis

 In order to undertake this activity, you can either use your existing knowledge or complete the research during your leisure time. What you will need to do is:

- Look at a range of television programmes or advertisements.
- Look at the images in a range of PlayStation or PC games.
- Look at a range of daily newspapers (the tabloids are the best to use).

From your observations, complete a chart similar to the one below.

	Selected images, signs and symbols	The meanings attached to the images, signs and symbols	Effect on a citizen's ability to participate successfully in society
Television programme or advertisement			
PlayStation or PC game			
Daily newspaper			

What conclusions can be made about any possible effects on a citizen's ability to participate successfully in society?

A subjective process

Before moving away from the use of content analysis, it is necessary to raise a number of criticisms related to this form of research. The first criticism is that the process of semiological analysis is a very subjective one and there is no proof that one citizen's interpretation of images, signs and symbols is going to be the same as another's. Since there is no proof, it is impossible to apply generalised statements in the form of 'all citizens will interpret ...'. The process implies that there is only one way in which images, signs and symbols can be interpreted, whereas in fact, many of them can be interpreted in different ways, not only by different audiences, but also when the mood of the researcher changes or the context of the images, signs and symbols changes. Another major problem associated with this approach is that the researcher has to be 'culturally competent'. The implication of this is that it is only possible for the researcher to analyse material if he or she 'knows the code'.

Critics of semiological analysis point out that, although there can be little doubt that there have been changes in the use of images, signs and symbols to convey meanings, this method cannot explain why those changes occurred.

Pluralist model and New Right approaches

The central component of pluralist approaches to the media is the acceptance that the media are biased and will have an impact on their audience. However, the notion of pluralism implies multiplicity. It is argued that, since the media

- portray a wide range of images, sign and symbols,
- present different opinions,
- present a wide and diverse range of differing points of view, and
- are comprehensive when they make judgments,

there is not a problem for citizens, because they can simply select what they want to listen to, read or view. The providers of the media argue that they need to be profitable, so they broadcast and publish what an audience wants. If there are differences in what the audience wants, this is not a problem because there is a wide range of different newspapers, magazines, and television channels with a wide range of styles and content. If a citizen cannot be satisfied within the mainstream of the media, there are thousands of specialist magazines catering for every minority interest imaginable.

Approaches to citizenship that have been influenced by the ideas from the New Right perspective have a belief in the necessity of a free market. A free market would, by definition, be unregulated. This would allow a range of media to enter the market, each with their own biases and interpretations of reality. Citizens would have the freedom to choose, from the wide range of interpretations available, which media presentation of reality was the one that reflected their point of view or was the one they wanted to adopt. The issue of bias is not a problem, first due to the range and scope of the media available, and, secondly, because citizens have the right to choose which media they wish to interact with.

The problem faced by the New Right approach becomes apparent with the next logical step in the application of the free market. When there is a free market, market forces will create a range of media that are successful and a range of media that are unsuccessful. The free market will ultimately ration the range and scope of the market and thus, by definition, limit the choice available for citizens.

Pluralist approaches, in general, have a range of problems surrounding the issue of choice. If there is a large number of radio stations that are all playing the same music, where is the choice? If those people who are playing the music all come from the same social background, where is the choice? If the radio stations are in competition with each other for listeners, there is the likelihood that they will all have to adapt the content of their programmes in order to attract the greatest number of listeners. This will mean adopting the 'lowest common denominator' approach and, if all radio stations do this, although it would be true to say that there is a choice between radio stations, it is not much of a choice if they all sound the same! The lack of choice and diversity in representing a wide range of views, attitudes and opinions would have a negative influence on some citizens' ability to participate successfully in society.

The process of 'agenda setting' and the work of 'gatekeepers'

Another way to illustrate the restricted and limited range of views and images within the media, which results in some citizens having less influence and a reduced capacity to participate effectively in society, is to look at the process of 'agenda setting' and the work of 'gatekeepers'. Although these terms are most often associated with the selection and prioritisation of stories in the news, they are equally relevant in discussing the relative empowerment of citizens.

The process of 'agenda setting' refers to the way in which the content of the media is selected and the relative importance that is placed on the items that are selected. In terms of the news, it is obvious that a television programme lasting 30 minutes cannot inform about every single event that has occurred since the previous broadcast. Out of all the possible events, a selection has to be made. The people who do the sifting and filtering before the journalist interprets and reports are the 'gatekeepers'. They 'open the gate' for some stories that then proceed to become an item of news in the next broadcast, and they 'close the gate' for other stories that are 'spiked'. The process of agenda setting and the role of the gatekeeper are mutually reinforcing.

Galtung and Ruge (in *The Manufacture of News – Social Problems, Deviance and the Mass Media*, by Cohen and Young, 1981) argued that the likelihood of any event's inclusion as 'news' rested on that event's 'news value'. Different events had different degrees of 'news value'. They developed an 11-point list of factors that influenced the news value of an event. The more news value attached to an event, the greater the likelihood of a positive reception from the gatekeepers, who would 'open the gate' and allow the story to become an item of news.

Gatekeepers, however, cannot divorce themselves from their culture, and this will influence not only the selection process, but, probably more importantly, the context in which some events will be reported. For example, if there is the expectation that event X will cause reaction Y, and the expected reaction does not occur, this non-event becomes newsworthy. A classic case of 'no news is good news'!

BobZ

News value

Being a successful gatekeeper involves making assumptions about what citizens want to know. This will again require the gatekeeper to make culturally relative judgments. The whole process of the selection of an event and the application of news values is a highly subjective activity. The decision as to whether an event has news value or not rests on culturally relative assumptions that gatekeepers make about citizens, described in Galtung and Ruge's work. These assumptions are:

- Big events are of greater interest and are of greater importance for citizens than small events.
- Most citizens will either not be interested in or will not comprehend detailed, technical or complicated stories.
- Citizens are more interested in events that involve fellow citizens or are 'close to home'. 'Home' can be interpreted in geographical or cultural terms.
- Citizens are more interested in events that do not challenge their preconceptions about the context in which the events take place.
- Citizens will become bored with repetition so, once an event has been reported, if there is no change in the event or a similar event occurs, reports will not continue as citizens will no longer be surprised.

- Citizens are more interested in any event when it involves certain groups of citizens. These groups could be members of any elite, celebrities, vicars and the royals.
- Citizens are more interested in bad news than good news.
- The event needs an element of 'human interest' as it is the effect on people's lives that will be of interest to citizens.
- A citizen has a limited attention span, so:
    - different events need to be reported in different ways to give the news pace, variety and interest;
    - once an event has been established as newsworthy, this will initially increase its news value, although if the event goes on too long, there will be a need to remove it from the news.
- Citizens need to have the report about the event direct from the source. Why does a reporter have to stand in the rain outside the House of Commons with background noise and interference, instead of reporting from a nice warm office?
- Television news needs pictures in order for the event to be interesting or understandable to citizens.

With so many assumptions influencing the content of news programmes, it might be more appropriate to call them 'olds', as there is little that is actually 'new' in them.

The content of the news media is socially constructed

For the student of citizenship, the importance of this debate becomes apparent when the next logical steps are taken. If what appears on a citizen's television news broadcast and in a citizen's newspaper is heavily influenced by cultural expectations and the role of gatekeepers, the content of the news media is socially constructed. Since it is these media that inform and provide 'knowledge', then 'knowledge' is also socially constructed and will also be culturally relative. Since 'knowledge' is socially constructed, it will reflect the biases, inconsistencies and assumptions that exist within society. It will also reflect differences in power and differences in the ability to impose interpretations on events. The result of the allocation of highly subjective news values is that some citizens will not only be empowered to a greater extent than others, but will also have the capacity to participate more effectively within society.

This conclusion mirrors the point made by the Glasgow University Media Group, who declared that the news serves to 'reproduce dominant assumptions about our society – the assumptions of the powerful about what is important, necessary and possible within it' (*More Bad News,* 1980).

The issue of agenda setting and bias within the media has been the focus of research by the Glasgow University Media Group for over 25 years, during which they have produced a series of books. Each study, using evidence gained through a systematic content analysis, focuses on the media's coverage of a particular issue. They conclude that the media help not only to create a single acceptable viewpoint, but also to maintain and promote that viewpoint. The media produce and create hegemony. John Eldridge, in *Getting the Message Across – News, Truth and Power* (1993), argues that it is actually impossible for the news media not to be biased, as they are actively involved with 'creating reality'.

Party political broadcasts and advertising

Another way in which reality can be created for citizens is through advertising in the media. Political parties are allowed to try to influence citizens through political adverts in the press and on billboards, and there are now strict limits on the level of advertising expenditure. Political parties cannot advertise on television or radio. Instead they are allocated free airtime which can be used to influence citizens. The amount of time allocated is partly determined by the number of candidates standing in the election. This can lead the broadcasters to a difficult position if a minority single-issue party is entitled under the rules to free airtime.

This situation arose in 2001 when the 'Pro-Life Alliance' produced an election broadcast that the BBC felt was unsuitable due to its 'shocking' images of abortions. For some citizens, the refusal to broadcast was political censorship by the BBC.

Another way in which citizens can be influenced by the media is through government advertising. In the first three months of 2001, the Government increased its expenditure on advertising by 157% compared to same period of time the previous year. Indeed, in the first three months of 2001, just prior to the General Election, the Government spent more than half of its entire advertising budget; £49 million was spent in March alone. Views about whether a government should spend citizens' money on advertising are hard to determine as opinions of the issue are a little difficult to establish. This difficulty is perfectly illustrated by contrasting two quotes from Tony Blair: in 1988, whilst in opposition, he expressed the view that the then Government was spending 'millions to promote the Conservative case on social security [and] privatisation'. In 2001, whilst in government, he expressed a different view that 'the vast bulk of the government advertisements are for campaigns that … make sure that people entitled to the child tax credit get it'. The implication for citizens behind these quotes is that politicians use the media not to empower citizens but simply to enhance their electability. It would seem that there is a difference between politicians and ordinary citizens after all. When a citizen bribes a politician that is called corruption; yet when a politician bribes a citizen, that is called democracy!

What do you understand by the following terms and concepts?

- Hegemony
- Dominant ideology
- Subjective
- Agenda setting

- Semiology
- Content analysis
- Deconstruction
- Social construction

The purpose of this activity is to research news values.

- Using the 11 factors outlined in Galtung and Ruge's work on news values, look at an edition of the news. How closely does the broadcast conform to Galtung and Ruge's news values?

The next activity is only possible if you have a satellite dish that will receive broadcasts intended for a different part of Europe or if you continue your Citizenship studies whilst on your foreign holiday.

- Look at news that is presented to a different audience. Can it be understood just by looking at the pictures? How similar is it to the domestic version of the news?

Name game

 Another way in which the media are able to distort one citizen's perceptions of another is through the manner in which they are addressed.

- Are they addressed with any prefix, for example 'Mr', 'Ms' or 'Mrs'?
- Are they referred to by their surname only?
- Are both first and surname used but without 'Mr', 'Ms' or 'Mrs'?
- Are they referred to by some shortened version of their name and, if they are, from where did this develop?

Examples of the style of reference during one week of March 2003 were 'IDS' for Mr Iain Duncan Smith, 'Ken' for the London Mayor, Mr Livingstone, and 'Becks' for Mr David Beckham. This was in contrast to Mr Blair and Prince Charles, whose names were not reconstructed to 'Our Tone' or 'Prince Chas'.

- From the media, find other examples of the variation in names attached to various citizens.
- Is it possible to draw any conclusions from your observations?

CHAPTER 20

The Creation of Differently Empowered Citizens through Stereotyping, Labelling and Image

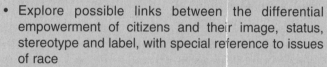

The aims of this chapter are to:

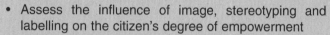

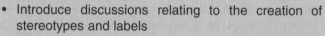

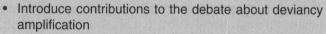

* Assess the influence of image, stereotyping and labelling on the citizen's degree of empowerment
* Introduce discussions relating to the creation of stereotypes and labels
* Introduce contributions to the debate about deviancy amplification
* Explore possible links between the differential empowerment of citizens and their image, status, stereotype and label, with special reference to issues of race
* Explore possible links between the differential empowerment of citizens and their race

An initial conclusion that could be drawn from the preceding debates and discussions is that the impact of socialisation, combined with the impact of the mass media, not only influences the ability of citizens to participate effectively in the local community and wider society, but ultimately helps to create differently empowered citizens. The reason for this is that these two influences help a citizen not only to construct their own identity but also to judge other citizens' identities.

Stereotypes and labels

One way in which the impact of socialisation and the mass media could influence a citizen's attitudes towards other citizens is through the use of labels and stereotypes. Although these are terms that are widely used, it is important to establish an exact meaning in order to avoid ambiguity.

A stereotype is 'a mental image held about a group of people and constructed on the basis of simplified, distorted or incomplete knowledge of [that group]' (E Cashmore and B Troyna, *Introduction to Race Relations*,

1968). A stereotype, in the mind of any citizen, is a form of packaging, a convenient shorthand, a simple tool to achieve the complex task of making sense of what is going on around them.

The difference between a stereotype and a label is, like a lot of things, not straightforward, and some would argue that there is no difference between the two terms. However, for the purposes of this book, it is felt that there is a difference and that the difference is significant enough to develop.

The term 'label' is directly related to the development of labelling theory. Labelling theory, developed from the work of the American sociologist Howard Becker in the 1960s, is an approach to the study of deviance. In an application of his approach, it is suggested that citizens can and will change their behaviour according to how that behaviour is labelled. Changes in behaviour will occur:

- through a citizen adopting a set of attitudes and patterns of behaviour that are associated with some socially identified category (label); or

- through a citizen's reaction to others, based on the assumption that other citizens' behaviour will be predictable and associated with a socially identified category (label).

Politicians and beards – the 'five o'clock shadow cabinet'!

Although this may sound like a silly piece of research, the conclusions should be quite illuminating.

1 Try to establish the following:
- When was the last time a Conservative member of the Cabinet had a beard?
- How many Conservative MPs have a beard?
- How many other politicians have a beard? Keep your results for the conclusion.

2 From any magazines, choose six pictures of men who are not famous. A good source for these types of picture is the magazine *Woman's Weekly*. Three of the men should be bearded and three clean-shaven.

Give each picture a name or a number.

Write six short manifestos, trying to make sure that the whole political spectrum is covered.

Ask a sample of people who they would vote for.

Can any conclusions be drawn from your results?

What cannot be denied is that stereotyping and labelling play, along with other factors, a crucial role in the process of the creation and maintenance of differently empowered citizens. The problem for the student of citizenship is in trying to establish the role of the media in this process, especially when there are so many possibilities, none of which are provable.

- Do stereotypes and labels already exist in society, and the media just use them?
- Do the media play an active role in the creation and maintenance of stereotypes and labels that are then adopted and used by other citizens?
- Are those citizens who have more power and influence able to access the media more easily and present their point of view?
- Do some citizens have nothing to contribute to debates, with the result that there is not much point in allowing them access to the media?
- Do the media merely report and represent reality as it actually exists?
- Do the media, through selective reporting and selective representation, change and distort reality?

In order to attempt to navigate a path through these possible examples, there is going to be a single focus, and all discussion, evidence and examples will be directed towards the central issue of developing possible conclusions to the important question of the empowerment of citizens.

Influences on empowerment

The degree of empowerment enjoyed by a citizen can be influenced by each of the following factors individually, or by a combination of some or all of them:

- The process of socialisation.
- The influence of social variables like class, sex/gender, sexuality, ethnicity, and age.
- The choice of how a citizen decides to present him or herself to others.
- The development of stereotypes and labels by the media and citizens.
- The successful application of stereotypes and labels by the media and citizens.
- The process of hegemony that may effectively alienate a citizen simply because of their point of view.
- The process of agenda setting in the reporting of news and events.
- The issue of bias in the reporting of news and events.

To initiate this discussion, let's look at the speech made by Peter Lilley at the Conservative Party Conference held at Brighton in October 1992:

This summer I announced tougher rules affecting so called 'New Age Travellers'. Most people were as sickened as I was by the sight of these spongers descending like locusts, demanding benefits with menaces. We are not in the business of subsidising scroungers.

And we've tightened up on the bogus asylum seekers. It's right to help genuine victims of persecution. But not those whose persecution is fraudulent. It's outrageous when people claim using a dozen different names. So we've clamped down on forged claims. And already nearly 20,000 have evaporated into thin air.

There are scores of other frauds to tackle. So, Mr Chairman, just like in *The Mikado,*

I've got a little list ...
Of benefit offenders who I'll soon be rootin' out
And who never would be missed,
They never would be missed.
There's those who make up bogus claims
In half a dozen names,
And councillors who draw the dole
To run left wing campaigns,
They never would be missed,
They never would be missed.
Young Ladies who get pregnant just to jump the housing list,
And Dads who won't support the kids of Ladies they have kissed.
And I haven't even mentioned
All those sponging Socialists
They'd none of them be missed,
They'd none of them be missed.
And I've got 'em on my list.

To take just one of the groups identified in the speech, that of the 'new age traveller', it is interesting to consider a number of issues. First, the name 'new age traveller'; where did it come from? When was it first used? How did the stereotypical image of social security fraud, long hair, tatty vans and buses come to be associated with the label 'new age traveller'?

Spot the stereotype and label

- From the speech made by Peter Lilley, identify how he categorises some groups of citizens through the use of stereotypes and labels.
- When a group of citizens has been stereotyped and labelled, certain types of behaviour become associated with those citizens. One effect of this is to influence the ability of some citizens to participate effectively in society. Complete the chart.
- What conclusions can be drawn?

Stereotyped and labelled citizens	Behaviour associated with the stereotype and label	Influence on ability to participate effectively in society

Development of stereotypes

One suggested answer to those questions is to look at the role and function of the media in their reporting of news and events. Older readers of this book will remember when it was free to visit Stonehenge, without restriction. Anybody could visit the monument at any time of the day or night. Some citizens attached significance to the monument at the time of the summer solstice and would make a pilgrimage to the site. However, once the monument became part of the tourist industry, with restricted access, it was impossible for those who continued to make a pilgrimage to get access. Although access was denied, the pilgrims still wanted to celebrate the summer solstice. The result was a sort of annual peaceful carnival.

Eventually, the media picked up the story and focused on concerns relating to noise, vandalism and drug use. There were soon calls from interested parties for the banning of these gatherings and calls for the police to do something about it. The result was a series of violent confrontations between the police and ... (for those reporting the story in the media there was now a problem: what is a collective noun for members of this group? If no name exists, their solution is to make one up!) ... thus the creation of 'new age travellers'.

This process provides a classic example of the role of the media first outlined in Stanley Cohen's study, *Folk Devils and Moral Panics*. Cohen asserts that the media, through a combination of the creation and use of stereotypes and labels, with the over-reporting of certain 'problems', actually increases the extent of the 'problem'.

Folk devils and moral panics

Cohen uses the terms 'folk devils' and 'moral panics'. 'Folk devils' are the social groups who come to represent a threat to social order, and a 'moral panic' occurs when there is a reaction to the group that is out of all proportion to the perceived threat posed by that group.

After the development of the label 'new age traveller' and the development of the idea of what these people would look like and how they would be expected to behave, that is, the development of the stereotype, the next stage in the process relates to how the media over-report the activities of this group.

The media, through the use of labels and stereotypes, now have the language and the context in which events involving these groups can be reported. Once the group starts to receive attention from news coverage, public knowledge about the group increases. This will increase the numbers of 'hangers-on', and the number of spectators attracted to the scene of the events. This increases the scale and scope of the event and, as a result of this increase, the event becomes more newsworthy and is elevated in importance amongst news stories. This process reinforces public perceptions, knowledge and awareness of the group, with the result that more examples are reported and more police efforts are made to remove and solve the problem. In short, there exists, in Cohen's terms, a spiral of 'deviancy amplification'. A problem has been created where one previously did not exist.

The importance of the process that has been outlined lies in the degree of media influence in the ability to empower some citizens more than others.

Some citizens might be effectively excluded from the reality of becoming an elected representative simply because of the development of a stereotype and the application of a label. It is, for example, only very recently that it has become socially acceptable for MPs to openly declare that their sexuality is not 'strictly heterosexual', and there is still considerable debate as to whether an MP should ever confess to indulging in any recreational drug taking activities in their past.

Another way in which the influence of the media could empower some citizens more than others is outlined in the diagram opposite. One example that might have been used to illustrate the activity above is the issue of race. The interaction between citizens in this area is a clear example of how different sets of assumptions and different attitudes can lead to an imbalance of power. There is clear evidence that a citizen's race and their degree of empowerment are linked, which affects the ability of some citizens to participate equally and effectively in the local community and wider society.

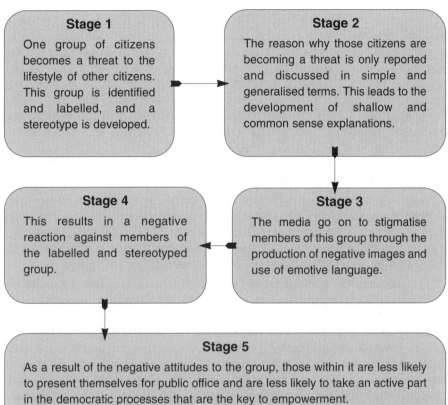

Stage 1

One group of citizens becomes a threat to the lifestyle of other citizens. This group is identified and labelled, and a stereotype is developed.

Stage 2

The reason why those citizens are becoming a threat is only reported and discussed in simple and generalised terms. This leads to the development of shallow and common sense explanations.

Stage 4

This results in a negative reaction against members of the labelled and stereotyped group.

Stage 3

The media go on to stigmatise members of this group through the production of negative images and use of emotive language.

Stage 5

As a result of the negative attitudes to the group, those within it are less likely to present themselves for public office and are less likely to take an active part in the democratic processes that are the key to empowerment.

Evidence to support this stage comes from the under-representation of some groups of citizens in the 'corridors of power' and the alarming extent to which some groups of citizens are not prepared to take part in the democratic and empowering process of voting in elections.

Race and empowerment

There is in existence an enormous range of evidence that could be used to demonstrate a simple link between a citizen's race and a citizen's likelihood of experiencing discrimination. However, this link is far from simple, and the issue of how a citizen's race influences their likelihood of experiencing discrimination is full of contradictions.

One simple approach is to produce a range of figures that immediately suggest that a citizen's chances of success in society are far from equal. Figures, for example, released by the Office for National Statistics in January 2001 revealed that the unemployment rate for white men was 6.9% of the workforce yet the unemployment rate for Bangladeshi men was 20.4%. Similarly for women, the unemployment rate for white women was 4.7% of the workforce whilst the unemployment rate for Bangladeshi and Pakistani women was 23.9%.

The problem, however, with figures like those above is that they are far too narrow, concentrating on only one element of a citizen's life. Figures produced for the Cabinet in 2002 by the Performance and Innovation Unit revealed that one in 20 Indian men are doctors compared with one in 200 white men, and 45% of Chinese men are employed in the professional sector compared to 25% of white and Indian men. Pakistani and Bangladeshi Muslims had a 400% greater chance of being unemployed than Hindus. Again, the student of citizenship could easily say that these are just figures and only concentrate on a narrow part of a citizen's life experience.

To fully appreciate the impact that a citizen's race can have on their degree of empowerment and their ability to participate equally and effectively in both the local community and wider society, it is necessary to look beyond any narrow set of figures and assess the total impact that a citizen's race can have on their ability to participate fully in society.

To illustrate this approach it is possible to look at a series of reports. In 2001, the King's Fund, an independent health thinktank, reported their findings that 'No aspect of a doctor's working life is untouched by racism. Discrimination begins in medical schools and affects the whole of a person's career. Harassment and bullying from both colleagues and patients are daily facts of life for black and Asian doctors'. The report has a wide focus and draws attention to different rates of promotion between white and non-white doctors and the greater proportion of white staff in the more 'glamourous' areas of hospital employment. The report also illustrated that non-white doctors experience abuse from patients, and racism and prejudice from colleagues who express doubt about their abilities and lifestyles. The report concluded that non-white staff were prevented from realising their full potential partly due to the fact that there is the daily threat or reality of racism.

From a different source, the report delivered to the Department of Health entitled 'Tackling Racial Harassment in the NHS' concluded that non-white staff in the NHS were more likely to be abused by their patients, ignored by colleagues and sidelined by management. Both these reports illustrate their points with statistics. However, the important point is not in the quoting of figures; when the whole picture is seen, it is clear that for some citizens, their ability to participate fully and equally in society is affected by the colour of their skin.

In education there appears to be a similar picture for students. The Ofsted report 'Improving Attendance and Behaviour', published in 2001, clearly identified that within a school, the length of fixed period exclusions varied considerably between black and white students for what were described as the same or similar incidents.

It is possible to develop the analysis further. In the week ending 3 December 2000, with an audience of 33 million citizens, the only ethnic minority faces to be seen in the most watched programmes on BBC2 were cartoon characters in *The Simpsons*.

The attention Delroy Lindo has received from the police illustrates how individual citizens can experience repeated attention from the authorities simply because of the colour of their skin. After being stopped 37 times by the police, an internal Metropolitan Police inquiry found that Lindo had been the subject of a sustained campaign of 'unwarranted police harassment'. The report established that racially derogatory comments were made to Lindo and his family, yet despite the unwarranted attention, no police officers faced charges or disciplinary action.

"GEORGE! YOU'RE ON HOLIDAY FROM THE POLICE – YOU DON'T HAVE TO KEEP STOPPING BLACK PEOPLE FOR NO REASON!"

Daily Mirror, 17 February 1999

Institutional racism

This weight of evidence has led various citizens to use the term 'institutional racism' when describing some elements of British society. As a term, 'institutional racism' was not very widely used until the publication of the Macpherson Report, in February 1999, on the investigation into the murder of the black teenager Stephen Lawrence. Institutional racism was defined by the Macpherson Report as:

> The collective failure of an organisation to provide adequate and professional service to people because of their colour, culture or ethnic origin. It can be seen or detected in processes, attitudes and behaviour which amount to discrimination through unwitting prejudice, ignorance,

thoughtlessness and racist stereotyping which disadvantages minority ethnic groups.

The report stated that the Metropolitan Police had displayed institutional racism in its failure to investigate adequately the murder of Stephen Lawrence. Added to this, in April 2000, Michael O'Drien, the Home Office Minister, announced that the Home Office was institutionally racist. This is not an insignificant statement bearing in mind that the Home Office is responsible for, amongst other things, immigration, the police and prison services.

Ethnic groups at different stages of the criminal process			
Ethnic appearance%	White	Black	Asian
Population aged 10 and over	94.5	1.8	2.7
Stop and search	85.2	8.2	4.4
Arrests	87.0	7.3	4.0
Prison population	81.2	12.3	3.0

Source: The Home Office Annual Statistics on Race in the Criminal Justice System, January 2001

www.homeoffice.gov.uk/rds/pdfs/s95race00.pdf

There can be no doubt that there is a link between race and the issue of empowerment. This link will continue until race ceases to be a factor in a citizen's life chances and an influence on their experiences. Until the black community are no longer marginalised, until racial harassment and racial attacks are a thing of the past, until police accountability is fully established and until the occupational culture within the police force changes, there will remain issues between race and the equal empowerment of citizens.

Image

An alternative approach to these issues as to whether the media has any influence on the degree of empowerment of citizens is to change the focus of the debate to issues relating to a citizen's image. Does a citizen's presentation of him or herself increase or decrease their ability to participate effectively in society?

An example can be found in Frank 'beard of the year' Dobson's plight in the campaign to be Mayor of London, when image consultants, using psychological research which suggests that men with beards are less trustworthy, attempted to persuade Mr Dobson to remove his beard.

Shave the beard or lose, Dobson warned

Whiskers galore: Frank Dobson.

Media image in political campaigns is of fundamental importance, and the image of a politician will have an enormous impact on their likelihood of achieving power. The extent of the importance attached to a politician's media image can be gauged from the following quotation:

> Today, politicians have become products to be packaged and sold. Their actions (speeches, interviews, and photo opportunities) are planned in detail. What they say, how they dress, their hairstyles, where they go, whom they meet, which politicians or party they attack, which section of the electorate they target, by whom they will be interviewed on television – all is decided for them after careful analysis (John Kingdom, *Government and Politics in Britain*, 1999, p 248).

The importance of image

The extent to which image is seen as being important in the process of winning power can be judged by the activities of the Labour Party Women's officer, Rachel McLean. She advised the 194 women who were listed in February 2000 as being able to apply for Labour seats at the 2001 election to 'Dress appropriately – smart and tidy, not too much make up (but some is better than none), wear a suit or smart skirt/trousers but try to include some colour which will make you memorable (eg a dark suit with a brighter top underneath), don't wear distracting earrings'.

Suitable images ...

© Crocodile Photos

So far in the discussion of any possible link between image and the likelihood of empowerment, the focus has been on those who wish to achieve or who already have achieved formal power. As a contrast to those wishing to achieve formal power, it is interesting to compare the campaigns of two teenage 'eco warriors' protesting against local issues, and a campaign by a group of mature professional women.

Eco-protesters claim victory

Two teenage eco-protesters who abandoned their protest claimed victory. Their representative said that this was a victory for all small protesters against 'the big boys' and would act as a warning to others.

Based on 'Eco-protesters leave campsite', Rosnruth's Free Press

The groups have had similar labels applied to them, either 'eco terrorist' or 'eco warrior', but differ considerably in their image, style and form of action. They have both had a degree of success, which raises questions about the importance and relevance of 'image' in the ability to achieve a successful conclusion to a campaign. The mere fact that the two campaigns have both had a degree of success may lead to the conclusion that there could be an 'expectation effect' occurring. If other citizens are expecting to meet with a campaigner who is unconventional in his or her image, they will not be disappointed when the 'anarchist weirdo' arrives. There is no conflict between what is expected and what has been delivered. When there is a conflict between the two, a campaigner may be less successful in their ability to achieve their aims. Although image is an important factor in empowering some citizens with greater influence, it is not the only factor. What may be of equal importance is a citizen's ability to successfully combine image with expert knowledge, content, style, sincerity, and the skills to organise, communicate and negotiate.

One leading direct action pressure group in the campaign against GM crops is called Genetix Snowball, which, in the words of Zoe Elford, is 'the acceptable face of direct action'.

'Do I look like an anarchist weirdo?'

Although they look like five typical twenty to fortysomething women leading everyday lives, they have been roughed up, arrested and banned from thousands of acres of English countryside. They have been condemned as eco-terrorists, scientific hooligans and farmland anarchists. America's biggest biotech companies have sued them for millions in damages and supermarket bosses want to ban them from their soft fruit aisles.

When a leading seed firm became the first genetically modified food tester to pull out of crop trials after being targeted by protesters, the finger of blame was pointed at Genetix Snowball.

In a pub in east London they are not easy to spot. Look for chunky-sweatered daughters of the soil and you will miss them. Don't even think about sandals and Greenham Common dreadlocks. Try the table in the corner that looks like a meeting of the Chelsea Women's Institute.

Their mail-order handbook – politely titled *A Guide to Safely Removing Genetically Modified Plants from Release Sites* – explains how to uproot oilseed rape with a minimum of fuss. 'Do not take too many plants and always bring an organic plant to replace what you take.'

If they are 'terrorists', these five go out of their way

to be civilised about it. 'We have all pledged to be non-violent. We want to build trust with the farmers', said Kathryn Tulip. Each has been arrested at least once and the legal battle against Monsanto threatens to be long and bitter.

They have more than 1000 supporters and even Prince Charles has 'wished the group well'.

Based on 'Do I look like an anarchist weirdo?', Arlidge and Nick Paton-Walsh, *The Observer*, 6 June 1999

Discussions relating to the issue of empowerment have so far focused on:

- elements of a citizen's social characteristics, their social class, gender/sex, sexuality, ethnicity and their age;
- the role of the media in the construction, projection of and judgments about a citizen's image.

However, it could be argued that a citizen's social characteristics combine to project an image, and a citizen's image is influenced by their social class, gender/sex, sexuality, ethnicity and age.

Spiral of empowerment

The empowerment of citizens is influenced by a set of social characteristics that help to create another set of criteria that reinforce the original set. This process can create two spirals: one of empowerment, accompanied by increasing influence, and a greater capacity to participate effectively in society, whilst the alternative spiral leads to a decrease in power, a decrease in the ability to influence others and a reduced capacity to participate effectively in society.

One criticism that could be applied to the idea that empowerment derives from the link between a citizen's social characteristics and their image is the argument that the two elements are in fact the same. What is actually being discussed is the status of a citizen, and it is a citizen's social status that determines their power, their influence and their capacity to participate effectively in society.

The importance of status

The term 'status' refers to the position that a citizen occupies within society. A citizen's position could relate to domestic categories like daughter/son, mother/father, or wife/husband. A citizen's position could equally relate to the status received through their occupation, for example teacher, carpenter or banker. Other sources of status could result from social activities like being captain of the local hockey team or a bass in the local choral society. In short, there are a thousand and one sources of status within modern society. Each of these statuses has attached to it a different degree of prestige, a different amount of social honour and a different amount of esteem.

Although there are countless sources of status, not every source will deliver an equal level of prestige, honour or responsibility. As a result of this process, some citizens will have a social standing that has more status than others. One result of a citizen's acquisition of social status within a community or society is the tendency for other citizens and social organisations to rank citizens according to their relative social status. Some citizens, it is felt, have a much higher status than others.

As a result of the ranking of social status within society, it could be argued that a hierarchy is formed, in which all those citizens who have a similar social status unite to form a social group. Access to one of these social groups is through the acquisition of the appropriate 'status symbols', that is, those commodities or possessions that would be regarded as proof that the citizens possess the necessary social skills, wealth and image to be a member of that social group.

The concept of social status can be used to explain not only how individual citizens come to be ranked within a community or society, but also how status can unite whole groups of similarly ranked citizens. Once groups of citizens are united according to their social status, it is possible to argue that there is a link between a citizen's social characteristics and their image, and that social status creates that link.

Status could be the key to empowerment

The results of an experiment undertaken by *The Observer* would lend support to the argument that status is the key that empowers citizens. In the experiment, eight fictitious characters were created, with each character writing a letter of complaint to five different firms.

THE TOFF   THE DISABLED WOMAN   THE VICAR   THE STUDENT

THE SOLICITOR   THE DOCTOR   THE SINGLE MOTHER   THE PENSIONER

The 40 letters, written or typed in different styles, were all posted from the same mail point on the same day, 4 January 1999, to the head office address of five firms – Tesco, McDonald's, West Anglia Great Northern Railway, Harrods, and Virgin Trains.

Of the eight fictitious characters, the solicitor received the best treatment, followed by a 'Right Honourable', a GP and a vicar. The pensioner, disabled woman and lone parent all trailed behind, with the student taking last place.

Janice Allen of the National Consumers' Council said: '[The] survey appears to show service providers treat consumers differently by way of status.'

THE TOFF

TESCO: Still waiting for reply about Christmas cracker complaint.

HARRODS: Personal phone call on 9 Jan to sort out complaint of missing Blue Jamaican Mountain coffee from hamper.

McDONALD'S: £10 voucher sent on 20 Jan after complaint that shooting party discovered two Big Macs and some fries missing from large order.

VIRGIN: Refund of 20 per cent on £40 ticket on condition of proof of purchase. Apology sent 15 January.

WAGN: £10 voucher without proof of purchase on £45.80 ticket for cancelled service.

THE DISABLED WOMAN

TESCO: £5 voucher for complaint about quality of Christmas crackers. Apology sent 14 Jan.

HARRODS: Offer to replace tin of biscuits sent first class and posted on 18 January.

McDONALD'S: £15 voucher after complaint about rude staff, a 15-minute wait and cold Big Mac meal. Apology sent 25 January.

VIRGIN: Refund of 20 per cent on proof of purchase of £35.50 ticket. Apology sent 25 January.

WAGN: £5 voucher for £16.10 ticket for cancelled service. Apology sent 23 January.

THE VICAR

TESCO: £8 voucher to compensate for damaged fruit. No proof of purchase necessary. Apology sent on 25 Jan.

HARRODS: Personal phone call, apology and offer of replacement for chipped cup. Call made 8 Jan.

McDONALD'S: Still waiting for reply after complaining of missing items from £20 order for the church choir and carol singers.

VIRGIN: Refund of 20 per cent on proof of purchase of £35.50 ticket for cancelled service. Apology sent 25 January.

WAGN: £10 voucher for £35.30 ticket, without proof of purchase, sent on 26 Jan.

THE STUDENT

TESCO: No reply after complaining about quality of £1.69 party poppers.

HARRODS: Invitation to contact the store to compensate for Blue Jamaican Mountain coffee missing from hamper. First-class letter sent on 10 January.

McDONALD'S: No reply after complaint about missing items from large order.

VIRGIN: No reply after request for compensation on £35.50 ticket.

WAGN: Still awaiting reply after letter was sent on 13 Jan promising to investigate complaint of cancelled service and request for £16.10 refund.

THE SOLICITOR

TESCO: £10 voucher for faulty Christmas crackers sent on 11 Jan.

HARRODS: Offer to replace chipped mug from Christmas hamper, sent on 8 Jan.

McDONALD'S: £5 voucher for two missing portions of fries. Apology sent 9 Jan.

VIRGIN: Offer of 20 per cent refund with proof of purchase for £40 ticket. First letter of apology sent 12 Jan.

WAGN: £10 voucher for cancelled train without proof of purchase of £48.80 ticket. First letter of apology sent 13 Jan.

THE DOCTOR

TESCO: £10 voucher for faulty Christmas crackers sent on 11 Jan.

HARRODS: Offer to replace chipped cup found in Christmas hamper. Letter sent 14 Jan.

McDONALD'S: Letter of apology sent on 25 Jan with pre-paid envelope to reply back and identify takeaway which missed portion of fries from order.

VIRGIN: Offer of 20 per cent refund with proof of purchase of £40 ticket for cancelled service. Apology sent 26 Jan.

WAGN: £10 refund on £48.80 ticket for cancelled train. No proof of purchase necessary. Apology sent 13 Jan.

THE SINGLE MOTHER

TESCO: Request for proof of packaging posted on 26 Jan after complaint about two bags of clementines bought Christmas week.

HARRODS: Tin of store's own shortbread biscuits and letter of apology sent on 19 Jan after complaint about broken biscuits.

McDONALD'S: £10 voucher for missing novelty gifts and two packs of fries from family order. Apology sent 1 February.

VIRGIN: Refund of 20 per cent on proof of purchase for £35.50 ticket. Apology sent 25 Jan.

WAGN: £5 voucher for £16.10 ticket on cancelled service. Apology sent 23 Jan.

THE PENSIONER

TESCO: Request for proof of packaging sent on 25 Jan after complaint about quality of £1.69 bag of clementines.

HARRODS: Offer to replace cracked coffee cup sent in Christmas hamper. First class letter sent on 12 Jan.

McDONALD'S: £5 voucher after complaint of missing fries from family order. Letter sent 31 January.

VIRGIN: Refund of 20 per cent on proof of purchase of £35.50 ticket. Apology sent 15 Jan.

WAGN: £10 voucher for £45.80 ticket. No request for proof of purchase. Apology sent on 23 January.

The Observer, 21 February 1999

The differential empowerment of citizens is linked to differential social status. Citizens are not born into a vacuum; they are born into a culture that has already empowered some citizens more than others. The process of socialisation, the role of the media and a citizen's individual social characteristics are the building blocks of social status on which a citizen's power, influence and ability to participate effectively rest.

What do you understand by the following terms and concepts?

- Labelling
- Stereotype
- Image
- Status
- New age traveller
- Anarchist

- Fraud
- Folk devil
- Moral panic
- Deviancy amplification
- Spiral of empowerment
- Formal power

The social construction of attitudes

 Suggest ways in which a citizen's attitudes to the variables in the first column could have been influenced through socialisation and the mass media.

The attitude of a citizen towards their:	Development of attitudes as a result of the impact of socialisation	Development of attitudes as a result of the impact of the mass media
• social class • gender/sex • sexuality • ethnicity • age		

 Does image matter?

- How important do you consider image to be in the process of creating differently empowered citizens?
- How much importance should be attached to a campaigner's image in his or her ability to influence others and achieve their desired aim?

Select the work of two or three pressure groups and asses the role of 'image' in their ability to be successful.

 A citizen's race will always directly influence their life chances.

> Read the following article.
>
> The Metropolitan Police were not interacting with John Sentamu as an individual, they were interacting with his social status.
>
> Try to find other examples where characteristics of a citizen influence the nature and the result of an interaction.

'Stupid cop' searches leading black bishop

Richard Reeves
Society Editor

AN INTERNATIONALLY respected black bishop who survived the Idi Amin regime has been 'stopped and searched' by London police, provoking outrage from the Church of England.

In an incident that adds to the controversy over the racial bias in stop and searches, the Bishop of Stepney, John Sentamu, was halted near Tower Bridge last week.

'He was a stupid cop,' said a spokesman for the Archbishop of Canterbury. 'Here is a man who has been a High Court judge, who escaped Amin, and is one of the leading lights of the Anglican communion, and PC Plod pulls him over.'

A leading church spokesman on issues of race and inequality since moving to Britain in 1974, Sentamu was briefly imprisoned in Uganda.

Questioned on the incident, a Metropolitan Police spokeswoman said: 'Why is this significant? Has he filed a complaint?'

Sentamu was asked to stop near Tower Bridge late at night earlier this week and asked where he was going.

The 52-year-old told the beat officer he was going home, and was asked to get out of his car. 'He ordered me to open the boot,' the bishop said. 'I knew when he started talking that he didn't have the right to make me open the boot without reasonable ground for suspicion.'

The clergyman, a trained lawyer, then asked the police officer for a written reason for the stop and search. 'I started to argue and he [the officer] became a bit ratty,' he said. 'He said, "If you co-operate you'll be all right".'

At that point the officer in question asked who he was. 'I am the Bishop of Stepney. He

John Sentamu was 'ordered to open his car without good reason'.

then said "Whoops" and was very polite after that.'

A spokesman for the City of London police said last night that no record of the incident had been made, but said the officers on duty would be questioned. If a search does not take place, there is no legal requirement for the incident to be recorded.

The incident will add to suspicions that the Metropolitan Police is struggling to rid itself of racist attitudes and practices, despite promises made in the wake of the Stephen Lawrence inquiry which found the force to be 'institutionally racist'.

Black men in London are at least 10 times as likely as whites to be stopped and searched – although officers are only allowed to search vehicles under anti-drug legislation if they have 'reasonable suspicion' that a crime may be underway.

'What had annoyed me was the lack of reasonable grounds to suspect me of anything,' Sentamu said. 'Middle-aged bishops are rarely a threat to the public.'

It is not the first time that Sentamu has had trouble with the police, having been stopped eight times in total.
Lords revolt on racism, page 5

CHAPTER 21

The Influence of Inequality and Poverty on a Citizen's Life Chances

The aims of this chapter are to:

- Explore the link between poverty, life chances and the empowerment of citizens
- Examine issues surrounding the defining and measuring of life chances
- Explore approaches that seek to explain the causes of poverty
- Introduce issues concerned with the definition of poverty

In her report, *The Health Divide* (1987), Margaret Whitehead asks:

> ... [can] lifestyle factors account for the observed differential in health between different social groups? The short answer is: no. When studies are able to control for factors like smoking and drinking, a sizeable proportion of the health gap remains ... In this context there is a growing body of evidence that material and structural factors, such as housing and income, can affect health.

In the report, *Literacy, Numeracy and Economic Performance* (1997), Dr Robinson, a research officer at the Centre for Economic Performance at the LSE, concluded that:

> Potentially the most powerful 'educational' policy might be one which tackles social and economic disadvantage. A serious programme to alleviate child poverty might do far more for boosting literacy and numeracy than any modest interventions in schooling.

In his book, *What Unemployment Means* (1981), A Sinfield writes:

> It is important to emphasise that most likely to be unemployed are people in low paying jobs, the very young and the oldest in the labour force, people from ethnic minorities, people from among the disabled and the handicapped, and generally those with the least skills and living in the most depressed areas. Unemployment strikes and strikes most harshly and frequently those who are amongst the poorest and least powerful in the labour force and society as a whole.

The link between poverty and a citizen's life chances

What is it that links these quotations? The common link between them is the suggestion that the evidence points towards a systematic and long standing link between poverty and a citizen's life chances. This link, which has enormous implications for issues surrounding citizenship, is suggested by the following:

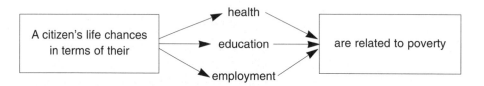

Before developing the discussion related to these areas, it is necessary to clarify what is meant by 'a citizen's life chances'.

Life chances

The term 'life chances' refers to a citizen's market situation and relates to the rewards that a citizen would expect to achieve throughout the course of his or her lifetime. So far so good, but what elements of a citizen's life should be included within a discussion on life chances? Should it include a citizen's happiness? Would how fast a citizen can run be appropriate as measure of life chances? Although these may be important, within the culture of the UK, they are not considered to be the most important or relevant determinants of how much a citizen would be expected to achieve throughout the course of his or her lifetime. Life chances are shaped by cultural expectations, and three of the most important influences on the life chances of a citizen are the citizen's health, the citizen's education and the citizen's occupation. Within the culture of the UK, it is a combination of these three factors that is seen to be crucially important in influencing how much a citizen will have achieved by the end of his or her life. It is these three factors that help to determine a citizen's rewards; it is these three factors that influence a citizen's life chances.

Another reason why these three factors are useful as indicators of a citizen's life chances is that, in any discussion related to life chances, the indicators that have been selected need to be measurable. Measurability is important in order to be able to make a comparison between different groups of citizens and to compare rates of change within the same group of citizens. For example:

Differences in health	These could be measured in terms of life expectancy, the chances of suffering from a long term illness or the chances of suffering a heart attack.
Differences in education	These could be measured in terms of the chances of passing GCSEs and AS levels, and the chances of receiving a university education.
Differences in employment	These could be measured in terms of the chances of experiencing redundancy, or of receiving appropriate pay in a safe working environment with benefits like sick pay, a pension scheme and paid holidays.

One final issue that needs to be raised in the discussion about a citizen's life chances relates to the distribution of rewards. These rewards are not infinite, they are rationed; there are only so many 'top jobs' in society and only so many university places. If a citizen is successful in achieving one of these rewards, it is often expressed in terms of 'winning'. To win implies that there is not only a race, but that there are also losers.

There are two types of races: those races in which all competitors start from the same point at the same time, and those races in which some competitors carry a handicap that could take the form of a longer distance to run or having to carry a heavy load. In the first race, the stakes are equal; in the second they are not.

If the life chances that a citizen could expect to achieve throughout the course of his or her lifetime are rationed, and there is a competitive nature to achievement, the most crucial question is whether all citizens start the race from the same set of starting blocks, or whether some citizens have a head start with a shorter course to run, and a pair of 'go faster' trainers to help them glide swiftly around the course whilst other citizens have a longer and more difficult course and a pair of weighted boots to slow them down.

If life chances do refer to the market situation and rewards that a citizen would expect to achieve throughout the course of his or her lifetime, do all citizens start this race from an equal position? Many would argue that the race is not equal, as inequalities from one generation stagger the starting line for the next. Not only do some citizens have a longer track to run, but less or older equipment to negotiate obstacles. Many citizens believe that a fair society requires not only an open road, but also an equal start.

This unequal distribution of life chances can be explained by returning to the concept, introduced earlier in the book, of cultural capital. With less cultural capital, the inability of some citizens to compete equally in the 'life chances race' creates an unequal distribution in the tokens of success.

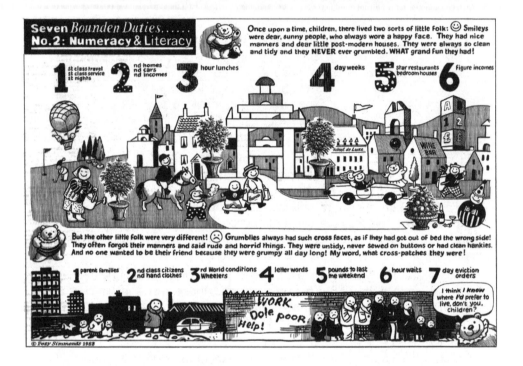

Issues of inequality and poverty

There can be no doubt that there is a link between a citizen's life chances and issues of inequality and poverty. What, however, is much more difficult to establish is the nature and the causes of the relationship. Does a citizen's reduced ability to experience success in his or her life chances result in an increase in the possibility of living in poverty, or does the fact that a citizen is living in poverty reduce his or her ability to achieve success in their life chances?

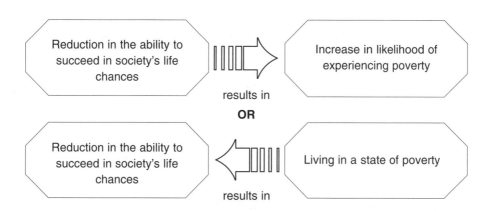

Influences on a citizen's life chances

Health

There has been an enormous amount of research into the relationship between the social conditions in which a citizen lives and the health of the citizen. A short historical diversion will highlight the name of Chadwick, whose report in 1842 on the *Sanitary Conditions of the Labouring Population* paved the way for a national system of water supply and sewage disposal that radically influenced the health of many Victorians. The evolution of the legislative changes developed into a National Health Service for all citizens that has often been used as evidence of the movement away from the situation in which a citizen's social origins were the most likely determinant of their life expectancy and their health. A National Health Service was seen as being a sign of progress towards achieving the ideal that the state, in undertaking some responsibility for citizens' health, was taking a step towards the removal of social class, sex, ethnicity or any other social variable as an influence on a citizen's chances for a long and healthy life, and a movement towards the goal of improving the health and life chances for all citizens in a fair and equal society.

	AGE	MEN				WOMEN			
		16–44	45–64	65 and over	Total	16–44	45–64	65 and over	Total
Heart and Circulatory System	Managerial and Professional	22	128	274	89	12	92	195	64
	Intermediate	22	139	345	108	17	127	312	116
	Routine and Manual	22	182	352	140	19	134	318	134
Respiratory System	Managerial and Professional	57	45	46	52	46	48	49	47
	Intermediate	52	46	107	58	47	50	69	53
	Routine and Manual	59	75	125	78	65	80	92	77
Musculo-skeletal System	Managerial and Professional	63	140	180	103	55	154	281	120
	Intermediate	64	199	237	132	54	169	376	160
	Routine and Manual	94	270	260	183	63	244	319	186

Source: Chronic sickness: rate per 1,000 reporting selected longstanding condition by age, sex and socio-economic classification, Great Britain. Office of National Statistics, 2001

© Daily Mirror

"BAD NEWS, I'M AFRAID...YOU'RE POOR!"

This cartoon suggests that the patient's health is linked to his wealth. There is a clear suggestion in the cartoon that the social origins and the social class of the patient are important factors that have an influence on his health. The weight of evidence tends to support this link.

Obesity and social class

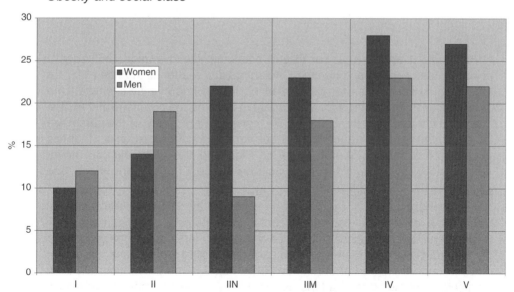

note: % with a Body Mass Index over 30. Based on Department of Health survey data for England.
Source: New Policy Institute, *Monitoring Poverty and Social Exclusion 1999*, December 1999

Smoking by sex/socio-economic group

% of persons aged 16 and over in each socio-economic group who smoke cigarettes.

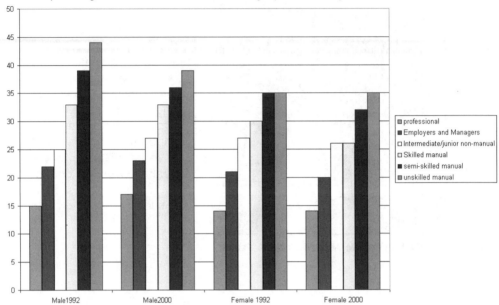

Source: *Living in Britain,* Office of National Statistics, 2001

Why would it appear that social and economic disadvantages influence a citizen's life chances and health? One suggested reason is that the NHS, for the majority of citizens, has done relatively little to improve life chances. One way to explain this point is for the student to imagine the purchase of their first car. The choice, from the same model, consists of two cars of the same age and with the same mileage. One car has experienced a rust problem that has been solved through liberal usage of filler, and the other car has never experienced any rust. Which car would be the best buy? There is only one sensible purchase to be made.

But what has this got to do with the issue of the NHS and life chances? Very often, citizens only come into contact with the health services after they have 'gone rusty', that is, after they have experienced a major health problem like a heart attack or a stroke. No matter how skilled the surgeon, he or she cannot undo a lifetime of unhealthy behaviour. Just as preventing rust from attacking a car is better than the use of filler in the motor trade, prevention is better than cure in the provision of health. However, in order to maintain a healthy lifestyle and prevent ill health, there needs to be a consideration of the factors that are most likely to influence a citizen's health and active life expectancy. These factors are social factors.

To explain how these social factors can influence a citizen's health, it is possible to use the example of diet. What a citizen chooses to eat is generally influenced by two considerations. First are the material considerations of how much an item costs and how much money they have to spend. Second are the cultural considerations of what they are used to eating, what they enjoy eating and, possibly, what they think is good for them.

Application of material and cultural considerations in the process of buying and eating bread	
Wholemeal stoneground	*White sliced loaf*
Higher price	Lower price
Lower accessibility (not easy to buy)	Higher accessibility (very easy to buy)
Not available in student canteen	Always available in student canteen
Don't like taste or weight	Yummy, yummy, yummy
Aware of importance of fibre in diet	Unaware of importance of fibre in diet
Never been part of the citizen's diet	Always been part of the citizen's diet

Some of the factors involved in the decision about what type of bread to choose are related to material considerations of wealth; others are related to cultural factors. A citizen might, for example, appreciate that the fibre content is important, but not have the money to afford that type of loaf; whilst another citizen might have the resources to afford the high fibre loaf, but choose to consume the white sliced loaf. When this example is transferred to the whole diet, it becomes clear that choices about diet are influenced by both material and cultural factors, and it is only when both sets of factors are combined that we can gain a complete understanding of how the life chances of some citizens are adversely influenced.

Education

There has also been an enormous amount of research into the relationship between the social conditions of a citizen's life and their achievements in the education system. The development of a free education system for all citizens was seen to be a measure of progress towards a fair and equal society; and the continuing emphasis placed on the importance of education as a way of achieving social justice is significant today. It is generally thought that there has been a movement away from a system in which social origins, in terms of class and gender, were the most likely determinant of a citizen's destination, towards a system in which educational success is related to talent and not privilege.

Such an education system would need to be modelled on the idea of a ladder on which all citizens could climb, all with an equal opportunity of reaching the top. Such an education system would ensure that citizens were given the employment opportunities that matched their talents. Social class, sex, ethnicity or any other variable would not influence the chances of success or failure.

The Twentieth Century School

School Report

Subject	Comment	Mark
English	Written work in class sometimes comes to a full stop	8/10
History	Too reliant on past efforts	6/10
Maths	Additional work required	7/10
Music	Sound progress	7/10
The UK education system	Must try much harder	6/10
Science	Needs to experiment with ideas	6/10

To what extent has this ideal been achieved? To answer this question we can look at the effects on citizens of the massive expansion of higher education in recent years. A research report by Steve Machin, director of the Centre for the Economics of Education at the DfES, published in 2003, shows that the main effect of the expansion (the aim of which was to give 50% of citizens under 30 a university education) has simply reinforced social class divisions. The result of the expansion policy in higher education has not been more citizens from poorer backgrounds attending university; it has in fact led to an increase in the number of less able children from more affluent backgrounds attending university. The report highlights that after the removal of student grants and the introduction of tuition fees, citizens from the poorest social class participating in higher education dropped to just 7% whilst, simultaneously, the participation by the most wealthy social class increased to 72%. The conclusion from the report – that higher ability citizens from poorer backgrounds are being disadvantaged whilst lower ability citizens from wealthy backgrounds are being advantaged – suggests that the education system has a long way to go in order to achieve the goal that a citizen's social origins are not the main determinant of his or her educational success.

The quotation at the start of this chapter suggested that there is evidence to support the view that social and economic disadvantages and poverty influence the educational achievements of citizens. It also suggested that the desire to improve literacy, numeracy and access to higher education would be more likely to be achieved if the money was spent on reducing poverty rather than imposing changes in schools. Much of the research tends to deliver the same conclusion: that there is a marked difference in educational attainment between citizens based on social variables. In some instances, not only is there a difference between citizens, but, more worryingly, these differences are becoming more pronounced. A considerable amount of research tends to deliver the same type of conclusion: that it is poverty and the social and economic disadvantages a citizen experiences that significantly influence their likelihood of educational success or failure. For many citizens, it would appear that it is these social factors that provide a far better barometer of potential educational achievement than any measure of IQ.

University wealth league				
		Oxbridge richest colleges		
University net assets		Income	Assets (£m)	(£m)
Cambridge	£1,230,757,000	Trinity Cambridge	19	310
Oxford	£807,435,000	St John's Cambridge	5.9	91
Edinburgh	£685,999,000	St John's Oxford	5.5	90
Glasgow	£407,517,000	Christ Church Oxford	4.7	90
Birmingham	£406,199,000	All Souls Oxford	3	61
Bristol	£319,315,000	New College	2.9	60
Source: Times Higher Education Supplement, July 2001		Source: The Sunday Times, November 1997		

Why should it be the case that poverty and social and economic disadvantages influence a citizen's educational achievement? One reason could be that the provision of state education has done relatively little to change and improve the life chances of those citizens who suffer the cumulative effects of a life in poverty and the most severe social and economic disadvantages. The provision of state education has merely tended to reaffirm the existing inequalities in life chances between citizens. In an attempt to explain this point, reference will again be made to the purchase of a car. This time, however, it will require a little more imagination, because it is a teacher who is buying the car, and the cars in question are magic cars that can talk.

The choice again is one car from a choice of two, the same model, the same age but with very different pasts. One car is spotlessly clean, painted in a pleasant shade of blue, with all the right equipment, plus extras, and is always well spoken, using complete and grammatically correct sentences. Whenever the teacher says, 'Time for school', the car responds with phrases learnt from its maker: 'And which way would you like to go: the quick route, the safest route or the scenic route?' The other car is an inferno of colours with fluffy dice hanging from the mirror. It does not have any extras and some of the essentials are missing. When spoken to, it can only grunt a few monosyllabic responses. Which of the two cars would most citizens expect to appeal to the teacher the most?

The difference between the two cars is in the range of equipment and the patterns of speech learnt from its past. To translate these differences from cars to citizens, these amount to differences between material factors and cultural factors. Some citizens have social and cultural capital that will help to empower them and improve their life chances, some citizens do not; and the education system reaffirms the existing inequalities.

Some of the factors influencing educational attainment are clearly related to material considerations of wealth. The differential access to the internet is a new example of the gap between 'have' and 'have not' citizens. The other set of factors is clearly related to issues of culture. When a citizen experiences disadvantages in both of these factors, the combination can be devastating for their potential educational achievement.

An interesting approach to this issue is to switch the discussion from the citizen to the system. So far, the discussion has been based on 'the' education system. The alternative approach would lead to the view that, in reality, there is not one education system, but at least two education systems, each one existing with its own set of cultural values, with its own financial parameters, and catering for its own 'type' of citizens. There is an education system for those citizens whose material and cultural background enhances their educability and there is an education system for those citizens whose material and cultural background handicaps their educability.

Employment

As a citizen's experience of education is usually linked to their future experience of employment, or lack of it, there must be some form of relationship between education and both attitudes towards employment and the material rewards from employment. The same combination of material factors and cultural factors is re-emerging, with the result that, for many citizens, the link between education and employment simply means converting the social and cultural capital from the education system into occupational power and prestige; or, alternatively, an extension to the frustrations, the sense of futility and the experience of powerlessness that were all characteristics of school life. The experience from one organisation that consistently denied the citizen status and a sense of achievement is transferred to another organisation that continues to deny the citizen the ability to gain a higher status and an enhanced sense of achievement. While some citizens think their school days are 'the best days of their life', others equate their school days with life in Colditz. Correspondingly, some citizens experience immense pleasure and satisfaction from their occupation whilst other citizens experience frustration and alienation.

	Selected evidence of the links between social factors and different employment experiences
Sexuality	In a report published by the Trades Union Congress, April 2000, it was revealed that 10% of lesbian and gay workers felt that they were treated less favourably than other staff: 12.5% of staff believed that employers should be able to sack staff simply because they are gay. *The Independent,* April 2000
Social class	The risk of unemployment is linked to social class. In spring 1993, unemployment rates for the ex-manual occupations was 7.4% higher than the unemployment rates for the non-manual occupations. *Employment Gazette,* 1994
Ethnicity	In research published in March 2000, evidence of discrimination in universities emerged, with black and Asian academics earning an average of £2,500 less than their white colleagues. *The Independent,* March 2000

The third quotation at the start of this chapter suggested that employment opportunities are not evenly spread among citizens in the UK. Groups of citizens who are characterised as the very young and the oldest in the labour force, who are characterised as being from an ethnic minority, who are characterised as being disabled, and those who are generally the poorest and least empowered citizens, are all more likely to experience relatively frequent periods of unemployment. Much of the research tends to deliver the same conclusion: there is a marked difference in the experience of employment and life chances among citizens based on social variables. For many citizens, it would appear that the social and economic disadvantages they experience prior to employment are going to influence their experience of employment. Not only does a citizen's social and cultural capital influence the link between the process of education and the experience of employment, but, combined with the other social variables of ethnicity, sexuality, age and gender, it also influences the likelihood of experiencing part time employment, anti-social hours of employment and, potentially, unemployment. Social and economic disadvantages would still seem to be a better indicator of a citizen's life chances and employment opportunities than any other set of factors.

The citizen and poverty

The quotations at the start of this chapter suggest that there is evidence of a standing link between poverty and a citizen's life chances. The consequences for those citizens who are living in a state of poverty are considerable. Many policies have come and gone with little or no impact on the lives of the citizens they were supposed to improve. In order to suggest solutions to the issue of poverty, many believe that there needs to be a greater understanding of the reasons why poverty exists in the first place.

The causes of poverty

When discussing the causes of poverty, the explanations that are suggested tend to fall into three different types. There are those explanations that:

- suggest that poverty is the fault of the citizen (individual explanations);

- suggest that poverty is built into the system (structural explanations);

- suggest that poverty is perpetuated through learnt norms and values (cultural explanations).

Individual explanations

Explanations which suggest that poverty is only ever going to be the fault of the individual citizen are generally not based on theoretical considerations within an ideological approach to the issue of poverty. These explanations are more likely to be associated with the 'irresponsible soapbox' approach to citizenship, in which the individual is seen as the cause of the problem so it should be the individual who solves the problem.

These explanations focus on the citizen's individual characteristics, or shortcomings, depending on the point of view, and use labels like 'lazy', 'idle', 'lack of initiative' and 'no money sense' as the causes of poverty.

Some who take this approach are a little more compassionate and suggest that those individual citizens who are sick, although it's still their fault, are more deserving than the other categories.

Structural explanations

Explanations which suggest that poverty is built into the system can be divided between those who argue from a social democratic perspective and those who argue from a Marxist/feminist point of view. Both of these viewpoints have been discussed previously. However, it is still relevant to apply them to explanations for the existence of poverty.

Those writers who support a social democratic perspective share the basic view that the free market is inevitably going to create inequalities in income that will result in some citizens living in a state of poverty. Poverty is an inevitable part of the system and, because of this, there must be some mechanisms put in place by the state to alleviate conditions for those citizens who find themselves in poverty. This is the justification for the range of welfare benefits.

One of the problems not previously discussed that is associated with the 'mix and match' approach to welfare benefit and taxation is the 'poverty trap'. The poverty trap is a term that is applied to those citizens who are working and receive one or more means tested benefits. The problem for these citizens occurs when they receive an increase in their pay from their employer. For many citizens, the increase in pay will result in a reduction in, or the removal of, a means tested benefit as a result of the higher wage. The outcome for these citizens is that either a very high percentage of every extra £1 earned is lost in taxation – in 1986, in some cases it was as much as 70–99p (Oppenheim and Harker, *Poverty: The Facts,* 1996) – or, worse still, an increase in pay results in a reduction in the citizen's final income.

Those writers who suggest that poverty is built into the system and who support views from the Marxist/feminist perspective would argue that poverty is a necessary and inevitable part of the system because the economic system needs a pool of permanently poor citizens to act as a form of motivation and encouragement for other citizens not to 'shirk their responsibilities towards work'. The system needs to have an incentive for those citizens who are in work to keep working. This is achieved by establishing poverty within the system and making sure it remains in the system.

Cultural explanations

Some explanations for the causes of poverty suggest that it is perpetuated from one generation of citizens to another through the process of socialisation. This version of the 'culture of poverty' owes much to the work of the American sociologist Oscar Lewis, who suggested that young citizens learn strategies for coping and survival which are very good for dealing with poverty but which do not lend themselves to taking advantage of opportunities (in education and training, for example) that would take these citizens out of the cycle of poverty. The culture of poverty suggests that, as a result of a citizen's learned norms and values, they develop an attitude that accepts the inevitability of their situation, which results in the lack of any attempt to initiate change and improvement.

A second version of this approach suggests that the cause of poverty is related to a culture of dependency. This approach is most often associated with those who work from a New Right point of view, who suggest that the continuation of poverty is the result of the benefits, particularly the universal benefits, provided by the welfare state. It is the benefits from the welfare state that provide the 'money for nothing' culture, which results, for some citizens, in the removal of any incentive to improve their own situation.

One conclusion that can be drawn from the combination of these different explanations for poverty is that there is very little agreement on the causes of poverty, or even on what constitutes poverty or how many citizens actually live in a state of poverty.

The following activity will help you to appreciate the complexity of the term 'poverty' and will illustrate the lack of agreement about it. Once you have completed it, repeat the questions with a number of other people.

1 What percentage of UK citizens do you think are living in poverty today?

2 Do you think this is this more or less than the percentage of citizens living in poverty in the UK 50 years ago?

3 Do you think is this more or less than the percentage of citizens living in poverty in the UK 150 years ago?

4 When estimating the percentage of citizens in poverty, did you use any of the following to arrive at your percentage:

- The basic biological necessities required for survival?

- A comparison with other parts of the world?

- A comparison between the richest and poorest parts of the UK?

- Some idea of what the citizens at that time would regard as being normal possessions?

- If you did use the idea that the possession of some items would be expected, what items did you have in mind for citizens

(a) Today?

(b) 50 years ago?

(c) 150 years ago?

5 Compare your results with other students who have completed the activity and see if there are any similarities in the findings.

6 What conclusions can be drawn from this activity?

It is very likely that no two students got the same results from this activity. It is, in fact, more than possible that the results will be so diverse that no conclusions can be drawn from them. This is nothing to worry about, because a look at the figures below will confirm that even the 'experts' cannot agree on the numbers, if any, of citizens who are living in a state of poverty.

There have been widely differing estimates of the number of citizens living in a state of poverty. The Breadline Europe study produced a report in March 2001, which used a definition developed at the 1995 World Summit at which 117 governments agreed on a definition of poverty. This report estimated that 5 million citizens, or 9% of all UK citizens, were living in a state of poverty. For some groups of citizens, the study found that their chances of living in a state of poverty were far greater, with 40% of all lone parents with one child, 54% of all lone parents with two or more children and 25% of lone pensioners all living in a state of poverty. Other estimates include the following:

- A report published by the Department of Work and Pensions in November 2002 shows that in central London, 53% of children, 36% of pensioners and 30% of working age adults are all living in a state of poverty. The report considers poverty to exist where, after housing costs are removed, income is less than 60% of the average national income. This report also found that some groups have a higher likelihood of living in poverty: for example, 73% of Pakistani and Bangladeshi children were found to be living in poverty.
- The Joseph Rowntree Foundation estimated in September 2001 that 4.5 million citizens, or 24% of households, were living in a state of poverty.
- The Institute for Public Policy Research estimated in March 2000 that 32% of children up to 15 years old were living in a state of poverty.
- The Centre for Analysis of Social Exclusion estimated in March 2000 that 2 million citizens were living in a state of poverty.

Not all share the view that there are considerable numbers of citizens living in a state of poverty. John Moore, when he was the 1989 Conservative Secretary of State for Social Security, stated that 'It is hard to believe that poverty stalks the land when even the poorest fifth of families spend nearly a tenth of their income on alcohol and tobacco' (May 1989), with the clear implication that no citizens are living in a state of poverty in modern Britain.

The reason for this range of speculation is that the term 'poverty' is based on many different sets of assumptions. These different assumptions will lead to considerable variations in the interpretation of what constitutes 'living in a state of poverty'. Different assumptions backed up with different evidence will result in different definitions. It is rather like an equation in which:

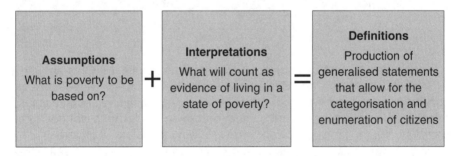

The assumptions that citizens can make about poverty fall into a number of different categories. One set of assumptions can view poverty in terms of basic needs or necessities. This could mean those basic biological necessities required in order to survive, essentially food and drink, and essential commodities like shelter and clothing.

An alternative approach is to make the assumption that poverty can only be established and measured if groups of citizens are compared with other groups of citizens. If one group of citizens can afford a range of goods and services, and have the ability to make choices about their lifestyle, whilst another group do not, it is possible to make comparisons between these groups. If the difference between the two groups is significant, the group that cannot afford to acquire the goods or use the services and do not have the ability to choose, compared to the other group, could be said to be living in poverty.

If you had to decide whether a group of citizens were or were not living in poverty:

- Which goods would you consider to be affordable?
- Which services would you consider to be affordable?
- What would be some of the choices that you would expect citizens to be able to make?

The difference in focus between these two approaches is considerable. The first approach to poverty views it in absolute terms, whilst the second approach needs to be able to compare groups of citizens in order to make a relative judgment about their position.

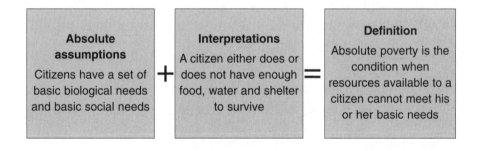

Absolute assumptions	Interpretations	Definition
Citizens have a set of basic biological needs and basic social needs	A citizen either does or does not have enough food, water and shelter to survive	Absolute poverty is the condition when resources available to a citizen cannot meet his or her basic needs

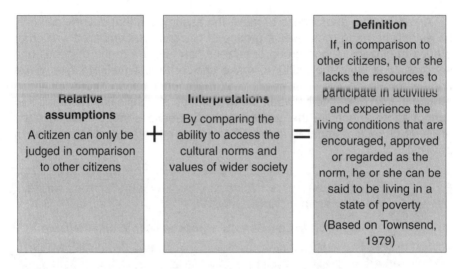

Relative assumptions		Interpretations		**Definition**
A citizen can only be judged in comparison to other citizens	**+**	By comparing the ability to access the cultural norms and values of wider society	**=**	If, in comparison to other citizens, he or she lacks the resources to participate in activities and experience the living conditions that are encouraged, approved or regarded as the norm, he or she can be said to be living in a state of poverty
				(Based on Townsend, 1979)

The two approaches to poverty are very distinctive in their focus. However, it is the implications that arise for those citizens living in a state of poverty when these approaches are applied that are important. After all, it is those citizens who are living in poverty who will face the consequences of the application of one specific approach.

Research the contribution to the study of poverty made by:

- Peter Townsend – Professor of International Social Policy at the LSE
- Seebohm Rowntree
- Charles Booth

If Rowntree was to repeat his work on poverty, with a poverty line being based on the monetary value of subsistence needs, what do you think he would include in his subsistence needs today?

Approaches to poverty based on an absolute definition

The advantages that many claim for approaches to poverty based on an absolute definition are that they are quick to work out, easy to apply and easy to understand. When the Beveridge Report was redefining the rules on the approach to welfare, it was an absolute approach that was largely adopted. The policies for dealing with poverty were based on a poverty line that was defined in monetary terms. To establish this line, based on the cost of essentials, was a relatively straightforward task for an uncritical civil service. Once established, the poverty line was easy to apply, since a citizen could only possibly be in one of two positions: on one side of the line if they had enough money not to be in poverty; on the other side of the line if they did not, and were living in a state of poverty. At a time when the norms and values regarding welfare benefits were also being redefined, this approach had the added advantage for politicians of being very easy to explain to citizens who had not been socialised into a culture of benefits.

The problems with this approach become apparent, however, as soon as it is applied to citizens. The single biggest problem is establishing the level at which any 'poverty line' should be set. If the poverty line is to be equated to a weekly sum of money, what should that sum of money be able to buy? What should or should not be on the 'shopping list'? Should the list only include goods needed for a citizen's survival, or should it include some luxuries? Who would be responsible for drawing up the shopping list? Would they be nutritional 'experts' who could knock up a nutritionally balanced meal from the scraps that are usually binned? Would they assume that all citizens need the same amount of daily calories? If it is to include a 'luxury', what is a luxury and will it be a luxury for all citizens? If a weekly sum of money is established, will it apply throughout the whole of the UK, ignoring regional variations in the cost of living?

Approaches to poverty based on a relative definition

The approaches to poverty that are based on the comparison of one group with another are referred to as relative approaches. The single biggest advantage of this approach is that it acknowledges that poverty is a socially constructed category. It is socially constructed because what counts as being in poverty will vary according to time, place and society. It is only possible to ascertain whether the condition of poverty is being experienced by a comparison of one social group with another.

Another advantage of this approach is that it does not isolate poverty from other citizenship issues, a point already established when discussing TH Marshall (see above, Chapter 3). Poverty is as important for those citizens not in poverty as it is for those who are in poverty, as it is the lifestyle and the life chances of those not in poverty that determine the nature, breadth and scope of those in poverty.

The final advantage of this approach relates directly to the criticisms of the absolute approach, as the relative approach does not rely on the construction of a single poverty line with all its associated problems.

One of the biggest problems associated with this approach can be developed from part of its definition. If relative poverty is said to exist when, in comparison with other citizens, a citizen lacks the resources to participate in the activities and experience the living conditions that are seen to be the norm, what exactly is the norm and how is the norm going to be established? When does a commodity change from being a luxury into a norm? Is the possession of a video recorder a luxury or a norm? If it is a norm, try putting an exact date on when this change occurred. What would be the situation if all citizens who wanted to own a video recorder owned one? Would the measure change to DVD machines? The process of trying to establish, measure and determine what constitutes 'the norm' is fraught with value judgments and problems, and could be subjected to all the criticisms associated with establishing, measuring and determining the poverty line in the absolute approach.

Another problem with this approach is that the number of citizens who appear to be living in a state of poverty can rapidly appear to increase at exactly the time when, in all likelihood, actual numbers are decreasing. This contradiction occurs because in times of an economic boom levels of deprivation tend to fall as incomes increase. However, with higher average incomes it then appears that there are more citizens, relatively, living in a state of poverty. The reverse is also true: if all citizens were suffering from malnutrition, since there would be no other group to compare them with, would that mean that nobody was living in a state of poverty?

When these points are combined, some critics of the relative approach to poverty argue that it does not actually measure poverty; what it does in fact measure is inequality, and the question is raised as to whether it is realistic to measure poverty in terms of the ability to possess a video recorder.

Poverty: a useful concept?

What is clear in any discussion relating to poverty is that no one approach is without its faults. Consequently, some argue that the best way to approach poverty is to select elements of each approach and combine them to help produce a reliable set of figures which shows how many citizens are, in fact, living in a state of poverty. One instant improvement would be to have a variable definition of poverty in which different groups of citizens would have different definitions of poverty. Although this sounds quite absurd, there is a logic behind the proposal that can be illustrated through issues surrounding the cost of child care. It could be argued that child care is cheaper when there are two adult citizens in a household as opposed to only one. For the two-citizen household, child care costs can often be reduced as citizens can use each other freely to undertake child care, an option that is not available for the one-citizen household.

The inability to arrive at a definition of poverty that has a measure of universal agreement returns students to the issue of numbers. How many citizens in the UK are living in poverty? This lack of agreement as to what constitutes living in a state of poverty will lead to the unhelpful, but technically correct, response that the number of citizens living in poverty will be dependent on how poverty is defined. Indeed, in August 2002, the Social Market Foundation, an organisation that advises governments, produced a pamphlet entitled 'Poor Measures', which warned the Blair Government that its ambitious plans to eliminate child poverty are more than likely to fail unless a more accurate definition of poverty is established.

Another issue that is often discussed relates to the causes of poverty. Again, the same problems emerge: it is difficult to establish why some citizens are more likely to experience living in a state of poverty when what counts as poverty cannot be universally determined.

Even when the internationally agreed definition of 'poverty' is used, there are still problems in establishing how many citizens are living in poverty. As discussed in the 2001 Breadline Europe study, the definition agreed by 117 governments at the 1995 World Summit links poverty to lack of food, safe drinking water, sanitation facilities, health, shelter, education and information, but, when applied, it still bases its data on the citizen's assessment of what are the absolute essentials of life, and it is only when households are lacking at least six of these essentials, not through choice but through lack of money, that they are categorised as living in poverty. Why six?

This may leave some students questioning the value of the concept of poverty and whether it has any value in the study of citizenship. In response to this point, it is important to affirm that any study of citizenship should include some reference to poverty. This does not have to be the type of reference that deals only in 'facts and statistics', but it is well worth examining poverty within an ideological context.

The importance of looking at poverty in an ideological context is because it is a tool that can be used to explain. Politicians, political parties, pressure groups and individual citizens all use poverty as an explanation for differences between citizens' life chances in health, education and employment. The problem, however, is that if poverty can be used as an ideological tool, it can be used differently by different sections of society. An ideological tool is no different from any other type of tool in the way that it can be put to different and unintended uses in order to achieve different results.

An alternative concept is that of 'social exclusion'. This is a broader concept than poverty, as it includes the issue of whether a citizen can participate effectively in the economic, social, political and cultural life to a degree that other citizens would regard as 'normal'. This concept was adopted by the Labour Party, which, when it returned to power in 1997, established the Social Exclusion Unit to co-ordinate the work of all government departments that have a potential impact on the life of any citizen at the margins of society.

Ending poverty

In an interesting article, Deborah Orr takes the consultative *Neighbourhood Renewal Strategy Report*, published by the Social Exclusion Unit in April 2000, and translates the report's key ideas from the language of 'excruciating politeness' into short 'bitesize' points. These key ideas are seen as a way in which those citizens who have experienced poverty can be given the help and support they need in order to get themselves out of their situation. This is a much more positive note, a note that suggests that there is hope and a future for all citizens. Read and digest the list opposite before completing the research exercise below.

 Research as many examples of material factors and cultural factors that could influence educational attainment as you can. Try to link these with the variables of social class, ethnicity, sexuality and gender. Use this research to complete the table.

Material factors that could influence educational attainment	Cultural factors that could influence educational attainment

Which set of factors, the material factors or the cultural, do you think plays the most significant role in influencing educational attainment?

Twenty ways out of poverty	
Key Idea 1	Improving citizens' skills through a second chance at education
Key Idea 2	Improving IT skills and knowledge and improving access to IT
Key Idea 3	Helping citizens into occupations, reducing unemployment and promoting re-employment
Key Idea 4	Promoting a positive view about the benefits of employment
Key Idea 5	Supporting and promoting business with the extra aim of keeping money in the community
Key Idea 6	Tackling crime, drugs and anti-social behaviour
Key Idea 7	Introducing neighbourhood wardens
Key Idea 8	Improving letting policies to remove the grouping of 'problem' citizens
Key Idea 9	Promoting art and sport in the community
Key Idea 10	Improving funding for projects that would benefit the community
Key Idea 11	Setting targets to improve the delivery of public services
Key Idea 12	Ensuring the public services have appropriate and adequate resources
Key Idea 13	Increasing the use of school facilities (also available outside school hours)
Key Idea 14	Increasing support for citizens from social workers and other agencies
Key Idea 15	Locating welfare agencies within the community
Key Idea 16	Locating financial services within the community
Key Idea 17	Encouraging local shopping facilities to return
Key Idea 18	Improving training for teachers, doctors and other professionals who work in the community
Key Idea 19	Co-ordinating policies between all the different agencies
Key Idea 20	Providing feedback of information to citizens in order to monitor improvements and changes in the community

Based on 'Thirty ways out of the poverty trap', *The Independent*, 14 April 2000

What do you understand by the following terms and concepts?

- Life chances
- Motivation
- Life expectancy
- Absolute poverty

- Powerlessness
- Relative poverty
- Cultural capital
- Educational attainment

A fair society requires not only an open road but also an equal start. Unless there are changes in the way society is organised, there is always going to be a link between a citizen's social class and their likelihood of experiencing either privilege or poverty.

It is impossible for any citizen in the UK today to experience deprivation and poverty.

CHAPTER 22

Citizenship and Community Involvement

Be active, be reflective, be successful

The aims of this chapter are to:

- Stress the importance of action and reflection to enhance progression
- Encourage the student of citizenship to extend their studies beyond the classroom
- Encourage the student of citizenship to evaluate their experiences
- Provide activities that will assist in the examination of AS Citizenship

Stage 1 – be active

No matter what else is happening, everybody, every day, has the potential not only to 'think citizenship', but also to be actively involved with citizenship issues. In reality this should not be new advice, as throughout your citizenship course there are plenty of opportunities to be active. Being active has the advantage of bringing the course alive and a lot of skills can be acquired from being active. It is much more enjoyable seeing a court in action than reading the transcript of the trial, and getting involved with political processes and the community will be more rewarding than just reading about pressure groups. Being active can also mean developing an awareness of what is going on around you, from the smallest element of your local community to the activities of multi-national organisations.

Developing awareness can also be achieved from using the media, and being active includes reading newspapers. It does not matter which one, as will become apparent later. Equally, watching television and listening to the radio, national and local, are other ways to be active.

Anybody can be active in the community and indeed many citizens are. However, there is little or no point in being active if you do not have a purpose or reason for being active. If you attend a court sitting without a reason, or if you read a newspaper or watch a television programme without thinking or reflecting, then the activity will only be of limited usefulness because once you have become active you need to combine it with stage two …

Stage 2 – be reflective

There is little point in reading about or watching an event if you do not reflect on it, and it is this reflective process that is probably the most important. Reflection allows the student of citizenship to make comments about their experience; not just comments, but informed comments. Through this process of reflecting, thinking and evaluating what you have actively been involved with, you will be able to understand why things happen in the way they do, why this process and not that process occurs and, from this reflection, you will be able to evaluate and to judge and to question the activities in which you have been involved. Those inside a group know why they act and behave in the way that they do. Outsiders do not understand why. They can describe, but they will not fully understand. Insider knowledge is invaluable in understanding the processes and actions of those inside. It allows you to see things from 'their point of view', to understand things from 'their point of view'. The insider can ask the questions that the outsider would not even have thought to ask.

Stage 1 – be active

There are many ways in which you can become more active. Some ideas are listed below.

- Visit the Courts of Justice. All have a public gallery.

- Visit areas of local public life. Councils publish their meetings for the year and all have a public gallery.

- Try to arrange a trip to the House of Commons when it is in session. You will need to contact your local MP. A tourist visit can be booked in advance during the summer recess.

- Keep a file of press cuttings that cover the major issues surrounding citizenship.

Stage 2 – be reflective

There are many ways in which you can improve your evaluative skills. Some ideas are listed below.

- Question all elements of your participation. Ask:
  - what is going on;
  - why it is going on;
  - who will benefit from the present arrangements.

- What if the citizens that you were working with changed ?

- What if the location changed?

- Are there any variables that may have influenced your experience?

- Become involved with a specific community group.
- Use the internet to establish cross-cultural links.
- Develop a statistics file to monitor any changes that are relevant to your study of citizenship.

- Can you make any generalisations about other citizens?
- Can you draw any conclusions from your activities?
- Are any key terms or concepts really of any use?
- Is there any hidden agenda?

Stage 3 – be successful

How is it possible to achieve success? One way success can be achieved is when stages one and two have been combined. You have become involved with some element of your community, reflected on your involvement and now, through this evaluation, you know more and can offer maybe a suggestion as to improvements for the future. The sum of the parts is of greater value than each individual part. For example, if you own the world's safest padlock but have lost the key, the padlock is of little real use. If you then found the world's most complicated key but did not have the padlock, this is also of little real use. However, if you own both the key and the padlock, you will always be able to lock away something secure in the knowledge that it will be safe. The sum of the parts is of greater value than each individual part.

Dilemmas facing the active citizen: a community action case study

Being different is not the same as being mad. However, for some citizens, the fact that they are different often means that they are excluded from what other citizens would regard as 'normal'. If they were asked to map out their life plan from the age of 16 to 60, most citizens would probably include elements of good health, completing their education, gaining rewarding employment, home ownership, partnership and family, as well as some of the luxuries of life: travel, the pursuit of some hobby or pastime, and ultimately a safe and reasonable pension. The exact nature of these life goals may vary from citizen to citizen, but for the majority, this path would represent a conventional life.

What happens, however, when a citizen chooses to be different? Some citizens will acknowledge the fact that each citizen has a right to be different, accept that citizen's alternative lifestyle and include them as part of their community. Some citizens will also acknowledge the fact that each citizen has a right to be different and argue that a citizen with an alternative lifestyle has the right to be different but not outside their house or in sight of their front room window. Communities inhabited by NIMBYs (Not In My Back Yard) provide a real dilemma for the active citizen.

'The Lady in the Van' is a work from the writer Alan Dennett which is based on the true story of Miss Shepherd, who lived for 15 years in a van parked on his drive. Ann Naysmith is another citizen who spurned the conventional house to live for nearly 30 years in a Ford Consul car parked in a west London street.

Miss Naysmith's accommodation has the potential to divide local citizens into:

- Those who see the car as an eyesore and a health hazard attracting rats and pigeons. The rubbish and litter make the whole street look a mess and ultimately the carhome devalues houses and makes them harder to sell.

- Those who see Miss Naysmith and her carhome as part of the local community and something to celebrate, as it represents community understanding and tolerance of someone who does not fit with conventional lifestyles.

Dilemma

 Ask yourself: which side of the fence would you be on?

The lifestyle of Miss Naysmith also has the potential to divide those citizens who have wider responsibilities.

- Bearing in mind that Miss Naysmith claims no benefits, is perfectly clean as she washes in a local doctor's surgery, recycles all her rubbish, obtains drinking water from a local shop and even grows plants on a small plot of land in a local car park which she swaps for food, is she actually doing anybody any harm?
- Alternatively, if your job involves a duty to care for local citizens, is it reasonable to claim that an unheated old car without any security is an appropriate and safe environment for anybody to live in?

Dilemma

 Ask yourself, would you try to include Miss Naysmith in the community and give her carhome an official postcode, which is essential as this allows citizens to register permanently with a doctor?

or

Would you try to move Miss Naysmith into some form of sheltered accommodation in order for her to live in warmth, security and with access to all the services that are regarded as 'normal'?

The outcome of the local council meeting discussing Miss Naysmith was to proceed with the legal processes to remove the car and to provide Miss Naysmith initially with bed and breakfast accommodation before moving her into a flat. When the legal processes were completed, the local council informed residents that the car was to be removed, and the police were on hand to ensure that the process was completed.

Dilemma

 Ask yourself, would you be secretly pleased, and watch the removal of the carhome?

or

Would you protest by forming a human shield to stop the removal of the carhome?

It was the usual pattern of Miss Naysmith's lifestyle to leave her carhome every morning at 8 am. This was the pattern on the day her carhome was to be removed. The consequence was that when she returned, her living accommodation for the last 30 years was no longer there.

Dilemma

Ask yourself, would you simply say that the local council had now stepped in and they must have everything under control?

or

Would you use a resident's car, with blacked out windows and a few blankets, as a temporary solution to provide some accommodation for Miss Naysmith?

The problem for citizens affected by the case of Miss Naysmith is what to do next. The possibilities are:

- Simply to do nothing; the 'it's not my problem' approach.
- To argue that her human rights under Article 8 of the Human Rights Act which states that 'Everyone has the right to respect for his [sic] private life, home and his [sic] correspondence' have been breached and to seek redress through the courts.
- To provide another car somewhere in the local area.
- To force Miss Naysmith to live a conventional lifestyle so that the 'problem' goes away.

Dilemma

Ask yourself: how would you organise some form of political action? How would you develop a campaign? What would its aims be? What methods would you adopt? Who would you encourage to participate? How would you use the media? How would you judge how effective your campaign had been?

All the questions above can be applied to your own involvement in a local issue, and all knowledge of community based forms of action, especially those using your own experiences, will provide by far the best way to discuss and evaluate effective community action.

Community involvement will arrive naturally from being a critical and questioning student. Being critical and questioning will also enable you to transform items of news into issues relating to citizenship. Every situation you find yourself in has the potential to illustrate the ways in which citizens interact.

The following extract raises many dilemmas facing the active citizen and many issues that directly relate to the study of citizenship.

The inner city borough of Sturdbrough is located in the east of the second largest city in the country. As with many inner city areas there are huge contrasts in nearly all aspects of the area. There have been considerable improvements in some parts of the borough, which are now occupied by the young rich who commute the short distance to their well paid jobs in the city centre. Other parts of the borough remain desperately poor. These are the areas occupied by a more transient population whose existence relies on less secure, less reliable and much lower paid work, if they are lucky. For many, however, even this work would be considered a luxury, for they have to rely on government benefits.

These divided groups of the rich and the poor were believed to be the two 'parallel worlds' making up the population of Sturdbrough.

That was until some recently published government research established that there is a large number of 'non-people' living in inner city areas like Sturdbrough. An alternative 'parallel world' has been discovered consisting of those people who officially do not exist. This group of people do not appear on any government list or register; they are 'invisible'. They are, however, real people with real rights.

Who are the largest group of people who inhabit this 'invisible' world? They consist, surprisingly, not of criminals on the run or anarchists out to destroy the fabric of society, but mainly 15–45 year old men who have slipped through the net. It is true that many are homeless and that there are some asylum seekers amongst the 'invisible', but other groups include, for example, the exploited, victims of discrimination, the abused and victims of domestic violence.

The borough of Sturdbrough feels that it has a responsibility to its 'invisible' people and especially to their children. Although people have the right to educate their children themselves, the official point of view is that it is better to be included within the norms and values of society rather than being excluded, and the borough of Sturdbrough is committed to reaching out to this 'invisible' population with the aim of including all citizens within its official figures.

Some issues could include:

- Approaches to the inclusion/ exclusion of citizens
- Responsibility to other citizens
- Reliability of official figures
- How to establish the 'real' number of citizens
- Education of all citizens
- Consensus/conflict in the community
- Cohesion/diversity in the community
- Exploitation of the most vulnerable citizens
- Welfare of all citizens

The examination and examination practice

One way to prepare for Module 3 is to look at the issue of resolving conflict in a community. All communities are different and all will have a number of citizens who are trying to achieve different objectives.

East Scraplington
campaigning for action in the local community

The village of East Scraplington is located to the south east of one of the largest cities in the country. It is a fairly long commute for the young, rich citizens who travel to their well paid jobs in the city centre. With its community of around 250 citizens, East Scraplington has quite distinct areas; some parts of the village have been considerably improved but some parts remain desperately poor.

This diversity is both a strength and a weakness for East Scraplington. When looked at as a whole, all the indicators point to 'an average village': average rates of employment/unemployment, average rates of crime, average rates of poverty and average rates of drug abuse/dealing. To the eyes of the outsider it appears a typical village.

Politics has never featured strongly amongst the citizens, and the local council has never been subjected to party politics with Miss Goodly-Twiner having been the Independent councillor for the last 37 years.

Until recently, the community would have been described as vibrant. A village school, a doctor's surgery, three public houses, a post office, a small number of shops that between them provided for all the everyday needs and even some emergencies. Doorstep milk deliveries, a weekly library service, and community events in the local village hall all contributed to the village's self-sufficiency. For the services that the village could not support, there was a twice daily bus service to and from the city from where inter-city bus and rail links are available. Even the village green with its cricket square played its part in the life of the village, being used regularly for community events.

Within the last four years, however, it all started to fall apart. The brewery closed down one pub and when the proprietor of the second died, the family decided to call it a day and turned the pub into a house. Budget measures reduced and then removed the bus service and a new Community Health Centre removed the village's GP and surgery. Due to the surplus of school places in the county, the village school was closed, with school children now being bussed to the suburbs of the city.

The opening of a 'business park', also to the south east of the city, meant a new supermarket that provided a range of goods and services that the local stores could not match. First one, then another and finally the last village shop closed its doors for the last time. The weekly library van's visit was reduced to once fortnightly and the dairy deliveries are now only twice a week.

Whilst the providers of these services have moved out, speculative buyers have moved in, buying cottages to rent out as 'holiday cottages' during the holiday season. E-commerce has also made some cottages attractive office spaces, a fact that was soon realised and exploited by an influx of home workers who work and live in the village but socialise in the city.

When a low-cost, high-density housing estate was developed to the south of the city, this had the effect of increasing the flow of traffic through the village as commuters and shoppers discovered that the lanes provide a fast alternative to the clogged-up ring road.

As the provision of services changed in the village so did its population. Without a school, the village became less attractive to the younger couples, who tended to move out. The elderly remained, with an influx of young, single, affluent workers. Speculative buyers of cottages were renting them out either as holiday lets or to the local authority to use to house the homeless, some asylum seekers, the exploited, victims of discrimination, the abused and victims of domestic violence. For some villagers, East Scraplington at night time is a dark and barren place with youngsters from the estate using the village green to undertake activities that are not always legal. Many of the elderly villagers now feel that East Scraplington is 'nice by day, but naughty by night', and they feel trapped inside their own homes.

The post office is now due to close down and some villagers have decided enough is enough. The post office has become a focal point in a local dispute that has split the village into four camps. Each section is described below with their campaign slogan.

1 Say NO to no PO

AIM – To reverse the decision to close the post office and to develop ways to keep the post office open.

This group is headed by Mr Peter Thorne, who, along with other pensioners, feels that the closure of the post office will have a detrimental effect on the lives of all pensioners.

2 Miss Goodly-Twiner is a Waste of Timer

AIM – To become an effective local councillor in order to represent all the interests of all villagers. This would be done through influencing the committees of the local council.

Ms M Redus, upwardly mobile and politically aware, wants to remove Miss Goodly-Twiner from the local council and is canvassing support for her campaign to become the local councillor.

3 East Scraplington Express Route

AIM – To improve the roads around and through the village so that villagers can get to the services and facilities available in the city quickly.

This group is headed by Mr John Webb, young, single and with business interests in the city, who works mainly through his computer terminal in his cottage in the village. He wants to improve the road access between East Scraplington and the city in order to get to the business park and to the pubs and restaurants in the city.

4 Real Villagers for a Real Village

AIM – To return the village to the type of community it was 30 years ago.

Mrs Dixie King, known as 'Mighty Mouth' to her friends, wants to remove all the 'spongers' and all those who live on welfare benefits from the village, as well as all holiday homes and cottages that are rented to holiday makers, converting them to 'Real Homes for Real Villagers'.

Listed below are some methods that are available to groups or individuals in order to try to influence opinion.

Each group devised a campaign to try to achieve their aim, although only one was successful.

Some possible methods available

- Bill posters
- Petitions
- Publishing a newsletter
- Writing to the local MP
- Holding a series of public meetings
- Processions

- Hand bills
- Website
- Briefing meetings
- Advertising in the press
- Employing a professional lobbyist

This activity not only provides valuable exam practice, but also allows, depending on the tactics adopted, a vast range of key skills to be achieved.

Group activity

Divide into four groups, with each group adopting one of the aims above.

- Using a range of media, devise a campaign that you think would be the most appropriate method to successfully achieve the group's aims.
- Each group should present their campaign to a neutral audience who then decides, as a result of the campaign, which groups would be successful and which groups would be unsuccessful.

Individual activity

- What do you think would be the most likely method to be adopted by each of the groups?
- What do you think would be the most appropriate method to successfully achieve each group's aims?
- Devise a campaign for one or more of these groups.

Present the campaigns to a small sample to see which of the four campaigns would be the most successful.

The AS Citizenship examination: 'what do points mean? ... Prizes!'

On the assumption that many students of citizenship will be hoping to pass their examination and continue into further education, there are some important things to remember apart from the obvious tips about systematic learning and revision.

The first tip is to remember that there exists a body of knowledge that constitutes Citizenship, which this book has aimed to investigate closely. If you are not sure exactly what the subject involves, look at the rationale and aims in the AS specification. You will find that you need to apply your body of knowledge of Citizenship to contemporary social and political debates that range from the smallest local concern, through national issues, to Europe-wide areas of concern. Not only are the issues that you study important, but of equal importance is how you apply your Citizenship skills to those issues. You will need to apply more than just your knowledge from your other subjects. Students following a course in Sociology or Government and Politics will not really be advantaged, as they will need to apply their Citizenship knowledge, not just their Sociology or Government and Politics knowledge, to the examination. Always remember that you will need to justify your responses. This is vital, as the examiner is unlikely to be a fount of all knowledge; they are human and cannot know all local examples. Therefore, justify why you have chosen something, why it provides a good illustration, why it is a good example, and so on.

A recipe for disaster is to think you can just apply your 'pre-determined common sense knowledge' to the examination or hope to use shallow media snippets. Also remember that the examination is not a soapbox or a platform from which you can air grievances or repeat prejudices. The 'of course, everyone knows' type of response will also only reveal a lack of Citizenship knowledge.

By far the best way to approach the subject is to 'get you hands dirty', be active and learn through experience, be practical and take an active role: 'to do is to know is to understand.' Learning through experience will be a way to find out the answers to the questions you would never have thought to ask.

So what should you aim to achieve? Apart from your best, the following descriptions may help.

Grade descriptions: what markers look for in students' work

The Grade A student

As a grade A student, you will be able to demonstrate an in-depth knowledge and critical understanding of Citizenship. This will involve Citizenship concepts and theories and knowledge of political institutions and processes. You will be able to provide accurate evidence and contemporary examples to substantiate and illustrate your Citizenship knowledge. You will have a substantial portfolio of evidence of your community involvement.

You will also be able to confidently apply a wide range of knowledge to unfamiliar situations, problems and issues using a substantial vocabulary appropriate to the study of Citizenship. You will be able to provide analysis that displays a sophisticated and detailed evaluation of evidence and arguments from a wide range of sources.

Your responses will be detailed and comprehensive. They will not only fully address the demands of any question, but will also show that you can organise and communicate arguments, justifications and conclusions from a diverse range of sources with clarity and purpose.

The Grade C student

As a grade C student, you will be able to demonstrate a sound knowledge and good understanding of Citizenship. This will involve Citizenship concepts and theories and knowledge of political institutions and processes. You will be able to provide clear evidence and relevant examples to substantiate and illustrate your Citizenship knowledge. You will have a reasonable portfolio of evidence of community involvement.

You will also be able to apply a good range of knowledge to unfamiliar situations, problems and issues using a vocabulary appropriate to the study of Citizenship. You will be able to provide analysis that displays effective evaluation of evidence and arguments from a range of sources.

Your responses will be reasonably comprehensive. They will not only address the demands of any question, but will also show that you can organise and communicate arguments, justifications and conclusions from a diverse range of sources adequately.

The Grade E student

As a grade E student, you will be able to demonstrate an outline of and a generally accurate understanding of Citizenship knowledge. This will involve Citizenship concepts and theories and knowledge of political institutions and processes. You will tend to provide anecdotal evidence with dated or inaccurate examples to illustrate your Citizenship knowledge. You will have some evidence of community involvement.

You will be able to apply some knowledge to unfamiliar situations, problems and issues, usually using a vocabulary appropriate to the study of Citizenship. You will also be able to provide limited analysis that displays some awareness of a range of evidence and arguments from a limited range of sources.

Your responses will be thinner and more descriptive and only marginally address the demands of any question, with arguments, justifications and conclusions being less well organised and from a narrow range of sources.

GOOD LUCK ALL CITIZENS

BIBLIOGRAPHY AND REFERENCES

Abercrombie, J and Warde, A, *Contemporary British Society*, 1988, Polity

Arlidge, J and Paton-Walsh, N, 'Do I look like an anarchist weirdo?', *The Observer*, 6 June 1999

Alton, D, *Citizen Virtues*, 1999, HarperCollins

Barnes, J, 'The worst reported war since the Crimean', *The Guardian*, 25 February 2002

Barrett, A, 'Every move you make. Every breath you take ...', *The Observer*, 30 June 2000

Becker, H, *Outsiders: Studies in the Sociology of Deviance*, 1997, Glencoe Illinois Free Press

Benn, T, 'Curbing the powers of PMs', *The Observer*, 15 July 1979

Bennetto, J, 'Thousands of new cameras filming street', *The Independent*, 18 January 2000

Bhattacharya, S, 'The Beat generation', *ES*, 21 January 2000

Biglono, I, 'Anti-terrorism legislation in the UK', 2002, Liberty

Bilton, T *et al*, *Introductory Sociology*, 3rd edn, 1981, Macmillan

Blair, A, 'My vision for Britain', *The Observer,* 10 November 2002

Blunkett, D, 'Need for citizenship education underlined by survey', Government press release 541/99

Blunkett, D, 'What does citizenship mean today?', Foreign Policy Centre, September 2002

Blunkett, D, 'It's not about cricket tests', *The Guardian*, 14 December 2001

Bourdieu, P, *Sociology in Question*, 1993, Sage

Bright, M, 'How a bomb in Libya led to a legal earthquake', *The Observer*, 23 July 2000

Bright, M, 'Why did the police stop this man 37 times?', *The Observer*, 10 December 2002

Brindle, D, 'Race bias in mental hospitals', *The Guardian*, 6 March 2000

Butler, D and Stokes, DE, *Political Change in Britain: The Evolution of Electoral Choice*, 1969, Macmillan

Butler, D and Kavanagh, D, *The General Election of 2001*, 2002, Palgrave

Campbell, D, 'Race discrimination rife within criminal justice say probation officers', *The Guardian*, 12 August 1996

Carter, H, 'Used in Europe since the last century', *The Guardian*, 4 July 2002

Carvel, J, '53% of London children "live in poverty"', *The Guardian*, 19 November 2002

Cashmore, E and Troyna, B, *Introduction to Race Relations*, 1968, Routledge

Cathcart, 'Murder in the dark', *New Statesman*, 10 April 1998

Clare, J, 'The Status Zero generation', *Daily Telegraph*, 13 October 1995

Clarke, C, 'Citizenship education can help support democracy', Government press release 275/99

Cohen, N, 'Blunkett's identity crisis', *The Observer*, 30 June 2002

Cohen, N, 'When justice is truly blind', *The Observer*, 4 August 2002

Cohen, N, 'Murmuring judges', *The Observer*, 16 July 2000

Cohen, N, 'No idea behind IDS', *The Observer*, 22 September 2001

Cohen N, 'Lies, damned lies and Jack Straw's statistics', *The Observer*, 6 February 2000

Cohen, S and Young, J, *The Manufacture of News – Social Problems, Deviance and the Mass Media*, 1981, Constable

Cohen, S, *Folk Devils and Moral Panics*, 1980, Martin Robertson

Cowley, J, 'Power, glory and the advance of the old school tie', *The Times*, 24 April 1997

Craig, I, 'Shock over "people who never vote"', *Manchester Evening News*, 2 December 1998

Criddle, B, 'MPs and candidates', in Butler, D and Kavanagh, D, *The British General Election of 1997*, 1997, Macmillan

Crowley, H, *Women and the Domestic Sphere in Social and Cultural Forms of Modernity*, 1992, Polity

Curtice, J and Steed, M, 'The results analysed', in Butler, D and Kavanagh, D, *The British General Election of 1997*, 1997, Macmillan

Deans, J, 'Blacks "are more likely target for police stop and search"', *Daily Mail*, 9 December 1998

Denscombe, M, *Sociology Update 1993, 1994, 1997, 1998, 1999*, Olympus

Dobraszczyc, U, *Sociology in Focus: Sickness, Health and Medicine*, 1989, Longman

Dudley, GF and Richardson, JJ, 'Arenas without rules and the policy change process: outsider groups and the British roads policy' (1989) Vol 46 Political Studies

Dyer, C, 'Blacks' jail risk "increased by biased judges"', *The Guardian*, 10 December 1992

Dyer, C, 'Judge selection found to lack transparency', *The Guardian*, 8 October 2002

Dyer, C, 'Judging the judges', *The Guardian*, 16 March 2001

Dyer, C, 'Justice in the spotlight', *The Guardian*, 13 February 2002

Dyer, C, 'The rights stuff', *The Guardian*, 2 October 2001

Elliot, V, '*Citizen's Charter* to get Blair treatment', *The Times*, 30 June 1998

Ellis, W, *The Oxbridge Conspiracy*, 1994, Penguin

Elvidge, J, *Getting the Message – News, Truth and Power*, 1993, Routledge

Evans, M, 'Shayler loses "public interest" argument', *The Times*, 17 May 2001

Evans, R and Hencke, D, 'Blair "big bang" theory to defy freedom act', *The Guardian*, 3 October 2001

Evans, R and Hencke, D, 'Whitehall silent on its progress in ending secrecy', *The Guardian,* 8 March 2002

Fisher, L and Jones, G, 'Who's climbing the career ladder?', *Daily Mirror*, 16 February 1999

Freedland, J, *Bring Home the Revolution: The Case for a British Republic*, 1998, Fourth Estate

Geddes, A *et al*, 'Candidate selection', *Contemporary Record*, April 1991

Giddens, A, *Sociology*, 2nd edition, 2002, Polity

Ginns, B, 'County Hall chief gains knighthood', *Kent on Sunday*, 12 January 2003

Glasgow University Media Group, *Bad News*, 1976, Routledge and Kegan Paul

Glasgow University Media Group, *More Bad News*, 1980, Routledge and Kegan Paul

Glasgow University Media Group, *Really Bad News*, 1982, Writers and Readers Co-operative

Glasgow University Media Group, *War and Peace News*, 1985, Open University Press

Goffman, E, *Asylums: Essays on the Social Situation of Mental Patients and Other Patients and Other Inmates*, 1968, Penguin

Goodwin, B, 'Journalists still get a raw deal in court', *The Guardian*, 19 July 2002

Graef, R, *Talking Blues*, 1989, Collins

Grant, M, *The British Media*, 1984, Comedia

Green, H, *Informal Carers, General Household Survey Supplement 1985*, HMSO

Greenslade, R, 'I arrest you for emailing', *The Guardian*, 31 July 2000

Griffith, J, *The Politics of the Judiciary*, 1991, Fontana

Harrison, G, 'Who pays for the party?', *The Observer*, 20 June 1993

Himmelweit, H *et al*, *How Voters Decide*, 1985, OUP

Hodge, M, 'The problem is alienation, not apathy', *The Guardian*, 24 March 2002

Hutton, W, 'How much longer will facts be sacred?' *The Observer*, 14 July 2002

Johnston, RJ and Pattie, CJ, *A Nation Dividing? The Electoral Map of Great Britain, 1979–1983*, 1988, Longman

Jones, L, 'Residents lied in election survey', *The Recorder*, 7 January 1999

Jones, S, *Policewomen and Equality*, 1986, Macmillan

Jorgensen, N *et al*, *Sociology: An Interactive Approach*, 1997, Collins

Joyce, P, *An Introduction to Politics*, 1999, Hodder and Stoughton

Kelso, P, 'Cautious welcome for citizenship classes', *The Guardian*, 27 October 2001

Kelso, P and Adams, G, 'As one in four homes go online, the digital divide widens', *The Guardian*, 11 July 2000

Kingdom, J, *Government and Politics in Britain*, 2nd edn, 1999, Polity

Kirby, M *et al*, *Sociology in Perspective*, 1997, Heinemann

Kirby, M, *Investigating Political Sociology*, 1995, Collins Educational

Klug, F, *Reinventing Community, The Rights and Responsibilities Debate*, 2002, Charter 88

Labour Research Department, 'Half of Tory MPs hold paid jobs outside parliament', 4 January 2003

Lacey, N, *Image and Representation: Key Concepts in Media Studies*, 1998, Macmillan

Leake, J and Brennan, Z, 'Oxbridge accounts reveal assets of £2bn', *The Sunday Times*, 16 November 1997

Leake, J and Craig, O, 'Eton richer than Spurs', *The Times*, 18 May 1997

Lewis, O, *La Vida*, 1968, Panther

Lilley, P, 'ID cards – a dumb idea and dangerous too', *The Observer*, 30 June 2002

Lister, R, *Citizenship: Feminist Perspectives*, 1997, Macmillan

Littlewood, R and Lipsedge, M, *Aliens and Alienists – Ethnic Minorities and Psychiatry*, 1982, Penguin

Lynn, J and Jay, A, *The Complete Yes Minister*, 1989, BBC

Machon, A and Wadham, J, untitled press statement issued 4 November 2002

Maguire, K, 'Party dress: Millbank's tips for women who want to be Labour MPs', *The Guardian*, 4 February 2000

Mandelson, P and Liddle, R, *The Blair Revolution: Can New Labour Deliver?*, 1996, Faber & Faber

March, DC, *The Welfare State*, 1970, Longman

Marshall, TH (ed), 'Citizenship and social class', in *Sociology at the Crossroads*, 1963, Heinemann

Marsland, D, 'Universal welfare provision creates a dependent population', *Social Studies Review*, November 1989

Mental Health Act Commission, *The Mental Health Act Commission Report*, March 2000

MORI Poll, 'What the nation thinks', *The Sun*, 1 March 1999

Morris, W, 'The racism that lies at the heart of this government', *The Independent*, 14 April 2000

National Youth Agency, *The Drop Out Society Report 1995*, National Youth Agency

Norton, C, 'Gays should be sacked, one in eight believes', *The Independent*, 19 April 2000

Norton-Taylor, R, 'What an ex-agent was not allowed to tell the jurors', *The Guardian*, 5 November 2002

Norton-Taylor, R, 'Shayler tells the jury, I'm gagged', *The Guardian*, 2 November 2002

Norton-Taylor, R and Wadham, J, 'The public has the right to the truth', *The Guardian*, 6 April 2002

O'Donnell, M, *Introductory Sociology*, 4th edn, 1997, Nelson

Oppenheim, C and Harker, L, *Poverty: The Facts*, 1996, Child Poverty Action Group

Orr, D, 'Thirty ways out of the poverty trap', *The Independent*, 14 April 2000

Outram, S, *Sociology in Focus: Social Policy*, 1989, Longman

Parry, G and Moyser, G, 'Political participation in Britain' (1993) Vol 3.2 *Politics Review*

Peek, L, 'No history question in British nationality quiz', *The Times*, 1 February 2003

Pinto-Duschinsky, M, *Elections and Parties Yearbook 1997*, 1997, Blackwell

Ponting, C, *The Right to Know: The Inside Story to the Belgrano Affair*, 1985, Sphere

Pyke, N, 'Caribbean boys fall far behind', *Times Educational Supplement*, 24 April 1996

Rayner, J and Wazir, B, 'Why did their loved ones die in custody?', *The Observer*, 9 January 2000

Reeves, R, Veash, N and Arlidge, J, 'Virtual chaos baffles police', *The Observer*, 20 June 1999

Reiner, R, 'Policing and the police', in *The Oxford Handbook of Criminology*, 1994, OUP

Reiner, R, *The Politics of the Police*, 2nd edn, 1993, Harvester Wheatsheaf

Ridley, Y, 'Poor, old, disabled? Don't complain', *The Observer*, 21 February 1999

Roberts, D *et al*, *British Politics in Focus*, 1997, Causeway

Robinson, G, *Literacy, Numeracy and Economic Performance*, 1997, Centre for Economic Performance at the LSE

Russell, B, 'Black academics – 2,500 earn less than whites', *The Independent*, 17 March 2000

Sebestyen, V, 'The case for and against the right to trial by jury', *ES*, 21 January 2000

Sinfield, A, *What Unemployment Means*, 1981, Martin Robinson

Smith, D and Gray, J, *Police and People in London*, 1985, Gower

Smithers, R, 'Punishment for Black pupils appears harsher', *The Guardian*, 1 March 2001

Susskind, *The Future of Law*, 1996, OUP

Taylor, P *et al*, *Sociology in Focus*, 1995, Causeway

Thatcher, M, *The Downing Street Years*, 1993, HarperCollins

Timmins, N, 'Moore says poverty levels are exaggerated', *The Independent*, 12 May 1989

Townsend, P, *Poverty in the UK*, 1979, Penguin

Travis, A, 'Anti-terror Bill dammed for catch-all powers', *The Guardian*, 14 November 2001

Travis, A, 'Compulsory ID cards back on the agenda and Blunkett puts his cards on the table', *The Guardian,* 4 July 2002

Travis, A, 'Night courts plan "a costly disaster"', *The Guardian*, 30 December 2002

Travis, A, 'Night courts shift to breakfast time', *The Guardian*, 28 January 2003

Travis, A, 'Tough and tender plan for immigrants', *The Guardian*, 8 February 2002

Travis, A, 'Un-British or vital? The ID debate', *The Guardian*, 25 September 2002

Travis, A, 'Citizenship classes for immigrants', *The Guardian*, 26 October 2001

Trowler, P, *Investigating Health, Welfare and Poverty*, 2nd edn, 1996, Collins

Trowler, P, *Investigating the Mass Media*, 2nd edn, 1996, Collins

Walford, G (ed), *Researching the Powerful in Education,* 1994, UCL Press

Watson-Smyth, K, 'UK is now "worst place in Europe to be growing up"', *The Independent*, 17 March 2000

Watt, N, 'Citizenship test to be practical', *The Guardian*, 1 February 2003

Wells, M, 'Hit TV shows "ignore ethnic minorities"', *The Guardian*, 2 April 2001

Welsh, I, 'New social movements' (2000) Vol 16 *Developments in Sociology*

West Kent Health Authority, *Report on the Patient's Charter April 1994 to March 1995*

White, M, 'Poll booth shake-up to beat voter apathy', *The Guardian*, 20 November 1999

White, M, 'The name game', *The Guardian*, 8 March 2000

Whitehead, M, *The Health Divide: Social Inequalities in Health*, 1987, Health Education Council

Whiteley, P *et al*, *True Blues: The Politics of the Conservative Party Membership*, 1994, OUP

Wintour, P and McKie, R, 'Shave the beard or lose, Dobson warned', *The Observer*, 12 March 2000

Woodward, W, 'Being sociable', *The Guardian*, 3 September 2002

Woodward, W, 'Top universities "waste state school talent"', *The Guardian*, 5 June 2000

Wright, P, *Spycatcher*, 1987, Viking

Young, W, Cameron, N and Tinsley, Y, *Juries in Criminal Trials*, Law Commission Preliminary Paper No 37

Useful websites

Alison Halford: www.alisonhalford.com

Charter 88: Unlocking Democracy: www.charter88.org.uk

Citizenship Foundation: www.citfou.org.uk

Commission for Racial Equality: www.cre.gov.uk

Commonwealth Institute: www.commonwealth.org.uk

Community Legal Service: www.justask.org.uk

Community service volunteers: www.csv.org.uk

Department of Health: Caring About Carers: www.doh.gov.uk/carers

Equal Opportunities Commission: www.eoc.gov.uk

European Parliament: www.europarl.org.uk

Government online: www.open.gov.uk

Institute for Citizenship: www.citizen.org.uk

Liberty: www.liberty-human-rights.org.uk

Magistrates Association: www.magistrates-association.org.uk

Modernising Public Services Group: www.servicefirst.gov.uk

Political parties: www.conservatives.com

www.greenparty.org.uk

www.labour.org.uk

www.libdems.org.uk

Tactical voting: www.tacticalvoter.net

INDEX